Lifelines
New and Collected

Lifelines

New and Collected

Letters From Famous People About Their Favourite Poem

Compiled by
Dónal O'Connor
Caroline Shaw
Stephanie Veitch

Forewords by
Seamus Heaney
Paul Durcan
Eavan Boland

Introduced and edited by
Niall MacMonagle

Wesley College
Dublin

This edition first published in 2010 by

Wesley College Dublin
Ballinteer
Dublin 16
www.wesleycollege.ie

to coincide with an exhibition of the original letters
in the National Library of Ireland

First published in 2006 by
TownHouse, Dublin
THCH Ltd
Mount Pleasant Business Centre
Mount Pleasant Avenue
Dublin 6

Compilers of previous editions: *Lifelines:* Joann Bradish, Jacki Erskine, Carolyn Gibson, Steven Given, Julie Grantham, Paula Griffin, Nicola Hughes, Jonathan Logue, Colette Lucy, Duncan Lyster, Joy Marshall, Alice McEleney; *Lifelines 2*: Ewan Gibson, Áine Jackson, Christopher Pillow; *Lifelines 3*: Ralph Croly, Caroline Dowling, Gareth McCluskey

1 2 3 4 5 6 7 8 9 10

ISBN PB: 978-0-9526317-5-0

Cover illustration: *Blue Rabbit* by Basil Blackshaw. Reproduced with the kind permission of the artist.

Cover design by Sin É Design

Text design and typesetting by Fiona Andreanelli

Printed by WS Bookwell, Finland, 2010

CONTENTS

For the children of the Developing World

'Children in famine . . . and the whole world
of loneliness, poverty, and pain make a
mockery of what human life should be.'

Bertrand Russell

FOREWORDS

Seamus Heaney, Lifelines

Towards the end of Ford Madox Ford's sequence of First World War novels, *Parade's End*, there is a scene where the protagonist, Tietjens, is preparing the soldiers under his command to sustain a barrage from the German artillery. His mind is vividly alert to the trench activity and the shelling which surround him, but it is equally receptive to memories and associations swimming in pell-mell from other, remoter strata of his consciousness. He remembers, for example, a gunner telling him that it had probably cost the two armies a total of three million pounds sterling to reduce a twenty-acre field between the lines to a pulverised nowhere; and this memory has itself been prompted by an earlier, random image of 'the quiet thing', the heavy-leaved, timbered hedge-rows around the parsonage at Bemerton, outside Salisbury, where the poet George Herbert had lived two centuries earlier. Inevitably, the sweetness and fortitude of Herbert's poetry come to mind then also, so that Tietjens's sense of value in the face of danger is both clarified and verified by the fleeting recollection of a couple of his favourite lines.

Jon Stallworthy directed my attention to this passage of Ford's after he had heard me refer to a similar moment in the life of George Seferis, when Seferis came to a realisation (recorded in his *Journals*) that the work of his fellow Greek poet, Constantine Cavafy, was 'strong enough to help'. And it seems relevant to cite both occasions here again, in the foreword to a book which testifies in its own uninsistent fashion to the ways in which individuals still continue to recognise that some part of the meaning of their lives is lodged in the words and cadences of cherished passages of verse.

Meaning and value, of course, do not always entail a lofty note and an earnest message: it has been said, for example, that it would be worth a poet's while to spend a lifetime at work in order to leave behind one limerick that might distract somebody walking the last few yards to the electric chair. Certainly the pages that follow reveal that people of great talents and responsibilities do not repose their imaginative trust only in the sonorities of the Bible or the canonical voice of Shakespeare; they also turn to less solemn achievements, such as Lewis Carroll's nonsense verse, or the devastatingly light touch of Stevie Smith, or the merry logic of the early Irish 'The Scholar and his Pet Cat' – chosen respectively by Amy Clampitt, Glenda Jackson and the late Cardinal Tomás Ó Fiaich.

Other choices, of course, were made because the contributor possessed a definite sense of the figure he or she must cut in the public eye: when Michael Holroyd selected 'Biography' by D J Enright, and Jeffrey Archer called for Kipling, and Sister Stanislaus picked 'Street Corner Christ', they did so in the knowledge that their poem would be read in the light of their known professions and commitments. And the same kind of compatibility operates in the case of critics like Helen Vendler and Christopher Ricks, whose choice of Stevens and Tennyson complements what we know about their literary preferences from other quarters. But when Conor Cruise O'Brien chose Milton's 'Ode on the Morning of Christ's Nativity' and Chaim Herzog picked 'The Lake Isle of Innisfree', they were declaring obliquely that as private persons they live within a field of cultural force which may be at some odds with the general perception of them as public figures.

Writers, on the other hand, live precisely at the intersection of the public and the private, and it is interesting to see how their choices indulge or deflect our natural wish to establish connections between the style of what they write and what they read. Almost every selection by a poet here is corroborative of some aspect of his or her own published work, and there is a corresponding aptness to the choices made by many of the prose writers: that V S Pritchett should go for Clough, Jennifer Johnston for Holub, Ben Kiely for Robinson and John Banville for Celan, makes sense immediately, but there's surely just a little bit of decoy activity going on when the realistic Drabble goes for the prophetic Blake and the comedian Lodge promotes the tragedian Yeats. (Yeats, incidentally, is chosen nineteen times – proof, if it were needed, that metrical force and direct utterance remain potent factors in establishing a poem's claim upon the affections.)

This anthology was a magnificent idea from the start. The initial dedication of the pupils and their teachers at Wesley College (and, in particular, of the student compilers of *Lifelines*) was admirable; and the end result is a book in which poems re-enter the world refreshed rather than jaded by their long confinement inside people's heads, a book that is surprisingly various and compulsively readable. It is, after all, greatly heartening to discover that the poems of Keats and Yeats are stored like imaginative fossil fuel in the minds of the President of Harvard and the President of the State of Israel respectively; and to be provided with such credible evidence that poetry does indeed survive, as W H Auden said it would, 'a way of happening, a mouth.'

Seamus Heaney, 1992

Paul Durcan, Lifelines 2

War and Famine are raging in Rwanda. Day and night, confronted on our TV screens and in the photographs of courageous reporters such as Frank Miller of *The Irish Times*, we feel that we are helpless witnesses to unspeakable suffering.

Unspeakable? Therein lies the deadly temptation proposed to us by the Satan of War and Famine. We are tempted to feel that, in the face of War and Famine, art is irrelevant, futile, indecent, blasphemous.

The truth is that War and Famine are man-made: something that we in Ireland know and remember with anger and grief, if not with bitterness and remorse. The demons of evil that have been raging in Ethiopia, Somalia, Sudan and Rwanda are not freaks of Nature; they are the handiwork of evil men who can be overcome only by the power of art. The Satanic Tempter's deepest desire is that we lose faith in the power of art and surrender to despair. In his beautiful poem 'The Harvest Bow', Seamus Heaney quotes W B Yeats, who was in turn quoting Horace: 'The end of art is peace.'

Only in what we call art lies our salvation. 'If anything is sacred, the human body is sacred' – Whitman quoted by Steven Berkoff. Art is the last repository of humane values – one might say, African values. In the West our consumerism has caused a spiritual famine which is spreading into Russia and Siberia. Only in art have old, perennial, humane values survived. We look to Africa for spiritual aid just as Africa looks to us for economic aid.

These truths have been translated into a practical programme of uniquely outstanding poetry anthologies by the students of Wesley College. Not only have significant sums of money accrued but the very anthologies themselves embody a personality and an ethos which have provoked an immediate, urgent, attentive, magnanimous response from individual contributors as well as from the general reading public.

Normally there is no class of book more slipshod, more boring, more prejudiced, more snobbish, more exclusive, more incestuous, more narrow-minded, more arid, more ignorant, more canonical, more soulless, more soul destroying, more anti-poetic than a poetry anthology. The shelves of bookshops are stacked with the spines of these prodigies of spinelessness – poetry anthologies. So what is the magic recipe of the Wesley students?

It is their belief, first, in the personal, individual, social character of art; secondly, in art as a primarily subjective encounter. Absolute values – *pace* Yeats, Eliot, Kavanagh – exist only in the context of subjective experience. What van Gogh wrote of painting is equally true of poetry: 'What lives in art and is eternally living is first of all the painter and then the painting.'

A work of art – a picture on the wall, a poem on the page, a nocturne in the concert hall, a film on the screen – is in itself only half-alive: that is to say, a poem ontologically (oops – but there is no other word for it) is only fifty per cent alive until it is read or heard by reader or auditor. It is only when art is encountered by an audience that art is fully born, wholly alive.

Which is why each reader brings to the same poem a new life, and therefore no poem reads the same way twice; no poem exists frigidly intact on a pedestal in a classroom. 'Dualism be damned. This is where it's at' – Niall Stokes.

The curse of the teaching of poetry in our schools and colleges has been the Tyranny of the One Meaning: viz, that a poem means one thing and one thing only, and that reading the wretched thing is merely a question of finding the right key with which to unlock the locker and zap – the meaning of the poem slips out into your lap and you pick it up by the tail and carry the poor thing up to the po-faced, freckled, red-haired, baldy old teacher who pats you on the pate and gives you a liquorice allsort and a kick in the pants. As well as needing to have many meanings, poetry needs to have no meaning. 'The pleasure you can take in them [words], that is nothing to do with their meaning' – Neil Jordan.

The letters in *Lifelines 2* are as vital and indispensable as the poems. Apart from the odd, stray, coy puff of conceit, the majority of the letters are passionate and startlingly honest: e.g. TV presenter Bibi Baskin – 'And yes, despite my profession, I do think the lovely evocative images of poetry do a much better job at it than the quick-flash images of television'; radio presenter Joe Duffy – 'I always came back to "The Windhover" mainly because it was the first poem to cast a sheltering shadow over my life.' Warm comic touches also, such as when that superb politician Mr Bertie Ahern TD, having chosen Kavanagh's Grand Canal poem, immediately protests his loyalty to the Royal Canal; or when Jeananne Crowley relates spending a week in Edinburgh, holding hands with Roger McGough.

Lifelines proved an extraordinarily popular book. How could the compilers of *Lifelines 2* hope to emulate it? They have surpassed themselves. This new anthology is even more exhilarating and distinctive.

Personally – how delighted I am to be able to wallow in that word aptly – I am astonished by the passages from Whitman, Poe, Lear, Millay, and Hill – none of whom featured in the first anthology. I rejoice in the ever-expanding recognition of Raymond Carver. I am grateful to contributors who are introducing me to poems I have not known before: e.g. Philip King for 'I am Stretched On Your Grave'; Deirdre Madden for 'Vaucluse'; Art Cosgrove for 'The Song of the Strange Ascetic'; Mark Joyce for 'Not Ideas About The Thing But The Thing Itself'; Edna Longley for 'Old Man'; Gwen O'Dowd for 'Chicory Chicory Dock'; Evelyn Conlon for 'I Gave Away That Kid'; James Hanley for 'Uh-Oh'; Emma Cooke for 'The Chess Board'; Proinnsías Ó Duinn for 'The Duck and the Kangaroo'; E Annie Proulx for 'Upon a Wasp Child With Cold'; Patrick McCabe for 'The Man From God-Knows-Where'; Neil Astley for 'September Song'.

I am grateful also to those contributors who have brought me back to rare poems read long ago: e.g. Pádraig J Daly for 'Swineherd'; Helen Dunmore for 'Buffalo Bill's'; Eilís Dillon for 'Bredon Hill'; Don Paterson for 'Soap Suds'; Bernard Farrell for 'The Cottage Hospital'; Charles Causley for 'The Faithless Wife' (which I first read twenty-five years ago in a translation by Michael Hartnett).

It is part of the unique recipe of *Lifelines 2* to be able to read all these new and familiar poems side by side with great classics such as 'The Lament for Art O'Leary' chosen by Seán Ó Tuama, and 'Epithalamion' chosen by Wendell Berry.

In the mid and late 1980s I was privileged to be invited to give poetry recitals in Wesley College. The response of the students was as memorable as it was moving, but most moving and memorable of all was the spectacle of the relationship between the students and their teachers. It was a palpable, visible current of electric affection and it is something I have never ceased to think about. When all is said and done, it is the individual schoolteacher who is the keystone. If every teacher and arts administrator was dedicated – in Dennis Potter's caustic, romantic sense of 'dedication' – the world would be a world without war and no child would go hungry.

When I was a boy I had the great good fortune to have a dedicated teacher, Fr Joseph Veale SJ. Three of Ireland's most popular writers – Brendan Kennelly, Roddy Doyle and Seamus Heaney – have been renowned in their very different ways as dedicated teachers. I think, and I am certain, that we owe an immeasurable debt not only to the students of Wesley College but to their teachers for throwing us – in a time of universal civil war – *Lifelines 2*.

For the epitome of everything that is marvellous about *Lifelines 2*, listen to Tess Gallagher's words on her husband Raymond Carver's poem 'What The Doctor Said': 'I love its spiritual dimension which is delivered so offhandedly that it takes hold of us the way sunlight takes hold of roses and weeds alike.'

Paul Durcan, 1994

Eavan Boland, Lifelines 3

I have been an admirer of this project since it began. In fact, when the first volume of poems – edited by Wesley students, chosen and commented on by various people, and all in an excellent and deserving cause – was published, I was almost taken aback by the charm, elegance and readability of the book. What's more, my own surprise surprised me. Like all working poets, anthologies have been a part of my life. Yet my relation to them, and I have no idea how representative this is, has never been simple. Most of them have almost no organising principle. Poems turn up in them randomly, scattered across their pages according to some non-specific agenda of taste or history. They create problems rather than solve them. They erase by fiat and preserve by diktat. By and large, I have come to feel about them as I do about family photograph albums. You have to trawl doggedly and patiently through far too many lost moments and inconclusive occasions to find the one perfect representation.

But this is different. These books have a design. They have a purpose and they get a result. What's more, somehow Ralph, Caroline and Gareth have enhanced the original version of both, so that the structure appears as fresh and convincing as ever, instead of just seeming a tired repetition. I have no idea of how this is done, and yet nothing appears like formula here. On the other hand, the form of this book resembles the others: public figures, from every part of the working community, have been asked for a favourite poem, and to give a reason for their choice. Artists, politicians, activists of all kinds have selected the poems, justified their selection and written back to the editors with both projects completed.

So what makes this different from the usual anthology? The answer to that question seems to me important. In giving it, I'll try – however inaccurately – to define some of the unease I feel about elements of the ethos surrounding contemporary poetry, which also has to do with my real appreciation of this book.

To return to my harsh words about anthologies, my resistance to them has to do with the fact that they so often reverse the process by which poetry is treasured, remembered and handed on from generation to generation. They substitute individual whim for the slow, measured communal sifting of poems. And yet that sifting is crucial. Take a poem like 'Dead Man's Dump' by Isaac Rosenberg, which Jon Silkin has chosen here. The poem is about the catastrophic violence of the First World War. About what Jon Silkin eloquently calls 'the spiritual problems of what killing each other entails'. I have remembered one line from the poem for years. *Will they come? Will they ever come?* But somehow the rest of it disappeared. Now here it is, with its powerful argument and discordant cadences, re-joining the line I remembered.

Therefore, so far from being an ordinary anthology, this book mirrors the almost-secret and yet definitive process by which poems are handed on. Take this poem, one reader says to another. Join the rest of it up to the single line you have half-remembered. And so a poem becomes a talisman, and a talisman becomes a treasure.

This makes an enchanting, readable book. But the enchantment shouldn't obscure the fact that this book also offers us a serious, interesting insight into the less glamorous, more democratic and, finally, more reliable way of handing on poetry. The difference between this book, with its personal selections and much-loved choices, and the average anthology, is the difference between a tradition and a canon. A tradition leads us towards the communal centre. A canon leads us away from it. The fact that so many poems here have been the loved companions of those who choose them tells us something about memory and association. It shows how obstinately poetry sets itself into feeling and recall. It also does something to recover the close affinities between music and poetry, because a lot of the poems here have been remembered by those who love them in the same way that a melody is remembered; something so woven into the associative fabric of their existence that it has become more life than literature.

Of course, that means that we're not likely to find too much Milton here, or Spenser or Crabbe or Bunting. By and large, the poems in this book have wheels and handles. They fit in the overhead compartment. They are the carry-ons of the poetry world. They are portable and manageable, which accounts for the fact that they tend not to get lost so easily.

This book, then, is just as engaging as the others – which is saying a great deal. The wonderful mixture of choice, memory and chance has lost none of its charm. Government ministers and priests and poets and actors and activists reveal themselves through poems. And the poems reveal ourselves to ourselves as part of this continuing process. Like everyone else who will read this book, I trust the choices here. They are too personal, quirky and definite to be anything but true. And this touches on one of the great pleasures of it all. Turning the pages, we ask ourselves why does this or that person, who we think of as hard-headed and practical, treasure and defend this or that poem, which seems so lyrical and other-worldly? Is this a voyeuristic or journalistic question? The very opposite, I think.

I congratulate the editors of the book, Ralph, Caroline and Gareth. To their commitment and the hours they spent on it we owe the final result. I congratulate Wesley, which has hosted this marvellous project, and Niall MacMonagle, who has fostered it. I hope, and suspect, that it will continue and strengthen, and there will be more books like this. I hope that I and other readers get more chances to be surprised into the kind of curiosity which makes us trace the advocacy to the poem, the reason to the rationale, the river to its source, till we find ourselves, all at once, at the magic heart of the original eco-system of poetry: its oldest habitat. The human spirit.

Eavan Boland, 1997

Coláiste Wesley,
Baile an tSaoir,
Baile Átha Cliath 16

Wesley College
Ballinteer
Dublin 16

The *Lifelines* books have been produced by Wesley pupils in an effort to raise money for those suffering in the developing world. These books have been a huge success and have more than fulfilled all the expectations of those who compiled them. We hope *Lifelines New and Collected* will be as widely successful as the other books and that it will help just as many people. It has been an amazing experience compiling this book and we hope you have as much fun reading it as we did putting it together.

Lifelines New and Collected combines a selection of new poems and letters, along with an assortment of entries from the previous three collections. It has been compiled by us in the same way as the other books, and, like those books, all the proceeds are going to those in need in the developing world. We have had many very interesting replies from the people we wrote to, and the poems are a great mixture of old and new. We hope you get as much pleasure, if not more, from this collection as the earlier ones.

There are many people who have helped us on our way in putting together this book. First our English teacher, Niall MacMonagle, who organised us and instructed us on our next step from day one. We would also like to thank Graham Darlington for setting up our e-mail, the office staff of Wesley College for all their assistance, our Principal Christopher Woods for his invaluable support and, of course, all the people who sent us their favourite poems for this book!

Dónal O'Connor
Stephanie Veitch
Caroline Shaw

INTRODUCTION

Lifelines began in a classroom here in Wesley, as a fund-raiser in April 1985, and first saw the light of day as a little Gestetnered, stapled booklet. Three other booklets – in March 1988, April 1990, May 1992 – followed, and their sell-out success resulted in the book *Lifelines*, published in autumn 1992. *Lifelines 2* appeared in 1994 and *Lifelines 3* in 1997. All royalties from these best-sellers were in aid of the Developing World, an important cause then as now.

Through the past twenty-one years, with their ups and downs, fads and fashions, crises and controversies, the *Lifelines* project reveals people's belief in poetry, proves its staying power. Poetry may never seem to be as popular as music or sport, the great enthusiasms of our time, but poetry, in its unique quiet way, endures and enriches.

'A letter,' says Emily Dickinson, 'always feels to me like immortality because it is the mind alone.' The letters accompanying the poems, from Ireland, Britain, India, Australia, New Zealand, Israel, the United States, Canada, the Czech Republic, reveal not only an extraordinary generosity – that so many replied in the first place is remarkable – but 'the mind alone' is revealed, what these minds chose and thought and felt at that particular time of their lives. When we think of those contributors who have since died, Dickinson's 'immortality' is particularly apt.

We couldn't include everyone in this book but Dónal O'Connor, Caroline Shaw, Stephanie Veitch and I hope that we've put together a readable, varied and manageable collection. In all, over six hundred and fifty people wrote to *Lifelines* [the original letters are in the National Library of Ireland] and the biggest difficulty, and the only regret, about this *New and Collected* edition was our not being able to include everyone.

The *Lifelines* project could not and would not have happened without the pupils and staff of Wesley College. Their energy, encouragement and support have been remarkable. Thanks to Christopher Woods, Graham Darlington, Carol Gee, Pauline Kinsella, Anne Quinn and Valerie Spendlove for their enthusiasm and help. A particular thank you to Seamus Heaney, Paul Durcan and Eavan Boland who responded immediately and with characteristic kindness when asked to write forewords. Thanks too to Townhouse publisher Treasa Coady who believed in the project from the beginning and transformed it into such beautiful books.

My own favourite poem? Yes, I've been asked by the pupils involved from the outset and now that this is the last of *Lifelines*, and at the publisher's request, here we go. There are three in particular: Philip Larkin's 'The Trees', Elizabeth Bishop's 'The Moose' and Yeats's 'Among School Children'. 'The Trees' means more to me with every spring and it's one of many poems that First Years in Wesley are invited to learn by heart when 'The trees are coming into leaf/Like something almost being said'. It has a beautiful sadness to it and a fine sense of the need to keep going. 'The Moose', for its convincing, beautiful descriptions and when Bishop says 'Life's like that./We know *it* (also death)' there is a steadying wisdom in both her affirmation and recognition. When the moose appears, unexpectedly, 'we all feel' that 'sweet/sensation of joy'. And Yeats. This is Yeats at his greatest. The setting is familiar and, though he speaks of disappointment, sorrow, heartbreak, he goes beyond and arrives at blossoming tree and dancer – nature and artist – exhilarating, liberating, heartening and celebratory images.

And then there's Joe Kane's wonder-filled poem where grammatical accuracy and conventions have been abandoned because they are irrelevant. 'The Boy Who Nearly Won The Texaco Art Competition' is the whoosh of the imagination at work. It reminds us that we were all young once and illustrates Thoreau's idea that 'Every child begins the world again'. This boy is a winner, no matter what the critics say.

Niall MacMonagle

The Boy Who Nearly Won the Texaco Art Competition.
for Ted Hughes

he took a large sheet
of white paper and on this
he made the world an african world
of flat topped trees and dried grasses
and he painted an elephant in the middle
and a lion with a big mane and several giraffes
stood over the elephant and some small animals to fill
in the gaps he worked all day had a bath this was saturday

on sunday he put six jackals
in the world and a great big snake
and buzzards in the sky and tickbirds
on the elephants back he drew down blue
from the sky to make a river and got the elephants
legs all wet and smudged and one of the jackals got drowned
he put red flowers in the front of the picture and daffodils in the bottom corners
and his dog major chewing a bone and mrs murphys two cats tom and jerry
and milo the milkman with a cigarette in the corner of his mouth
and his merville dairy float pulled by his wonder horse trigger
that would walk when he said click click and the holy family
in the top right corner with the donkey and cow
and sheep and baby jesus and got the 40A bus
on monday morning in to abbey street to hand
it in and the man on the door said
thats a sure winner

JOE KANE (B. 1952)

GRAHAM NORTON COMEDIAN

Dear Dónal, Caroline and Stephanie,

Many thanks for your letter. I have long been a fan of Lifelines *and am honoured to be included in its latest incarnation.*

'Favourite' is such a strange, fixed term that it scares me, especially for something like this where your choice is trapped between the covers of a book for all eternity. I've chosen a poem that I come back to again and again. 'Epic' by Patrick Kavanagh is one of the wisest poems I know. Whatever one is going through or experiencing in life, it always helps to try and see it in perspective. Everything matters and doesn't matter in equal measure depending on where one stands. It seems to me that remembering this will keep you sane and help your happiness.

Very best of luck with the book.

Graham Norton XX

['Patrick Kavanagh's *'Epic'* was also chosen by Anne Doyle in *Lifelines.* Anne Doyle wrote: *Very difficult to nominate an absolute favourite, but I'll go for Patrick Kavanagh's* 'Epic'. *Already I'm having second and third thoughts – so without further ado I'll wish you well and leave you with best regards.*]

Epic

I have lived in important places, times
When great events were decided: who owned
That half a rood of rock, a no-man's land
Surrounded by our pitchfork-armed claims.
I heard the Duffys shouting 'Damn your soul'
And old McCabe, stripped to the waist, seen
Step the plot defying blue cast-steel —
'Here is the march along these iron stones'.
That was the year of the Munich bother. Which
Was most important? I inclined
To lose my faith in Ballyrush and Gortin
Till Homer's ghost came whispering to my mind.
He said: I made the *Iliad* from such
A local row. Gods make their own importance.

PATRICK KAVANAGH (1904–1967)

13 May 1985

Dear Collette, Joy and Steven,

Impossible to choose one favourite but never mind, here is one of my favourites – the three stanzas by Blake that begin:

> Never seek to tell thy love.

I love this poem because it is sad – I have always liked sad poems best, I think – and because it is mysterious and yet compact and because it catches the difficulty and fragility of love. I don't really know what it means, but I respond to it very strongly.
I hope this arrives in time and good luck with your anthology.

Yours sincerely,

Margaret Drabble

Never Seek to Tell Thy Love

Never seek to tell thy love
Love that never told can be;
For the gentle wind does move
Silently, invisibly.

I told my love, I told my love
I told her all my heart,
Trembling, cold, in ghastly fears —
Ah, she doth depart.

Soon as she was gone from me
A traveller came by
Silently, invisibly —
O, was no deny.

WILLIAM BLAKE (1757–1827)

BERTIE AHERN POLITICIAN

25 February 1994

Like most other schoolboys, I suppose I did not really appreciate poetry at an early age. Having to learn line upon line of verse never really knowing what it meant was probably not the greatest way to instil an appreciation of poetry in a tender mind. However, like a good wine, an appreciation of poetry develops as the years go by. One of my children bought me a birthday present of the Complete Poems of Patrick Kavanagh *some years back. 'Canal Bank Walk' became one of my favourites. This is not to say that I do not have a deep love of the Royal Canal which flows through my native Northside, but I passed by that very area which Kavanagh wrote about every day for five years when I was Minister for Labour. I can certainly tell you there were many evenings of long negotiations when I looked out my window and wished that I was walking up its leafy banks which seem to have a distinctive colour for every season. Kavanagh seems to capture all the movement and emotion of the canal which he so eloquently put to verse. I am obviously not the only one who has been attracted by its beauty, it has always proved a popular place for walkers, lunchtimers or those who simply want to sit and watch the world go by.*

Bertie Ahern, TD
Minister for Finance

Canal Bank Walk

Leafy-with-love banks and the green waters of the canal
Pouring redemption for me, that I do
The will of God, wallow in the habitual, the banal,
Grow with nature again as before I grew.
The bright stick trapped, the breeze adding a third
Party to the couple kissing on an old seat,
And a bird gathering materials for the nest for the Word,
Eloquently new and abandoned to its delirious beat.
O unworn world enrapture me, encapture me in a web
Of fabulous grass and eternal voices by a beech,
Feed the gaping need of my senses, give me ad lib
To pray unselfconsciously with overflowing speech,
For this soul needs to be honoured with a new dress woven
From green and blue things and arguments that cannot be proven.

PATRICK KAVANAGH (1904–1967)

Dear Dónal, Caroline and Stephanie,

You're right! It's not easy to pick a favourite poem. But here's one:

'My Last Duchess' *by Robert Browning*

This is one of the best examples of a dramatic monologue in poetic form. I am often rather fogged – and even quite bored – by Browning, but this piece is simply brilliantly put together, and seems very modern. The reader discovers a complete scene: the speaker, the listener, the dead woman, even the curtain. What I value about this poem is that, although it's an unfolding story with an emerging secret, it's not a script for an actor to read aloud; in fact, an actorly interpretation might well ruin it. I admire it much more on the page than I would as a speech. 'This grew; I gave commands;/Then all smiles stopped together. There she stands/As if alive.' Also, you have to admire those fabulous semicolons. I do hope they weren't added by a later editor.

   Hope you can use that.

With best wishes,

Lynne Truss

My Last Duchess

Ferrara

That's my last Duchess painted on the wall,
Looking as if she were alive. I call
That piece a wonder, now: Frà Pandolf's hands
Worked busily a day, and there she stands.
Will't please you sit and look at her? I said
'Frà Pandolf' by design, for never read
Strangers like you that pictured countenance,
The depth and passion of its earnest glance,
But to myself they turned (since none puts by
The curtain I have drawn for you, but I)
And seemed as they would ask me, if they durst,
How such a glance came there; so, not the first
Are you to turn and ask thus. Sir, 'twas not
Her husband's presence only, called that spot
Of joy into the Duchess' cheek: perhaps
Frà Pandolf chanced to say 'Her mantle laps
Over my Lady's wrist too much,' or 'Paint
Must never hope to reproduce the faint
Half-flush that dies along her throat:' such stuff

Was courtesy, she thought, and cause enough
For calling up that spot of joy. She had
A heart – how shall I say? – too soon made glad,
Too easily impressed; she liked whate'er
She looked on, and her looks went everywhere.
Sir, 'twas all one! My favour at her breast,
The dropping of the daylight in the West,
The bough of cherries some officious fool
Broke in the orchard for her, the white mule
She rode with round the terrace – all and each
Would draw from her alike the approving speech,
Or blush, at least. She thanked men, – good! but thanked
Somehow – I know not how – as if she ranked
My gift of a nine-hundred-years-old name
With anybody's gift. Who'd stoop to blame
This sort of trifling? Even had you skill
In speech – (which I have not) – to make your will
Quite clear to such an one, and say, 'Just this
Or that in you disgusts me; here you miss,
Or there exceed the mark' – and if she let
Herself be lessoned so, nor plainly set
Her wits to yours, forsooth, and made excuse,
– E'en then would be some stooping, and I choose
Never to stoop. Oh sir, she smiled, no doubt,
Whene'er I passed her; but who passed without
Much the same smile? This grew; I gave commands;
Then all smiles stopped together. There she stands
As if alive. Will't please you rise? We'll meet
The company below, then. I repeat,
The Count your master's known munificence
Is ample warrant that no just pretence
Of mine for dowry will be disallowed;
Though his fair daughter's self, as I avowed
At starting, is my object. Nay, we'll go
Together down, sir. Notice Neptune, though,
Taming a sea-horse, thought a rarity,
Which Claus of Innsbruck cast in bronze for me!

ROBERT BROWNING (1812–1889)

Golden Stockings

Golden stockings you had on
In the meadow where you ran;
And your little knees together
Bobbed like pippins in the weather
When the breezes rush and fight
For those dimples of delight;
And they dance from the pursuit
And the leaf looks like the fruit.

I have many a sight in mind
That would last if I were blind;
Many verses I could write
That would bring me many a sight.
Now I only see but one,
See you running in the sun;
And the gold-dust coming up
From the trampled buttercup.

OLIVER ST JOHN GOGARTY (1878–1957)

One small page found in my father's wallet after he died had a poem written on it that he had obviously carried around with him. It was well-worn and anonymous, about a little girl. It was only when Ulick O'Connor's diaries were published that I discovered the author. The poem was by Oliver St John Gogarty. It was called 'Golden Stockings' and Oliver St John Gogarty wrote it for his daughter Brenda.

It was my father's way of remembering his young daughter, Betty, who died of pneumonia in the tenements in 1942.

Bill Cullen

ANDREW MOTION

POET

1 May 1985

Dear Collette Lucy, Joy Marshall and Steven Given,

Thank you for your letter, and for inviting me to help you further your excellent idea.

'They Flee from Me' by Thomas Wyatt is a poem I admire enormously. Although very well-known, its long exposure to the public gaze has done nothing to dim the power of its eroticism, or to weaken the ways in which private feelings are related to public issues. And the marvellously adroit irregularities of its metre guarantee (among other things) that the freshness never fades from its conversational tone.

Good wishes,

Andrew Motion

They Flee from Me

They flee from me, that sometime did me seke
With naked fote stalkyng within my chamber,
Once I have seen them gentle, tame, and meke,
That now are wild, and do not once remember
That sometime they have put them selves in danger,
To take bread at my hand, and now they range,
Busily sekyng in continuall change.

Thanked be fortune, it hath bene otherwise
Twenty tymes better: but once especiall,
In thinne aray, after a pleasant gyse,
When her loose gowne did from her shoulders fall,
And she me caught in her armes long and small,
And therwithall, so swetely did me kysse,
And softly sayd: deare hart, how like you this?

It was no dreame: for I lay broade awakyng.
But all is turnde now through my gentlenesse,
Into a bitter fashion of forsakyng:
And I have leave to go of her goodnesse,
And she also to use newfanglenesse.
But, sins that I unkyndly so am served:
How like you this, what hath she now deserved?

THOMAS WYATT (1503–1542)

[This poem was also chosen by William Wall in *Lifelines 3*. William Wall wrote:
*My favourite poem is called 'They flee from me that sometime did me seek . . .' by Thomas Wyatt,
a remarkable sixteenth-century poet.*

*Why? That is hard to say. I like the wit, the plaintive tone, the sensuality, the simple directness
of it. Wyatt was an interesting man and I suppose I have as much affection for the man behind
the poem as the poem itself. Many people could say the same, for example, about Seamus Heaney.
Wyatt was first and foremost a diplomat as well as a poet of great skill and sensitivity. He was
probably Anne Boleyn's lover before Henry set his cap at her and this may have got him into
trouble. At any rate, he was eventually charged with adultery and though he was not executed he
was imprisoned! Dangerous times! He died shortly after his release on his last diplomatic mission.*]

8 January 1992

Dear Nicola Hughes, Paula Griffin and Alice McEleney

Yeats's poem 'Memory' has always been a favourite.

Memory

One had a lovely face,
And two or three had charm,
But charm and face were in vain
Because the mountain grass
Cannot but keep the form
Where the mountain hare has lain.

W B YEATS (1865–1939)

This short and apparently simple poem has something of the quality of a Japanese haiku – a great deal said in a few words, on whatever level it is being understood.

With good wishes,

Doris Lessing

[Brian Farrell also chose '*Memory*' in *Lifelines*. Brian Farrell wrote:
There is no simple answer to 'what is your favourite poem?' Choose any one and you forego so many others. I'd be tempted to say the Shakespeare sonnet – 'Shall I compare thee to a summer's day' – must rank high. I first read the first two lines in an article and it haunted me until I captured the full text. Or there's

Time was away and somewhere else
And you were there and I was there
And time was away

(Don't trust me on the lines) – that sticks in my mind because on one occasion, rather exuberantly, I met Paddy Kavanagh and said that it must be wonderful to be able to write something like that; he grunted and eventually said 'Yes, only I didn't do it.' Among all the modern Irish poets there is so much richness to choose – forced to choose just one, I think I'd plump for Austin Clarke:

Men that had seen her
Drank deep and were silent,
The women were speaking
Wherever she went –

Still among the lyrics it's hard to pass Byron – 'We'll go no more a roving . . .' That's a name that turns your mind to satire. There's Byron's own:

(So, we'll go no more a roving
So late into the night)
I met murder on the way
He wore a face like Castlereagh

and the deliciously bitchy poet on verse-makers:

Some people praise the restraint you show.
I'm with them there, of course.
You use the snaffle and the bit alright
But where's the bloody horse.

And, for some reason – maybe the tum-te-tum tone – I think of something entirely different like Belloc's still splendid Don John of Austria.

But, in the end of it all, push me into some dark anthological corner and hold me up to poetic ransom and I think it would be back to Yeats's 'Memory'. Out of all that rich, musical, magnificent cornucopia of words it's difficult to do better than a poem I first heard from Dr Roger McHugh when I was a freshman student in University College thirty-five years ago.]

MELVIN BURGESS   NOVELIST

2006

Sorry, I'm late!

My favourite poem changes all the time, but just now it is 'The Garden Seat' by Thomas Hardy. I usually like rather jangled poems, but this one is very beautiful. I read it out at her funeral when my mum died. I don't know why it felt right, I don't normally like Hardy's poems as much as this one. I love the repetition and the mysterious nature of it. The fact that the ghosts don't affect the seat means that they can't be harmed either, and that's a comforting idea.

Hope this edition does as well as the others

Melvin Burgess

The Garden Seat

Its former green is blue and thin,
And its once firm legs sink in and in;
Soon it will break down unaware,
Soon it will break down unaware.

At night when reddest flowers are black
Those who once sat thereon come back;
Quite a row of them sitting there,
Quite a row of them sitting there.

With them the seat does not break down,
Nor winter freeze them, nor floods drown,
For they are as light as upper air,
They are as light as upper air!

THOMAS HARDY (1840–1928)

Hi Dónal, Caroline and Stephanie,

Hope this will be OK and all best with the project.

The Haw Lantern

The wintry haw is burning out of season,
crab of the thorn, a small light for small people,
wanting no more from them but that they keep
the wick of self-respect from dying out,
not having to blind them with illumination.

But sometimes when your breath plumes in the frost
it takes the roaming shape of Diogenes
with his lantern, seeking one just man;
so you end up scrutinized from behind the haw
he holds up at eye-level on its twig,
and you flinch before its bonded pith and stone,
its blood-prick that you wish would test and clear you,
its pecked-at ripeness that scans you, then moves on.

SEAMUS HEANEY (B. 1939)

According to my diary, it's the ninth of December, 1985. I'm in my third year studying English at Trinity. Fiona, my flat-mate from UCD, has tipped me off that there's a reading that evening by Seamus Heaney in UCD's Lit Soc. It's the days before smokeless fuel and when I take my bike out of the communal hallway after dinner, the night smells of smog and coal. Also, for the first time I can ever recall, there is a sea-fog in the centre of Dublin. It's drifted all the way in from Dublin Bay to Windsor Road, Ranelagh, where our flat is, and the faint light from the dynamo on my bike cannot pierce it. I cycle out through Donnybrook and on to the Stillorgan dual-carriageway as if invisible, objects looming up out of the gloaming. I can hear fog-horns moaning in the bay like sea-monsters. I find myself thrilling to this strange, unsettling thick darkness, where everything familiar looks utterly unfamiliar. Near UCD, I start seeing other bikes; their red back-lights floating along in front of me.

Since the place is so packed, nobody on the door knows who's meant to be there and who's a chancer waif-and-stray from elsewhere, so I blag my way in with no trouble. I've never seen any university Lit Soc reading so full. I stand at the back. Condensation trickles down the windows. Outside, the fog presses against the windows. Inside, cigarette smoke fills the room with its acrid fug. The fluorescent light slices hard and unforgiving through it all.

Seamus Heaney arrives, easy, gracious; commanding silence as soon as he walks in the door. It's the first time I've heard him reading in person. It's mesmeric. Towards the end of the reading, he tells us that he has only that morning finished a poem, and that he wants to read it now for the first time in public – to us. There is a pleased, excited, anticipatory buzz. We're only broke arts students, in a grotty, smoky, overheated, overcrowded room where the windows are running with water, but we're being made to feel like a valued audience. We listen even more attentively. The poem is 'The Haw Lantern', and the following year, when it is published, we will discover that it is the title poem of his new collection.

I cycle home, images from 'The Haw Lantern' poem in my head. The small red lights from the backs of the roaming shapes of bikes go floating past me in the darkness; wintry haws, burning out of season.

Rosita Boland

SIMON ARMITAGE POET

1992

Dear Nicola, Paula and Alice,

Many thanks for your invitation. Good luck with the project.

'The More Loving One' by W H Auden (1907–1973). Favourite poems come and go, and although I wouldn't claim that this is the greatest piece ever written, it has stayed with me longer than most. On the face of it, I'm attracted to its casual but compelling tone, its shifting rhythms and acoustics, its brevity, as well as its sentiments, which I can more or less subscribe to. The second stanza is exceptional – my heart goes off like a flash-bulb every time I read it. More than this, whilst the poem would be at home in any anthology of modern verse, it would be equally as comfortable on a toilet door or the back of a bus seat, and none the worse for it.

Very best,

Simon Armitage

The More Loving One

Looking up at the stars, I know quite well
That, for all they care, I can go to hell.
But on earth indifference is the least
We have to dread from man or beast.

How should we like it were stars to burn
With a passion for us we could not return?
If equal affection cannot be,
Let the more loving one be me.

Admirer as I think I am
Of stars that do not give a damn,
I cannot, now I see them, say
I missed one terribly all day.

Were all stars to disappear or die
I should learn to look at an empty sky
And feel its total dark sublime,
Though this might take me a little time.

W H AUDEN (1907–1973)

JUNG CHANG WRITER

4 February 1994

Dear Ewan, Áine and Christopher,

Thank you for your letter. I would be happy to help you with your anthology, and enclose one of my favourite poems.

I first read this poem by the eighth-century Chinese poet Tu Fu in 1969, when at the age of 16 I was sent to work as a peasant in a village at the edge of the Himalayas. My mother was in detention, and my father was in a labour camp. I was consumed by anxiety about what was happening to them. This poem gave expression to my longings to hear from them, and moreover, by transforming tragedy into great beauty, it helped keep me from feeling bitter or depressed.

Yours sincerely,

Jung Chang

Midnight

By the West Pavilion, on a thousand feet of cliff,
Walking at midnight under my latticed window.
Flying stars pass white along the water,
Transparent beams of moonset flicker on the sand.
At home in its tree, notice the secret bird:
Safe beneath the waves, imagine the great fishes.
From kinsmen and friends at the bounds of heaven and earth
Between weapon and buffcoat seldom a letter comes.

TU FU (712–770)

DERMOT HEALY WRITER

1997

Dear Folk,

Thank you for your letter. The poems I like best are anonymous – the name of the author has been written away by time, so no autobiography clings weighing the text down with all kinds of Hi-fal-la.

The other type of poems I like are songs, or maybe songs that are not considered poems. 'Dónal Óg' could have been a song once, but 'Frankie and Johnny' still is, and, best of all, it is anonymous, despite the fact that it's comparatively recent.

Good luck with the enterprise,

Dermot Healy

Frankie and Johnny

Frankie and Johnny were lovers.
O my Gawd how they did love!
They swore to be true to each other,
As true as the stars above.
He was her man but he done her wrong.

Frankie went down to the hock-shop,
Went for a bucket of beer,
Said: 'O Mr Bartender
Has my loving Johnny been here?
He is my man but he's doing me wrong.'

'I don't want to make you no trouble,
I don't want to tell you no lie,
But I saw Johnny an hour ago
With a girl named Nelly Bly,
He is your man but he's doing you wrong.'

Frankie went down to the hotel,
She didn't go there for fun,
'Cause underneath her kimona
She toted a 44 Gun.
He was her man but he done her wrong.

Frankie went down to the hotel.
She rang the front-door bell,
Said: 'Stand back all you chippies
Or I'll blow you all to hell.
I want my man for he's doing me wrong.'

Frankie looked in through the key-hole
And there before her eye
She saw her Johnny on the sofa
A-loving up Nelly Bly.
He was her man; he was doing her wrong.

Frankie threw back her kimona,
Took out a big 44,
Root-a-toot-toot, three times she shot
Right through that hardware door.
He was her man but he was doing her wrong.

Johnny grabbed up his Stetson,
Said: 'O my Gawd Frankie don't shoot!'
But Frankie pulled hard on the trigger
And the gun went root-a-toot-toot.
She shot her man who was doing her wrong.

'Roll me over easy,
Roll me over slow,
Roll me over on my right side
'Cause my left side hurts me so.
I was her man but I done her wrong.'

'Bring out your rubber-tired buggy,
Bring out your rubber-tired hack;
I'll take my Johnny to the graveyard
But I won't bring him back.
He was my man but he done me wrong.

'Lock me in that dungeon,
Lock me in that cell,
Lock me where the north-east wind
Blows from the corner of Hell.
I shot my man 'cause he done me wrong.'

It was not murder in the first degree,
It was not murder in the third.
A woman simply shot her man
As a hunter drops a bird.
She shot her man 'cause he done her wrong.

Frankie said to the Sheriff,
'What do you think they'll do?'
The Sheriff said to Frankie,
'It's the electric-chair for you.
You shot your man 'cause he done you wrong.'

Frankie sat in the jail-house,
Had no electric fan,
Told her sweet little sister:
'There ain't no good in a man.
I had a man but he done me wrong.'

Once more I saw Frankie,
She was sitting in the Chair
Waiting for to go and meet her God
With the sweat dripping out of her hair.
He was a man but he done her wrong.

This story has no moral,
This story has no end,
This story only goes to show
That there ain't no good in men.
He was her man but he done her wrong.

Anonymous

Happy to participate!

A favourite poem is Andrew Marvell's 'To His Coy Mistress'. I think of it as the world's best chat-up, and have always been amused by how the poet tries to wear down this poor girl. But the famous image of 'time's winged chariot hurrying near', has haunted me throughout my life.

I also love a silly one – it's a chat between two gargoyles!

> Splodge be my name
> Splurge be mine
> Here we squat
> In foul or fine

Francesca Simon

To His Coy Mistress

> Had we but world enough, and time,
> This coyness, lady, were no crime.
> We would sit down and think which way
> To walk, and pass our long love's day;
> Thou by the Indian Ganges' side
> Shouldst rubies find; I by the tide
> Of Humber would complain. I would
> Love you ten years before the Flood;
> And you should, if you please, refuse
> Till the conversion of the Jews.
> My vegetable love should grow
> Vaster than empires, and more slow;
> An hundred years should go to praise
> Thine eyes, and on thy forehead gaze;
> Two hundred to adore each breast,
> But thirty thousand to the rest;
> An age at least to every part,
> And the last age should show your heart.
> For, lady, you deserve this state,
> Nor would I love at lower rate.
> But at my back I always hear
> Time's wingèd chariot hurrying near;
> And yonder all before us lie
> Deserts of vast eternity.
> Thy beauty shall no more be found,
> Nor, in thy marble vault, shall sound
> My echoing song; then worms shall try

That long preserv'd virginity,
And your quaint honour turn to dust,
And into ashes all my lust.
The grave's a fine and private place,
But none I think do there embrace.
⠀⠀⠀Now therefore, while the youthful hue
Sits on thy skin like morning dew,
And while thy willing soul transpires
At every pore with instant fires,
Now let us sport us while we may;
And now, like amorous birds of prey,
Rather at once our time devour
Than languish in his slow-chapp'd power.
Let us roll all our strength, and all
Our sweetness, up into one ball;
And tear our pleasures with rough strife
Thorough the iron gates of life:
Thus, though we cannot make our sun
Stand still, yet we will make him run.

ANDREW MARVELL (1621–1678)

['*To His Coy Mistress*' was also chosen by Ita Daly and Macdara Woods in *Lifelines*. Ita Daly wrote:

The poem I have chosen is 'To His Coy Mistress' *by Andrew Marvell. Marvell is one of my favourites and I have chosen this poem because it is sensuous, witty and wise. I share its philosophy and I admire its execution. A comfort on dark winter nights.*

Macdara Woods wrote:

Andrew Marvell's 'To His Coy Mistress' *is a poem I keep coming back to because it is one of those texts, like Thomas Mann's* Death In Venice, *which goes on quietly growing by itself while you are away from it. Which may be just another way of saying that the older I get the more relevant this poem appears to become. It is about human contact and human vulnerability, with an acute perception of mortality and decay, and yet it is hopeful – and even heroic – because it says that human contact and the full endorsement of it, despite the inevitability of heartbreak, is all we have got and is worthwhile. This is all we can do in the end, be human, and courage lies in being human in spite of that. In Beckett's words:* 'You must go on. I can't go on. I'll go on.' *Somehow, in spite of logic, age, decay and death do not rob life – or love – of meaning.*]

Seamus Heaney may have written better poems than 'Mid-Term Break', but he has surely never written one more touching or moving than this account of his coming home from boarding school for the funeral of his four-year-old brother who had been knocked down and killed by a car.

This simple 22-line poem conveys such a powerful impression of the sense of loss created by the sudden death of a child on the parents and on the child's siblings.

It brings us back to an era when many more children in rural Ireland went away to school and when funerals were a lot more formal and ritualised than now – with the teenage Heaney expressing his embarrassment as old men stood up to shake his hand and tell them they were 'sorry for my trouble'.

Anyone who has ever lost a sibling at an early age or even who has been at a funeral of a young child will be able to identify with the sense of bewildered loss and confusion expressed by Heaney.

Best wishes,

Pat Rabbitte TD

Mid-Term Break

I sat all morning in the college sick bay
Counting bells knelling classes to a close.
At two o'clock our neighbours drove me home.

In the porch I met my father crying—
He had always taken funerals in his stride—
And Big Jim Evans saying it was a hard blow.

The baby cooed and laughed and rocked the pram
When I came in, and I was embarrassed
By old men standing up to shake my hand

And tell me they were 'sorry for my trouble'.
Whispers informed strangers I was the eldest,
Away at school, as my mother held my hand

In hers and coughed out angry tearless sighs.
At ten o'clock the ambulance arrived
With the corpse, stanched and bandaged by the nurses.

Next morning I went up into the room. Snowdrops
And candles soothed the bedside; I saw him
For the first time in six weeks. Paler now,

Wearing a poppy bruise on his left temple,
He lay in the four-foot box as in his cot.
No gaudy scars, the bumper knocked him clear.

A four-foot box, a foot for every year.

SEAMUS HEANEY (B. 1939)

13 February 1997

Dear Ralph, Caroline and Gareth,

I'm afraid I've taken a long time answering your letter, but you must forgive me, because it unfortunately took a long time to arrive. Your anthology Lifelines *was a wonderful idea, and I very much regret that it must be too late now for me to contribute, but if by any chance it's not, I should like to say that my favourite poem (or one of them, because I care a lot about poetry) is Yeats's 'The Stare's Nest by My Window', and I hardly need to explain why it means so much to me, as there must be many millions all over the world who make the same prayer for honey-bees to come to the empty house. In fact, I daresay it's been suggested to you often already. But meantime, I should like to send you all my best wishes for* Lifelines 3.

Penelope Fitzgerald

The Stare's Nest by My Window

The bees build in the crevices
Of loosening masonry, and there
The mother birds bring grubs and flies.
My wall is loosening; honey-bees,
Come build in the empty house of the stare.

We are closed in, and the key is turned
On our uncertainty; somewhere
A man is killed, or a house burned,
Yet no clear fact to be discerned:
Come build in the empty house of the stare.

A barricade of stone or of wood;
Some fourteen days of civil war;
Last night they trundled down the road
That dead young soldier in his blood:
Come build in the empty house of the stare.

We had fed the heart on fantasies,
The heart's grown brutal from the fare;
More substance in our enmities
Than in our love; O honey-bees,
Come build in the empty house of the stare.

W B YEATS (1865–1939)

2006

Hi Dónal, Caroline and Stephanie,

I'm not really into poetry but I do have a favourite poem. It's called 'Self-Pity' by D H Lawrence.

Best of luck with the project,

Derek

Self-Pity

I never saw a wild thing
sorry for itself.
A small bird will drop frozen dead from a bough
without ever having felt sorry for itself.

D H LAWRENCE (1885–1930)

BILLY COLLINS   POET

2006

The best known Coleridge poems are the so-called 'mystery poems'. 'Kubla Khan', 'Christabel' and 'The Rime of the Ancient Mariner' enjoy regular appearances in textbooks and anthologies and are frequent visitors to classrooms all over the English-speaking world. But his other style and form at work in the 'conversation poems' set the direction more clearly for the lyric poems written in the post-Romantic and modern periods. This less intimidating group, named by broadening the title of 'The Nightingale: A Conversation Poem', includes such poems as 'Frost at Midnight', 'The Aeolian Lyre', and my favorite, 'This Lime-Tree Bower My Prison'. Each of these poems opens in a simple domestic setting – at home by a fire, in a cottage garden, in a backyard bower – then each rises by the incremental power of the imagination from the level of casual conversation to higher levels of intense meditation and sometimes dizzying speculation.

What other poem opens so casually as this one? 'Well . . .' is a far cry from 'A drowsy numbness pains my sense . . .' 'Well . . .' is a common opening for rockabilly songs, but not for a poem composed in the waning years of the 18th century. But a mere 30 lines pass after this off-hand exhalation before we find this heightened apostrophe to the sun:

'Ah! slowly sink/Behind the western ridge, thou glorious Sun!' And a dozen lines later, the scope of the poet's consideration has widened to include the 'Almighty Spirit, when yet he makes/Spirits perceive his presence.'

By a bit of rhetorical sleight-of-hand, Coleridge manages in the poem to be in two places at once. Left behind by his friends, he must remain home while they take a walk. Imprisoned at home in a leafy bower by his cottage, he manages to join his friends – Charles Lamb and the Wordsworths – through an act of imaginative projection. Further, he is able to describe both the imagined walk and his present surroundings with equal focus. The detail of the 'blue clay stone' in the 'roaring dell' is no less a specific image than 'the solitary humble-bee' that sings 'in the bean flower.' Coleridge achieves a kind of out-of-body travel while remaining somehow sharply attentive to his homely surroundings.

In the poem's climactic lines, the poet's imaginative reach unites him and his beloved Lamb through the overhead flight of the 'last rook', which forms the third point of a connective triangle, a scene of shared witnessing.

The poem is finally a thrilling example of the power of a lyric poem to escalate from a commonplace beginning to a transcendent ending.

It is also the best poem I know on the subject of friendship despite Lamb's letter of response in which he – a Londoner – denies any need for the therapeutic influence of nature and orders Coleridge to never again refer to him as 'gentle-hearted Charles'.

Billy Collins

This Lime-Tree Bower My Prison

Well, they are gone, and here must I remain,
This lime-tree bower my prison! I have lost
Beauties and feelings, such as would have been
Most sweet to my remembrance even when age
Had dimmed mine eyes to blindness! They, meanwhile,
Friends, whom I never more may meet again,
On springy heath, along the hill-top edge,
Wander in gladness, and wind down, perchance,
To that still roaring dell, of which I told;
The roaring dell, o'erwooded, narrow, deep,
And only speckled by the mid-day sun;
Where its slim trunk the ash from rock to rock
Flings arching like a bridge;—that branchless ash,
Unsunn'd and damp, whose few poor yellow leaves
Ne'er tremble in the gale, yet tremble still,
Fann'd by the water-fall! and there my friends
Behold the dark green file of long lank weeds,
That all at once (a most fantastic sight!)
Still nod and drip beneath the dripping edge
Of the blue clay-stone.

　　　Now, my friends emerge
Beneath the wide wide Heaven—and view again
The many-steepled tract magnificent
Of hilly fields and meadows, and the sea,
With some fair bark, perhaps, whose sails light up
The slip of smooth clear blue betwixt two Isles
Of purple shadow! Yes! they wander on
In gladness all; but thou, methinks, most glad,
My gentle-hearted Charles! for thou hast pined
And hunger'd after Nature, many a year,
In the great City pent, winning thy way
With sad yet patient soul, through evil and pain

And strange calamity! Ah! slowly sink
Behind the western ridge, thou glorious Sun!
Shine in the slant beams of the sinking orb,
Ye purple heath-flowers! richlier burn, ye clouds!
Live in the yellow light, ye distant groves!
And kindle, thou blue Ocean! So my friend
Struck with deep joy may stand, as I have stood,
Silent with swimming sense; yea, gazing round
On the wide landscape, gaze till all doth seem
Less gross than bodily; and of such hues
As veil the Almighty Spirit, when yet he makes
Spirits perceive his presence.

    A delight
Comes sudden on my heart, and I am glad
As I myself were there! Nor in this bower,
This little lime-tree bower, have I not mark'd
Much that has sooth'd me. Pale beneath the blaze
Hung the transparent foliage; and I watch'd
Some broad and sunny leaf, and lov'd to see
The shadow of the leaf and stem above
Dappling its sunshine! And that walnut-tree
Was richly ting'd, and a deep radiance lay
Full on the ancient ivy, which usurps
Those fronting elms, and now, with blackest mass
Makes their dark branches gleam a lighter hue
Through the late twilight: and though now the bat
Wheels silent by, and not a swallow twitters,
Yet still the solitary humble-bee
Sings in the bean-flower! Henceforth I shall know
That Nature ne'er deserts the wise and pure;
No plot so narrow, be but Nature there,
No waste so vacant, but may well employ
Each faculty of sense, and keep the heart
Awake to Love and Beauty! and sometimes
'Tis well to be bereft of promis'd good,
That we may lift the soul, and contemplate
With lively joy the joys we cannot share.
My gentle-hearted Charles! when the last rook
Beat its straight path across the dusky air
Homewards, I blest it! deeming its black wing
(Now a dim speck, now vanishing in light)
Had cross'd the mighty Orb's dilated glory,
While thou stood'st gazing; or, when all was still,
Flew creeking o'er thy head, and had a charm
For thee, my gentle-hearted Charles, to whom
No sound is dissonant which tells of Life.

SAMUEL TAYLOR COLERIDGE (1772–1834)

24 March 1997

Dear Ralph, Caroline and Gareth,

Thanks for asking me to contribute to Lifelines 3. *My favourite poem is* 'Long Distance II' *by poet/playwright Tony Harrison.*

Long Distance II

Though my mother was already two years dead
Dad kept her slippers warming by the gas,
put hot water bottles her side of the bed
and still went to renew her transport pass.

You couldn't just drop in. You had to phone.
He'd put you off an hour to give him time
to clear away her things and look alone
as though his still raw love were such a crime.

He couldn't risk my blight of disbelief
though sure that very soon he'd hear her key
scrape in the rusted lock and end his grief.
He *knew* she'd just popped out to get the tea.

I believe life ends with death, and that is all.
You haven't both gone shopping; just the same,
in my new black leather phone book there's your name
and the disconnected number I still call.

TONY HARRISON (B. 1937)

The father's 'still raw love' lies at the heart of this extraordinarily moving poem, opposed by the rational poet's 'blight of disbelief' at such grief-stricken self-delusion. The opposition between reason and emotion collapses at the end with the haunted sceptic persistently dialling a discontinued phone number: a perfectly alienated, late-century metaphor for the confusion and pain of bereavement. A masterpiece.

All the best with the anthology,

Declan Hughes

My favourite poem is 'Wind' by Ted Hughes.

I grew up in a large farmhouse in the middle of the Laggan Valley in East Donegal. My bedroom (which had single-glazed windows when I was young) faces a back garden which has a massive oak tree. As a child I used to fall asleep at night during the winter months listening to the strong winds blowing up the valley and whistling through the bare branches of the large oak tree.

The fierce winds rustling through the tree really sounded like waves on the sea and I used to use my child's eye to pretend that the house was really a ship rocking about on the moonlit sea. This would send me off to sleep every night. This is why I love 'Wind' by Ted Hughes . . . 'This house has been far out at sea all night'.

I was very happy to get your letter and to take part in the project.

Ann Quinn

Wind

This house has been far out at sea all night,
The woods crashing through darkness, the booming hills,
Winds stampeding the fields under the window
Floundering black astride and blinding wet

Till day rose; then under an orange sky
The hills had new places, and wind wielded
Blade-light, luminous and emerald,
Flexing like the lens of a mad eye.

At noon I scaled along the house-side as far as
The coal-house door. I dared once to look up –
Through the brunt wind that dented the balls of my eyes
The tent of the hills drummed and strained its guyrope,

The fields quivering, the skyline a grimace,
At any second to bang and vanish with a flap;
The wind flung a magpie away and a black–
Back gull bent like an iron bar slowly. The house

Rang like some fine green goblet in the note
That any second would shatter it. Now deep
In chairs, in front of the great fire, we grip
Our hearts and cannot entertain book, thought,

Or each other. We watch the fire blazing,
And feel the roots of the house move, but sit on,
Seeing the window tremble to come in,
Hearing the stones cry out under the horizons.

TED HUGHES (1930–1998)

14 January 1994

Dear Ewan Gibson, Áine Jackson and Christopher Pillow,

Thank you for your letter about your Lifelines *anthology. I'm glad you've had so much success in raising money for Third World causes – congratulations. Very hard to choose a favourite poem, but this is one of my favourites:* 'Buffalo Bill's' *by E E Cummings. I like it because it's funny and moving and uses the word 'defunct' quite brilliantly. It has made a permanent home in my imagination. It has to be read aloud, and I like poems to be read aloud.*

All best wishes,

Helen Dunmore

Buffalo Bill's
defunct
      who used to
      ride a watersmooth-silver
                  stallion
and break onetwothreefourfive pigeonsjustlikethat
                                 Jesus

he was a handsome man
                  and what i want to know is
how do you like your blueeyed boy
Mister Death

E E CUMMINGS (1894–1962)

RICHARD DAWKINS

SCIENTIST

3 February 1997

Dear Mr Croly, Miss Dowling and Mr McCluskey,

Thank you for your letter.

This poem from A Shropshire Lad *has been in my head ever since 1977 when the great evolutionary scientist W D Hamilton quoted it in his long, thoughtful – and poetic – review of my first book. Like many Housman poems it is about life's transience but, in a Darwinian mind, it also evokes life's continuation as an endless cycle of recombination and permutation – not just of atoms (as Housman would have realised) but of coded information (as he presumably did not).*

Yours sincerely,

Richard Dawkins

from *A Shropshire Lad*

XXXII
From far, from eve and morning
    And yon twelve-winded sky,
The stuff of life to knit me
    Blew hither: here am I.

Now — for a breath I tarry
    Nor yet disperse apart —
Take my hand quick and tell me,
    What have you in your heart.

Speak now, and I will answer;
    How shall I help you, say;
Ere to the wind's twelve quarters
    I take my endless way.

A E HOUSMAN (1859–1936)

My favourite poem is 'Les Sylphides' by Louis MacNeice. He is my favourite poet. I love this poem because it is a strange mixture of the romantic and the sardonic. It is a warning not to be carried away by youthful infatuation and still it has an awareness of how beautiful such an infatuation is.

Rosaleen Linehan

Les Sylphides

Life in a day: he took his girl to the ballet;
Being shortsighted himself could hardly see it —
    The white skirts in the grey
    Glade and the swell of the music
    Lifting the white sails.

Calyx upon calyx, canterbury bells in the breeze
The flowers on the left mirror to the flowers on the right
    And the naked arms above
    The powdered faces moving
    Like seaweed in a pool.

Now, he thought, we are floating — ageless, oarless —
Now there is no separation, from now on
    You will be wearing white
    Satin and a red sash
    Under the waltzing trees.

But the music stopped, the dancers took their curtain,
The river had come to a lock — a shuffle of programmes —
    And we cannot continue down
    Stream unless we are ready
    To enter the lock and drop.

So they were married — to be the more together —
And found they were never again so much together,
    Divided by the morning tea,
    By the evening paper,
    By children and tradesmen's bills.

Waking at times in the night she found assurance
Due to his regular breathing but wondered whether
    It was really worth it and where
    The river had flowed away
    And where were the white flowers.

LOUIS MacNEICE (1907–1963)

Dear Pupils,

My favourite poem is 'No Coward Soul is Mine' *by Emily Brontë. It is a perfect expression of her nature, defying the death that would come in two years. It is full of feminine passion and courage. It vindicates all lives that are cut short with apparent meaninglessness and is the only poem I know worthy of this anthology.*

Medbh McGuckian

No Coward Soul is Mine

No coward soul is mine,
No trembler in the world's storm-troubled sphere!
I see Heaven's glories shine,
And Faith shines equal, arming me from Fear

O God within my breast,
Almighty ever-present Deity!
Life, that in me hast rest,
As I, Undying Life, have power in thee!

Vain are the thousand creeds
That move men's hearts, unutterably vain;
Worthless as withered weeds,
Or idlest froth amid the boundless main,

To waken doubt in one
Holding so fast by thy infinity,
So surely anchored on
The steadfast rock of Immortality.

With wide-embracing love
Thy spirit animates eternal years,
Pervades and broods above,
Changes, sustains, dissolves, creates and rears.

Though earth and moon were gone,
And suns and universes ceased to be,
And thou wert left alone,
Every Existence would exist in thee.

There is not room for Death,
Nor atom that his might could render void;
Since thou art Being and Breath
And what thou art may never be destroyed.

EMILY BRONTË (1818–1848)

'The Wild Swans at Coole' *by William Butler Yeats*

I can speak many of Yeats's poems by heart, but I can not recall consciously sitting down to learn them. I've simply absorbed them – as any person growing up in Ireland might absorb and retain the sound of the surf on Erris Head, or the thick scent of meadowsweet after a shower of rain in a Monaghan sheugh, or the image of those all-seeing two-faced stone figures by the shores of Lough Erne. I suppose that my response to 'The Wild Swans at Coole' *is tempered by many things: the story of the Gregory family, unusual in that its members were good landlords as well as distinguished people in public life; geology and topography, because of that extraordinary limestone landscape into which the Coole lakes are hollowed; ornithology, naturally – even if you exclude the mythological connotations of swans (which is impossible!) they are never anything short of being 'brilliant creatures'; and literary history, for it was at Coole Park that Yeats and Lady Gregory wrestled with the intractabilities of the Abbey Theatre. Almost twenty years after his first visit to Coole, we find the poet looking back on a period of intense creativity, on an era of cataclysmic political and social change in Ireland, on disillusion, broken dreams, and towards an uncertain future in which the imagination may not take flight in the way it used to do.*

Christopher Fitz-Simon

The Wild Swans at Coole

The trees are in their autumn beauty,
The woodland paths are dry,
Under the October twilight the water
Mirrors a still sky;
Upon the brimming water among the stones
Are nine-and-fifty swans.

The nineteenth autumn has come upon me
Since I first made my count;
I saw, before I had well finished,
All suddenly mount
And scatter wheeling in great broken rings
Upon their clamorous wings.

I have looked upon those brilliant creatures,
And now my heart is sore.
All's changed since I, hearing at twilight,
The first time on this shore,
The bell-beat of their wings above my head,
Trod with a lighter tread.

Unwearied still, lover by lover,
They paddle in the cold
Companionable streams or climb the air;
Their hearts have not grown old;
Passion or conquest, wander where they will,
Attend upon them still.

But now they drift on the still water,
Mysterious, beautiful;
Among what rushes will they build,
By what lake's edge or pool
Delight men's eyes when I awake some day
To find they have flown away?

W B YEATS (1865–1939)

IRIS MURDOCH   NOVELIST

22 April 1985

A Summer Night
(To Geoffrey Hoyland)

Out on the lawn I lie in bed,
Vega conspicuous overhead
        In the windless nights of June,
As congregated leaves complete
Their day's activity; my feet
        Point to the rising moon.

Lucky, this point in time and space
Is chosen as my working place,
        Where the sexy airs of summer,
The bathing hours and the bare arms,
The leisured drives through a land of farms
        Are good to a newcomer.

Equal with colleagues in a ring
I sit on each calm evening
        Enchanted as the flowers
The opening light draws out of hiding
With all its gradual dove-like pleading,
        Its logic and its powers:

That later we, though parted then,
May still recall these evenings when
        Fear gave his watch no look;
The lion griefs loped from the shade
And on our knees their muzzles laid,
        And Death put down his book.

Now north and south and east and west
Those I love lie down to rest;
        The moon looks on them all,
The healers and the brilliant talkers
The eccentrics and the silent walkers,
        The dumpy and the tall.

She climbs the European sky,
Churches and power-stations lie
        Alike among earth's fixtures:
Into the galleries she peers
And blankly as a butcher stares
        Upon the marvellous pictures.

To gravity attentive, she
Can notice nothing here, though we
        Whom hunger does not move,
From gardens where we feel secure
Look up and with a sigh endure
        The tyrannies of love:

And, gentle, do not care to know,
Where Poland draws her Eastern bow,
        What violence is done,
Nor ask what doubtful act allows
Our freedom in this English house,
        Our picnics in the sun.

Soon, soon, through dykes of our content
The crumpling flood will force a rent
        And, taller than a tree,
Hold sudden death before our eyes
Whose river dreams long hid the size
        And vigours of the sea.

But when the waters make retreat
And through the black mud first the wheat
        In shy green stalks appears,
When stranded monsters gasping lie,
And sounds of riveting terrify
        Their whorled unsubtle ears,

May these delights we dread to lose,
This privacy need no excuse
        But to that strength belong,
As through a child's rash happy cries
The drowned parental voices rise
        In unlamenting song.

After discharges of alarm
All unpredicted let them calm
        The pulse of nervous nations,
Forgive the murderer in his glass,
Tough in their patience to surpass
        The tigress her swift motions.

W H AUDEN (1907–1973)

This marvellously beautiful elegiac song, full of magisterial images, expresses both fear and hope. It also conjures up, with great tenderness and feeling, a particular occasion. This connection of vast moral vistas with individual situations is typical poetic magic.

Iris Murdoch

Oifig an Taoisigh
22 April 1985

Dear Collette,

Many thanks for your letter. I must admit I find your plan to raise money for the Third World very original, as this is the first occasion on which I have been asked for my favourite poem.

    I have, from time to time, come across a poem I have enjoyed reading, but quite frankly, on considering your letter, I found it difficult to pinpoint any one particular poem. However, I am particularly fond of the enclosed extract from The Book of Ecclesiastes, *the words of which I find thought-provoking and profound, and like to reflect on in the rare moments when I can tear myself away from the hurly-burly of political life. I hope this will be of assistance to you.*

    Wishing you, Joy and Steven every success with the undertaking,

Yours sincerely,

Garret FitzGerald

extract from *The Book of Ecclesiastes*

All things have their season, and in their times
    all things pass under heaven.
A time to be born and a time to die.
A time to plant, and a time to pluck up that which is planted.
A time to kill, and a time to heal.
A time to destroy, and a time to build.
A time to weep, and a time to laugh.
A time to mourn, and a time to dance.
A time to scatter stones, and a time to gather.
A time to embrace, and a time to be far from embraces.
A time to get, and a time to lose,
A time to keep, and a time to cast away.
A time to rend, and a time to sew.
A time to keep silence, and a time to speak.
A time of love and a time of hatred.
A time of war, and a time of peace.
What hath men more of his labour?

Dear Ralph, Caroline and Gareth,

Congratulations on a splendid idea and a very worthwhile project. I take off my proverbial hat to you.

I'm delighted to be able to send on one of my favourite poems. I decided that, rather than picking something well-known, I'd go for a more obscure poet – Wendell Berry, a writer/farmer from Kentucky. (Another one of his poems which you might enjoy is the tiny political lyric called 'The Mad Farmer's Liberation Song': 'Instead of reading Chairman Mao/I think I'll go and milk my cow')!

Anyway, enclosed is my favourite poem of Berry's and my response to it.

With very best wishes for you and your project,

Yours sincerely,

Colum McCann

A Meeting

In a dream I meet
my dead friend. He has,
I know, gone long and far,
and yet he is the same
for the dead are changeless.
They grow no older.
It is I who have changed,
grown strange to what I was.
Yet I, the changed one,
ask: 'How you been?'
He grins and looks at me.
'I been eating peaches
off some mighty fine trees.'

WENDELL BERRY (B. 1934)

Wendell Berry is a farmer who lives in the farmlands of Kentucky. Once – while I was travelling across the United States on a bicycle – I carried his poems with me for thousands of miles. (Other poets I carried in my pannier bags were Dylan Thomas, Gary Snyder, Jim Harrison and Seamus Heaney.) Late at night I would learn the poems off by heart. The rhythms have clicked with me ever since. I think this particular poem, 'A Meeting', is sad, wise, funny, poignant and just unspeakably beautiful.

I recently read it at a funeral service for a friend of mine – strangely enough, not far from the service, a man was out on the street selling peaches. He was grinning at the world.

12 January 1992

Dear Mss Hughes, Griffin and McEleney,

Thank you for your invitation to nominate a favourite poem for your Lifelines *anthology. When I settled down to think what it might be, I realised that I had at least thirty favourite poems; but some of them were very long and some so obvious that they have doubtless been chosen by many other contributors. So in the end I set aside my Pope and Wordsworth and Tennyson and my Yeats and Hopkins and Heaney and Elizabeth Bishop, and picked a rather less well-known item by Thom Gunn (it comes from his book* The Passages of Joy, *published by Faber and Faber in 1982).*

With all good wishes for your project.

Yours sincerely,

Alan Hollinghurst

Night Taxi

for Rod Taylor,
wherever he is

Open city
uncluttered as a map.
I drive through empty streets
scoured by the winds
of midnight. My shift
is only beginning and I am fresh
and excitable, master of the taxi.
I relish my alert reflexes
where all else
is in hiding. I have
by default it seems
conquered me a city.

My first address: I
press the doorbell, I lean back
against the hood, my headlights
scalding a garage door, my engine
drumming in the driveway,
the only sound on the block.
There the fare finds me
like a date, jaunty,
shoes shined, I am
proud of myself, on my toes,
obliging but not subservient.

I take short cuts, picking up
speed, from time to time
I switch on the dispatcher's
litany of addresses,
China Basin to Twin Peaks,
Harrison Street to the Ocean.

I am thinking tonight
my fares are like affairs
—no, more like tricks to turn:
quick, lively, ending up
with a cash payment.
I do not anticipate a holdup.
I can make friendly small talk.
I do not go on about Niggers,
women drivers or the Chinese.
It's all on my terms but
I let them think it's on theirs.

Do I pass through the city
or does it pass through me?
I know I have to be loose,
like my light embrace of the wheel,
loose but in control
—though hour by hour I tighten
minutely in the routine,
smoking my palate to ash,
till the last hour of all
will be drudgery, nothing else.

I zip down Masonic Avenue,
the taxi sings beneath the streetlights
a song to the bare city, it is
my instrument, I woo with it,
bridegroom and conqueror.

I jump out to open the door,
fixing the cap on my head
to, you know, firm up my role,
and on my knuckle
feel a sprinkle of wet.

Glancing upward I see
high above the lamppost
but touched by its farthest light
a curtain of rain already blowing
against black eucalyptus tops.

THOM GUNN (1929–2004)

I know of no more beautiful evocation of a city at night than that in 'Night Taxi'. In this case the city is San Francisco, where Thom Gunn lives, and to read these fluent but watchful lines is to see again its plunging hills and the glittering panorama of its bay. 'Loose but in control' might sum up the poet's technique: the voice is natural, unforced, though capable of a kind of exaltation; and the subject matter, if rare – even unprecedented – in poetry, is deliberately routine. Yet it seems to me a great elegaic poem, the stronger and the more poignant for the way it only glances at its theme, which I take to be the transience of experience, of sexual happiness, of our brief tenancy of our spot on earth. The poet, the taxi-driver, the dedicatee ('wherever he is') have made their passage through this ghostly cityscape. The last lines hauntingly combine imagery of radiance and of dissolution.

AMY CLAMPITT POET

16 January 1990

Dear Joann Bradish, Jacki Erskine, and Carolyn Gibson,

You ask me to name my favourite poem. Like many other people, I have too many favorites to settle for very long on any single one. But since I first encountered it at the age of four or five, one of those favorites has always been 'Jabberwocky' from Through the Looking-Glass, *the second of the Alice books by Lewis Carroll. It is one of the few poems I can recite from memory without stumbling, and that is strange since it is studded with words that came out of nowhere and mean nothing in particular. As Alice herself put it, '. . . it seems to fill my head with ideas – only I don't know exactly what they are.' Anyhow, the sound of those words is somehow magical and ridiculous both at once. And the sound, after all, is what makes a good poem worth remembering.*

Sincerely yours,

Amy Clampitt

Jabberwocky

'Twas brillig, and the slithy toves
      Did gyre and gimble in the wabe:
All mimsy were the borogoves,
      And the mome raths outgrabe.

'Beware the Jabberwock, my son!
      The jaws that bite, the claw that catch!
Beware the Jubjub bird, and shun
      The frumious Bandersnatch!'

He took his vorpal sword in hand:
      Long time the manxome foe he sought—
So rested he by the Tumtum tree,
      And stood awhile in thought.

And, as in uffish thought he stood,
      The Jabberwock, with eyes of flame,
Came whiffling through the tulgey wood,
      And burbled as it came!

One, two! One, two! And through and through
      The vorpal blade went snicker-snack!
He left it dead, and with its head
      He went galumphing back.

'And, hast thou slain the Jabberwock?
      Come to my arms, my beamish boy!
O frabjous day! Callooh! Callay!'
      He chortled in his joy.

'Twas brillig, and the slithy toves
      Did gyre and gimble in the wabe:
All mimsy were the borogoves,
      And the mome raths outgrabe.

LEWIS CARROLL (1832–1898)

11 February 1988

Dear Julie, Jonathan and Duncan,

'Street Corner Christ' *is a poem very close to my own heart and given the nature of your cause, I feel an appropriate contribution. I have kept my comments to the bare minimum and although my few lines do not do justice to this poem it is my heartfelt wish that in helping to raise funds for Ethiopia they may allow justice to be done elsewhere.*

If there is any other way in which I can be of assistance please don't hesitate to contact me. With kindest regards,

Yours sincerely,

Sr Stanislaus Kennedy

At first reading, the reader is struck by the simple poignancy of this poem and touched by the sadness which tinges the poet's description of his subject matter – 'an uncouth ballad seller with tail-matted hair'.

But to be merely touched by the images which predominate the verse and not to recognise the harsh criticism which the poet is levelling at society, would not do Kavanagh justice. It would be similar in fact, to becoming 'as blind and deaf' as the 'pieties' within the poem whose narrowness of vision prohibits them from seeing the truth.

Indeed, acceptance of such criticism is integral to identifying with the poet and to understanding and empathising with the message of the poem. It was Christ, after all, who said 'whatever you do to the least of these my brethren, you do unto me'. Surely, it follows, then, that if it takes a little bit of poetic licence to bring these words home to us and to help all those who seek to find their own street corner Christ in the 'rags of a beggar', then God Bless Paddy Kavanagh!

Street Corner Christ

I saw Christ today
At a street corner stand,
In the rags of a beggar he stood
He held ballads in his hand.

He was crying out: 'Two for a penny
Will anyone buy
The finest ballads every made
From the stuff of joy?'

But the blind and deaf went past
Knowing only there
An uncouth ballad seller
With tail-matted hair.

And I whom men call fool
His ballads bought,
Found Him whom the pieties
Have vainly sought.

PATRICK KAVANAGH (1904–1967)

PAT KENNY BROADCASTER

Dear Julie, Jonathan and Duncan,

I found it quite impossible to nominate an all-time favourite. So much depends on the mood, the weather, the circumstance. Because I work with the spoken word all the time, I have an infatuation with its beauty whether it's in the sonnets of Shakespeare, the lyricism of Yeats or in the words of some popular songs. However, my first realisation that poetry didn't, wasn't always about nature, life, love or despair came with the discovery of Sir John Betjeman. It also helped me to realise as a schoolboy that you didn't have to be dead to be recognised as a poetic genius. I can recommend any of his poems to your readers, but perhaps 'Business Girls' captures the world of bedsit London, and to some extent Dublin, to perfection.

Yours sincerely,

Pat Kenny

Business Girls

From the geyser ventilators
Autumn winds are blowing down
On a thousand business women
Having baths in Camden Town.

Waste pipes chuckle into runnels
Steam's escaping here and there,
Morning trains through Camden cutting
Shake the Crescent and the Square.

Early nip of changeful Autumn,
Dahlias glimpsed through garden doors,
At the back precarious bathrooms
Jutting out from upper floors;

And behind their frail partitions
Business women lie and soak,
Seeing through the draughty skylight
Flying clouds and railway smoke.

Rest you there, poor unbelov'd ones,
Lap you loneliness in heat.
All too soon the tiny breakfast,
Trolley bus and windy street!

JOHN BETJEMAN
(1906–1984)

May 2006

Dear Editors,

Apologies for replying at the last minute – had hoped to get back to you sooner, but . . .

It is, of course, near impossible to pick a favourite poem, but put to the wall my choice is Eavan Boland's 'The Lost Land'. Other contributors may well choose the same poem.

Good luck with the project, and very well done.

All best,

Denyse Woods (and also Denyse Devlin!)

The first time I read Eavan Boland's 'The Lost Land', it hit me in about three different places. The first two lines always get me in the gut, because I too have two daughters and they are all I ever wanted from the earth. That someone has found the words to pinpoint this most primeval and visceral experience is baffling, and exciting.

When 'The Lost Land' was published in 1998, I transcribed the first three lines on to cards and gave them to my daughters. They were small then, and could not understand. They are older now, and almost understand. If they become mothers themselves, they will understand.

And then the powerful reminder that we are not only mothers: 'Or almost all.' It immediately made me think of Ireland – and there it was, in the next line: 'I also wanted one piece of ground.'

As the daughter of a diplomat, I spent my childhood abroad. I wasn't even born here. But when I was sixteen, and quasi-Australian after three years over there, my father took me to Connemara. This, he seemed to be saying, is yours.

> So I could say, *mine. My own.*
> And mean it.

My father took me away from Ireland; he also gave it back to me.

When we finally moved back here, I had no sooner found my bearings than I had to leave again, to work. So the sense of absence in this poem is not, for me, about my daughters, who have not yet left me, or Ireland; it is about my own extended absences from a place I almost didn't find. I have been the daughter on the mailboat, 'shadows falling/on everything they had to leave?/And would love forever?' I was drawn to the Arab world, but Ireland kept pulling on me, as it does. In Baghdad, 'At night, on the edge of sleep' Dublin came to me and I would imagine myself walking its pavements (Merrion Square, for some reason) and try to feel the city beneath my feet. In London, an Irish friend, hearing that I hoped to go home one day, shook her head and said, 'You'll burn your bridges.' And when I married an Englishman, I very nearly did light that match. In the mid-Eighties, it seemed as if Ireland itself was the mailboat, sailing away. It was something of a sinking ship at the time, everyone jumping off, but I was prepared to go down with it. I could not allow myself to be exiled permanently, made restless and homeless by my peripatetic childhood and my choice of partner. It was sheer luck that, unlike me, my husband had no spiritual need to be in his homeland. We took a huge leap, and made it.

Now I have my 'piece of ground'. I have been able to watch my daughters grow up here. I can stand on cliffs in Mayo, or on hills in Kerry, or even in my adopted home of Cork – also 'One city trapped by hills. One urban river' – and rejoice. I sit on beaches, bewitched by the sight of our dark and mysterious headlands sloping down into the Atlantic – 'An island in its element' – and think, 'Mine. All mine.' I am greedy, and no doubt sentimental, about Ireland. I don't indulge the greed, but I allow it. It helps me think, and write.

When I took that ferry, to come home to Ireland, I was expecting our first child, who is now eighteen and may soon leave. How can I not be deeply moved, now and always, by a poem that ends: 'Ireland. Absence. Daughter.'

The Lost Land

I have two daughters.

They are all I ever wanted from the earth.

Or almost all.

I also wanted one piece of ground:

One city trapped by hills. One urban river.
An island in its element.

So I could say *mine. My own.*
And mean it.

Now they are grown up and far away

and memory itself
has become an emigrant,
wandering in a place
where love dissembles itself as landscape.

Where the hills
are the colours of a child's eyes,
where my children are distances, horizons:

At night,
on the edge of sleep,
I can see the shore of Dublin Bay,
its rocky sweep and its granite pier.

Is this, I say
how they must have seen it,
backing out on the mailboat at twilight,

shadows falling
on everything they had to leave?
And would love forever?
And then

I imagine myself
at the landward rail of that boat
searching for the last sight of a hand.

I see myself
on the underworld side of that water,
the darkness coming in fast, saying
all the names I know for a lost land.

Ireland. Absence. Daughter.

EAVAN BOLAND (B. 1944)

NICK HORNBY NOVELIST

3 February 1994

Dear Ewan Gibson, Áine Jackson and Chris Pillow,

My favourite poem is 'Gravy', by Raymond Carver, from the book A New Path to the Waterfall. *Carver was dying of cancer when he wrote the poem, but I love its absolute determination to celebrate: he had nearly died of alcoholism ten years before, but gave up drinking, met the woman with whom he spent the last, very happy, decade of his life, and produced several volumes of wonderful short stories and poems. So 'Gravy' is about being given a second chance, and appreciating that chance for what it was. I find it very moving and very humbling, because I know that this was written by someone who was a better human being than more or less all of us.*

I hope this is OK, and let me know if I can be of any further help (I'd like to buy one, for example).

Best wishes and good luck,

Nick Hornby

Gravy

No other word will do. For that's what it was. Gravy.
Gravy, these past ten years.
Alive, sober, working, loving and
being loved by a good woman. Eleven years
ago he was told he had six months to live
at the rate he was going. And he was going
nowhere but down. So he changed his ways
somehow. He quit drinking! And the rest?
After that it was *all* gravy, every minute
of it, up to and including when he was told about,
well, some things that were breaking down and
building up inside his head. 'Don't weep for me,'
he said to his friends. 'I'm a lucky man.
I've had ten years longer than I or anyone
expected. Pure gravy. And don't forget it.'

RAYMOND CARVER (1939–1988)

21 June 1997

Dear Editors,

Firstly, may I apologise for the very long delay in responding to your letter, but I'm afraid the newsroom in The Irish Times *is somewhat like Bedlam and my own desk bears close resemblance to a combat zone!*

I decided to select not a poem, but a letter, for this edition of Lifelines. *It is a most unusual letter, written by Chief Seattle of the Duwamish tribe in Washington State to the US President, Franklin Pierce, in 1854, in response to an offer from the federal government to purchase the Indian lands and relocate his tribe on a reservation.*

Chief Seattle's letter has its own lyricism and delivers a powerful message about how we all need to care for the natural world – our environment – particularly in its much-quoted phrases about how 'the Earth is sacred' and 'all things are connected'. There are some who may think, on reading it, that the Chief goes somewhat over the top in places, but I don't believe so.

'Continue to contaminate your bed, and you will one night suffocate in your own waste', he warned. Who could doubt the veracity of this metaphor for what we are doing to the world? It is, I'm afraid, all too true. We need to learn about treading softly on the Earth, as Chief Seattle clearly did, and try a little harder to pass on what we have inherited to succeeding generations of humanity in as close as possible to an uncontaminated state.

By the way, I also like a quote from Big Jim Larkin, who led the workers of Dublin during the 1913 lock-out. It is emblazoned on a bronze plaque on the plinth of Oisín Kelly's marvellous statue of Larkin in the middle of O'Connell Street and reads as follows: 'The great appear to be great because we are on our knees; let us rise.'

Yours sincerely,

Frank McDonald

The Earth Is Sacred

How can you buy or sell the sky, the warmth of the land? The idea is strange to us. If we do not own the freshness of the air and the sparkle of the water, how can you buy them?

Every part of this earth is sacred to my people. Every shining pine needle, every sandy shore, every mist in the dark woods, every clearing and humming insect is holy in the memory and experience of my people. The sap which courses through the trees carries the memories of the red man. The white man's dead forget the country of their birth when they go to walk among the stars. Our dead never forget this beautiful earth, for it is the mother of the red man. We are part of the earth and it is part of us. The perfumed flowers are our sisters; the deer, the horse, the great eagle, these are our brothers. The rocky crests, the juices in the meadows, the body heat of the pony, and man – all belong to the same family.

So, when the Great Chief in Washington sends word that he wishes to buy our land, he asks much of us. The Great Chief sends word he will reserve us a place so that we can live comfortable among our own people. He will be our Father and we will be his children. So we will consider your offer to buy our land. But it will not be easy. For this land is sacred to us.

The shining water that moves in the streams and rivers is not just water but the blood of our ancestors. If we sell you the land, you must remember that it is sacred, and you must teach your children that each ghostly reflection in the clear water of the lakes tells of events and memories in the life of my people. The water's murmur is the voice of the father's father.

Kindness to the Rivers

The rivers are our brothers, they quench our thirst. The rivers carry our canoes, and feed our children. If we sell you our land, you must remember, and teach your children, that the rivers are our brothers, and yours, and you must henceforth give the rivers the kindness you would give a brother.

We know that the white man does not understand our ways. One portion of land is the same to him as the next, for he is a stranger who comes in the night and takes from the land whatever he needs. The Earth is not his brother, but his enemy, when he has conquered it, he moves on. He leaves his father's graves behind, and he does not care. He kidnaps the earth from his children, and he does not care. His father's graves, and his children's birthright, are forgotten. He treats his mother, the earth, and his brother, the sky, as things to be bought, plundered, sold like sheep or bright beads. His appetite will devour the earth and leave behind only a desert. I do not know. Our ways are different from yours. The sight of your cities pains the eyes of the red man. But perhaps it is because the red man is a savage and does not understand. There is no quiet place in the white man's cities; no place to hear the unfurling of leaves in spring, or the rustle of the insect's wings. The clatter only seems to insult the ears. And what is there to life if a man cannot hear the lonely cry of the whippoorwill, or the argument of the frogs around a pond at night? The Indian prefers the soft sound of the wind darting over the face of a pond, and the smell of wind itself, cleansed by the midday rain, or scented with the pinon pine.

The Air Is Precious

The air is precious to the red man, for all things share the same breath – the beast, the tree, and the human. The white man does not seem to notice the air he breathes. Like a man dying for many days he is numb to the stench. But if we sell you our land you must remember that the air is precious to us, that the air shares its spirit with all the life it supports. The wind that gave our grandfather his first breath also receives his last sigh. And if we sell you our land, you must keep it apart and sacred, as a place where even the white man can go to taste the wind that is sweetened by the meadow's flowers.

All Things Are Connected

So we will consider your offer to buy our land. If we decide to accept, I will make one condition; the white man must treat the beasts of this land as his brothers. I have seen a thousand rotting buffaloes on the prairie, left by the white man who shot them from a passing train. I am a savage and I do not understand how the smoking iron horse can be more important than the buffalo that we kill only to stay alive. What is man without the beasts? If all the beasts were gone, man would die from great loneliness of spirit, for whatever happens to the beast also happens to man. All things are connected. Whatever befalls the earth befalls the sons of earth. The white man, too, shall pass – perhaps sooner than other tribes. Continue to contaminate your bed, and you will one night suffocate in your own waste. When the buffalo are all slaughtered, the wild horses all tamed, the secret corners of the forest heavy with scent of many men, and the view of ripe hills blotted by talking wires, where is the thicket? Gone. Where is the eagle? Gone. And what is it to say goodbye to the swift pony and the hunt? It is the end of living and the beginning of survival.

CHIEF SEATTLE (?1786–1866)

BERYL BAINBRIDGE   NOVELIST

1997

I have chosen 'Dover Beach' by Matthew Arnold because I used to recite it as a child while roaming the shore at Formby, Lancashire. The sadness and morbidity of the last verse appealed to me. It still does.

Beryl Bainbridge

Dover Beach

The sea is calm tonight.
The tide is full, the moon lies fair
Upon the straits — on the French coast the light
Gleams and is gone; the cliffs of England stand,
Glimmering and vast, out in the tranquil bay.
Come to the window, sweet is the night air!
Only, from the long line of spray
Where the sea meets the moon-blanched land,
Listen! you hear the grating roar
Of pebbles which the waves draw back, and fling,
At their return, up the high strand,
Begin, and cease, and then again begin,
With tremulous cadence slow, and bring
The eternal note of sadness in.

Sophocles long ago
Heard it on the Aegean, and it brought
Into his mind the turbid ebb and flow
Of human misery; we
Find also in the sound a thought,
Hearing it by this distant northern sea.

The Sea of Faith
Was once, too, at the full, and round earth's shore
Lay like the folds of a bright girdle furled.
But now I only hear
Its melancholy, long, withdrawing roar,
Retreating to the breath
Of the night wind, down the vast edges drear
and naked shingles of the world.

Ah, love, let us be true
To one another! for the world, which seems
To lie before us like a land of dreams,
So various, so beautiful, so new,
Hath really neither joy, nor love, nor light,
Nor certitude, nor peace, nor help for pain;
And we are here as on a darkling plain
Swept with confused alarms of struggle and flight,
Where ignorant armies clash by night.

MATTHEW ARNOLD (1822–1888)

['*Dover Beach*' was chosen by Mary O'Donnell in *Lifelines*. Mary O'Donnell wrote:
I find it hard to pin down an overall favourite poem, as what I think is my favourite poem one year changes to something completely different the next.

However, lurking at the back of my mind forever and ever is Matthew Arnold's 'Dover Beach' which I fell in love with as a student when I heard it read aloud in 1974 by the Professor of English in Maynooth College, Fr John McMacken. The poem was read with passion and feeling and love and that's exactly what I've carried within me about it ever since.

It's like listening to a Beethoven symphony – deeply romantic and probing, and even if Arnold mourns the demise of 'The Sea of Faith' which once 'round earth's shore/Lay like folds of a bright girdle furled', the whole emotional sweep and mood of the poem carries the reader to the climactic pain and resolution of the final stanza – still for me, utterly believable, magnificent and something you live your way into!]

PAUL MULDOON

Dear Ewan Gibson,

One of my favourite poems is 'The Taxis' by Louis MacNeice. I love its negotiation of the thin line between nursery-rhyme and nightmare, between humour and horror, between delight and dread, that's quite unlike anything I know.
   With best wishes for your wonderful project.

Yours sincerely,

Paul Muldoon

The Taxis

In the first taxi he was alone tra-la,
No extras on the clock. He tipped ninepence
But the cabby, while he thanked him, looked askance
As though to suggest someone had bummed a ride.

In the second taxi he was alone tra-la
But the clock showed sixpence extra; he tipped according
And the cabby from out his muffler said: 'Make sure
You have left nothing behind tra-la between you'.

In the third taxi he was alone tra-la
But the tip-up seats were down and there was an extra
Charge of one-and-sixpence and an odd
Scent that reminded him of a trip to Cannes.

As for the fourth taxi, he was alone
Tra-la when he hailed it but the cabby looked
Through him and said: 'I can't tra-la well take
So many people, not to speak of the dog'.

LOUIS MacNEICE (1907–1963)

18 January 1994

Dear Ewan, Áine and Christopher,

I have chosen the poem 'Manners' by Elizabeth Bishop, which I love for its obvious simplicity. It records an age and a state of mind entirely without cynicism: a secure, small world in which no-one can lose his way. The child-like speaking voice is brilliantly achieved with rudimentary, sing-song rhymes which accommodate the jolly generosity and good faith of the child and her grandfather.

I also like it for its not-so-obvious complexities. Hovering at the edge of its simplicity is something much darker, suggested by the obscured faces of the passengers in the cars: a future in which the values of the child and her grandfather will be as outmoded as their wagon seat; an impersonal, technological world which will have no place for the gentle intimacy of manners. The poem marks the belated transition from the nineteenth to the twentieth centuries, and from innocence to painful experience. Its success lies, I think, in doing so without the slightest trace of either rhetoric or sentiment.

I wish you success with your new Lifelines, *and congratulations on your work so far.*

Best wishes,

Vona Groarke

Manners

For a Child of 1918

My grandfather said to me
as we sat on the wagon seat,
'Be sure to remember to always
speak to everyone you meet.'

We met a stranger on foot.
My grandfather's whip tapped his hat.
'Good day, sir. Good day. A fine day.'
And I said it and bowed where I sat.

Then we overtook a boy we knew
with his big pet crow on his shoulder.
'Always offer everyone a ride;
don't forget that when you get older,'

my grandfather said. So Willy
climbed up with us, but the crow
gave a 'Caw!' and flew off. I was worried.
How would he know where to go?

But he flew a little way at a time
from fence post to fence post, ahead;
and when Willy whistled he answered.
'A fine bird,' my grandfather said,

'and he's well brought up. See, he answers
nicely when he's spoken to.
Man or beast, that's good manners.
Be sure that you both always do.'

When automobiles went by,
the dust hid the people's faces,
but we shouted 'Good day! Good day!
Fine day!' at the top of our voices.

When we came to Hustler Hill,
he said that the mare was tired,
so we all got down and walked,
as our good manners required.

ELIZABETH BISHOP (1911–1979)

JOHN BOYNE NOVELIST

2006

Dear Dónal, Caroline & Stephanie,

Thanks for the invitation to contribute to the new Lifelines *collection, which my publisher forwarded on to me; I actually only live about two minutes away from Wesley College.*

I have chosen a very short poem of only four lines which I've always loved entitled 'First Fig' by the American poet Edna St Vincent Millay.

On dark winter evenings, when huddled around tables with good friends, this poem always comes into my mind. It says so much in so few words. The importance of living for the moment, the pleasure that can be taken from transient things, the understanding that all things are transient: life, love, the glow of a candle. Most importantly the juxtaposition in the third line of friends and foes suggests a laying down of arms for a brief moment, for no other reason than to appreciate something beautiful. And what better place to suggest such an idea than in a poem?

Best wishes,

John Boyne

First Fig

My candle burns at both ends;
    It will not last the night;
But, ah, my foes, and oh, my friends —
    It gives a lovely light!

EDNA ST VINCENT MILLAY (1892–1950)

8 January 1997

Dear Ralph, Caroline and Gareth,

Thank you very much for your invitation to contribute to Lifelines 3: *I have been a great admirer of the previous volumes and I wish this one every possible success.*

As for my 'favourite poem' . . . I have to say that I do not honestly have one favourite poem. Rather, there are hundreds of poems which appeal to me in more or less equal measure and if I were forced to single out any one of them my choice would probably depend to some extent on the mood I was in, the day of the week, the time of day, what I had been doing, reading or thinking about over the previous few hours. I very much like poems which speak to me directly, moving me by the intensity of the experience which they describe. In contemporary Irish poetry I am particularly fond of the work of Paula Meehan and one of her poems which I find especially touching is 'Buying Winkles'. It is a poem about love, about warmth, about the intimacy of mother and daughter, abstractions all given wonderful concrete expression in the details of the setting, characterisation and dialogue. The note of pride in the closing line – 'like torches' – is a triumphant conclusion to this beautifully observed and brilliantly reported anecdote.

With every good wish.

Yours sincerely,

Robert Dunbar

Buying Winkles

My mother would spare me sixpence and say,
'Hurry up now and don't be talking to strange
men on the way.' I'd dash from the ghosts
on the stairs where the bulb had blown
out into Gardiner Street, all relief.
A bonus if the moon was in the strip of sky
between the tall houses, or stars out,
but even in rain I was happy — the winkles
would be wet and glisten blue like little
night skies themselves. I'd hold the tanner tight
and jump every crack in the pavement,
I'd wave up to women at sills or those
lingering in doorways and weave a glad path through
men heading out for the night.

She'd be sitting outside the Rosebowl Bar
on an orange-crate, a pram loaded
with pails of winkles before her.
When the bar doors swung open they'd leak
the smell of men together with drink
and I'd see light in golden mirrors.
I envied each soul in the hot interior.

I'd ask her again to show me the right way
to do *it*. She'd take a pin from her shawl —
'Open the eyelid. So. Stick it in
till you feel a grip, then slither him out.
Gently, mind.' The sweetest extra winkle
that brought the sea to me.
'Tell yer Ma I picked them fresh this morning.'

I'd bear the newspaper twists
bulging fat with winkles
proudly home, like torches.

PAULA MEEHAN (B. 1955)

['*Buying Winkles*' was also chosen by Ferdia MacAnna in *Lifelines*. Ferdia McAnna wrote:
My favourite poem of the moment is 'Buying Winkles' *from Paula Meehan's collection,* The Man
Who Was Marked by Winter. *I like it because it is direct, simple and beautiful, and because it
conjures up images of a child's experience of the adult world. Each time I read it, I find something
new to savour. Most of all though, I like this poem because of its strong cinematic flavour. Reading
it is a bit like being inside an imaginary Fellini film set in Dublin – there is colour, dash, charm,
light and character as well as an ever-present tinge of danger.*

*I love this kind of work. I think it gives poetry a good name. Also, I think Paula Meehan is a
great writer.*]

JOHN NEILL ARCHBISHOP

2006

God's Grandeur

The world is charged with the grandeur of God.
    It will flame out, like shining from shook foil;
    It gathers to a greatness, like the ooze of oil
Crushed. Why do men then now not reck his rod?
Generations have trod, have trod, have trod;
    And all is seared with trade; bleared, smeared with toil;
    And wears man's smudge and shares man's smell: the soil
Is bare now, nor can foot feel, being shod.

And for all this, nature is never spent;
  There lives the dearest freshness deep down things;
And though the last lights off the black West went
  Oh, morning, at the brown brink eastward, springs—
Because the Holy Ghost over the bent
  World broods with warm breast and with ah! bright wings.

GERARD MANLEY HOPKINS (1844–1889)

This poem speaks to me of two truths – we live in God's world and we have made a mess of it. The signs of the second truth are easy to see – pollution, violence, exploitation and despair.

As a Christian, I see that this is only part of the picture. God is still active in the world, bringing that eternal light of new life into the darkness which we have made.

I rejoice that I live in the world that God has made.

†John Neill

CATHAL Ó SEARCAIGH POET

Tír Chonaill
1 Márta 1994

My Dear Ewan, Áine, Christopher,

Maith domh an mhoill. Istigh tá an dán atá roghnaithe agam . . . 'Afterlives' le Derek Mahon. Tá obair ar dóigh á dhéanaimh agaibh agus mólaim go hard na spéire sin. Tá súil agam go mbeidh an rath agus an ráchaint cheanna ar an eagrán reatha de Lifelines *agus a bhí ar na cinn eile. Is léir go ndeachaigh ann smaoineadh agus an saothair i bhfeidhm ar an phobal. Ádh mór oraibh triúr.*

Le dea ghuí.

Cathal Ó Searcaigh

Some people invoke spirits. They are called spiritualists. Some people invoke themselves. They are called poets. I belong to the second calling. In recent times, though, I'm becoming more mediumistic. I'm letting ancestral voices speak through me. This implies, for me anyway, a longing for origins . . .a yearning for home, an attachment to place and an awareness of its past. Home is the Gaelic-speaking community of Gleann An Átha, situated in the shadow of Mt Errigal, between Dún Lúiche and Gort 'a Choirce in North West Donegal. This is the territory of my people, the terrain of my imagination, my soulscape. Home! I became acutely aware of that word thanks to Derek Mahon's poem. This is how it happened. In the mid-Seventies I was 'on the stray' in London, drifting aimlessly, taking a walk on the wild side of life and of love. It was the first time I looked down into that terrible dark pool – the dubhlinn of the self. At times like that you realise that you're an abyss. Within there's a deep unfathomable darkness. You get dizzy looking down into yourself – into that Chasm of Silence. A poem becomes a shout of defiance yelled in the face of that Silence. I found out that it was much more rewarding to write bad poems than to read really great poems . . . until somebody gave me a copy of Derek Mahon's collection The Snow Party. *'Afterlives', the first poem in that collection, was a revelation, particularly the second part of it. The first time I read the word 'home' there in*

---

the last line, I got what I can only describe as a 'shock of recognition'. It was an awakening for me, an awakening from the anonymity of the city. I felt the word as a fierce longing to be reunited with something which I felt to be cut off from. Suddenly I felt deprived and dispossessed in the faceless society of the streets and I craved for a new sense of communion with my own hill-farming community. The word was a discovery for me, but what is discovery only what we remove the cover from. It has always been there . . .only concealed. That poem sent me home to my own land and my own language. It was the beginning of my homecoming. For Mahon it's a poem about coming back to a turbulent and troubled city. On the rough seas of sectarian strife, poetry becomes, for some, the buoy of the Spirit. Gúrú maith agaibh:

  le gean,
till the desert sands freeze and the camels come
  skating home.

Afterlives
for James Simmons

I

I wake in a dark flat
To the soft roar of the world.
Pigeons neck on the white
Roofs as I draw the curtains
And look out over London
Rain-fresh in the morning light.

This is our element, the bright
Reason on which we rely
For the long-term solutions.
The orators yap, and guns
Go off in a back street;
But the faith does not die

That in our time these things
Will amaze the literate children
In their non-sectarian schools
And the dark places be
Ablaze with love and poetry
When the power of good prevails.

What middle-class cunts we are
To imagine for one second
That our privileged ideals
Are divine wisdom, and the dim
Forms that kneel at noon
In the city not ourselves.

II

I am going home by sea
For the first time in years.
Somebody thumbs a guitar
On the dark deck, while a gull
Dreams at the masthead,
The moon-splashed waves exult.

At dawn the ship trembles, turns
In a wide arc to back
Shuddering up the grey lough
Past lightship and buoy,
Slipway and dry dock
Where a naked bulb burns;

And I step ashore in a fine rain
To a city so changed
By five years of war
I scarcely recognise
The places I grew up in,
The faces that try to explain.

But the hills are still the same
Grey-blue above Belfast.
Perhaps if I'd stayed behind
And lived it bomb by bomb
I might have grown up at last
And learnt what is meant by home.

DEREK MAHON (B. 1941)

9 February 1997

Dear Ralph Croly, Caroline Dowling and Gareth McCluskey,

Thanks for the invitation to participate in Lifelines 3 *and accept my admiration for the work you're doing.*

Now to my (favourite?) favorite poem. It's Wilfred Owen's 'Anthem for Doomed Youth'. *It's a powerful anti-war poem from a man killed just before the 'Great War' ended. In it he fuses the sounds, images and rituals of war and religion so that the activity of war becomes its own requiem. Its diction is sombre and stately as a death march.*

I hope this helps.

Sincerely,

Frank McCourt

Anthem for Doomed Youth

What passing-bells for these who die as cattle?
  Only the monstrous anger of the guns.
  Only the stuttering rifles' rapid rattle
Can patter out their hasty orisons.
No mockeries now for them; no prayers nor bells,
  Nor any voice of mourning save the choirs, —
The shrill, demented choirs of wailing shells;
  And bugles calling for them from sad shires.

What candles may be held to speed them all?
  Not in the hands of boys, but in their eyes
Shall shine the holy glimmers of good-byes.
  The pallor of girls' brows shall be their pall;
Their flowers the tenderness of patient minds,
And each slow dusk a drawing-down of blinds.

WILFRED OWEN (1893–1918)

30 January 1994

Dear Ewan, Áine and Christopher,

Thanks for your invitation to contribute to the latest Lifelines. *I bought and loved the last one. I have lots of favourite poems; I love* 'The Green Eye of the Little Yellow God' *and the* 'Tale of Mad Carew' *because they remind me of long car drives with my father as a child when we four in the back seat were held a captive audience to a circular recitation of them both.*

I love 'Raglan Road' – *plain and unsung; I love especially the titles of Paul Durcan's poems as in* 'On Seeing Two Bus Conductors Kissing Each Other in the Middle of the Street' *or,* 'Making Love outside Áras an Uachtaráin'.

But the poem that maybe moves me most is that one by Seamus Heaney when he is evoking the memory of his mother and the time when she and he peeled potatoes together at the kitchen sink. 'Never closer than at that moment' *I think he says in the poem which unfortunately I cannot put my hand to but you should be able to find it without too much difficulty.*

I remember moments like that with my own mother; I hope my daughter does the same.

Best wishes for another bestseller,

Emily O'Reilly

from *Clearances*—

a sonnet sequence in memoriam MKH, 1911–1984

When all the others were away at Mass
I was all hers as we peeled potatoes.
They broke the silence, let fall one by one
Like solder weeping off the soldering iron:
Cold comforts set between us, things to share
Gleaming in a bucket of clean water.
And again let fall. Little pleasant splashes
From each other's work would bring us to our senses.

So while the parish priest at her bedside
Went hammer and tongs at the prayers for the dying
And some were responding and some crying
I remembered her head bent towards my head,
Her breath in mine, our fluent dipping knives —
Never closer the whole rest of our lives.

SEAMUS HEANEY (B. 1939)
(from 'Clearances', an eight-sonnet sequence)

[This sonnet was also chosen by Kathleen Watkins in *Lifelines* and by Sean Hughes in *Lifelines 2*. Kathleen Watkins wrote:

I love these lines because they are so simple and clear and one can see vivid pictures when reading them. Most people would probably identify with them also. To enjoy poetry, which I do very much, I must understand it perfectly and the pictures always have to be very clear.

Sean Hughes wrote:

'Clearances' – *Seamus Heaney from* The Haw Lantern, *my favourite poem of all time. I read it at least four times a year and each time it says more and more. I envy his touch, I envy the moments he remembers, I envy his love of life and this of course leaves me with the utter need to express my love for my mother before her time comes. A rich, soft, beautiful poem.*]

Roy Foster

26 January 1994

Dear Lifelines,

I hope this is in time: sorry for delay. Keep up the good work.

Yours sincerely,

Roy Foster
Carroll Professor of Irish History

Favourites change all the time. It would have to be Yeats (though Louis MacNeice's 'Autumn Journal' runs him close). While I love the grandeur of 'Byzantium' and the historical complexity of 'Meditations in Time Of Civil War', at the moment I'm very drawn to the deceptive simplicity of his early lyrics and ballads. I would choose 'The Fiddler Of Dooney' for the wonderful Yeatsian music of names, and its subversive twist. Also, my mother (who loved Sligo and Yeats) used to recite it to us when we were small, so it appeals on an irrational level too: as Yeats himself said, you can refute Hegel but not the saint or the song of sixpence.

The Fiddler of Dooney

When I play on my fiddle in Dooney,
Folk dance like a wave of the sea;
My cousin is priest in Kilvarnet,
My brother in Mocharabuiee.

I passed my brother and cousin:
They read in their books of prayer;
I read in my book of songs
I bought at the Sligo fair.

When we come at the end of time
To Peter sitting in state,
He will smile on the three old spirits,
But call me first through the gate;

For the good are always the merry,
Save by an evil chance,
And the merry love the fiddle,
And the merry love to dance:

And when the folk there spy me,
They will all come up to me,
With 'Here is the fiddler of Dooney!'
And dance like a wave of the sea.

W B YEATS (1865–1939)

20 January 1997

Dear Ralph, Caroline and Gareth,

Gerald Manley Hopkins's 'Spring and Fall: to a young child' *is a deep favourite of mine. It catches life's sadness, and has a certain serenity about it. I have written two novels for which these lines are the epigram; they are called* Goldengrove Unleaving. *My own daughter is called Margaret after the girl in this poem.*

Spring and Fall

to a young child

Márgarét, áre you gríeving
Over Goldengrove unleaving?
Léaves, líke things of man, you
With your fresh thoughts care for, can you?
Ah! ás the heart grows older
It will come to such sights colder,
By and by, nor spare a sigh
Though worlds of wanwood leafmeal lie;
And yet you *will* weep, and know why.
Now no matter, child, the name:
Sórrow's spríngs áre the same.
Nor mouth had, no nor mind, expressed
What heart heard of, ghost guessed:
It is the blight man was born for,
It is Margaret you mourn for.

GERALD MANLEY HOPKINS (1844–1889)

I wish you every good luck with the project in such a good cause,

Yours faithfully,

Jill Paton Walsh

['*Spring and Fall*' was also Niamh Bhreathnach's choice in *Lifelines 3*. Niamh Bhreathnach wrote:

My favourite poem is 'Spring and Fall: to a young child', *by Gerard Manley Hopkins.*

Hopkins is a favourite poet of mine because he had uniqueness of style which gives a freshness and vitality to his poetry. For me, this particular poem captures a very real sense of the transition from childhood to adulthood – Spring to Fall. In the Romantic tradition, Hopkins uses nature as a means to express his theme. The imagery of nature, combined with Hopkins's unique rhythmic style, make this a poem which never fails to please when read silently or aloud.]

17 January 1990

Who my favourite poet is, and what my favourite poem is, are questions to be sidestepped as nimbly as good manners permit: the answers vary almost from moment to moment. However, Patrick Kavanagh and the poems of Patrick Kavanagh occupy an elevated place in the list at all times.

I came to know of him first in the 1940s when I read his epic poem The Great Hunger *and then in person when I met him during the 1950s in the company of Peadar O'Donnell who was editing* The Bell *at the time. After that, there were casual meetings in the coffee shops of Bewleys and Mitchells and in Sunday pubs. His work, in both prose and poetry, became a must.*

The poem I have selected here is from Come Dance With Kitty Stobling and Other Poems, *first published in 1960. It is 'In Memory of My Mother'. I found if deeply moving when I first read it and it continues to evoke the same admiration and emotion whenever I return to it, especially on the repetition at the beginning of the last verse of the line:*

> O you are not lying in the wet clay . . .

What a tender, brooding sorrow hovers over it.
Sincerely,
James Plunkett

In Memory of My Mother

I do not think of you lying in the wet clay
Of a Monaghan graveyard; I see
You walking down a lane among the poplars
On your way to the station, or happily

Going to second Mass on a summer Sunday –
You meet me and you say:
'Don't forget to see about the cattle –'
Among your earthiest words the angels stray.

And I think of you walking along a headland
Of green oats in June,
So full of repose, so rich with life –
And I see us meeting at the end of a town

On a fair day by accident, after
The bargains are all made and we can walk
Together through the shops and stalls and markets
Free in the oriental streets of thought.

O you are not lying in the wet clay,
For it is a harvest evening now and we
Are piling up the ricks against the moonlight
And you smile up at us – eternally.

PATRICK KAVANAGH (1904–1967)

24 April 2006

Dear Dónal, Caroline & Stephanie,

Further to your recent letter, I would be delighted to participate in the Lifelines *project and the poem I have selected is* 'A Nation Once Again' *by Thomas Davis. The reason I chose this poem is that it was the first poem I learned in school and I could empathise with the sentiments of the poet.*

Good luck with the project.

Yours sincerely,

Dermot F Desmond

A Nation Once Again

When boyhood's fire was in my blood
  I read of ancient freemen
For Greece and Rome who bravely stood,
  Three hundred men and three men.
And then I prayed I yet might see,
  Our fetters rent in twain,
And Ireland, long a province, be
  A Nation once again.

And from that time, through wildest woe,
  That hope has shone, a far light;
Nor could love's brightest summer glow
  Outshine that solemn starlight:
It seemed to watch above my head
  In forum, field and fane;
Its angel voice sang round my bed,
  'A Nation once again.'

It whispered, too, that 'Freedom's ark
  And service high and holy,
Would be profaned by feelings dark
  And passions vain or lowly:
For Freedom comes from God's right hand,
  And needs a godly train;
And righteous men must make our land
  A Nation once again.'

So, as I grew from boy to man,
    I bent me to that bidding —
My spirit of each selfish plan
    And cruel passion ridding;
For, thus I hoped some day to aid —
    Oh! can such hope be in vain? —
When my dear country shall be made
    A Nation once again.

THOMAS DAVIS (1814–1845)

CAROL SHIELDS   NOVELIST

Canada
22 January 1997

Dear Ralph, Caroline and Gareth,

First, I congratulate you on this wonderful project. Second, I thank you for giving me a chance to think about what my favourite poem really is; there are so many. But I've always loved the American poet Emily Dickinson and her elliptical, eccentric and truthful work. There was, and is, no one like her. In a sense, she remakes language, using verbs for nouns, adjectives for verbs, and she establishes rhythms that are vigorous, startling and utterly original. Her poems offer the remarkable compression that the best and most directly affecting poetry possesses. Poetry should go off like a flashbulb, and her poems do. Here's one of my favourites.

Tell all the Truth but tell it slant —
Success in Circuit lies
Too bright for our infirm Delight
The Truth's superb surprise

As Lightning to the Children eased
With explanation kind
The Truth must dazzle gradually
Or every man be blind —

EMILY DICKINSON (1830–1886)

With best wishes to all concerned in this effort,
Carol Shields

MICHAEL COADY

16 January 1994

Dear Friends,

Thank you for your recent letter. I know of the very successful Lifelines *project and admire it. Thank you for your invitation to contribute towards a further collection.*

I would find it next to impossible to nominate any one particular poem as my favourite above all others, but I suggest one which has long been a favourite.

I remember being immediately entranced by John Montague's love-lyric 'All Legendary Obstacles' *when I opened* The Irish Times *to discover it one Saturday morning well over twenty years ago. Such potent memorability must be significant. The drama of Montague's poem is a primary one of journeying, of waiting and encounter, of hope and uncertainty and desire. Its personal intimacies are set against a great sweeping landscape – mountains, rain, the dark – and the poem's technique is strikingly cinematic. Its eye is one which has been consciously or unconsciously schooled by the camera, as we all have in this century. As in some classic film, the visual and emotional charge of the last 'scene' remains haunting and unforgettable.*

With best wishes,

Michael Coady

All Legendary Obstacles

All legendary obstacles lay between
Us, the long imaginary plain,
The monstrous ruck of mountains
And, swinging across the night,
Flooding the Sacramento, San Joaquin,
The hissing drift of winter rain.

All day I waited, shifting
Nervously from station to bar
As I saw another train sail
By, the San Francisco Chief or
Golden Gate, water dripping
From great flanged wheels.

At midnight you came, pale
Above the negro porter's lamp.
I was too blind with rain
And doubt to speak, but
Reached from the platform
Until our chilled hands met.

You had been travelling for days
With an old lady, who marked
A neat circle on the glass
With her glove, to watch us
Move into the wet darkness
Kissing, still unable to speak.

JOHN MONTAGUE (B. 1929)

MARY LOHAN ARTIST

8 May 2006

Dear Dónal, Caroline and Stephanie,
Thank you for your invitation to contribute to the Lifelines *project.*

A joy I thought! A favourite poem! This was soon to become a difficult task, as I visited and revisited old favourites. In the end, and because I had to choose one, I settled on Elizabeth Bishop's 'The Fish'. I could have chosen almost anything of this poet's work.

I love her spare style, painterly descriptions and the vague and not so vague underlying darkness in her work. I choose 'The Fish' because it is imprinted on my mind through the poet's voice caught on radio, one evening . . . never to be forgotten. Her slow, soft tones painted the picture for me, the forensic detail – 'coarse white flesh packed in like feathers' – the feeling of looking into his eyes like – 'the lenses of old scratched isinglass' – not meeting the gaze of course. That would not be bearable. Finally, she exposes all of the Fish, this wonderful pierced hero – 'a five-haired beard of wisdom trailing from his jaw'.

Of course, we identify with this brave, battle-worn, vulnerable, sullen and probably very fed-up fish! The whole picture is brilliantly captured – the physical colour, place, time past and future possible – a terrific ending, a fanfare – 'until everything was rainbow, rainbow, rainbow! And I let the fish go.'

Thank you again and all the best,

Mary Lohan

The Fish

I caught a tremendous fish
and held him beside the boat
half out of water, with my hook
fast in a corner of his mouth.
He didn't fight.
He hadn't fought at all.
He hung a grunting weight,
battered and venerable
and homely. Here and there
his brown skin hung in strips
like ancient wallpaper,
and its pattern of darker brown

was like wallpaper:
shapes like full-blown roses
stained and lost through age.
He was speckled with barnacles,
fine rosettes of lime,
and infested
with tiny white sea-lice,
and underneath two or three
rags of green weed hung down.
While his gills were breathing in
the terrible oxygen
— the frightening gills,
fresh and crisp with blood,
that can cut so badly —
I thought of the coarse white flesh
packed in like feathers,
the big bones and the little bones,
the dramatic reds and blacks
of his shiny entrails,
and the pink swim-bladder
like a big peony.
I looked into his eyes
which were far larger than mine
but shallower, and yellowed,
the irises backed and packed
with tarnished tinfoil
seen through the lenses
of old scratched isinglass.
They shifted a little, but not
to return my stare.
— It was more like the tipping
of an object toward the light.
I admired his sullen face,
the mechanism of his jaw,
and then I saw
that from his lower lip
— if you could call it a lip —
grim, wet, and weaponlike,
hung five old pieces of fish-line,
or four and a wire leader
with the swivel still attached,
with all their five big hooks
grown firmly in his mouth.
A green line, frayed at the end
where he broke it, two heavier lines,

and a fine black thread
still crimped from the strain and snap
when it broke and he got away.
Like medals with their ribbons
frayed and wavering,
a five-haired beard of wisdom
trailing from his aching jaw.
I stared and stared
and victory filled up
the little rented boat,
from the pool of bilge
where oil had spread a rainbow
around the rusted engine
to the bailer rusted orange,
the sun-cracked thwarts,
the oarlocks on their strings,
the gunnels—until everything
was rainbow, rainbow, rainbow!
And I let the fish go.

ELIZABETH BISHOP (1911–1979)

NEIL RUDENSTINE ACADEMIC

9 January 1992

Dear Ms Hughes et al,

I am happy to contribute to Lifelines, *but I should say that I have no single favorite poem – and many of the poems that are most important to me are not quite 'poems' in the usual sense, and are much too long for an anthology. The Iliad, The Canterbury Tales, The Divine Comedy, Paradise Lost, and many other works would fall into this category.*

Poems shift their meanings – and their importance – at different times, in different periods of our life, and on different occasions. So no single poem – or even a few – will really be adequate. Choosing one poem is impossible, but it would be possible at least to say that John Keats's 'Ode to Autumn' is one of the very great poems in English, and is very important to me personally: it says much about growth and maturity; age and death and bleakness; richness and fruition and indulgence; and finally about the way in which all these perceptions, feelings, and ideas can be held together in consciousness, in such a way as to evoke their power and yet reconcile and give resolution to what may seem irreconcilable in them. It also does this, not so much by explicit statement, but by the wonderfully modulated tones of the poet, the images captured, and the implicit meanings that those images suggest.

Sincerely,

Neil Rudenstine

To Autumn

I

Season of mists and mellow fruitfulness,
     Close bosom friend of the maturing sun,
Conspiring with him how to load and bless
     With fruit the vines that round the thatch-eves run:
To bend with apples the mossed cottage-trees,
     And fill all fruit with ripeness to the core;
          To swell the gourd, and plump the hazel shells
     With a sweet kernel; to set budding more,
And still more, later flowers for the bees,
Until they think warm days will never cease,
          For summer has o'er-brimmed their clammy cells.

II

Who hath not seen thee oft amid thy store?
     Sometimes whoever seeks abroad may find
Thee sitting careless on a granary floor,
     Thy hair soft-lifted by the winnowing wind;
Or on a half-reaped furrow sound asleep,
     Drowsed with the fume of poppies, while thy hook
          Spares the next swath and all its twinèd flowers:
And sometimes like a gleaner thou dost keep
     Steady thy laden head across a brook;
     Or by a cyder-press, with patient look,
          Thou watchest the last oozings hours by hours.

III

Where are the songs of Spring? Aye, where are they?
     Think not of them, thou hast thy music too,—
While barrèd clouds bloom the soft-dying day,
     And touch the stubble-plains with rosy hue;
Then in a wailful choir the small gnats mourn
     Among the river sallows, borne aloft
          Or sinking as the light wind lives or dies;
And full-grown lambs loud bleat from hilly bourn;
     Hedge-crickets sing; and now with treble soft
     The red-breast whistles from a garden-croft;
And gathering swallows twitter in the skies.

JOHN KEATS (1795–1821)

[Keats's 'To Autumn' was also chosen by John Carey and Seán Lysaght in *Lifelines 2* and by Myrtle Allen and Matthew Dempsey in *Lifelines 3*.

John Carey wrote:
I suppose my 'favourite' poem – that is, the one I happen to be thinking of about most, varies from time to time. But the poem I say over to myself most often, I think, is Keats's 'To Autumn'. I love

it because of its calming rhythms, and because, though it is about dying, it is not sad, but rich and comforting.

Seán Lysaght wrote:

John Keats's 'To Autumn' has stayed with me since I first read it about twenty years ago, at the age of fifteen. The poem embodies a truth that I have only lately realised for myself: that the poet does not have to parade his/her own private emotions to write effectively. At this late stage in his career, with the knowledge that he is soon going to die, Keats transcends the psychological drama of the Odes by writing a poem descriptive of the dying year. His art achieves great serenity here; at the same time, it communicates the full pathos of his personal situation.

Myrtle Allen wrote:

I have been chef in my restaurant since 1964, only recently retiring to take up an equally onerous occupation. Chefs running restaurants get very, very little free time to read anything, even their post, so, sadly, poetry has not come into my life.

All I can say is that, when I go to pick my produce from the garden, the orchards, the glasshouses or, formerly, from beds of watercress by streams, on one of those lovely mellow, golden days in September, I always say to myself, 'Season of mists and mellow fruitfulness'!

Matthew Dempsey wrote:

If the autumn is fine and the harvest good, then, as a farmer, it has to be Keats's 'To Autumn']

GLENN PATTERSON NOVELIST

19 January 1997

Dear Ralph, Caroline and Gareth,

Thank you for your letter. I enclose a brief paragraph (at least I hope it's brief enough) on my favourite poem, Louis MacNeice's 'Snow'.

May I take this opportunity to congratulate the three of you on your decision to take on this latest Lifelines *project and to wish you every success with its publication.*

Yours sincerely,

Glenn Patterson

Snow

The room was suddenly rich and the great bay-window was
Spawning snow and pink roses against it
Soundlessly collateral and incompatible:
World is suddener than we fancy it.

World is crazier and more of it than we think,
Incorrigibly plural. I peel and portion
A tangerine and spit the pips and feel
The drunkenness of things being various.

And the fire flames with a bubbling sound for world
Is more spiteful and gay than one supposes —
On the tongue on the eyes on the ears in the palms of one's hands —
There is more than glass between the snow and the huge roses.

LOUIS MACNEICE (1907–1963)

I am torn between this and another MacNeice poem, Canto IV of the 'Autumn Journal'
sequence. I settle for 'Snow' because it was the first poem that really got through to me,
that worked on me as a poem and not as an object of study. I was in the lower sixth in
a school in Belfast, in an English class displaced from its usual room to a large lecture
theatre. Somewhere in the course of the lesson – I have always thought it was when
we reached the lines 'I peel and portion/A tangerine and spit the pips and feel/The
drunkenness of things being various' – I started to feel as though my eyes, or perhaps, more
properly, my ears, were opening. My teacher of the time still tells me she remembers me
saying, with a sort of awe, 'Oh, God, I see it.' An epiphany experienced while reading a
poem describing an epiphany. These moments it seems to me, moments when everything
appears to come together, are the moments most worth living for; certainly they are the
moments most worth writing for. I think what happened the day I read 'Snow' was that I
started wanting to be a writer.

['*Snow*' was also chosen by Andy O'Mahony in *Lifelines*. Andy O'Mahony wrote:
While I find it impossible to select one favourite poem in preference to all others, what I have done
is chosen a poem that I was reminded of when recently reading Gabriel Garcia Marquez' novel
Love in the Time of Cholera.

This novel intoxicated me with its richness: there's a potent sense in it of the plurality of things
both natural and man-made. Reading it brought to mind a phrase of Louis MacNeice's, 'the
drunkenness of things being various' from a poem called 'Snow' written in January 1935.

On re-reading the poem I realised that I had forgotten the expression 'incorrigibly plural'
which also captures (though clearly not as memorably) my reaction to the world of Marquez.
The occasion of this epiphany for MacNeice was the peeling of a tangerine in a room framed by a
bay-window of snow and pink roses. It's only now it has dawned on me the number of tangerines I
enjoyed not in the snow but in the sunshine while reading Love in the Time of Cholera.]

CHARLES TYRRELL ARTIST

1994

Dear Ewan, Áine and Christopher,

I hope I'm not too late with my response to your request. The poem I chose is Paul Durcan's
'*The Mantelpiece' from his last collection* – Give me Your Hand.
Best of luck with the project.

Yours sincerely,

Charles Tyrrell

This recent poem by Paul Durcan was written in response to a painting I've long admired
by Edouard Vuillard called 'The Mantelpiece'. Vuillard and his contemporary and fellow
Frenchman Pierre Bonnard were masters at painting the intimate, incidental domestic
situation and transforming it into something a lot more profound. I fear that this
painting of the mantelpiece will never be quite the same for me now that Paul Durcan has
applied his whacky imagination to it. The last line takes the biscuit.

The Mantelpiece
after Vuillard

Staring into the marble, I stray into it
Exploring its pores, its veins, its stains, its moles.
A block of marble on legs of marble.
Is it an altar?
Am I going to die?
Where is she? Will she ever come back?
Who is she? What is her name?
What kind of a woman
Would have an altar for a mantelpiece?
Would rescue a down-and-out at her gate
And put him to sleep in her own bed?

When she does come back in the late afternoon
She does not speak except to say
'It's May!'
She puts a glass vase of Queen Anne's lace
And daisies on the mantelpiece,
A single poppy, a bramble blossom,
Medicine bottles with labels
Prescribing for me when and how to take them.
She reiterates 'It's May!'
As if she herself is the May.
She hands me a book entitled 'Howard's End'.
How does she know that my name is Howard?
She puts out a clothes horse
Draping it with white cotton nighties.
I put out a finger with which to trace the marble
But trace her instead—trace her cheekbone.
Is your mantelpiece an altar?
She smiles: Are you my spring lamb?
I am.

That was five and a half years ago.
The world that is the case is everything and new.
O my drowned spring lamb!
O my wild, wild mantelpiece!

PAUL DURCAN (B. 1944)

5 February 1997

Dear Ralph, Caroline and Gareth,

Thank you for inviting me to contribute to Lifelines 3.

Adrian Mitchell is one of my favourite poets. He writes wonderful poems on a huge range of subjects in plain yet magical language. I love his funny poems, but the one I have chosen is one of his most sad.

He wrote 'Especially When It Snows' for Boty Goodwin, his adopted daughter, who died in 1995 when she was just 29 years old. I find this a most beautiful poem, full of love and tenderness and grief.

I knew Boty, so this poem is particularly moving for me.

Wishing you every success with the book.

Yours sincerely,

P J Lynch

Especially When It Snows
(for Boty)

especially when it snows
and every tree
has its dark arms and widespread hands
full of that shining angelfood

especially when it snows
and every footprint
makes a dark lake
among the frozen grass

especially when it snows darling
and tough little robins
beg for crumbs
at golden-spangled windows

ever since we said goodbye to you
in that memorial garden
where nothing grew
except the beautiful blank-eyed snow

and little Caitlin crouched to say goodbye to you
down in the shadows

especially when it snows
and keeps on snowing

especially when it snows
and down the purple pathways of the sky
the planet staggers like King Lear
with his dead darling in his arms

especially when it snows
and keeps on snowing

ADRIAN MITCHELL (B. 1932)

GREG DELANTY POET

17 January 1990

Dear Joann, Jacki and Carolyn,

Thank you for giving me the privilege to take part in your blessed and much needed work. Outside of the essential purpose of helping the Third World, you've also given poetry a purpose and prove it can make something happen.

It's impossible for me to pick a single favourite poem. I must have hundreds. Instead of picking a poem by well-known authors from the Old Sod, I thought I'd choose a poem from ones I've read recently, which are mostly by US poets. I would have liked to have put in Hayden Carruth's 'Marshall Washer', John Engels's 'The Comet', and Donald Hall's 'Kicking the Leaves', but they are all too long. I would also have liked to have chosen poems written in Irish given me by Louis de Paor . . . I could go on and on.

In the end I don't know whether I'll send Kenneth Rexroth's 'Blues' or Carolyn Forché's 'The Colonel'. They both seem fitting, especially the latter for the Colonels are everywhere, including Ireland, not just in El Salvador. And the Colonels are certainly partly responsible for the plight of the Third World. 'Blues' is a flower of art which nourishes us and helps us keep going when we are brought low by whatever circumstances.

Best wishes,

Greg Delanty

Blues

The tops of the higher peaks
Of the Sierra Nevada
Of California are
Drenched in the perfume of
A flower which grows only there —
The blue *Polemonium*
Confertum eximium,
Soft, profound blue, like the eyes
Of impregnable innocence;
The perfume is heavy and
Clings thickly to the granite
Peaks, even in violent wind;

The leaves are clustered,
Fine, dull green, sticky, and musky.
I imagine that the scent
Of the body of Artemis
That put Endymion to sleep
Was like this and her eyes had the
Same inscrutable color.
Lawrence was lit into death
By the blue gentians of Kore.
Vanzetti had in his cell
A bowl of tall blue flowers
From a New England garden.
I hope that when I need it
My mind can always call back
This flower to its hidden senses.

KENNETH REXROTH (1905–1982)

The Colonel

WHAT YOU HAVE HEARD is true. I was in his house. His wife carried a tray of coffee and sugar. His daughter filed her nails, his son went out for the night. There were daily papers, pet dogs, a pistol on the cushion beside him. The moon swung bare on its black cord over the house. On the television was a cop show. It was in English. Broken bottles were embedded in the walls around the house to scoop the kneecaps from a man's legs or cut his hands to lace. On the windows there were gratings like those in liquor stores. We had dinner, rack of lamb, good wine, a gold bell was on the table for calling the maid. The maid brought green mangoes, salt, a type of bread. I was asked how I enjoyed the country. There was a brief commercial in Spanish. His wife took everything away. There was some talk then of how difficult it had become to govern. The parrot said hello on the terrace. The colonel told it to shut up, and pushed himself from the table. My friend said to me with his eyes: say nothing. The colonel returned with a sack used to bring groceries home. He spilled many human ears on the table. They were like dried peach halves. There is no other way to say this. He took one of them in his hands, shook it in our faces, dropped it into a water glass. It came alive there. I am tired of fooling around he said. As for the rights of anyone, tell your people they can go fuck themselves. He swept the ears to the floor with his arm and held the last of his wine in the air. Something for your poetry, no? he said. Some of the ears on the floor caught this scrap of his voice. Some of the ears on the floor were pressed to the ground.

CAROLYN FORCHÉ (B. 1950)

Dáil Éireann,
Baile Átha Cliath 2
12 February 1997

*I knew that this poem was the right one to submit. As soon as I read it, it struck a chord.
I have on a couple of occasions been made feel inadequate, due to lack of material
possessions, especially when I was much younger. For that reason, I detest when people
judge others, without making an attempt to get to know them. We are probably all guilty
and need to be reminded that we are all vulnerable.*

Kind regards,

Mildred Fox, TD

On the Elevator Going Down

A Caucasian gets on at
        the 17th floor.
He is old, fat and expensively
        dressed

I say hello / I'm friendly.
        He says, 'Hi'.

Then he looks very carefully at
        my clothes.

I'm not very expensively dressed.
I think his left shoe costs more
than everything I am wearing.

He doesn't want to talk to me
        any more.

I think that he is not totally aware
that we are really going down
and there are no clothes after you have
been dead for a few thousand years.

He thinks as we silently travel
down and get off at the bottom
        floor
that we are going separate
        ways.

RICHARD BRAUTIGAN (1933–1984)

16 February 1988

Dear Julie, Jonathan and Duncan,

I was pleased to have your letter and to read about the book you are putting together. I am particularly pleased to be asked to contribute as both my parents went to Wesley College, and I have lovely memories of several visits to Dublin.

One of my favourite poems is 'Adlestrop' by Edward Thomas. I love it because of its essential Englishness and because it reminds me of the time of steam trains and that special hiss that announced their arrivals and departures. It is a very nostalgic poem about a part of England that I know well, and I hope its inclusion will introduce the poem to lots of new readers.

With best wishes,

Judi Dench

Adlestrop

Yes, I remember Adlestrop —
The name, because one afternoon
Of heat the express-train drew up there
Unwontedly. It was late June.

The steam hissed. Someone cleared his throat.
No one left and no one came
On the bare platform. What I saw
Was Adlestrop — only the name

And willows, willow-herb, and grass,
And meadowsweet, and haycocks dry,
No whit less still and lonely fair
Than the high cloudlets in the sky.

And for that minute a blackbird sang
Close by, and round him, mistier,
Farther and farther, all the birds
Of Oxfordshire and Gloucestershire.

EDWARD THOMAS (1878–1917)

New York
7 February 1994

Dear Ewan, Áine and Christopher,

Thank you for your letter which has been forwarded to me.
I'm delighted to be offered a second chance. I chose a poem for the first Lifelines, *wrote a note about it and then shamefully forgot to post it.*

I'll choose the same poem 'Tyger Tyger Burning Bright' by William Blake (to my surprise no one else chose it for the first volume).

Here are some reasons: first of all it has such compression; it sounds as clenched and muscular and fluid as a tiger. It is as ringingly memorable as a nursery rhyme and is apparently simple but full of complication – a lot of matter packed in a small container.

With best wishes toward another odd and wonderful anthology,

Barrie Cooke

The Tyger
from *Songs of Experience*

Tyger! Tyger! burning bright
In the forests of the night,
What immortal hand or eye
Could frame thy fearful symmetry?

In what distant deeps or skies
Burnt the fire of thine eyes?
On what wings dare he aspire?
What the hand, dare seize the fire?

And what shoulder, and what art,
Could twist the sinews of thy heart?
And when thy heart began to beat,
What dread hand? and what dread feet?

What the hammer? what the chain?
In what furnace was thy brain?
What the anvil? what dread grasp
Dare its deadly terrors clasp?

When the stars threw down their spears,
And water'd heaven with their tears,
Did he smile his work to see?
Did he who made the Lamb make thee?

Tyger! Tyger! burning bright
In the forests of the night,
What immortal hand or eye,
Dare frame thy fearful symmetry?

WILLIAM BLAKE (1757–1827)

BRIAN LYNCH   WRITER

2006

Dear Dónal O'Connor, Caroline Shaw and Stephanie Veitch,

Thank you for the kind invitation.

The poem I have chosen is 'To Mary' by William Cowper (1731–1800), the hero of my novel The Winner of Sorrow. *Cowper suffered from a seasonal bi-polar disorder – in the winter months he was inclined to suicidal depressions. He wrote the poem for Mrs Mary Unwin, a widow who had been taking care of him for almost twenty years. Seventeen of these years were spent in the lace-making town of Olney on the river Ouse in Buckinghamshire. (Their house, Orchardside, is now a museum.)*

Mrs Unwin was a skilled needlewoman, a skill which is replicated in the poem – read it aloud and you can hear in the clipped regularity of the metre and the rhyme the click of knitting needles. The needles 'rust disused and shine no more' because shortly after the couple had moved to Weston Underwood, just a mile up the river, Mrs Unwin was struck down by a stroke, an illness for which the poet blamed himself.

There is a less visible guilt in the poem. While Cowper was writing it, he was aware that tenderness towards one person can be wounding to another. In the relationship between him and Mary there was a third person, Lady Harriot Hesketh. Harriot was kindly and well-intentioned, but a terrible bossy-boots – it was she who obliged the couple to move from Olney to Weston. Although she was Cowper's first cousin, Harriot seems to have been in love with him. She was certainly madly jealous of Mrs Unwin: the fourteen repetitions of Mary's name were dagger blows to her heart – or they would have been had Cowper shown her the poem, but he didn't show it, he kept it a secret, and when Harriot found the manuscript amongst his papers many years later she was shocked, wounded, incredulous.

At the end of the novel, as he is dying, I imagine Cowper musing thus: 'To have written verses that even one person could not read aloud without tears, yes, that was adequate.' This poem has often made my eyes wetten. I wish your readers, too, the joy of its grief.

Sincerely,

Brian Lynch

To Mary

The twentieth year is well-nigh past
Since first our sky was overcast;
Ah, would that this might be the last,
           My Mary!

Thy spirits have a fainter flow,
I see thee daily weaker grow –
'Twas my distress that brought thee low,
           My Mary!

Thy needles, once a shining store,
For my sake restless heretofore,
Now rust disused and shine no more,
           My Mary!

For though thou gladly wouldst fulfil
The same kind office for me still,
Thy sight now seconds not thy will,
           My Mary!

But well thou played the housewife's part,
And all thy threads with magic art
Have wound themselves about this heart,
           My Mary!

Thy indistinct expressions seem
Like language uttered in a dream,
Yet me they charm, what'er the theme,
           My Mary!

Thy silver locks, once auburn bright,
Are still more lovely in my sight
Than golden beams of glorious light,
           My Mary!

For could I view nor them nor thee,
What sight worth seeing could I see?
The sun would rise in vain for me,
           My Mary!

Partakers of thy sad decline,
Thy hands their gentle force resign;
Yet, gently pressed, press gently mine,
           My Mary!

And then I feel that I still hold
A richer store ten thousandfold
Than misers fancy in their gold,
           My Mary!

Such feebleness of limb thou prov'st,
That now at every step thou mov'st,
Upheld by two; yet still thou lov'st,
                    My Mary!

And still to love, though pressed with ill,
In wintry age to feel no chill,
With me is to be lovely still,
                    My Mary!

But ah! by constant heed I know,
How oft the sadness that I show
Transforms thy smiles to looks of woe,
                    My Mary!

And should my future lot be cast
With much resemblance of the past,
Thy worn-out heart will break at last,
                    My Mary!

WILLIAM COWPER (1731–1800)

PETER FALLON   POET

9 May 1990

To: The Editors of Lifelines

I don't know how I'd single out one poem as a favourite. So many verses are central to my life as a writer, an editor, a reader. Still I appreciate opportunities to attempt to direct people to patterns of words which I've come to love. Perhaps, in this case, I am asking that familiar words be reconsidered, thought about again. Thousands of times I've heard the 'Hail Mary' transformed into, at best, a kind of mantra, at worst, the sound of no sense. Yet the words are lovely in their pure praise of a woman, a mother – maybe all women – and the phrase which has always delighted me, that is 'the fruit of thy womb', for an offspring, a welcomed child, has again and again been submerged in the interminable decades of a million galloping rosaries. One thoughtful recitation of this prayer would be worth those millions. Perhaps it's the editor in me which would propose to alter the order of the first section of the piece so that it ends 'Blessed is Jesus, the fruit of thy womb', to recover its special emphasis.

Now I'm no holy Joe, but the plain beauty of this homage came to me first on my uncle's farm when I was a boy, when we congregated each evening and slumped as much as we were allowed on the arms of the drawing-room chairs and my brother Bernard (or BP if you like), on holidays from prep school in England, knelt straight upright and spoke his pieces with the clear impression that he'd be a bishop at least if not the Pope! Somehow the arch loveliness of the words and ideas filtered through to me then. I thought them perfectly married. I still do.

Thank you for asking me.

Very best wishes,

Peter Fallon

Hail Mary, full of grace,
the Lord is with thee.
Blessed art thou amongst women
and blessed is the fruit of thy womb, Jesus.

Holy Mary, mother of God,
pray for us sinners,
now and at the hour of our death. Amen.

MARK HADDON NOVELIST

2006

Dear Caroline, Dónal and Stephanie,
Apologies for the speed at which I am doing this.

A Complaint by Night of the Lover not Beloved

Alas! so all things now do hold their peace,
    Heaven and earth disturbed in no thing.
The beasts, the air, the birds their song do cease;
    The nightes chare the stars about doth bring;
Calm is the sea; the waves work less and less.
    So am not I, whom love, alas! doth wring,
Bringing before my face the great increase
    Of my desires, whereat I weep and sing,
In joy and woe, as in a doubtful ease.
    For my sweet thoughts sometime do pleasure bring;
But by and by, the cause of my disease
    Gives me a pang, that inwardly doth sting,
        When that I think what grief it is again,
        To live and lack the thing should rid my pain.

HENRY HOWARD, EARL OF SURREY (1517–1547)

Great poems seem to change when you're not watching. Sometimes I will reread a poem that has never touched me before and find that it has come alive in my absence. On other occasions I reread a poem I love and find that it has gone into hibernation. Consequently, I have a different favourite poem every week.

This week it happens to be Henry Howard's 'A Complaint by Night of the Lover not Beloved'.

Explaining why is difficult. It has to be difficult, I think, because if you can explain precisely why a poem moves you, then it has failed to transport you to that strange place beyond all words which is the ambition of all good poetry.

If I had to point to anything in the poem it would be the gorgeously knotty word order which mirrors the poet's own turmoil ('The nightes chare the stars about doth bring'); that lovely phrase 'the waves work less and less' which is somehow psychological, mechanical and perfectly observed all at the same time; and that amazing second line, 'Heaven and earth disturbed in no thing', which I always find profoundly eerie.

Best wishes,

Mark Haddon

CHARLIE BIRD JOURNALIST

2006

Hope I'm not to late. The poem I would like included is 'Pangur Bán' by Anonymous, translated by Robin Flower.

    This may be a simple poem, but each of the eight verses has a beautiful flow. It is a poem from which some of the lines stick in the mind years after one has read it.

Charlie Bird

Pangur Bán

I and Pangur Bán my cat,
'Tis a like task we are at:
Hunting mice is his delight,
Hunting words I sit all night.

Better far than praise of men
'Tis to sit with book and pen;
Pangur bears me no ill will,
He too plies his simple skill.

'Tis a merry thing to see
At our tasks how glad are we,
When at home we sit and find
Entertainment to our mind.

Oftentimes a mouse will stray
In the hero Pangur's way;
Oftentimes my keen thought set
Takes a meaning in its net.

'Gainst the wall he sets his eye
Full and fierce and sharp and sly;
'Gainst the wall of knowledge I
All my little wisdom try.

When a mouse darts from its den
O how glad is Pangur then!
O what gladness do I prove
When I solve the doubts I love!

So in peace our tasks we ply,
Pangur Bán, my cat, and I;
In our arts we find our bliss,
I have mine and he has his.

Practice every day has made
Pangur perfect in his trade;
I get wisdom day and night
Turning darkness into light.

ANONYMOUS (EIGHTH OR EARLY NINTH CENTURY)
Translated by Robin Flower

['*Pangur Bán*' (or '*The Monk and his Pet Cat*', the title of the translation chosen by the late Cardinal Tomás Ó Fiaich in *Lifelines*, was also chosen by Moy McCrory in *Lifelines 2*.

Cardinal Ó Fiaich wrote:

I have many favourite poems and the one I would mention to you is 'Pangur Bán' *where an old monk in his scriptorium philosophises on the meaning of life for himself and his pet cat Pangur Bán. Every time I read the poem I can see the two of them in my mind's eye as each goes about his work.*

Moy McCrory wrote:

A favourite poem is always one of those nightmare questions because whatever I choose I will be missing out thousands that I love equally.

   However, a significant poem for me has to be 'Pangur Bán'. *(I'm thinking of the Robin Flower translation). This has been a favourite since childhood. Its simple, lyric quality and its clearness gives it a childlike simplicity which is deceptive. You can't hear it without being whisked back in time, the listener shares the scriptorium with the frozen scribe, who finds his mind wandering late in the night, watching his white Pangur chase mice. And that final irreverent gesture, to scribble it down the side of St Paul's Epistle, makes it both profane, vernacular and sacred.*

   I think this is a writer's poem, comparing the hunting of words to Pangur's hunting. As such it serves as a hymn for anyone who has sat up late trying to get the exact phrase, that word which always eludes.]

Dear Editors,

First of all, congratulations on carrying on the marvellous work of your predecessors in helping to alleviate famine in the Third World.

I haven't got just one favourite poem; I have a nucleus of poems that I love and that I turn to at different times and for different reasons.

The one I'm nominating for Lifelines 3 *is* 'Musée des Beaux Arts' *by W H Auden. This poem contemplates beauty, suffering and human indifference in a clear-eyed way. By being a beautiful thing itself, it assuages pain to some degree. It does make something happen.*

Every success with Lifelines 3.

Sincerely,

Marie Heaney

Musée des Beaux Arts

About suffering they were never wrong,
The Old Masters: how well they understood
Its human position; how it takes place
While someone else is eating or opening a window or just walking dully along;
How, when the aged are reverently, passionately waiting
For the miraculous birth, there always must be
Children who did not specially want it to happen, skating
On a pond at the edge of the wood:
They never forgot
That even the dreadful martyrdom must run its course
Anyhow in a corner, some untidy spot
Where the dogs go on with their doggy life and the torturer's horse
Scratches its innocent behind on a tree.

In Brueghel's *Icarus*, for instance: how everything turns away
Quite leisurely from the disaster; the ploughman may
Have heard the splash, the forsaken cry,
But for him it was not an important failure; the sun shone
As it had to on the white legs disappearing into the green
Water; and the expensive delicate ship that must have seen
Something amazing, a boy falling out of the sky,
Had somewhere to get to and sailed calmly on.

W H AUDEN (1907–1973)

['Musée des Beaux Arts' was also Terry Prone's choice in *Lifelines 3*. Terry Prone wrote:
My favourite is one of Auden's. Favourite because it underlines the tension between what is heroic, what is tragic, what is unique, and what is routine, what is driven by the imperative of the 'little round of deeds and days'. It's usually an unregistered and unacknowledged tension – with today's trivia triumphant . . . I love it, too, because once you know the poem, you know the painting in a quite different way.]

BRIAN KEENAN   WRITER

1994

Dear Friends,

Please excuse this long delay in replying to your request. I have been travelling much of late and busy with work.

  Like most people, I have many favourite poems and this changes with each new collection I read. So here it is for what it's worth. 'Spring in the City' by Pablo Neruda.

  I have always been a traveller, always part of me an exile. I know the streets of which Neruda writes. I have been down them one hundred thousand times. These streets are metaphorical as well as literal. Like a wonderful impressionist painting, they are closely observed and sensuous. They pose questions. And they are the eternal questions loosely grasped at, about identity, place, meaning and purpose.

  Like a fine work of art, Neruda's poems are simple and direct yet they hold you, and you re-read them again and again.

  I have always believed all life is a journey. With Neruda, one can travel into many landscapes. The metaphysical, the existential and the simply exquisite landscape of Chile and South America.

Yours,

Brian Keenan

La Primavera Urbana

Se gastó el pavimento hasta no ser
sino una red de sucios agujeros
en que la lluvia acumuló sus lágrimas,
luego llegaba el sol como invasor
sobre el gastado piso
de la ciudad sin fin acribillada
de la que huyeron todos los caballos.
Por fin cayeron algunos limones
y algún vestigio rojo de naranjas
la emparentó con árboles y plumas,
le dio un susurro falso de arboleda
que no duraba mucho,
pero probaba que en alguna parte
se desnudaba entre los azahares
la primavera impúdica y plateada.

Era yo de acquel sitio? De la fría
contextura de muro contra muro?
Pertenecía mi alma a la cerveza?
Eso me preguntaron al salir
y al entrar en mí mismo, al acostarme,
eso me preguntaban las paredes,
la pintura, las moscas, los tapices
pisados tantas veces
por ostros habitantes parecidos
a mí hasta confundirse:
tenían mi nariz y mis zapatos,
la misma ropa muerta de tristeza,
las mismas uñas pálidas, prolijas,
y un corazón abierto como un mueble
en que se acumularon los racimos,
los amores, los viajes y la arena,
es decir, todo lo que sucediendo
se va y se queda inexorablemente.

PABLO NERUDA (1904–1973)

Spring in the City

The sidewalk has been worn till it is only
a network of dirty holes
in which the tears of the rain gathered;
then came the sun, an invader
over the wasted ground
of the endlessly riddled city
from which all the horses fled.
At last, some lemons fell
and a red vestige of oranges
connected it with trees and feathers,
whispered falsely of orchards
which did not last long
but showed that somewhere
the shameless, silvered spring
was undressing among the orange blossoms.

Was I from that place? From the cold
texture of adjoining walls?
Did my spirit have to do with beer?
They asked me that when I went out,
when I entered myself again, when I went to bed,
they were asking me that, the walls,
the paint, the flies, the carpets
trodden so many times
by other inhabitants
who could be confused with me.
they had my nose and my shoes,
the same dead, sorrowing clothes,
the same pale, neat nails,
and a heart as open as a sideboard
in which accumulated bundles,
loves, journeys, and sand.
That's to say, everything in its happening
goes and stays inexorably.

Translated by Alistair Reid

8 January 1992

Dear Nicola, Paula and Alice,

Thank you for your letter. Your Lifelines *project sounds very worthwhile though I wish you had said exactly which Third World charities you support: as an atheist, I prefer not to be associated with any which have a religious basis.*

My favourite poem is Shelley's 'Ozymandias' because it creates such an unforgettable picture of the ruined statue in the desert and quietly reminds us that all human pomp and power is transient and that even the greatest self-importance ends in dust. I love the commonplace, buttonholing way it opens, and then the grandeur of its climax. A few years ago I saw the ruined Pharaonic statue near Luxor which the poem is supposed to be based on: a bitter disappointment because it is beside a busy tourist road. But the glory of the poem remains.

Yours sincerely,

Lynn Barber

Ozymandias

I met a traveller from an antique land
Who said: Two vast and trunkless legs of stone
Stand in the desert. Near them on the sand,
Half sunk, a shatter'd visage lies, whose frown
And wrinkled lip and sneer of cold command
Tell that its sculptor well those passions read
Which yet survive, stamp'd on these lifeless things,
The hand that mock'd them, and the heart that fed;
And on the pedestal these words appear:
'My name is Ozymandias, king of kings:
Look on my works, ye Mighty, and despair!'
Nothing beside remains. Round the decay
Of that colossal wreck, boundless and bare,
The lone and level sands stretch far away.

PERCY BYSSHE SHELLEY (1792–1822)

['*Ozymandias*' was also chosen by Michael Scott in *Lifelines 3*. Michael Scott wrote:
There are two poems I keep going back to, two poems I can recite by heart, both – I believe – first heard in my childhood: Shelley's 'Ozymandias' and Thomas Hardy's 'Lyonesse'. In truth, however, I never remember learning these verses. In each, the sense of magic and mystery, of suggested secrets and hinted wonders appeals to me, and I try to instil that same sense of wonder into my own writing. I do know that, when I started to write, many years ago, I pinned the poem, 'Lyonesse', to the wall above my desk. It is still there.]

14 January 1994

Dear Áine, Ewan and Chris,

I've chosen one of Wallace Stevens's last poems 'Not Ideas about the Thing but the Thing Itself', it still makes me dizzy when I read it. Thanks for the invite to contribute. It's a wonderful project, good luck with it.

Yours

Mark Joyce

Not Ideas about the Thing but the Thing Itself

At the earliest ending of winter,
In March, a scrawny cry from outside
Seemed like a sound in his mind.

He knew that he heard it,
A bird's cry, at daylight or before,
In the early March wind.

The sun was rising at six,
No longer a battered panache above snow . . .
It would have been outside.

It was not from the vast ventriloquism
Of sleep's faded papier-mâché . . .
The sun was coming from outside.

That scrawny cry—it was
A chorister whose c preceded the choir.
It was part of the colossal sun,

Surrounded by its choral rings,
Still far away. It was like
A new knowledge of reality.

WALLACE STEVENS (1879–1955)

24 April 2006

Dear Dónal, Caroline and Stephanie,

Many thanks for asking me to contribute. I remember buying a copy of the first Lifelines *in a bookshop on Grafton Street in 1992, I think, when I was sixteen, and poring over it. It's no exaggeration to say that that book opened a door between me and poetry. Here were politicians, actors, writers and, most importantly to me, poets speaking directly and without embarrassment about this strange thing poetry, about its seriousness and pleasures and importance. Without opening the books – and one of them is right now in the bookcase across the room – I can remember that Heaney chose Yeats's 'Cuchulain Comforted', Longley opted for a section of Hart Crane's 'Voyages', Hughes went for Gregory's version of 'Dónal Óg', Armitage picked Auden's 'The More Loving One', Durcan decided on Ellen Gilchrist . . . I met so many poets in those books. Mahon had chosen 'The Moose' and it was where I first read that cool, calm tone of Elizabeth Bishop. Many of the poets in those books became my favourites too. Aside from the admirable charitable cause,* Lifelines *was immensely important for me as a book, as I'm certain it was for many others. Many congratulations on keeping it going.*

Now that I come to it though, picking a favourite poem is difficult. I could mention any of the poems Blu-tacked around my house: Allen Curnow's 'Continuum', Frank O'Hara's 'Animals', Les Murray's 'The Quality of Sprawl', Wallace Stevens's 'The Poems of Our Climate', Berryman's 'Dream Song 14', Mark Doty's 'A Green Crab's Shell', Jorie Graham's 'Reading Plato' . . . but on the basis that your book is a good place for people to meet poets beyond, perhaps, the borders of their usual reading, I'll choose the Polish poet Zbigniew Herbert and his poem 'The Envoy of Mr Cogito'.

The poem is a howl and also a prayer, both charge sheet and primer, a war cry against war. It has a Beckettian authority that says I can't go on, I'll go on. *It knows the pointlessness but insists on effort, on attaining the good. I love its necessary ironies, its unabashed abstractions and the tiny apprehensible details. As with much Polish poetry of this century, it has an earned, lived drama about it. It's not an everyday poem perhaps (it's not on my fridge), but it is very much a serious, powerful poem about how to live well in the world, in the 'kingdom without limit', and when I read the seventh and eighth lines something in me clicks.*

All the best and good luck,

Nick Laird

The Envoy of Mr Cogito

Go where those others went to the dark boundary
for the golden fleece of nothingness your last prize

go upright among those who are on their knees
among those with their backs turned and those toppled in the dust

you were saved not in order to live
you have little time you must give testimony

be courageous when the mind deceives you be courageous
in the final account only this is important

and let your helpless Anger be like the sea
whenever you hear the voice of the insulted and beaten

let your sister Scorn not leave you
for the informers executioners cowards — they will win
they will go to your funeral and with relief will throw a lump of earth
the woodborer will write your smoothed-over biography

and do not forgive truly it is not in your power
to forgive in the name of those betrayed at dawn

beware however of unnecessary pride
keep looking at your clown's face in the mirror
repeat: I was called—weren't there better ones than I

beware of dryness of heart love the morning spring
the bird with an unknown name the winter oak
light on a wall the splendour of the sky
they don't need your warm breath
they are there to say: no one will console you

be vigilant—when the light on the mountains gives the sign—arise
            and go
as long as blood turns in the breast your dark star

repeat old incantations of humanity fables and legends
because this is how you will attain the good you will not attain
repeat great words repeat them stubbornly
like those crossing the desert who perished in the sand

and they will reward you with what they have at hand
with the whip of laughter with murder on a garbage heap

go because only in this way will you be admitted to the company of
            cold skulls
to the company of your ancestors: Gilgamesh Hector Roland
the defenders of the kingdom without limit and the city of ashes

Be faithful Go

ZBIGNIEW HERBERT (1924–1998)
translated by John Carpenter and Bogdana Carpenter

J M Coetzee

Zbigniew Herbert, 'The Envoy of Mr Cogito' – A poem of courage for the dark twentieth century.

John Coetzee

[Both Nick Laird and J M Coetzee chose Zbigniew Herbert's 'The Envoy of Mr Cogito' for *Lifelines New and Collected*.]

Laurie Lee

20 January 1988

Dear Julie, Jonathan, Duncan,

'Stopping by Woods on a Snowy Evening' *(Robert Frost) for its atmosphere and rhyme-scheme, timelessly satisfying. For its gauche imperfections –*

> 'Whose woods these are I think I know,
> His house is in the village though;'

Well, does he or doesn't he?
   And for the shattering repetition of the two last lines. A stumbling accident of writing, according to Frost, as most revelations are.

Laurie Lee

Stopping By Woods on a Snowy Evening

Whose woods these are I think I know,
His house is in the village though;
He will not see me stopping here
To watch his woods fill up with snow.

My little horse must think it queer
To stop without a farmhouse near
Between the woods and frozen lake
The darkest evening of the year.

He gives his harness bells a shake
To ask if there is some mistake.
The only other sound's the sweep
Of easy wind and downy flake.

The woods are lovely, dark and deep,
But I have promises to keep,
And miles to go before I sleep,
And miles to go before I sleep.

Robert Frost (1874–1963)

[*'Stopping by Woods on a Snowy Evening'* was also chosen by Kate Atkinson and Declan McGonagle in *Lifelines 3*:

Kate Atkinson wrote:

Like all really good poems it defies absolute interpretation, so that although I think that I partly understand it I know it contains something inaccessible that will always defy interpretation. Also – another trait of a good poem for me – it is, on the surface, very simple; the language Frost uses is plain and monosyllabic, almost childlike in places – 'Whose woods these are I think I know' and also familiar and domestic – 'My little horse must think it queer'. There is a constant use of assonance and all those lovely long open vowel sounds – 'The only other sound's the sweep/Of easy wind and downy flake' – that build up into an overall effect that's strangely hallucinatory and incantational, especially in that wonderful final stanza. It's a poem that reveals the numinous and the mystical at the heart of the ordinary.

Declan McGonagle wrote:

This is practically a love poem where the poet acknowledges the importance of the relationship between mankind and nature.

That he is able to convey very profound meaning in such direct, understandable language is a measure of the strength of his vision. As I know from my schooldays, the poem communicates very clearly and is easily remembered. The rhythm and cadence of the poet's 'voice' is insistent but also lulling as well. The poem is really a description of a moment of stillness when meaning in life is perceptible in a flash of understanding before we move on again towards an inevitable end.]

NUALA O'FAOLAIN   WRITER

2006

Dear Editors,

I got this poem years ago from a book of essays by Joseph Brodsky called On Grief and Reason. *This is a difficult poem, and I don't know that I could have loved it as I do now when I was young. But I am beginning to lose the people I love to death, and I'm conscious, now, of my own inevitable death. This poem reverses the myth of Orpheus and Eurydice – in which Orpheus, rescuing his beloved Eurydice from the underworld, is forbidden to look back as he leads her out but does look back, and loses her. In this poem she turns back. Perhaps she has even already turned before he looks back.*

She hardly notices him. Death is a completely different thing from life, Rilke is saying. It is another condition. Human motives, such as Orpheus's love, can mean nothing to a person as full of death as the living are of life.

The grave beauty of this poem – especially the lines beginning 'She was already loosened like long hair' – is respectful towards death in a way that makes it less oppressive. It, in fact, comforts me with its beauty. I hope a few readers will keep it somewhere in their minds.

It was written by Rainer Maria Rilke and I don't know who did the translation here, that I copied from somewhere years ago.

In haste, much thanks, much admiration for Wesley's great achievements in this area.

Nuala

Orpheus. Eurydice. Hermes

That was the strange unfathomed mine of souls.
And they, like silent veins of silver ore,
were winding through its darkness. Between roots
welled up the blood that flows on to mankind,
like blocks of heavy porphyry in the darkness.
Else there was nothing red.

But there were rocks
and ghostly forests. Bridges over voidness
and that immense, gray, unreflecting pool
that hung above its so far distant bed
like a gray rainy sky above the landscape.
And between meadows, soft and full of patience,
appeared the pale strip of the single pathway,
like a long line of linen laid to bleach.

And on this single pathway they approached.

In front the slender man in the blue mantle,
gazing in dumb impatience straight before him.
His steps devoured the way in mighty chunks
they did not pause to chew; his hands were hanging,
heavy and clenched, out of the falling folds,
no longer conscious of the lightsome lyre,
the lyre which had grown into his left
like twines of rose into a branch of olive.
It seemed as though his senses were divided:
for, while his sight ran like a dog before him,
turned round, came back, and stood, time and again,
distant and waiting, at the path's next turn,
his hearing lagged behind him like a smell.
It seemed to him at times as though it stretched
back to the progress of those other two
who should be following up this whole ascent.
Then once more there was nothing else behind him
but his climb's echo and his mantle's wind.
He, though, assured himself they still were coming;
said it aloud and heard it die away.
They still were coming, only they were two
that trod with fearful lightness. If he durst
but once look back (if only looking back
were not undoing of this whole enterprise
still to be done), he could not fail to see them,
the two light-footers, following him in silence:

The god of faring and of distant message,
the traveling-hood over his shining eyes,
the slender wand held out before his body,
the wings around his ankles lightly beating,
and in his left hand, as entrusted, *her*.

She, so belov'd, that from a single lyre
more mourning rose than from all women-mourners—
that a whole world of mourning rose, wherein
all things were once more present: wood and vale
and road and hamlet, field and stream and beast—
and that around this world of mourning turned,
even as around the other earth, a sun
and a whole silent heaven full of stars,
a heaven of mourning with disfigured stars—
she, so beloved.

But hand in hand now with that god she walked,
her paces circumscribed by lengthy shroudings,
uncertain, gentle, and without impatience.
Wrapt in herself, like one whose time is near,
she thought not of the man who went before them,
nor of the road ascending into life.
Wrapt in herself she wandered. And her deadness
was filling her like fullness.
Full as a fruit with sweetness and with darkness
was she with her great death, which was so new
that for the time she could take nothing in.

She had attained a new virginity
and was intangible; her sex had closed
like a young flower at the approach of evening,
and her pale hands had grown so disaccustomed
to being a wife that even the slim god's
endlessly gentle contact as he led her
disturbed her like a too great intimacy.

Even now she was no longer that blond woman
who'd sometimes echoed in the poet's poems,
no longer the broad couch's scent and island,
nor yonder man's possession any longer.

She was already loosened like long hair,
and given far and wide like fallen rain,
and dealt out like a manifold supply.

She was already root.

And when, abruptly,
the god had halted her and, with an anguished
outcry, outspoke the words: He has turned round!—
she took in nothing, and said softly: Who?

But in the distance, dark in the bright exit,
someone or other stood, whose countenance
was indistinguishable. Stood and saw
how, on a strip of pathway between meadows,
with sorrow in his look, the god of message
turned silently to go behind the figure
already going back by that same pathway,
its paces circumscribed by lengthy shroudings,
uncertain, gentle, and without impatience.

RAINER MARIA RILKE (1875–1926)
translated by J B Leishman

DEIRDRE MADDEN   NOVELIST

22 February 1994

Dear Ewan, Áine and Christopher,

Thank you for your letter. I read and enjoyed earlier Lifelines *anthologies, and I'm happy to contribute to the latest issue.*

My favourite poem is 'Vaucluse', *by my husband Harry Clifton. It relates to a time before we were married, when I was spending some months in the south of France, and Harry came out to visit me. We went to Aix-En-Provence together, and to Marseilles. It's a marvellous poem, and it means a great deal to me.*

Good luck with Lifelines.

All best wishes,

Deirdre Madden

Vaucluse

Cognac, like a gold sun
Blazed in me, turning
The landscape inside out—
I had left the South
An hour ago, and the train
Through Arles, through Avignon,
Fed on electricity
Overhead, and quickened my mind
With infinite platforms, cypress trees,
Stone villages, the granaries
Of Provence, and I saw again

France, like a blue afternoon
Genius makes hay in, and drink improves—
The worked fields, the yellow sheaves
In shockwaves, perceived
And lit from within, by love.
By then, I suppose,
You had made your own connections,
My chance, eventual girl,
And half Marseilles had closed
For the hot hours—the awnings of cafés
With nothingness in their shadows,
And the drink put away
For another day
Not ours . . . .
                    I see, I remember
Coldly now, as I see ourselves
And the merchants from Africa, glozening
Liquor on the shelves
Of celebration, everyone dozing
In transmigratory dreams
Of heroin, garlic, and cloves—
And how we got there, you and I,
By trade route or intuition, seems,
Like charts for sale on the Occident streets
As fabulous, as obsolete
As a map of the known world.

But then again, how kind he was,
The dark *patron* . . . and it lasted,
That shot of cognac,
An hour, till the train
Occluded in grey rain
Above Lyons, and the Rhône Valley
Darkened. I would carry
Your books, your winter clothes
Through stations, streets of Paris
To a cold repose
In the North. We would meet again
In months to come, and years,
Exchanging consciousness, reason and tears
Like beggars. Transfigured,
Not yet fallen from grace
I saw us, not as we are
But new in love, in the hallowed place
Of sources, the sacred fountains
Of Petrarch and René Char.

HARRY CLIFTON (B.1952)

25 April 2006

Dear Dónal, Caroline & Stephanie,

Many thanks for inviting me to participate in your latest Lifelines *project. I am delighted and flattered to be asked. I have always greatly admired the idea behind the enterprise; it does so much for Concern (and for poetry). You deserve all the support you can get, and I hope you make a hatful of money.*

Like so many of your contributors, I find it extremely difficult to select a favourite poem. I know it is traditional for everyone who participates to moan how hard it is to choose, but I hadn't realised how demanding the task was until your letter came in. Right now this instant, and in no particular order, I love Eavan Boland's 'The Necessity for Irony', *Seamus Heaney's* 'Postscript', *Paul Durcan's* 'Ulysses', *Greg Delanty's* 'Aceldama', *Zbigniew Herbert's* 'Nothing Special', *Don Paterson's* 'Imperial', *Clive James's* 'Johnny Weismuller Dead in Acapulco', *Michael Coady's* 'Though There are Torturers', *Sheenagh Pugh's* 'Sometimes', *Sheila O'Hagan's* 'Mozart's Kitchen', *Ted Hughes's* 'Full Moon and Little Frieda', *Pat Boran's* 'Neighbours', *Robert Frost's* 'Stopping by Woods on a Snowy Evening', *Patrick Kavanagh's* 'Inniskeen Road: July Evening', *Tom Waits's* 'Kentucky Avenue', *Bob Dylan's* 'Like a Rolling Stone', *U2's* 'One', *Bruce Springsteen's* 'Born to Run' . . . *I could run and run myself but I'd better stop.*

I've selected 'Lemonade' *by the late, great Raymond Carver. In her introduction to his posthumous collected poems entitled* All Of Us, *his widow Tess Gallagher quotes Czeslaw Milosz:* 'When it hurts we return to the banks of certain rivers'. *She said that for Ray poems were like rivers, places of recognition and healing. What a brilliant description. So I'm picking* 'Lemonade' *because it's a poem I return to again and again; and every time I do return to this particular river I'm moved once more by its elegance and clarity, its beauty and strength; and above all by Carver's pure compassion.*

Once again the best of luck with your project.

Every good wish,

John O'Donnell

Lemonade

When he came to my house months ago to measure
my walls for bookcases, Jim Sears didn't look like a man
who'd lose his only child to the high waters
of the Elwha River. He was bushy-haired, confident,
cracking his knuckles, alive with energy, as we
discussed tiers, and brackets, and this oak stain
compared to that. But it's a small town, this town,
a small world here. Six months later, after the bookcases
have been built, delivered and installed, Jim's
father, a Mr Howard Sears, who is 'covering for his son'
comes to paint our house. He tells me – when I ask, more

out of small-town courtesy than anything, 'How's Jim?' –
that his son lost Jim Jr in the river last spring.
Jim blames himself. 'He can't get over it,
neither,' Mr Sears adds. 'Maybe he's gone on to lose
his mind a little too,' he adds, pulling on the bill
of his Sherwin-Williams cap.
    Jim had to stand and watch as the helicopter
grappled with, then lifted, his son's body from the river
with tongs. 'They used like a big pair of kitchen tongs
for it, if you can imagine. Attached to a cable. But God always
takes the sweetest ones, don't He?' Mr Sears says. 'He has
His own mysterious purposes.' 'What do *you* think about it?'
I want to know. 'I don't want to think,' he says. 'We
can't ask or question His ways. It's not for us to know.
I just know He taken him home now, the little one.'

He goes on to tell me Jim Sr's wife took him to thirteen foreign
countries in Europe in hopes it'd help him get over it. But
it didn't. He couldn't. 'Mission unaccomplished,' Howard says.
Jim's come down with Parkinson's disease. What next?
He's home from Europe now, but still blames himself
for sending Jim Jr back to the car that morning to look for
that thermos of lemonade. They didn't need any lemonade
that day! Lord, lord, what was he thinking of, Jim Sr has said
a hundred – no, a thousand – times now, and to anyone who will
still listen. If only he hadn't made lemonade in the first
place that morning! What could he have been thinking about?
Further, if they hadn't shopped the night before at Safeway, and
if that bin of yellowy lemons hadn't stood next to where they
kept the oranges, apples, grapefruit, and bananas.
That's what Jim Sr had really wanted to buy, some oranges
and apples, not lemons for lemonade, forget lemons, he hated
lemons – at least now he did – but Jim Jr, he liked lemonade,
always had. He wanted lemonade.

'Let's look at it this way,' Jim Sr would say, 'those lemons
had to come from someplace, didn't they? The Imperial Valley,
probably, or else over near Sacramento, they raise lemons
there, right?' They had to be planted and irrigated and
watched over and then pitched into sacks by field workers and
weighed and then dumped into boxes and shipped by rail or
truck to this god-forsaken place where a man can't do anything
but lose his children! Those boxes would've been off-loaded
from the truck by boys not much older than Jim Jr himself.
Then they had to be uncrated and poured all yellow and
lemony-smelling out of their crates by those boys, and washed

and sprayed by some kid who was still living, walking around town, living and breathing, big as you please. Then they were carried into the store and placed in that bin under that eye-catching sign that said Have You Had Fresh Lemonade Lately? As Jim Sr's reckoning went, it harks all the way back to first causes, back to the first lemon cultivated on earth. If there hadn't been any lemons on earth, and there hadn't been any Safeway store, well, Jim would still have his son, right? And Howard Sears would still have his grandson, sure. You see, there were a lot of people involved in this tragedy. There were the farmers and the pickers of lemons, the truck drivers, the big Safeway store. . . . Jim Sr, too, he was ready to assume his share of responsibility, of course. He was the most guilty of all. But he was still in his nosedive, Howard Sears told me. Still, he had to pull out of this somehow and go on. Everybody's heart was broken, right. Even so.

Not long ago Jim Sr's wife got him started in a little
wood-carving class here in town. Now he's trying to whittle bears
and seals, owls, eagles, seagulls, anything, but
he can't stick to any one creature long enough to finish
the job, is Mr Sears's assessment. The trouble is, Howard Sears
goes on, every time Jim Sr looks up from his lathe, or his
carving knife, he sees his son breaking out of the water downriver,
and rising up – being reeled in, so to speak – beginning to turn and
turn in circles until he was up, way up above the fir trees, tongs
sticking out of his back, and then the copter turning and swinging
upriver, accompanied by the roar and whap-whap of
the chopper blades. Jim Jr passing now over the searchers who
line the bank of the river. His arms are stretched out from his sides,
and drops of water fly out from him. He passes overhead once more,
closer now, and then returns a minute later to be deposited, ever
so gently laid down, directly at the feet of his father. A man
who, having seen everything now – his dead son rise from the river
in the grip of metal pinchers and turn and turn in circles flying
above the tree line – would like nothing more now than
to just die. But dying is for the sweetest ones. And he remembers
sweetness, when life was sweet, and sweetly
he was given that other lifetime.

RAYMOND CARVER (1938–1988)

25 January 1988

Dear Miss Grantham,

Many thanks for your letter.

My favourite poem is 'The Thousandth Man' by Rudyard Kipling because it reflects my own attitude to loyalty and friendship. I am a great admirer of Kipling because he had a great command of the language as well as being a first-class storyteller.

May I wish your project every success,

Yours sincerely,

Jeffrey Archer

The Thousandth Man

One man in a thousand, Solomon says,
Will stick more close than a brother.
And it's worth while seeking him half your days
If you find him before the other.
Nine hundred and ninety-nine depend
On what the world sees in you,
But the Thousandth Man will stand your friend
With the whole round world agin you.

'Tis neither promise nor prayer nor show
Will settle the finding for 'ee.
Nine hundred and ninety-nine of 'em go
By your looks, or your acts, or your glory.
But if he finds you and you find him,
The rest of the world don't matter;
For the Thousandth Man will sink or swim
With you in any water.

You can use his purse with no more talk
Than he uses yours for his spendings,
And laugh and meet in your daily walk
As though there had been no lendings.
Nine hundred and ninety-nine of 'em call
For silver and gold in their dealings;
But the Thousandth Man he's worth 'em all,
Because you can show him your feelings.

His wrong's your wrong, and his right's your right
In season or out of season.
Stand up and back it in all men's sight—
With *that* for your only reason!

Nine hundred and ninety-nine can't bide
The shame or mocking or laughter,
But the Thousandth Man will stand by your side
To the gallows-foot—and after!

RUDYARD KIPLING (1865–1936)

['*The Thousandth Man*' was also Patricia Scanlan's choice in *Lifelines*. Patricia Scanlan wrote: *The name of my favourite poem is Rudyard Kipling's* 'The Thousandth Man'. *I particularly like this poem because of the way it describes a true and real friendship where a person is accepted for who and what they are, warts and all. In this poem a friend is always there to share the good times and the bad 'to the gallows-foot — and after!'*

I am lucky to have some great friends and I like this poem so much I used it as my theme for my first novel, City Girl.]

EAMONN SWEENEY — NOVELIST

7 January 1997

Dear Ralph, Caroline and Gareth,

Thanks very much for asking me to pick my favourite poem for Lifelines; *it's a great honour. Thinking about which poem I'd pick if I was ever asked is like choosing my top-ten records for* Desert Island Discs *or selecting a World football team to play Mars in the Inter-Galactic Cup, something I've thought of many a night when it would have been more in line to be doing some work.*

The fact is that every time I pick a favourite poem, it's different. So this choice reflects what I think tonight, it would have been another poem yesterday and it will be another one tomorrow. The reason I've answered you this quickly is to end the torment of choosing just one poem. Already, I'm thinking of the poems by Paul Durcan, Seamus Heaney and Robert Lowell, among others, which I could have picked.

The poem I've gone for is 'Iola, Kansas' *by the American poet Amy Clampitt from her collection* Westward. *It strikes a chord with me for many reasons. It evokes the mind-numbing atmosphere of the long-distance bus-ride (and reminds me of the trek from London to Holyhead when I was too broke to travel back to Ireland any other way except by bus and ferry). It paints a great picture of the neglected heartland of America. And, in the end, it celebrates the unifying joy which seemingly minor pleasures can bring to people's hearts. I love this poem.*

Thanks again for asking me for a contribution and best of luck with the anthology. I think the work done by the Lifelines *people over the past few years has been admirable. Keep it going and best of luck in the future to the three of you.*

Yours sincerely,

Eamonn Sweeney

Iola, Kansas

Riding all night, the bus half empty, toward the interior,
among refineries, trellised and turreted illusory cities,
the crass, the indispensable wastefulness of oil rigs
offshore, of homunculi swigging at the gut of a continent:

the trailers, the semis, the vans, the bumper stickers,
slogans in day-glo invoking the name of Jesus, who knows
what it means: the air waves, the brand name, the backyard
Barbie-doll barbecue, graffiti in video, the burblings,

the dirges: *heart like a rock, I said Kathy I'm lost,*
the scheme is a mess, we've left Oklahoma, its cattle,
sere groves of pecan trees interspersing the horizonless
belch and glare, the alluvium of the auto junkyards,

we're in Kansas now, we've turned off the freeway,
we're meandering, as again night falls, among farmsteads,
the little towns with the name of a girl on the watertower,
the bandstand in the park at the center, the churches

alight from within, perpendicular banalities of glass
candy-streaked purple-green-yellow (who is this Jesus?),
the strangeness of all there is, whatever it is, growing
stranger, we've come to a rest stop, the name of the girl

on the watertower is Iola: no video, no vending machines,
but Wonder Bread sandwiches, a pie: 'It's boysenberry,
I just baked it today', the woman behind the counter
believably says, the innards a purply glue, and I eat it

with something akin to reverence: free refills from
the Silex on the hot plate, then back to our seats,
the loud suction of air brakes like a thing alive, and
the voices, the sleeping assembly raised, as by an agency

out of the mystery of the interior, to a community —
and through some duct in the rock I feel my heart go out,
out here in the middle of nowhere (the scheme is a mess)
to the waste, to the not knowing who or why, and am happy.

AMY CLAMPITT (1920–1994)

MIKE MURPHY

3 March 1988

Dear Julie Grantham,

My apologies for the delay in replying to your letter – I'm afraid that it just got mislaid and I have only found it today.

My choice of poem would be 'Elegy in a Country Churchyard' *by Thomas Gray because in my opinion it is one of the gentlest, most provocative poems ever written. I don't need yoga, valium, or any other relaxant. When necessary I recite the first few verses and I feel the better for it.*

Kind regards,

Mike (Murphy)

from *Elegy Written in a Country Churchyard*

The curfew tolls the knell of parting day,
The lowing herd wind slowly o'er the lea,
The plowman homeward plods his weary way,
And leaves the world to darkness and to me.

Now fades the glimmering landscape on the sight,
And all the air a solemn stillness holds,
Save where the beetle wheels his droning flight,
And drowsy tinklings lull the distant folds;

Save that from yonder ivy-mantled tow'r
The moping owl does to the moon complain
Of such, as wand'ring near her secret bow'r,
Molest her ancient solitary reign.

Beneath those rugged elms, that yew-tree's shade,
Where heaves the turf in many a mould'ring heap,
Each in his narrow cell forever laid,
The rude forefathers of the hamlet sleep.

The breezy call of incense-breathing Morn,
The swallow twitt'ring from the straw-built shed,
The cock's shrill clarion, or the echoing horn,
No more shall rouse them from their lowly bed.

THOMAS GRAY (1716–1771)

Jerusalem
15 February 1988

Dear Julie, Jonathan and Duncan,

Many thanks for your letter dated January 1988. I am very happy to help you in your efforts to raise money for famine victims in Ethiopia. I congratulate you on the success of your efforts, following the production of Lifelines *I and wish you every success in your further endeavours to help the starving people in the Third World.*

It is very difficult, indeed, for me to choose a particular poem or poet. A very deep appreciation and love of poetry was instilled in me when I was a pupil at Wesley College. The result is that I have far too many favourite poets and favourite poems and it is, therefore, not easy for me to choose one. However, since I am contributing to an effort in Ireland let me say that one of my favourite poets is W B Yeats. His poem that has remained with me as a favourite is 'The Lake Isle of Innisfree'. *I believe that few poems have given life to a rustic scene as has this poem. Everything, as it were, comes to life – the beauty of the quietness of the glade in which he will build a small cabin, the bees, the cricket, the shimmer and glimmer of the morning and the night and the birds. All this against the background of the lake with the water lapping by the shores. Yeats was certainly one of the greatest poets of our time. He succeeded in his beautiful poems to bring to life so many aspects of nature, of life and of art. All this against the background of his deep love for Ireland and its legends and his idealistic devotion to the cause of the Irish Revolution. W B Yeats is, in my mind, a poet who will survive the ages and who belongs to eternity.*

With best wishes,

Yours sincerely,

Chaim Herzog

The Lake Isle of Innisfree

I will arise and go now, and go to Innisfree,
And a small cabin build there, of clay and wattles made:
Nine bean-rows will I have there, a hive for the honey-bee,
And live alone in the bee-loud glade.

And I shall have some peace there, for peace comes dropping slow,
Dropping from the veils of the morning to where the cricket sings;
There midnight's all a glimmer, and noon a purple glow,
And evening full of the linnet's wings.

I will arise and go now, for always night and day
I hear lake water lapping with low sounds by the shore;
While I stand on the roadway, or on the pavements grey,
I hear it in the deep heart's core.

W B YEATS (1865–1939)

['The Lake Isle of Innisfree' was Darina Allen's choice in *Lifelines* and Paddy Cole's choice in *Lifelines 2*.

Darina Allen wrote:

My favourite poem is 'The Lake Isle of Innisfree' by W B Yeats. This is a wonderfully evocative poem. I can escape in my mind's eye to this idyllic peaceful isle where peace comes dropping slow and there are no telephones.]

Paddy Cole wrote:

My favourite poem is a W B Yeats. It's called 'The Lake Isle of Innisfree'.

As I lead a very hectic life, with a lot of travelling, this poem to me depicts everything that is relaxing and tranquil.

I think the last line in the first verse is fabulous as I can just imagine a 'bee-loud glade'. I love to fish, and have done since I was a young boy with my father, so this poem is about everything outdoors that I love to get away to.

And I shall have some peace there, for peace comes dropping slow

I often would think of that line, and of course 'And evening full of the linnet's wings'.]

RODDY DOYLE NOVELIST

28 February 1997

Dear Mr Croly, Ms Dowling and Mr McCluskey,

Here is my poem. I hope it's of use to you. Good luck with the project.

Yours,

Roddy Doyle

Base Details

If I were fierce, and bald, and short of breath,
    I'd live with scarlet Majors at the Base,
And speed glum heroes up the line to death.
    You'd see me with my puffy petulant face,
Guzzling and gulping in the best hotel,
    Reading the Roll of Honour. 'Poor young chap,'
I'd say — 'I used to know his father well;
    Yes, we've lost heavily in this last scrap.'
And when the war is done and youth stone dead,
I'd toddle safely home and die — in bed.

ROUEN, 4 MARCH 1917
Siegfried Sassoon (1886–1967)

I first read 'Base Details' in 1974. It was one of the Inter Cert poems, along with 'The Dong with the Luminous Nose' and twenty-odd other poems about spring and waterfalls and the love of God. I'll never forget the first reading. The teacher read it like he read everything, like he was looking for a dentist's name in the phone book. But the poem hit me between the eyes, almost smashed my glasses. Its anger and sarcasm were mine. The language was fresh and ordinary; there was nothing old-fashioned or dainty about it. Each word seemed to invite dozens of images and meanings. It was honest and brutal, clever and funny. And it was a poem about modern war. There is nothing romantic or heroic about it – except for the heroism of the poet.

NUALA NÍ DHOMHNAILL   POET

1992

I have to confess that I chose this poem because I am a bit of a Sylvia Plath affectionado, especially of the later poems which many have termed hysterical, and self-dramatising. I am not frightened or repelled by these powerful poems; rather I find they are the nearest thing I have ever read to some of my own states of mind, writ large. I read these poems as extremely honest and clear-eyed expressions of women's emotions in a society that frustrates the self-fulfilment of women. Literary critics, men for the most part, and especially covert upholders of the old order, are particularly baffled by these poems. They pretend to be irritated by them. Mostly, actually, they are frightened out of their skins.

For all its seeming artlessness, this poem is actually very finely crafted. Plath has come far from the careful, formal stylization of, say, 'The Colossus', but has lost nothing in transit. The poem fairly buzzes with energy, not the least of which is the energy of simple, colloquial words and phrases – 'coffin of a midget', 'a square baby', 'I have simply ordered a box of maniacs', yet the whole is greater than the parts, being as it is almost one long sustained metaphor. Muriel Rukeyseyer asked once:

> 'What would happen if one woman told the truth about her life?
> The world would split open.'

In the terrible tension of containing the clamour of the host of my own interior selves, so as not to destroy the world, I am often that bee box. I am like a walking keg of dynamite. As in Plath's poem, a whole swarm of dark little angry things are barely contained within my skin. A great African Queen would lose her cohorts if I ever took the lid off. And nobody knows as well as I do how they can sting. It is perhaps interesting that the phrase used in Irish for acting on a sudden impulse is 'do phrioch an bheach mé, – *'the bee stung me'. In view of Sylvia Plath's untimely death, the last line of the poem is particularly poignant and prophetic – 'The box is only temporary.' It would make you wonder if the price to pay for leaving all the bees out is always as great as it had to be in her case.*

The Arrival of the Bee Box

I ordered this, this clean wood box
Square as a chair and almost too heavy to lift.
I would say it was the coffin of a midget
Or a square baby
Were there not such a din in it.

The box is locked, it is dangerous.
I have to live with it overnight
And I can't keep away from it.
There are no windows, so I can't see what is in there.
There is only a little grid, no exit.

I put my eye to the grid.
It is dark, dark,
With the swarmy feeling of African hands
Minute and shrunk for export,
Black on black, angrily clambering.

How can I let them out?
It is the noise that appals me most of all,
The unintelligible syllables.
It is like a Roman mob,
Small, taken one by one, but my god, together!

I lay my ear to furious Latin.
I am not a Caesar.
I have simply ordered a box of maniacs.
They can be sent back.
They can die, I need feed them nothing, I am the owner.

I wonder how hungry they are.
I wonder if they would forget me
If I just undid the locks and stood back and turned into a tree.
There is the laburnum, its blond colonnades,
And the petticoats of the cherry.

They might ignore me immediately
In my moon suit and funeral veil.
I am no source of honey
So why should they turn on me?
Tomorrow I will be sweet God, I will set them free.

The box is only temporary.

Sylvia Plath (1932–1963)

Now just to show that I have no particular prejudice against formalism as such, my second choice is, on the surface at least, a very different kind of poem – Derek Mahon's 'Antarctica'. Once before a reading I asked Derek to read this poem as a special favour and he said he felt a bit of a dolt reading it, hearing all those rhymes and repetitions clanging heavily about his ears. But he still read it for me, and then I knew at once why I loved this poem, because it suddenly dawned on me that the dull thud of the repetitions is an absolutely intrinsic part of the poem itself. If every poem, as opposed to every piece of verse, is an invocation or an evocation of the muse, then it must be the Goddess Durga who is called into being here, the Snow Queen, mistress of the cold impenetrable regions of the psyche, that inner tundra. It is a region I have travelled in myself, where the bouncing common-sense ego on which our civilization is built perishes in a vertiginous swoon. Therefore, as Derek Mahon says himself, this is a feminist poem, because it chronicles the moment when the more-than-faintly-ridiculous heroic male ego finally snuffs it. The rigidity of the metre and the constant repetitions are a very symptom of the state of the soul. The psyche is an ice box, a house in mid winter with the heat turned off. In this state you wander about, metaphorically, in furs and highboots, in a frozen stupor, stamping your feet and repeating yourself constantly. The pipes, the conduits of emotion, are frozen solid, rigid like the lines of the poem. Thus for me 'Antarctica' is the supreme example of a formal poem that is not merely emptily so, but where the metre and strict rhyming scheme play an essential part in building up the reality enacted.

Tá súil agam go ndéanfaidh an méid seo cúis,

Nuala x x x

Antarctica

'I am just going outside and may be some time.'
The others nod, pretending not to know.
At the heart of the ridiculous, the sublime.

He leaves them reading and begins to climb,
Goading his ghost into the howling snow;
He is just going outside and may be some time.

The tent recedes beneath its crust of rime
And frostbite is replaced by vertigo:
At the heart of the ridiculous, the sublime.

Need we consider it some sort of crime,
This numb self-sacrifice of the weakest? No,
He is just going outside and may be some time —

In fact, for ever. Solitary enzyme,
Though the night yield no glimmer there will glow,
At the heart of the ridiculous, the sublime.

He takes leave of the earthly pantomime
Quietly, knowing it is time to go:—
'I am just going outside and may be some time.'
At the heart of the ridiculous, the sublime.

DEREK MAHON (B. 1941)

EÓIN O'CONNOR ARTIST

When I was asked to pick a favourite poem, I initially found the task quite a daunting one, but as soon as I had added 'The Arrival of the Bee Box' to my already extensive list, it forced all other choices into submission.

Rarely gentle or subtle, Plath's powerful work excites me like no other poet I have yet read and this poem in particular has all the ingredients of her highly personal and acutely observed views on life. Themes of pain and death, mingled with her fantastic descriptions of the natural world, create new glimpses of a darker and shadowed existence.

This box of bees, so full of danger and fear, cannot help but exhilarate in every sense. Putting one's ear up to this swarming mass with nothing to protect you, only a thin veil, conjures up the extraordinary power of nature, but in an intimate and teasing way. The mystery and awe surrounding this gentle swarm hints at an otherworldliness, where we become the insignificant observer.

Eóin O'Connor

KATE THOMPSON NOVELIST

2006

Dear Dónal, Caroline and Stephanie,

Many thanks for inviting me to contribute to Lifelines. *I remember the previous volumes and, coincidentally, I tracked one down very recently when BBC Radio 4 was making a documentary about the poem 'Dónal Óg' and I wanted to remind myself of Ted Hughes's reasons for selecting it.*

As you say, it's very difficult to choose a favourite poem, but I have a particular fondness for 'Naming of Parts' by Henry Reed. It is more than sixty years since it was written, but it remains completely fresh and original and I have never encountered anything quite like it. The contrast between the hard, cold weaponry within and the natural world without is effortlessly achieved. This is poetry which brings the reader's senses into play; poetry which you can see and hear and smell. Without mentioning death or bloodshed, 'Naming of Parts' gets right to the heart of the political insanity of warfare and the personal cost to those enlisted to participate in it.

Hope this is the kind of thing you need. Don't hesitate to contact me again if you have any queries or further requests. Good luck with the project – I very much look forward to seeing the finished volume.

With best wishes,

Kate Thompson

Naming of Parts

Today we have naming of parts. Yesterday,
We had daily cleaning. And tomorrow morning,
We shall have what to do after firing. But to-day,
Today we have naming of parts. Japonica
Glistens like coral in all of the neighbouring gardens,
      And to-day we have naming of parts.

This is the lower sling swivel. And this
Is the upper sling swivel, whose use you will see,
When you are given your slings. And this is the piling swivel,
Which in your case you have not got. The branches
Hold in the gardens their silent, eloquent gestures,
      Which in our case we have not got.

This is the safety-catch, which is always released
With an easy flick of the thumb. And please do not let me
See anyone using his finger. You can do it quite easy
If you have any strength in your thumb. The blossoms
Are fragile and motionless, never letting anyone see
      Any of them using their finger.

And this you can see is the bolt. The purpose of this
Is to open the breech, as you see. We can slide it
Rapidly backwards and forwards: we call this
Easing the spring. And rapidly backwards and forwards
The early bees are assaulting and fumbling the flowers:
      They call it easing the Spring.

They call it easing the Spring: it is perfectly easy
If you have any strength in your thumb: like the bolt,
And the breech, and the cocking-piece, and the point of balance,
Which in our case we have not got; and the almond-blossom
Silent in all of the gardens and the bees going backwards and forwards,
      For today we have naming of parts.

HENRY REED (1914–1986)

20 April 2006

Dear Stephanie, Caroline and Dónal,

Thank you for your letter. It's very flattering to be asked to contribute to Lifelines.

A favourite poem is 'Burnt Norton' *from* Four Quartets *by T S Eliot. I especially like the first movement.*

It starts with a cool logic as a meditation on time, but he soon seems to drift off into the dream. He is shown a glimpse of some devastating truth by a bird, at which point he wakes up back in his complicated world. As well as many other things it could be seen as a poem about the process of poetry.

Best of luck with your wonderful project.

Jonathan Hunter

Burnt Norton

from *Four Quartets*

I
Time present and time past
Are both perhaps present in time future,
And time future contained in time past.
If all time is eternally present
All time is unredeemable.
What might have been is an abstraction
Remaining a perpetual possibility
Only in a world of speculation.
What might have been and what has been
Point to one end, which is always present.
Footfalls echo in the memory
Down the passage which we did not take
Towards the door we never opened
Into the rose-garden. My words echo
Thus, in your mind.
                    But to what purpose
Disturbing the dust on a bowl of rose-leaves
I do not know.
                    Other echoes
Inhabit the garden. Shall we follow?
Quick, said the bird, find them, find them,
Round the corner. Through the first gate,
Into our first world, shall we follow
The deception of the thrush? Into our first world.

There they were, dignified, invisible,
Moving without pressure, over the dead leaves,
In the autumn heat, through the vibrant air,
And the bird called, in response to
The unheard music hidden in the shrubbery,
And the unseen eyebeam crossed, for the roses
Had the look of flowers that are looked at.
There they were as our guests, accepted and accepting.
So we moved, and they, in a formal pattern,
Along the empty alley, into the box circle,
To look down into the drained pool.
Dry the pool, dry concrete, brown edged,
And the pool was filled with water out of sunlight,
And the lotos rose, quietly, quietly,
The surface glittered out of heart of light,
And they were behind us, reflected in the pool.
Then a cloud passed, and the pool was empty.
Go, said the bird, for the leaves were full of children,
Hidden excitedly, containing laughter.
Go, go, go, said the bird: human kind
Cannot bear very much reality.
Time past and time future
What might have been and what has been
Point to one end, which is always present.

T S ELIOT (1888–1965)

HELEN VENDLER ACADEMIC

Harvard University
4 March 1990

Dear Students of Wesley College,

I am sorry to be answering you so late. I was in Japan for a month, and am only catching up.

My favorite poem is 'The Auroras of Autumn' by Wallace Stevens (1879–1955), our American great modernist poet. In it, Stevens confronts the exhaustion and destruction of everything we hold dear, and praises the sublimity of the human mind, which rises to meet and master, if only by imagination, the disasters of reality. This great hymn to change, even if change entails our own destruction, is Stevens's summarium in excelsis: 'Hear what he says, The dauntless master, as he starts the human tale.' This quotation, from Stevens's poem 'Puella Parvula', always comes to my mind when I re-read 'The Auroras of Autumn': it is the human tale of the innocent human being pitted against an impersonal but innocent necessitarian law of change.

Yours truly,

Helen Vendler
Kenan Professor of English

from *The Auroras of Autumn*

II
Farewell to an idea . . . A cabin stands,
Deserted, on a beach. It is white,
As by a custom or according to

An ancestral theme or as a consequence
Of an infinite course. The flowers against the wall
Are white, a little dried, a kind of mark

Reminding, trying to remind, of a white
That was different, something else, last year
Or before, not the white of an aging afternoon,

Whether fresher or duller, whether of winter cloud
Or of winter sky, from horizon to horizon.
The wind is blowing the sand across the floor.

Here, being visible is being white,
Is being of the solid of white, the accomplishment
Of an extremist in an exercise . . .

The season changes. A cold wind chills the beach.
The long lines of it grow longer, emptier,
A darkness gathers though it does not fall

And the whiteness grows less vivid on the wall.
The man who is walking turns blankly on the sand.
He observes how the north is always enlarging the change,

With its frigid brilliances, its blue-red sweeps
And gusts of great enkindlings, its polar green,
The color of ice and fire and solitude.

III
Farewell to an idea . . . The mother's face,
The purpose of the poem, fills the room.
They are together, here, and it is warm,

With none of the prescience of oncoming dreams,
It is evening. The house is evening, half dissolved.
Only the half they can never possess remains,

Still-starred. It is the mother they possess,
Who gives transparence to their present peace.
She makes that gentler that can gentle be.

And yet she too is dissolved, she is destroyed.
She gives transparence. But she has grown old.
The necklace is a carving not a kiss.

The soft hands are a motion not a touch.
The house will crumble and the books will burn.
They are at ease in a shelter of the mind

And the house is of the mind and they and time,
Together, all together. Boreal night
Will look like frost as it approaches them

And to the mother as she falls asleep
And as they say good-night, good-night. Upstairs
The windows will be lighted, not the rooms.

A wind will spread its windy grandeurs round
And knock like a rifle-butt against the door.
The wind will command them with invincible sound.

VII
Is there an imagination that sits enthroned
As grim as it is benevolent, the just
And the unjust, which in the midst of summer stops

To imagine winter? When the leaves are dead,
Does it take its place in the north and enfold itself,
Goat-leaper, crystalled and luminous, sitting

In highest night? And do these heavens adorn
And proclaim it, the white creator of black, jetted
By extinguishings, even of planets as may be,

Even of earth, even of sight, in snow,
Except as needed by way of majesty,
In the sky, as crown and diamond cabala?

It leaps through us, through all our heavens leaps,
Extinguishing our planets, one by one,
Leaving, of where we were and looked, of where

We knew each other and of each other thought,
A shivering residue, chilled and foregone,
Except for that crown and mystical cabala.

But it dare not leap by chance in its own dark.
It must change from destiny to slight caprice.
And thus its jetted tragedy, its stele

And shape and mournful making move to find
What must unmake it and, at last, what can,
Say, a flippant communication under the moon.

WALLACE STEVENS (1879–1955)

21 January 1994

Dear Ewan, Áine and Christopher,

Well done you three and I will of course join in in your grand venture.

My favourite poem is Gerard Manley Hopkins's lovely sonnet 'Pied Beauty'. My introduction to this poet's work came away back in 1978 when a fan in London sent me his own well-thumbed copy of Hopkins's poetry. He suggested that I read 'The Caged Skylark' and I did, enjoying the comparison between the bird in the cage with my boy-poet's predicament as I sat confined within my frame. But as I sat there thinking, my glance fell on the opposite page and I began to read 'Pied Beauty'. Remember now that I was just thirteen at the time and had never heard of Hopkins but as I gazed through this poem's kaleidoscope I was captivated, I had never ever experienced such musical language or such magical images.

Christy Nolan

P.S. Great good luck with your Lifelines*!*

Pied Beauty

Glory be to God for dappled things—
    For skies of couple-colour as a brinded cow;
        For rose-moles all in stipple upon trout that swim;
Fresh-firecoal chestnut-falls; finches' wings;
    Landscape plotted and pieced—fold, fallow, and plough;
    And áll trádes, their gear and tackle and trim.

All things counter, original, spare, strange;
    Whatever is fickle, freckled (who knows how?)
        With swift, slow; sweet, sour; adazzle, dim;
He fathers-forth whose beauty is past change:
        Praise him.

GERARD MANLEY HOPKINS (1844–1889)

[*'Pied Beauty'* was also chosen by Anna Scher in *Lifelines*. Anna Scher wrote:
Speaking as an Irish-Jewish integrationist, this poem really appeals to the warts-and-all in me as it celebrates individuality, its uniqueness and all the 'oddballness' that goes with it.]

An Irish Airman Foresees His Death

I know that I shall meet my fate
Somewhere among the clouds above;
Those that I fight I do not hate,
Those that I guard I do not love;
My country is Kiltartan Cross,
My countrymen Kiltartan's poor,
No likely end could bring them loss
Or leave them happier than before.
Nor law, nor duty bade me fight,
Nor public men, nor cheering crowds,
A lonely impulse of delight
Drove to this tumult in the clouds;
I balanced all, brought all to mind,
The years to come seemed waste of breath,
A waste of breath the years behind
In balance with this life, this death.

W B YEATS (1865–1939)

The history of World War I and II is of great interest to me. The incredible bravery of the men who flew during the conflict, when so many of them were certain they would never return, was an extraordinary feature of those times. Yeats captures that feeling wonderfully in this poem.

Hope that this favourite poem of mine will work for your booklet.

Every good wish for the Lifelines *Project.*

George Hook

Missionaries of Charity
Calcutta

13 February 1990

Dear Joann Bradish, Jacki Erskine and Carolyn Gibson,

Thank you for your letter of 1 January 1990. I am sure God is very pleased with your desire to serve the sick and save the lives of children through Lifelines. I feel nothing can be better than Christ's own words 'Whatever you do to the least of my brothers you do it to ME.' Jesus cannot deceive us – we can be sure that whatever we do for His poor, sick and suffering people, we do it for Him, and to Him. The same applies if we are unkind, uncharitable and unforgiving, we do it to Christ.

I am praying for you and wish you a year of true Peace – that comes from loving and caring and from respecting the rights of every human being – even the unborn child.

God bless you

[For the 1992 edition of *Lifelines*, Mother Teresa requested that the following paragraph be added to her first letter.]

12 June 1992

The prayer for Peace of St Francis of Assisi is so beautiful and simple that we pray it daily after Mass. I would like to include it now. My prayer for you is that you may make this prayer your own and put it into your life and so become an instrument of Jesus's peace – the true peace that comes from loving and sharing and respecting everyone as a child of God – my Brother – my Sister.

God bless you

Mother Teresa, MC

Prayer for Peace

Lord, make me a channel of Thy peace; that where there is hatred, I may bring love; that where there is wrong, I may bring the spirit of forgiveness; that where there is discord, I may bring harmony; that where there is error, I may bring truth; that where there is doubt, I may bring faith; that where there is despair, I may bring hope; that where there are shadows, I may bring light; that where there is sadness, I may bring joy.

Lord, grant that I may seek rather to comfort than to be comforted, to understand than to be understood; to love than to be loved; for it is by forgetting self that one finds; it is by forgiving that one is forgiven; it is by dying that one awakens to eternal life.

Amen.

22 January 1990

Dear Misses Bradish, Erskine and Gibson,

I would nominate as my favourite poem 'Among School Children' by W B Yeats. It deals with some of the most fundamental human emotions: love, nostalgia, regret, and the longing for what Yeats called elsewhere 'unity of being', but which he figured here in the wonderful final stanzas in the symbols of the chestnut tree and the dancer. What I particularly admire about the poem is the extraordinary range of diction, from the most down-to-earth and colloquial, to the most sublime; and the way a natural-seeming utterance is fitted into a most complex stanzaic form.

Yours sincerely,

David Lodge

Among School Children

I

I walk through the long schoolroom questioning;
A kind old nun in a white hood replies;
The children learn to cipher and to sing,
To study reading-books and histories,
To cut and sew, be neat in everything
In the best modern way — the children's eyes
In momentary wonder stare upon
A sixty-year-old smiling public man.

II

I dream of a Ledaean body, bent
Above a sinking fire, a tale that she
Told of a harsh reproof, or trivial event
That changed some childish day to tragedy —
Told, and it seemed that our two natures blent
Into a sphere from youthful sympathy,
Or else, to alter Plato's parable,
Into the yolk and white of the one shell.

III

And thinking of that fit of grief or rage
I look upon one child or t'other there
And wonder if she stood so at that age —
For even daughters of the swan can share
Something of every paddler's heritage —
And had that colour upon cheek or hair,
And thereupon my heart is driven wild:
She stands before me as a living child.

IV

Her present image floats into the mind —
Did Quattrocento finger fashion it
Hollow of cheek as though it drank the wind
And took a mess of shadows for its meat?
And I though never of Ledaean kind
Had pretty plumage once — enough of that,
Better to smile on all that smile, and show
There is a comfortable kind of old scarecrow.

V

What youthful mother, a shape upon her lap
Honey of generation had betrayed,
And that must sleep, shriek, struggle to escape
As recollection or the drug decide,
Would think her son, did she but see that shape
With sixty or more winters on its head,
A compensation for the pang of his birth,
Or the uncertainty of his setting forth?

VI

Plato thought nature but a spume that plays
Upon a ghostly paradigm of things;
Solider Aristotle played the taws
Upon the bottom of a king of kings;
World-famous golden-thighed Pythagoras
Fingered upon a fiddle-stick or strings
What a star sang and careless Muses heard:
Old clothes upon old sticks to scare a bird.

VII

Both nuns and mothers worship images,
But those the candles light are not as those
That animate a mother's reveries,
But keep a marble or a bronze repose.
And yet they too break hearts — O Presences
That passion, piety or affection knows,
And that all heavenly glory symbolise —
O self-born mockers of man's enterprise;

VIII
Labour is blossoming or dancing where
The body is not bruised to pleasure soul,
Nor beauty born out of its own despair,
Nor blear-eyed wisdom out of midnight oil.
O chestnut-tree, great-rooted blossomer,
Are you the leaf, the blossom or the bole?
O body swayed to music, O brightening glance,
How can we know the dancer from the dance?

W B Yeats (1865–1939)

['*Among School Children*' was also chosen in *Lifelines* by Brian Lenihan TD, then Tánaiste and
Minister for Defence. His Private Secretary, Brian Spain wrote on 24 April 1990:
An appropriate poem favoured by An Tánaiste is by William Butler Yeats and is titled 'Among
School Children'. *The last four lines relate to the unity of being, embracing the harmony of
existence, which gives meaning to life.*
*The essential message for children to learn and retain for life is the unity of being. This is
the basis of conviction, integrity and the rejection of anarchy, insecurity and fragmentation. It
emphasises the harmony of existence which gives meaning and purpose to life.*]

HERMIONE LEE
ACADEMIC

2 February 1994

Dear Ewan Gibson, Áine Jackson and Christopher Pillow,

Thank you for asking me to choose my favourite poem for Lifelines. *In response, I
realized that many of my favourite poems are elegies: Tennyson's* 'In Memoriam',
Milton's 'Lycidas', *Auden's magnificent* 'In Memory of W B Yeats' *(the un-cut
version), Donne's heartbreakingly formal* 'Nocturnall Upon S. Lucies Day', *Henry
King's poignant* 'The Exequy', *and Peter Porter's beautiful echoing of it in* 'An
Exequy'; *Hardy's 1912–1913* Poems, *love-poems for the wife he had stopped loving;
and Stevie Smith's* 'Harold's Leap', *a dignified tribute to a brave failure. I like these
poems in memory of dead wives, friends and poets because, like a biography or a
love-letter, they tell the story of a relationship between the writer and the lost subject,
who is re-found in the poem; and because of the problem they all confront, of turning
a grief into a shape. I chose Emily Dickinson's extraordinary version of elegy, which
boldly abandons the conventions for a ruthlessly detailed, exact account of the moment
of death, and its effect on the living. As in all her greatest poems, what looks domestic,
small, and 'narrow', opens out into a terrifying, 'awful' space. The poem has no title. It
was written in about 1866 and first published in 1890.*
With best wishes for the success of Lifelines.

Yours sincerely,

Hermione Lee

The last Night that She lived
It was a Common Night
Except the Dying—this to Us
Made Nature different

We noticed smallest things—
Things overlooked before
By this great light upon our Minds
Italicized—as 'twere.

As We went out and in
Between Her final Room
And Rooms where Those to be alive
Tomorrow were, a Blame

That Others could exist
While She must finish quite
A Jealousy for Her arose
So nearly infinite—

We waited while She passed—
It was a narrow time—
Too jostled were Our Souls to speak
At length the notice came.

She mentioned, and forgot—
Then lightly as a Reed
Bent to the Water, struggled scarce—
Consented, and was dead—

And We—We placed the Hair—
And drew the Head erect—
And then an awful leisure was
Belief to regulate—

EMILY DICKINSON (1830–1886)

MARITA CONLON-McKENNA NOVELIST

29 January 1994

Dear Áine, Ewan and Christopher,

Thank you for your letter, I am delighted that there will be a new edition of Lifelines. 'Nightfeed' by Eavan Boland is one of my old favourites.

I first read this poem when I was awash with babies and buggies and sticky fingers – my own fine collection of 'daisies'. Its sheer simplicity took my breath away, and to hear a poet speak of life's cycle and that love which is so often ignored in poetry – mother and child.

My second poem would be 'Digging' by Seamus Heaney. His poetry tends to leave an invisible bruise that hurts for a long long time afterwards.

Good luck with the book.

Marita Conlon-McKenna

Night Feed

This is dawn.
Believe me
This is your season, little daughter.
The moment daisies open,
The hour mercurial rainwater
Makes a mirror for sparrows.
It's time we drowned our sorrows.

I tiptoe in.
I lift you up
Wriggling
In your rosy, zipped sleeper.
Yes, this is the hour
For the early bird and me
When finder is keeper.

I crook the bottle.
How you suckle!
This is the best I can be,
Housewife
To this nursery
Where you hold on,
Dear life.

A silt of milk
The last suck.
And now your eyes are open,
Birth-coloured and offended.
Earth wakes.
You go back to sleep.
The feed is ended.

Worms turn.
Stars go in.
Even the moon is losing face.
Poplars stilt for dawn
And we begin
The long fall from grace.
I tuck you in.

EAVAN BOLAND (B. 1944)

Digging

Between my finger and my thumb
The squat pen rests; snug as a gun.

Under my window, a clean rasping sound
When the spade sinks into gravelly ground:
My father, digging. I look down

Till his straining rump among the flowerbeds
Bends low, comes up twenty years away
Stooping in rhythm through potato drills
Where he was digging.

The coarse boot nestled on the lug, the shaft
Against the inside knee was levered firmly.
He rooted out tall tops, buried the bright edge deep
To scatter new potatoes that we picked
Loving their cool hardness in our hands.

By God, the old man could handle a spade.
Just like his old man.

My grandfather cut more turf in a day
Than any other man on Toner's bog.
Once I carried him milk in a bottle
Corked sloppily with paper. He straightened up
To drink it, then fell to right away
Nicking and slicing neatly, heaving sods
Over his shoulder, going down and down
For the good turf. Digging.

The cold smell of potato mould, the squelch and slap
Of soggy peat, the curt cuts of an edge
Through living roots awaken in my head.
But I've no spade to follow men like them.

Between my finger and my thumb
The squat pen rests.
I'll dig with it.

SEAMUS HEANEY (B.1939)

[*'Digging'* was also nominated by Feargal Quinn in *Lifelines 3* and by John Hegarty for
Lifelines New and Collected. John Hegarty's letter appears on page 231. Feargal Quinn wrote:
*Each of us has a memory of our parents. My memory of my father — like that of Seamus Heaney
— is of him at work. Seamus's memory of his father was of him digging. The tool was a spade. My
memory of my father was of him making his guests welcome. His tool was a smile.*

   *'My God, the old man could handle a spade' – that was Mr Heaney Senior.
My father achieved success in being a good host. A spade or a smile – either will do!*]

JOSEPH O'CONNOR NOVELIST

28 January 1992

Dear Nicola, Paula, Alice,

Thanks very much for your recent note about the Lifelines IV *book. It sounds like a good idea, and I'm happy to be involved.*

Warmest best wishes,

Joseph O'Connor

I don't really have one favourite poem but I like Raymond Carver's 'Happiness' a lot. I like the clarity of it. It's lucid and atmospheric and very moving. For me, what makes a poem work is the sense that it had *to be written. Carver's poems and short stories are alive with that quality.*

Happiness

So early it's still almost dark out.
I'm near the window with coffee,
and the usual early morning stuff
that passes for thought.
When I see the boy and his friend
walking up the road
to deliver the newspaper.
They wear caps and sweaters,
and one boy has a bag over his shoulder.
They are so happy
they aren't saying anything, these boys.
I think if they could, they would take
each other's arm.
It's early in the morning,
and they are doing this thing together.
They come on, slowly.
The sky is taking on light,
though the moon still hangs pale over the water.
Such beauty that for a minute
death and ambition, even love,
doesn't enter into this.
Happiness. It comes on
unexpectedly. And goes beyond, really,
any early morning talk about it.

RAYMOND CARVER (1938–1988)

TRACEY EMIN ARTIST

Tracey Emin Studio, London
2006

Dear Organisers of Lifelines,

If it is not too late, Tracey Emin would like to contribute to your project. Her favourite poem, which is also at the front of her book Strangeland *is:*

> I poured out my worries to a friend
> Hoping that it would make me feel better
> But what I told him became an open secret
> Fireflies in the dark.

AHMAD IBU-AL-QAF (11TH CENTURY)

Tracey says: 'I love this poem and I always will – it reminds me of my life.'
Best wishes,

Alexandra Hill

DON PATERSON POET

1994

Dear Ewan,

Re your enquiry for Lifelines *anthology—one of my favourite poems is MacNeice's 'Soap Suds'; from the poet's point of view it's a technical miracle, MacNeice's foot hard on the brakes one minute, hard on the accelerator the next, freezing time then speeding it up outrageously and most importantly, taking the reader along for the ride. Poems, like cars, are really time-machines, and no poem I can think of demonstrates better the terrifying capabilities they possess.*
Best wishes,

Don Paterson

Soap Suds

> This brand of soap has the same smell as once in the big
> House he visited when he was eight: the walls of the bathroom open
> To reveal a lawn where a great yellow ball rolls back through a hoop
> To rest at the head of a mallet held in the hands of a child.
>
> And these were the joys of that house: a tower with a telescope;
> Two great faded globes, one of the earth, one of the stars;
> A stuffed black dog in the hall; a walled garden with bees;
> A rabbit warren; a rockery; a vine under glass; the sea.

To which he has now returned. The day of course is fine
And a grown-up voice cries Play! The mallet slowly swings,
Then crack, a great gong booms from the dog-dark hall and the ball
Skims forward through the hoop and then through the next and then

Through hoops where no hoops were and each dissolves in turn
And the grass has grown head-high and an angry voice cries Play!
But the ball is lost and the mallet slipped long since from the hands
Under the running tap that are not the hands of a child.

LOUIS MacNEICE (1907–1963)

MARK SWORDS ARTIST

2006

Dear Editors,

Thank you for the opportunity to select a poem for New and Collected Lifelines. *I have chosen the attached poem* 'Tableau', *written by my father, Martin Swords. I enclose a short comment on my choice.*

Tableau

Polished pride of place
The massive table, heart
Of the home, the only decent
Thing we ever bought.
Solid as a six-year marriage
Set with a cloth at the sunny end
For tea, two.
The rest littered with work,
A warm scarf half
Knitted, a stocking with a ladder.
Letters from the front.
My pen, my paper,
'Dearest Harry . . .' Nothing more.
A sodden handkerchief
My beads. Our picture.
And staring starkly back at me
A passion from Passchendaele
'. . . in action . . .'
How can I fill this table,
Alone.

MARTIN SWORDS

It may be a cliché, but there is something in the view that some people prefer radio to television, because the pictures are better! Given a choice, imagination is a powerful way of seeing. I like this poem because, although short, it presents a very powerful picture and story. I can see this table, this room. I can see the woman before, during and after the incident in the poem. You may see a different picture, that's OK.

Mark Swords

DERMOT BOLGER WRITER

12 January 1997

Dear Editors,

I write to you with a guilty conscience as I was asked to contribute to Lifelines 2 *and the question of my favourite poem so perplexed me that I missed all the deadlines involved.*

One is inclined to try to think of the best poem you ever read, which is really an impossible question, because poems are like snares waiting to trap you at certain moments of your life. Like good jokes told at a bad time, they often pass you by, whereas at another moment of your life they would leap from the page to transfix you.

So the poem I have finally picked is not the best poem I have ever read and nor is the poet, for that matter, a major figure – although, if he had been allowed to live, perhaps he might well have become one. But he was vitally important to me when I was the age that you are now, when I was finishing secondary school and looking out, both excitedly and somewhat fearful, at the adult world, utterly uncertain as to what course my life would take.

Back then there were no Writers-in-Schools schemes, the explosion of Irish writing now occurring could not have even been guessed at, and there wasn't even a public library in the suburb of Finglas where I grew up. I had never read a modern poet and had little notion that such people existed (and even less notion that if you threw a rock over your shoulder in Dublin you were likely to hit one).

All I knew was that I wished to write poems and that this desire and practice was regarded as odd locally. Adolescence is confusing at the best of times and poetry made me feel especially isolated. At such times of great loneliness (I mainly lived alone in a house by myself from the age of fifteen) you reach for any straw which makes you feel less alone or less foolish and so at the age of fifteen I stumbled upon the poetry of Francis Ledwidge.

Ledwidge had been born in great poverty in Slane, County Meath. His father died when he was very young and his mother had to slave in the fields to keep him and his younger brother Joe with him in her small cottage there. After school he helped her, working for local farmers, but at the age of fourteen it seemed that a new life was opening up for him when she managed to apprentice him to a Dublin grocer in Rathfarnham. But Ledwidge was so homesick there that one night he was moved to write his first poem, 'Behind the Closed Eye', and was so exhilarated and awed by this experience that he secretly packed his clothes and walked the thirty-five miles home to Slane that night, arriving home at dawn to find his young brother already awake, instinctively knowing that something special was happening.

I was moved by the idea of a poem being powerful enough to change the course of somebody's life and even more so when I discovered that Ledwidge had rested at every milestone along that road home. Because, near my house in Finglas, one of those self-same milestones had somehow survived the planners and still existed. I would walk there late at night and sit where Ledwidge had sat, at much the same age as me, equally fearful and uncertain about his future, but knowing (as his fingers touched that hand-written poem in his pocket) that poetry would be the centre of his life from now on.

Ledwidge worked as a farm boy, a labourer, a road-mender and a miner, among other jobs in the years that followed, perpetually writing poems of often intense beauty in those free moments he had. He only lived to see one book of his poems in print before being killed in the First World War in his late twenties. Yet today he is still read and remembered by so many and the street benches in Slane do not refer to the powerful family who owned the great castle there, but simply read 'Ledwidge Country'.

It would be nice if I could say that 'Behind the Closed Eye' was a great poem and I have picked it here. It's not, however, and the one I have picked (and the one I recite in my mind every time I pass through Slane) is one written by him much later, on his last visit home from the war before his death in fact. It is an elegy on the death of a local Slane boy, Jack Tiernan, who had worked at driving cattle for a local farmer just as Ledwidge himself once had, and whom Francis used to meet on his morning walks.

Only a few months after this was written, Ledwidge himself was dead and now the older I get the more I read it as an elegy for the young Francis Ledwidge himself, for that child who rested on a milestone in the village of Finglas with nothing before him except the dark country road and a return to bleak poverty, but with his life transformed by the gift of poetry.

Yours sincerely,

Dermot Bolger

A Little Boy in the Morning

He will not come, and still I wait.
He whistles at another gate
Where angels listen. Ah, I know
He will not come, yet if I go
How shall I know he did not pass
Barefooted in the flowery grass?

The moon leans on one silver horn
Above the silhouettes of morn,
And from their nest-sills finches whistle
Or stooping pluck the downy thistle.
How is the morn so gay and fair
With his whistling in its air?

The world is calling, I must go.
How shall I know he did not pass
Barefooted in the shining grass?

FRANCIS LEDWIDGE (1887–1917)

2 March 1994

Dear Ewan, Áine and Christopher,

Thank you for inviting me to contribute to your second Lifelines *book.*

   Congratulations on your stunning initiative and energy. I hope this volume will be as big a success as the last.

All good wishes,

Maureen Gaffney

The poem I have chosen is 'Martial Cadenza' *by Wallace Stevens, one of the great modern American poets. For me, this poem has an indelible association with a very great and beloved friend, Barry Heffernan, from Shanagarry, near Midleton, County Cork, who died tragically in November 1979 at the age of 28. We were friends at that time in our lives when we walked and talked with that peculiar and irresistible intensity of youth and it was he who introduced me to the work of Stevens. For me, this poem gives a vivid presence to that lost time. In the critic Helen Vendler's phrase, it provokes 'a sharp and relieving pang', conjuring up again that time of last protests and affirmations of desire. Time flashes again,*

> '. . .as if evening found us young, still young,
> Still walking in a present of our own.'

So Barry, wherever you are in that world without time, this is for you, with love.

Martial Cadenza

I
Only this evening I saw again low in the sky
The evening star, at the beginning of winter, the star
That in spring will crown every western horizon,
Again . . . as if it came back, as if life came back,
Not in a later son, a different daughter, another place,
But as if evening found us young, still young,
Still walking in a present of our own.

II
It was like sudden time in a world without time,
This world, this place, the street in which I was,
Without time: as that which is not has no time,
Is not, or is of what there was, is full
Of the silence before the armies, armies without
Either trumpets or drums, the commanders mute, the arms
On the ground, fixed fast in a profound defeat.

III

What had this star to do with the world it lit,
With the blank skies over England, over France
And above the German camps? It looked apart.
Yet it is this that shall maintain — Itself
Is time, apart from any past, apart
From any future, the ever-living and being,
The ever-breathing and moving, the constant fire,

IV

The present close, the present realized,
Not the symbol but that for which the symbol stands,
The vivid thing in the air that never changes,
Though the air change. Only this evening I saw it again,
At the beginning of winter, and I walked and talked
Again, and lived and was again, and breathed again
And moved again and flashed again, time flashed again.

WALLACE STEVENS (1879–1955)

EAMON KELLY   SEANCHAÍ

1994

In County Kerry when I was a child, a garda came once a year to take down the stock and tillage census. He stood his bicycle outside our door. He sat at our kitchen table writing in his ledger, while his peaked cap rested on the newel post of the stairs. I admired the silver buttons of his uniform and the case by his left hip which held his baton. Unlike Seamus Heaney's constable, he had no gun.

Once, when rain and darkness threatened, we guessed the number of cocks, hens, pigs, dry heifers and cultivated acres in a distant farm and saved him the bother of peddling up a long boreen.

Eamon Kelly

A Constable Calls

from *Singing School*

His bicycle stood at the window-sill,
The rubber cowl of a mud-splasher
Skirting the front mudguard,
Its fat black handlegrips

Heating in sunlight, the 'spud'
Of the dynamo gleaming and cocked back,
The pedal treads hanging relieved
Of the boot of the law.

His cap was upside down
On the floor, next his chair.
The line of its pressure ran like a bevel
In his slightly sweating hair.

He had unstrapped
The heavy ledger, and my father
Was making tillage returns
In acres, roods, and perches.

Arithmetic and fear.
I sat staring at the polished holster
With its buttoned flap, the braid cord
Looped into the revolver butt.

'Any other root crops?
Mangolds? Marrowstems? Anything like that?'
'No.' But was there not a line
Of turnips where the seed ran out

In the potato field? I assumed
Small guilts and sat
Imagining the black hole in the barracks.
He stood up, shifted the baton-case

Further round on his belt,
Closed the domesday book,
Fitted his cap back with two hands,
And looked at me as he said goodbye.

A shadow bobbed in the window.
He was snapping the carrier spring
Over the ledger. His boot pushed off
And the bicycle ticked, ticked, ticked.

SEAMUS HEANEY (B. 1939)

25 January 1997

Dear Editors,

Thank you for your letter. My favourite poem is W B Yeats's 'Circus Animals' Desertion'. I admire the poem's boldness in expressing the realisation that a long life has been spent in self-deception and that the only reality is the human heart.

With best wishes,

Brenda Maddox

The Circus Animals' Desertion

I

I sought a theme and sought for it in vain,
I sought it daily for six weeks or so.
Maybe at last, being but a broken man,
I must be satisfied with my heart, although
Winter and summer till old age began
My circus animals were all on show,
Those stilted boys, that burnished chariot,
Lion and woman and the Lord knows what.

II

What can I but enumerate old themes?
First that sea-rider Oisín led by the nose
Through three enchanted islands, allegorical dreams,
Vain gaiety, vain battle, vain repose,
Themes of the embittered heart, or so it seems,
That might adorn old songs or courtly shows;
But what cared I that set him on to ride,
I, starved for the bosom of his faery bride?

And then a counter-truth filled out its play,
The Countess Cathleen was the name I gave it;
She, pity-crazed, had given her soul away,
But masterful Heaven had intervened to save it.
I thought my dear must her own soul destroy,
So did fanaticism and hate enslave it,
And this brought forth a dream and soon enough
This dream itself had all my thought and love.

And when the Fool and Blind Man stole the bread
Cuchulain fought the ungovernable sea;
Heart-mysteries there, and yet when all is said
It was the dream itself enchanted me:
Character isolated by a deed
To engross the present and dominate memory.
Players and painted stage took all my love,
And not those things that they were emblems of.

III
Those masterful images because complete
Grew in pure mind, but out of what began?
A mound of refuse or the sweepings of a street,
Old kettles, old bottles, and a broken can,
Old iron, old bones, old rags, that raving slut
Who keeps the till. Now that my ladder's gone,
I must lie down where all the ladders start,
In the foul rag-and-bone shop of the heart.

W B Yeats (1865–1939)

Melvyn Bragg — Writer

7 April 1997

Dear Ralph, Caroline and Gareth,

Further to your letter, the delay for which I apologise profusely. If I am not too late, please find below my contribution towards Lifelines 3, *'I Wandered Lonely as a Cloud' by William Wordsworth.*

For me, what gives the poem its deep tap root into our minds is Wordsworth's description of the process which he calls 'the inward eye', on which images 'flash' (influence of his studies in electricity at the time) to bring back or provoke a remembering. With best wishes,

Yours sincerely,

Melvyn Bragg

I Wandered Lonely as a Cloud

I wandered lonely as a cloud
That floats on high o'er vales and hills,
When all at once I saw a crowd,
A host, of golden daffodils;
Beside the lake, beneath the trees,
Fluttering and dancing in the breeze.

Continuous as the stars that shine
And twinkle on the milky way,
They stretched in never-ending line
Along the margin of a bay:
Ten thousand saw I at a glance,
Tossing their heads in sprightly dance.

The waves beside them danced, but they
Out-did the sparkling waves in glee:
A poet could not but be gay,
In such a jocund company:
I gazed — and gazed — but little thought
What wealth the show to me had brought:

For oft, when on my couch I lie
In vacant or in pensive mood,
They flash upon that inward eye
Which is the bliss of solitude;
And then my heart with pleasure fills,
And dances with the daffodils.

WILLIAM WORDSWORTH (1770–1850)

[*I Wandered Lonely as a Cloud*' was also chosen by Ollie Campbell in *Lifelines*. Ollie Campbell wrote:

My favourite poem is 'Daffodils' by William Wordsworth. It is simple (like myself!) and for me is synonymous with being at peace. It is springtime, the sun is out though it is not too warm, pretty girls are wearing their summer frocks for the first time AND the rugby season is nearing its club climax! Though excitement is in the air I feel calm and I feel good in myself and with the world. That's what 'Daffodils' does for me.]

I am so sorry I have been so slow. But poetry offers such a vast store and I can only suggest now that perhaps fate had deliberately had a hand, and the delay meant Fergus could be honoured and remembered in your wonderful book.

Regards,

Eileen Battersby

Selecting a favourite poem is as difficult as choosing a favourite piece of music, such is the diversity of music and poetry. Also, so much depends on the mood of a given moment. Poetry may not be quite as emotive as music, but it is a form of music, just as music is poetry – which is why I have at times offered Mozart's Great Mass in C, *or Beethoven's* Violin Concerto *as my favourite poem. However much I might complain about having to whittle down a vast list of personal favourite poems, it is extremely pleasing to be asked, particularly for a cause as big-hearted as this project. What to choose? Work by Thomas Hardy, Shakespeare, John Donne, Akhmatova, Louis MacNeice, Mandelstam, Heaney, Wallace Stevens, Ovid, Robert Frost or Derek Mahon? Having pondered over so many poems for so long, having tested the patience of the* Lifelines *compilers as I constantly changed my mind or mood, from Elizabethan sonnet, to Keats, to Emily Dickinson, to Austin Clarke, my mind was made up for me by a tragic event – the death of a greatly beloved and respected colleague, Fergus Pyle, a former editor of* The Irish Times *and one of the most remarkable individuals I have ever known, a man of immense personal charm, exuberance and daunting intellectual range. He died on 11 April after a short, viciously cruel two-month illness. Since then, lines from* Richard II *continue to run through my mind:*

> For God's sake let us sit upon the ground
> and tell sad stories of the death of kings

Richard's powerful, moving, exasperated lament is, of course, concerned with kingship and the swift betrayals which result in the loss of power. A betrayal of life caused Fergus's death, and for anyone who knew him, he was a king. He was also very, very human, a committed European who loved art, music, history, ideas and life itself. Not even the most eloquent elegy seems sufficient.

Few poets match art and life as well as that most human of writers, Philip Larkin, who worked in the library of Queen's University Belfast, a city whose tragic history was recorded and analysed so brilliantly by Fergus Pyle in his reports from there. Although I had considered selecting Dylan Thomas's dramatically defiant ode, 'And Death Shall Have No Dominion', it is Larkin's thoughtful meditation, 'And Now The Leaves Suddenly Lose Strength', which best catches the atmosphere of numbed loss, more accurately perhaps than any epic or elegy. This poem, with its theme of day's end, winter's arrival and life's passing, expresses, for me, some sense of the emptiness left by the death of a dear friend.

For Fergus Pyle (1935–1997).

And Now the Leaves Suddenly Lose Strength

And now the leaves suddenly lose strength.
Decaying towers stand still, lurid, lanes-long,
And seen from landing windows, or the length
Of gardens, rubricate afternoons. New strong
Rain-bearing night-winds come: then
Leaves chase warm buses, speckle statued air,
Pile up in corners, fetch out vague broomed men
Through mists at morning.
                              And no matter where goes down,
The sallow lapsing drift in fields
Or squares behind hoardings, all men hesitate
Separately, always, seeing another year gone —
Frockcoated gentleman, farmer at his gate,
Villein with mattock, soldiers on their shields,
All silent, watching the winter coming on.

3 November 1961

PHILIP LARKIN (1922–1985)

['*And Now the Leaves Suddenly Lose Strength*' was also chosen by Maura Treacy in *Lifelines 2*.
Maura Treacy wrote:
*Thank you for your letter inviting me to choose my favourite poem. With so many long-standing
favourites already spoken for in the other* Lifelines, *I've chosen a comparatively recent discovery:
'And Now the Leaves Suddenly Lose Strength' by Philip Larkin.*

*Though written in 1961, this poem wasn't published until after Larkin's death in 1985 – which
suggests that he had some reservations about it. Now, I don't mean to vex his ghost by choosing a
poem he wouldn't publish himself, but I love this one.*

*And I'm intrigued as to why he withheld it all those years. It's not as if there's anything too
gruesomely personal here. And I'm sure it wasn't mislaid – it hadn't slipped down behind a
drawer or anything – because he methodically filed everything. Maybe he was jaded, even a little
embarrasssed: maybe he thought, Autumn leaves, they've been done to death. And indeed that
is so. But he needn't have let that stop him: it's not everybody can make dead leaves 'chase warm
buses, speckle statued air . . .'*

*I think this is a fine poem from beginning to end, and – apart from anything else – an
impeccable setting for that brilliant, faceted word, 'rubricate', which encapsulates not just the
colours of Autumn, but all the ritual that attends the dying year.*]

21 March 1994

Dear Ewan Gibson, Áine Jackson, Christopher Pillow,

I have found great difficulty in choosing a favourite poem, it is a bit like being a child when we asked each other what was our favourite colour. (I always said black as I felt it was left out.) Really, even then I didn't like the idea of favourites. And, it is impossible with poetry.

Poems feed us in different ways, at different times. I can be bowled over by a poem. They can hit me in the guts, have music that entrances and enwraps me in its magic.

I so wanted to put in a poem by Emily Dickinson, or Robert Frost, or William Blake, or Agnes Nemes Nagy, a poem by John B Keane, Emily Brontë, and so many more. T S Eliot was very important to me in my teens. Shakespeare, how can I do without him? Bawdy and raw Chaucer, the poetry of the medieval mystery plays. The wonderful lyric poems of Fleur Adcock, and her humour! The many women poets of now that need to be heard.

I chose 'Limbo', by Seamus Heaney. When I first read it in the 1970s it shook and moved me. It is not a comfortable poem, it is bleak but beautifully made as we expect always from Heaney. The terrible fact of 'Limbo' is still here with us, babies still die as it seems to their mothers there is no loving place for their children or themselves. Until this ends forever, how are we a civilized or a Christian nation? Because two babies were found dead in the last few months is the reason why I have chosen 'Limbo'. This fact and the poem are both terrible and real.

A true poet has many voices, singing of life and death, love and hate, warmth, sensuousness, and the cruelty of this world. Seamus Heaney has all these voices. In 'Limbo' he shows a beautiful and a chill power.

My thanks for inviting me to make a contribution to your book. I wish you very well in such a warming venture, it is good to be part of it.

Yours sincerely,

Anne Le Marquand Hartigan

Limbo

Fishermen at Ballyshannon
Netted an infant last night
Along with the salmon.
An illegitimate spawning,

A small one thrown back
To the waters. But I'm sure
As she stood in the shallows
Ducking him tenderly

Till the frozen knobs of her wrists
Were dead as the gravel,
He was a minnow with hooks
Tearing her open.

She waded in under
The sign of her cross.
He was hauled in with the fish.
Now limbo will be

A cold glitter of souls
Through some far briny zone.
Even Christ's palms, unhealed,
Smart and cannot fish there.

SEAMUS HEANEY (B. 1939)

13 January 1990

Dear Joann Bradish, Jackie Erskine, Carolyn Gibson,

I enclose a photocopy of a scrap of paper I have carried around with me for many years now. I cannot remember how it came into my possession, why it was typed out, or who wrote the piece. The sentence in Italian beneath it leads me to believe it may have been a libretto to an Opera?

I am very attached to this scrap and every time I move to a new city and set up home again, it goes up on the mantelpiece straight away. There it sits amidst the photos and gegaws ready to make my own blood freeze every time I catch sight of it.

Is there some way you can reproduce it in your book as it is, i.e. a fragment? This is part of its importance for me. Even though it was torn out of something else for its 'written' words, it has since then become and 'object' too, a talisman.

Good luck with Lifelines III.

Sincerely yours,
Alice Maher

Pallid the Sun

Pallid the Sun
& turbid grows the Air.
Thy Soul'd imperilled;
Man, for Death prepare.
Thy Heart turns sick
With Terror & Remorse;
Thy Blood turns thick
& freezes to its Course.
Thy Life to Loathing turns,
Eclipsed by Sin:
Loathing thy Self,
Thine Enemy Within.

Fino a sera la rosa cremata

e sangue, sangue, un coro d'

(Until the
is bl . . . .)

ANONYMOUS

Dáil Éireann
28 January 1994

Dear Ewan, Áine and Christopher,

I chose the poem 'Prayer' by Carol Ann Duffy because it is written about moments that we all experience in daily life. These moments are hard to define. They touch our memory and our imagination and remind us of our universal humanity. I often read this poem. Like the moments themselves, 'Prayer' is powerful enough to stop me in my tracks.

I wish you all the very best with your anthology Lifelines. *It is a wonderful project and I hope that you are as successful as you were the last time.*

Good luck with the project.

Yours sincerely,

Liz
Cllr Liz McManus, TD
Democratic Left

Prayer

Some days, although we cannot pray, a prayer
utters itself. So, a woman will lift
her head from the sieve of her hands and stare
at the minims sung by a tree, a sudden gift.

Some nights, although we are faithless, the truth
enters our hearts, that small familiar pain;
then a man will stand stock-still, hearing his youth
in the distant Latin chanting of a train.

Pray for us now. Grade I piano scales
console the lodger looking out across
a Midlands town. Then dusk, and someone calls
a child's name as though they named their loss.

Darkness outside. Inside, the radio's prayer—
Rockall. Malin. Dogger. Finisterre.

CAROL ANN DUFFY (B. 1955)

MIROSLAV HOLUB POET

Praha
Československo
9 January 1992

Dear Nicola Hughes, Paula Griffin, Alice McEleney,

*I am not sure that I read your letter correctly: should it be my poem or any poem?
I have chosen my own poem for the only reason that I must give my own poems more
thought and that I must spend much more time with them. The poem 'Masterpiece' was
published in* the London Poetry Review *last Fall. And here is my comment.*

*Among my own poems I like this one this year: it was written recently and therefore
belongs to my actual self. It is childish enough to be a real poem and, which is most
important, is not that gloomy as most poems written today anywhere.*

Best wishes to your project,

Miroslav Holub

Masterpiece

The only masterpiece
I ever created
was a picture of the moth Thysania agrippina
in pastel on grey paper.

Because I was never
much good at painting. The essence of art
is that we aren't very good at it.

The moth Thysania agrippina
rose from the stiff grey paper
with outstretched, comb-like antennae,

with a plush bottom resembling the buttocks
of the pigwidgeons of Hieronymus Bosch,
with thin legs on a shrunken chest
like those on Breughel's grotesque figures
in 'Dulle Griet', it turned into Dulle Griet
with a bundle of pots and pans in her bony hand,

it turned into Bodhiddharma
with long sleeves,

it was Ying or Shade
and Yang or Light, Chwei or Darkness
and Ming or Glow, it had
the black colour of water, the ochre colour of earth,
the blue colour of wood.

I was as proud of it as an Antwerp councillor,
or the Tenth Patriarch from the Yellow River,

I sprinkled it with shellac, which is
the oath that painters swear on Goethe's Science of Colours,

and then the art teacher took it to his study

and I forgot all about it
the way Granny used to forget
her dentures in a glass.

MIROSLAV HOLUB (1923–1998)
(Translated by Dana Hábová and David Young)

[When Miroslav Holub read the *Lifelines IV* pamphlet he felt that he had
misunderstood the request and was uneasy about having submitted one of his own
poems. He asked if the following letter and choice might also be included]

Dear Paula, Nicola and Alice,

*The term 'favourite poem' is very plastic, almost like the sea-god Proteus. The answer, for
me, depends even on the nature of the person who asked.*

*For three beautiful girls, I would rather pick something very manly, like something from
Ted Hughes or Galway Kinnell.*

*But, realising I have to answer as a Czech among Irish and English people, Vladimir
Holan occurs to me, and this poem which was so close to our Poetry of Everyday that it
reads like something deeply related, something I would wish to have written.*

Miroslav Holub

Resurrection

Is it true that after this life of ours we shall one day be awakened
by a terrifying clamour of trumpets?
Forgive me, God, but I console myself
that the beginning and resurrection of all of us dead
will simply be announced by the crowing of the cock.

After that we'll remain lying down a while . . .
The first to get up
will be Mother . . . We'll hear her
quietly laying the fire,
quietly putting the kettle on the stove
and cosily taking the teapot out of the cupboard.
We'll be home once more.

VLADIMIR HOLAN (1905–1980)
(Translated by George Theiner)

BERNARD O'DONOGHUE

Wadham College, Oxford
12 January 1997

Dear Ralph, Caroline and Gareth,

Thank you very much for writing to me about Lifelines; *I am full of admiration for the project and very honoured to be asked to contribute to it.*

My favourite poem (most of the time, anyway) is Austin Clarke's 'The Planter's Daughter'. *The first thing I admire about it is the way that it keeps a loose rein on emotion (as in the closing exclamation 'And O she was the Sunday/In every week') by a light but firmly held form, drawn distantly from Old Irish. Even more though I suppose I admire its mystery: its distant and understated politics and universality. The fact that the planter's house is recognised by the trees means his daughter is entitled to be proud: we see that, though it is said with great lightness. This order of things is as universal as the fact that a fire draws a crowd in on a bad night; it's a social fact. And it is a rather conformist fact which, just this once, doesn't matter.*

Congratulations on the enterprise and good luck with the book.

With very best wishes,

Bernard O'Donoghue

The Planter's Daughter

When night stirred at sea
And the fire brought a crowd in,
They say that her beauty
Was music in mouth
And few in the candlelight
Thought her too proud,
For the house of the planter
Is known by the trees.

Men that had seen her
Drank deep and were silent,
The women were speaking
Wherever she went —
As a bell that is rung
Or a wonder told shyly
And O she was the Sunday
In every week.

AUSTIN CLARKE (1896–1974)

[*'The Planter's Daughter'* was chosen by Mary McEvoy in *Lifelines*. Mary McEvoy wrote:
I hope my reply isn't too late. My favourite poem, without a shadow of a doubt, is 'A Subaltern's Love-Song / Miss Jane Hunter Dunn' *by John Betjeman. If you need a second choice, I suppose it's* 'The Planter's Daughter' *by Austin Clarke.*]

140 LIFELINES NEW AND COLLECTED

FERGAL KEANE BROADCASTER

BBC, Hong Kong
30 April 1997

Dear Ralph and colleagues,

Sorry for the long delay in replying – I have been travelling extensively.

  Raymond Carver is one of my favourite writers and I think his poetry is every bit as good as the short fiction for which he is better known. The poem I have chosen, 'Hummingbird', is taken from his last collection, A New Path to the Waterfall. *It was written when he was dying from cancer. Raymond Carver was a recovered alcoholic – his work is full of compassion, tenderness, regret and love. This particular poem appeals because of its simplicity – it is short but manages to say a great deal. There is a hint of sadness – we know that time is slipping away and perhaps the poet's words gather force because we know this.*

  I think Lifelines *is a wonderful project. You should be proud, because you care about your world and are willing to try and change it.*

My best wishes,

Fergal

Hummingbird

For Tess

Suppose I say *summer*,
write the word 'hummingbird',
put it in an envelope,
take it down the hill
to the box. When you open
my letter you will recall
those days and how much,
just how much, I love you.

RAYMOND CARVER (1938–1988)

The Alligator Girls

Remembering John Crowe Ransom

Are you to tell me where my soul is cast
Or in an alligator or a god.

Or would you like to bring the girls at ransom
Over to a have a picnic beside the sweet
Clear water. This is the very day for it.
Bring your apricot brandy over. Tell the girls
The mill is off and to come on over
And we'll all put our toes in the sweet river.

An afternoon by the river with two sisters
Is something special. We shouted Gator Gator
And out came May and Bonnie lifting their skirts
Prancing with mock terror out of the shallows
To lovingly berate us. That was when
I worked in America as a young man.

I am told the river had alligators in it.
May and Bonnie are grown up and dead.
But we had some great fun, didn't we?

W S GRAHAM (1918–1986)

This poem is almost too sad for me to even read. It is also funny and I can imagine W S Graham standing in some remote American river, yelling 'Gator, Gator' at two local girls in his Scottish accent. But then, as I'm chuckling to myself, I go on to the last three lines and my smile evaporates. W S Graham is a genius at saying devastating things in a simple way.

I hope your Poetry anthology sells well!

Sincerely,

Julie O'Callaghan

'I am Stretched on Your Grave' *was translated from the Irish by Frank O'Connor in a book of translations called* The Little Monasteries. *I got a copy of* The Little Monasteries *in 1976 and was immediately struck by Frank O'Connor's translation of* 'Tá mé Sínte ar Do Thuama'. *The poem stuck in my memory and I began tossing the words at concerts with Scullion, of whom I was a member at the time. I later became aware of the Irish* sean-nós *song which I heard sung by the late Diarmaid Ó Suilleabháin, a great singer from Cúil Aodha. It is a love song without parallel. It captures that terrible sense of loss when a loved one dies.*

Best regards,

Philip King

I am Stretched on Your Grave

I am stretched on your grave
And would lie there forever
If your hands were in mine
I'd be sure we'd not sever.
My appletree, my brightness
'Tis time we were together
For I smell of the earth
And am worn by the weather.

When my family thinks
That I'm safe in my bed
From night until morning
I am stretched at your head.
Calling out into the air with
Tears hot and wild
My grief for the girl that
I loved as a child.

Do you remember the
Night we were lost
In the shade of the blackthorn
And the chill of the frost.
Thanks be to Jesus we
Did what was right
And your maidenhead still
Is a pillar of light.

The priests and the friars
Approach me in dread
Because I still love you
My love, and you're dead.
I still will be your shelter
Through rain and through storm
But with you in your cold grave
I cannot sleep warm.

I am stretched on your grave
And would lie there forever
If your hands were in mine
I'd be sure we'd not sever.
My appletree, my brightness
'Tis time we were together
For I smell of the earth
And am worn by the weather.

ANONYMOUS (EIGHTEENTH CENTURY)
Translated from the Irish by Frank O'Connor
(1903–1966)

Dear Ewan, Áine and Christopher,

Thank you so much for your letter inviting me to be part of Lifelines. *May this edition prove to be as successful as its predecessors.*

The poem I have chosen is 'The Cottage Hospital' by John Betjeman.

I could stick a pin into the contents of any John Betjeman collection and chances are that I'd like (and probably love) the selection. 'The Cottage Hospital' wasn't always a favourite but now, with time passing, I find that it has become more relevant and, perhaps, more frightening.

Apart from its theme and expression, I greatly admire its structure. The third stanza may initially seem remote and unconnected, but when the work is taken as a unit and the seeds so cleverly sown bear fruit, then everything falls perfectly into place. The poem, I think, holds the same attraction for me as the flame does for the moth. It is more than slightly dangerous.

With every good wish,

Bernard Farrell

The Cottage Hospital

At the end of a long-walled garden
    in a red provincial town,
A brick path led to a mulberry—
    scanty grass at its feet.
I lay under blackening branches
    where the mulberry leaves hung down
Sheltering ruby fruit globes
    from a Sunday-tea-time heat.
Apple and plum espaliers
    basked upon bricks of brown;
The air was swimming with insects,
    and children played in the street.

Out of this bright intentness
    into the mulberry shade
Musca domestica (housefly)
    swung from the August light
Slap into slithery rigging
    by the waiting spider made
Which spun the lithe elastic
    till the fly was shrouded tight.
Down came the hairy talons
    and horrible poison blade
And none of the garden noticed
    that fizzing, hopeless fight.

Say in what Cottage Hospital
    whose pale green walls resound
With the tap upon polished parquet
    of inflexible nurses' feet
Shall I myself be lying
    when they range the screens around?
And say shall I groan in dying,
    as I twist the sweaty sheet?
Or gasp for breath uncrying,
    as I feel my senses drown'd
While the air is swimming with insects
    and children play in the street?

JOHN BETJEMAN (1906–1984)

Dear Dónal, Caroline and Stephanie ,

It is an honour to be asked to contribute to Lifelines, *which is now such a distinguished fixture on the Irish literary calendar. I'd like to include a poem called 'The Day We Drove Down La Nicolière' by my sister Elizabeth Walsh Peavoy about her daughter. When it was previously anthologised in* A Part of Ourselves: Laments for Lives that Ended too Soon, *edited by Siobhán Parkinson (A&A Farmar, 1997) it was accompanied by a note by Elizabeth giving its provenance: 'Our third child, Eliza, died in Mauritius where the family was living. She was fourteen months old when she died, on 30 June 1979, and was buried in St Pierre Cemetery. Her name is inscribed on our family headstone in Navan, County Meath.'*

I have it in a book beside my bed and I often read it. It reminds me of the days I spent with Elizabeth almost 30 years ago on the beautiful island of Mauritius just after Eliza died, walking together in the Pamplemousse botanical gardens and visiting St Pierre Cemetery. I am always bowled over by its complete acknowledgment of the finality of death, a finality that no amount of graveyard roses can assuage. Eliza may be gone with her 'almost smiles', but somehow death has been outwitted by the poet who makes the reader remember her so indelibly.

Caroline Walsh

The Day We Drove Down La Nicolière

After you died I had nothing but regret
a bunch of graveyard roses no use
to anyone least of all you. Yet I remember
the day we drove down la Nicolière
and you too sick for anything least of all
driving down a mountain pass. I had never
seen anything that sick before as you dear
and didn't know quite what to fear
yet I feared and fought holding your will
to live in mine for you now I alone
must hold a bunch of Christmas Roses

hard to believe in that existence beyond
graveyards, but you had a mouth pink peony
cheeks a nose and eyes for laughter
and pearly hands for reaching out and grasping
the silver strings from heaven pulling you.
Why the hurt so great to have the child
one loves depart for what they say
becomes a better life leaving her spoon
bowl there with saccharine poetry to scar
and simplify our hearts. Gone with white dress
my dear and your almost smiles.

ELIZABETH WALSH PEAVOY (B. 1945)

Carcanet
3 February 1997

Dear Ralph, Caroline and Gareth,

Thank you for your letter dated January 1997. I am delighted that you are continuing with the excellent Lifelines *project.*

The poem I would choose is by Elizabeth Bishop. It is called 'Questions of Travel' and is included in her book of the same title published in this country by Chatto and Windus. I like the poem because it is a meditation full of rich and exotic detail but unlike so many travel poems it does not take liberties with those details: the world to which she has travelled and the worlds through which she travels are not her worlds and there is a continuous sense of difference and exclusion. The conclusion of the poem is wonderful because it recognises that the traveller finds herself only in herself and though the various details that she sees are rich and wonderful, they do not provide stability or happiness. It is a poem that is at once beautiful, amusing and 'altering', because if you come to terms with it you come to terms with a very basic human truth.

   Good luck with your project.

Yours sincerely,

Michael Schmidt

Questions of Travel

There are too many waterfalls here; the crowded streams
hurry too rapidly down to the sea,
and the pressure of so many clouds on the mountaintops
makes them spill over the sides in soft slow-motion,
turning to waterfalls under our very eyes.
— For if those streaks, those mile-long, shiny, tearstains,
aren't waterfalls yet,
in a quick age or so, as ages go here,
they probably will be.
But if the streams and clouds keep travelling, travelling,
the mountains look like the hulls of capsized ships,
slime-hung and barnacled.

Think of the long trip home.
Should we have stayed at home and thought of here?
Where should we be today?
Is it right to be watching strangers in a play
in this strangest of theatres?
What childishness is it that while there's a breath of life
in our bodies, we are determined to rush
to see the sun the other way around?

The tiniest green hummingbird in the world?
To stare at some inexplicable old stonework,
inexplicable and impenetrable,
at any view,
instantly seen and always, always delightful?
Oh, must we dream our dreams
and have them, too?
And have we room
for one more folded sunset, still quite warm?

But surely it would have been a pity
not to have seen the trees along this road,
really exaggerated in their beauty,
not to have seen them gesturing
like noble pantomimists, robed in pink.
— Not to have had to stop for gas and heard
the sad, two-noted, wooden tune
of disparate wooden clogs
carelessly clacking over
a grease-stained filling-station floor.
(In another country the clogs would all be tested.
Each pair there would have identical pitch.)
— A pity not to have heard
the other, less primitive music of the fat brown bird
who sings above the broken gasoline pump
in a bamboo church of Jesuit baroque:
three towers, five silver crosses.
— Yes, a pity not to have pondered,
blurr'dly and inconclusively,
on what connection can exist for centuries
between the crudest wooden footwear
and, careful and finicky,
the whittled fantasies of wooden cages.
— Never to have studied history in
the weak calligraphy of songbirds' cages.
— And never to have had to listen to rain
so much like politicians' speeches:
two hours of unrelenting oratory
and then a sudden golden silence
in which the traveller takes a notebook, writes:

'Is it lack of imagination that makes us come
to imagined places, not just stay at home?
Or could Pascal have been not entirely right
about just sitting quietly in one's room?

Continent, city, country, society:
the choice is never wide and never free.
And here, or there . . . No. Should we have stayed at home,
wherever that may be?'

ELIZABETH BISHOP (1911–1979)

KATHARINE WHITEHORN JOURNALIST

The Observer
24 January 1997

Dear Ralph Croly, Caroline Dowling and Gareth McCluskey,

Thank you for your letter. It's very hard to say which is my favourite poem, as over the years this has obviously changed. I think at the moment probably my favourite is the Shakespeare sonnet that begins 'That time of year thou mayst in me behold . . .' But previous favourites have included W B Yeats's 'Second Coming', Browning's 'One Word More' and Henry Reed's 'A Map of Verona'. Good luck to the project.

Yours cordially,

Katharine Whitehorn

LXXIII

That time of year thou mayst in me behold
When yellow leaves, or none, or few, do hang
Upon those boughs which shake against the cold,
Bare ruin'd choirs, where late the sweet birds sang.
In me thou seest the twilight of such day
As after sunset fadeth in the west,
Which by and by black night doth take away,
Death's second self, that seals up all in rest.
In me thou seest the glowing of such fire
That on the ashes of his youth doth lie,
As the death-bed whereon it must expire,
Consum'd with that which it was nourish'd by.
This thou perceiv'st, which makes thy love more strong,
To love that well which thou must leave ere long.

WILLIAM SHAKESPEARE (1564–1616)

18 January 1988

Dear Julie Grantham, Jonathan Logue and Duncan Lyster,

Thanks for your letter inviting me to choose a favourite poem and give a reason for my choice. Good luck with the book which I hope makes a lot of money for Ethiopia.

I like this poem because it brings together neatly and wittily, and with considerable feeling, the arguments against what James Joyce called literary 'biografiends' such as myself. It's a humane and appealing case that D J Enright pleads, and one that any biographer should confront before deciding whether to write someone's Life. *One possible defence may be found in Pope's* Essay on Man:

> 'Know then thyself, presume not God to scan;
> The proper study of mankind is man.'

Best wishes,

Michael Holroyd

Biography

Rest in one piece, old fellow
May no one make his money
Out of your odd poverty

Telling what you did
When the streets stared blankly back
And the ribbon fell slack

The girls you made
(And, worse, the ones you failed to)
The addled eggs you laid

Velleities that even you
Would hardly know you felt
But all biographers do

The hopes that only God could hear
(That great non-tattler)
Since no one else was near

What of your views on women's shoes?
If you collected orange peel
What *did* you do with the juice?

Much easier than your works
To sell your quirks
So burn your letters, hers and his—
Better no Life at all than this.

D J Enright (b. 1920)

Eilís Dillon Writer

1994

Dear Ewan Gibson, Áine Jackson, Christopher Pillow,

Thank you for asking me to contribute to your poetry anthology, which I have admired for the last few years. The poem I have chosen is a great favourite, called 'Bredon Hill' (pronounced Breedon). The poet is A E Housman and it is one from A Shropshire Lad, *one of the gentlest collections of poems in the English language, celebrating a dearly loved place.*

Bredon Hill

from *A Shropshire Lad*

XXI
In summertime on Bredon
   The bells they sound so clear;
Round both the shires they ring them
   In steeples far and near,
   A happy noise to hear.

Here of a Sunday morning
   My love and I would lie,
And see the coloured counties,
   And hear the larks so high
   About us in the sky.

The bells would ring to call her
   In valleys miles away:
'Come all to church, good people;
   Good people, come and pray.'
   But here my love would stay.

And I would turn and answer
    Among the springing thyme,
'Oh, peal upon our wedding,
    And we will hear the chime,
    And come to church in time.'

But when the snows at Christmas
    On Bredon top were strown,
My love rose up so early
    And stole out unbeknown
    And went to church alone.

They tolled the one bell only,
    Groom there was none to see,
The mourners followed after,
    And so to church went she,
    And would not wait for me.

The bells they sound on Bredon,
    And still the steeples hum,
'Come all to church, good people'—
    Oh, noisy bells, be dumb;
    I hear you, I will come.

A E HOUSMAN (1859–1936)

Housman himself told how that wonderful 'coloured', came to him in a dream, first as 'painted', then as 'coloured', a completely satisfactory adjective. The other delightful aspect of this poem is the sense of certainty that one gets in a ballad.

   Music to this was written by Vaughan Williams. I have heard it sung by Sidney MacEwan.

Eilís Dillon

[*'Bredon Hill'* was also chosen by the late Sir John Gielgud in *Lifelines.* John Gielgud wrote: *My favourite poem is* 'Bredon Hill' *from A E Housman's* A Shropshire Lad, *as I spoke it for my first audition in 1921 when I got a scholarship at my first Dramatic School, and used to recite it at troop concerts during the war, and once very successfully in a television talk show in America not many years ago.*]

Dear Nicola, Paula and Alice, Thank you for the invitation to take part in Lifelines. I am delighted to be able to help Third World people in this way, all the more since I have recently been in Zambia, one of these poor countries, and have seen how desperately they need the help of those of us who live easier, more comfortable lives.

The poem I have chosen is by C P Cavafy, a twentieth-century Greek poet (he died in 1933), and one I find wonderfully illuminating. On the surface it is about a particular journey, one of the most famous in all literature, Odysseus's ten-year-long travels that took him home to Ithaca after the Trojan Wars. But as you read you become Odysseus yourself, the journey is yours. The poem is here in translation, so perhaps we have lost some of the quality, but even so it says with marvellous clarity and compassion how important it is to live your life fully; it is the journey itself that matters, wherever it takes you. How gently and with what simplicity he says at the end 'you must surely have understood by then what Ithacas mean'.

My greetings to you all and my best wishes for the success of your project.

Lauris Edmond

Ithaca

When you start on your journey to Ithaca,
then pray that the road is long,
full of adventure, full of knowledge.
Do not fear the Lestrygonians
and the Cyclopes and the angry Poseidon.
You will never meet such as these on your path,
if your thoughts remain lofty, if a fine
emotion touches your body and your spirit.
You will never meet the Lestrygonians,
the Cyclopes and the fierce Poseidon,
if you do not carry them within your soul,
if your soul does not raise them up before you.

Then pray that the road is long.
That the summer mornings are many,
that you will enter ports seen for the first time
with such pleasure, with such joy!
Stop at Phoenician markets,
and purchase fine merchandise,
mother-of-pearl and corals, amber and ebony,
and pleasurable perfumes of all kinds,
buy as many pleasurable perfumes as you can;
visit hosts of Egyptian cities,
to learn and learn from those who have knowledge.

Always keep Ithaca fixed in your mind.
To arrive there is your ultimate goal.
But do not hurry the voyage at all.
It is better to let it last for long years;
and even to anchor at the isle when you are old,
rich with all that you have gained on the way,
not expecting that Ithaca will offer you riches.
Ithaca has given you the beautiful voyage.
Without her you would never have taken the road.
But she has nothing more to give you.

And if you find her poor, Ithaca has not defrauded you.
With the great wisdom you have gained, with so much experience,
you must surely have understood by then what Ithacas mean.

CONSTANTINE P CAVAFY (1863-1933)
Translated by Rae Dalven

PAULA MEEHAN   POET

9 January 1992

Dear Nicola, Paula and Alice,

I came across the earlier Lifelines *and they were invariably good reads and I'm delighted to put my own spake in. I tend to get haunted by poems – they won't let me alone and hang around in my head for ages. At any given time there will be a number clamouring for attention. Some insinuate themselves so completely that when I'm making my own poems stray lines will cross over and I'll even think I've written them myself. This must be what they mean by influence.*

A poem I go back to again and again is Eavan Boland's 'The Journey' from the collection of the same name. It gives me a huge amount of comfort and courage, apart altogether from its music, which I love. It calls up all the great poems about guided underground quests and also challenges the tradition, for the shades the speaker meets on her journey with Sappho are not the dead heroes but ordinary women and children who have largely been edited out of history.

Good luck with your project. I hope you make a rake of money.

Paula x

The Journey

For Elizabeth Ryle

*Immediately cries were heard. These were the loud wailing of infant souls weeping at the
very entrance-way; never had they had their share of life's sweetness for the dark day had
stolen them from their mothers' breasts and plunged them to a death before their time.*

—Virgil, *The Aeneid, Book VI*

And then the dark fell and 'there has never'
I said 'been a poem to an antibiotic:
never a word to compare with the odes on
the flower of the raw sloe for fever

'or the devious Africa-seeking tern
or the protein treasures of the sea-bed.
Depend on it, somewhere a poet is wasting
his sweet uncluttered metres on the obvious

'emblem instead of the real thing.
Instead of sulpha we shall have hyssop dipped
in the wild blood of the unblemished lamb,
so every day the language gets less

'for the task and we are less with the language.'
I finished speaking and the anger faded
and dark fell and the book beside me
lay open at the page Aphrodite

comforts Sappho in her love's duress.
The poplars shifted their music in the garden,
a child startled in a dream,
my room was a mess—

the usual hardcovers, half-finished cups,
clothes piled up on an old chair—
and I was listening out but in my head was
a loosening and sweetening heaviness,

not sleep, but nearly sleep, not dreaming really
but as ready to believe and still
unfevered, calm and unsurprised
when she came and stood beside me

and I would have known her anywhere
and I would have gone with her anywhere
and she came wordlessly
and without a word I went to her

down down down without so much as
ever touching down but always, always
with a sense of mulch beneath us,
the way of stairs winding down to a river

and as we went on the light went on
failing and I looked sideways to be certain
it was she, misshapen, musical—
Sappho—the scholiast's nightingale

and down we went, again down
until we came to a sudden rest
beside a river in what seemed to be
an oppressive suburb of the dawn.

My eyes got slowly used to the bad light.
At first I saw shadows, only shadows.
Then I could make out women and children
and, in the way they were, the grace of love.

'Cholera, typhus, croup, diptheria'
she said, 'in those days they racketed
in every backstreet and alley of old Europe.
Behold the children of the plague'.

Then to my horror I could see to each
nipple some had clipped a limpet shape—
suckling darknesses—while others had their arms
weighed down, making terrible pietàs.

She took my sleeve and said to me, 'be careful.
Do not define these women by their work:
not as washerwomen trussed in dust and sweating,
muscling water into linen by the river's edge

'nor as court ladies brailled in silk
on wool and woven with an ivory unicorn
and hung, nor as laundresses tossing cotton,
brisking daylight with lavender and gossip.

'But these are women who went out like you
when dusk became a dark sweet with leaves,
recovering the day, stooping, picking up
teddy bears and rag dolls and tricycles and buckets—

'love's archaeology—and they too like you
stood boot deep in flowers once in summer
or saw winter come in with a single magpie
in a caul of haws, a solo harlequin.'

I stood fixed. I could not reach or speak to them.
Between us was the melancholy river,
the dream water, the narcotic crossing
and they had passed over it, its cold persuasions.

I whispered, 'let me be
let me be at least their witness,' but she said
'what you have seen is beyond speech,
beyond song, only not beyond love;

'remember it, you will remember it'
and I heard her say but she was fading fast
as we emerged under the stars of heaven,
'there are not many of us; you are dear

'and stand beside me as my own daughter.
I have brought you here so you will know forever
the silences in which are our beginnings,
in which we have an origin like water,'

and the wind shifted and the window clasp
opened, banged and I woke up to find
the poetry books stacked higgledy piggledy,
my skirt spread out where I had laid it—

nothing was changed; nothing was more clear
but it was wet and the year was late.
The rain was grief in arrears; my children
slept the last dark out safely and I wept.

EAVAN BOLAND (B. 1944)

JOHN MACKENNA WRITER

8 January 1994

Dear Áine, Ewan and Christopher,

Thank you for your letter and kind invitation to nominate some poem/poems for the new
Lifelines. *I hope it is every bit as successful as the previous editions. I'm enclosing two poems – if
you are stuck for space I'd go with the John Clare poem* 'I Am'. *I might have nominated two
others – Byron's* 'We'll Go No More a Roving' *and Tennyson's* 'Crossing the Bar' *– and, I
think, the Lord's Prayer but I'm moving towards taking up more than enough space in that!*

The John Clare poem was the piece that inspired me to write the novel Clare *about his
life. I think its strength is its honesty. It comes from the heart and isn't at all self-pitying.
It tells his story briefly and bitterly. The Raymond Carver poem closes his posthumous
collection* A New Path to the Waterfall *and was written in his last days. It speaks so
much of hope and life and optimism and satisfaction. I think it's wonderful.*

All the best, again, with your book – may it sell a million.

Good things,

John MacKenna

I Am

I am: yet what I am none cares or knows,
    My friends forsake me like a memory lost;
I am the self-consumer of my woes,
    They rise and vanish in oblivious host,
Like shades in love and death's oblivion lost;
And yet I am, and live with shadows tost

Into the nothingness of scorn and noise,
    Into the living sea of waking dreams,
Where there is neither sense of life nor joys,
    But the vast shipwreck of my life's esteems;
And een the dearest—that I loved the best—
Are strange—nay, rather stranger than the rest.

I long for scenes where man has never trod;
    A place where woman never smiled or wept;
There to abide with my Creator, GOD,
    And sleep as I in childhood sweetly slept:
Untroubling and untroubled where I lie;
The grass below—above the vaulted sky.

JOHN CLARE (1793–1864)

So We'll Go No More a Roving

So we'll go no more a roving
    So late into the night,
Though the heart be still as loving,
    And the moon be still as bright.

For the sword outwears the sheath,
    And the soul wears out the breast,
And the heart must pause to breathe,
    And Love itself have rest.

Though the night was made for loving,
    And the day returns too soon,
Yet we'll go no more a roving
    By the light of the moon.

GEORGE GORDON, LORD BYRON (1788–1824)

Crossing the Bar

Sunset and evening star,
    And one clear call for me!
And may there be no moaning of the bar,
    When I put out to sea.

But such a tide as moving seems asleep,
    Too full for sound and foam,
When that which drew from out the boundless deep
    Turns again home.

Twilight and evening bell,
    And after that the dark!
And may there be no sadness of farewell,
    When I embark;

For though from out our bourne of Time and Place
    The flood may bear me far,
I hope to see my Pilot face to face
    When I have crost the bar.

ALFRED, LORD TENNYSON (1809–1892)

The Lord's Prayer

Our Father, who art in heaven,
hallowed be thy Name;
thy kingdom come;
thy will be done;
on earth as it is in heaven.
Give us this day our daily bread.
And forgive us our trespasses,
as we forgive those who trespass against us.
And lead us not into temptation;
but deliver us from evil.
For thine is the kingdom,
the power, and the glory,
for ever and ever.

Amen.

Late Fragment

And did you get what
you wanted from this life, even so?
I did.
And what did you want?
To call myself beloved, to feel myself
beloved on the earth.

RAYMOND CARVER (1939–1988)

['*Late Fragment*' was chosen by Jo Slade and Madeleine Keane in *Lifelines 2* and by Molly McCloskey in *Lifelines 3*.

Jo Slade wrote:
I am delighted to send you a copy of my favourite poem as requested. I have had many favourite poems at different times of my life. At this particular time this short poem by Raymond Carver called 'Late Fragment' *seems to express one common desire of all people, to be loved.*

Madeleine Keane wrote:
One of my favourite poems is Raymond Carver's 'Late Fragment'. *I love it because, for me, it encapsulates what people search for all their lives, namely the secret of life. And for me the secret of life is loving and being loved, something your wonderful and worthwhile project is all about.*

Molly McCloskey wrote:
I don't know that 'favourite' is the word I would use, but it's one that's stayed with me since I read it last year — 'Late Fragment' *by Raymond Carver. Unadorned, and yet quite powerful, like so much of his writing. In light of the circumstances of his life, and written when he knew that he was dying, it's full — in those few lines — of reconciliation, acceptance and gratitude. So, though it reads like an epitaph, it feels strangely inclusive.*]

BERNADETTE KIELY   ARTIST

8 May 2006

Dear Dónal, Caroline and Stephanie,

Thank you for inviting me to contribute to your New and Collected Lifelines. *I am delighted to be part of your project.*

The poem I have chosen is 'The Terrain of Suffering: Frida Kahlo in Ireland' *by Kerry Hardie.*

It's difficult to put how I feel about the poem into words except to say that I see it as a beautifully evocative 'painted' poem that expresses something I immediately recognise and feel a connection with.

Thank you again and every good luck with the book.

With best wishes,

Bernadette

The Terrain of Suffering: Frida Kahlo in Ireland

1
Frida Kahlo looked in the mirror,
painted what she saw.
Monkeys and cats are familiars.
Bones lie about her neck.

Broad leaves mass behind her
(hairy. Or veined, or urgent as flame.)
A dead bird — its spread wings —
hangs from a collar of thorns.

Once, a greater detachment
paints four green parrots, topaz-eyed.
No leaves. A cigarette.
Each time her blouse is white.

2
Over the rotting posts
the torn nets of the fruit cage
blow like waves. The daffodils
thrust up their pointed leaves.

Kahlo's familiars
look like her devils.
In Ireland she'd have worn a velvet dress
and thought on long grey slugs and leaves

like spears. Trailing the wet fields in draggled hems,
the fading colours would have quelled her eyes.
Behind her,
ink-blue hills, rain coming.

KERRY HARDIE (B. 1951)

EVELYN CONLON   NOVELIST

10 January 1994

Dear Ewan, Áine and Christopher,

I want to cheat because it's not possible to have one favourite poem, however I won't. Grace Paley is known as a surprising and satisfying short-story writer. Her poetry could never be as good, only because it becomes the blueprint for something more marvellous; stories that tell an entire history in two pages, tragically but with wipe-the-floor wit. Born in 1922, she has always been politically active in feminist and anti-war causes. She once described herself as a co-operative anarchist and a combative pacifist; this poem is an illustration of the latter stance. Hope you enjoy it and good luck with your book.

Evelyn

I Gave Away That Kid

I gave away that kidlike he was an old button
    Here old button get off of me
    I don't need you anymore
    go on get out of here
    get into the army
    sew yourself onto the colonel's shirt
    or the captain's fly   jackass
    don't you have any sense
    don't you read the papers
    why are you leaving now?

That kid walked out of here like he was the cat's pyjamas
    what are you wearing p j's for   you damn fool?
    why are you crying   you couldn't
    get another job anywhere anyways
    go march to the army's drummer
    be a man like all your dead uncles
    then think of something else to do

Lost him, sorry about that the president said
    he was a good boy
    never see one like him again
    Why don't you repeat that your honor
    why don't you sizzle up the meaning
    of that sentence for your breakfast
    why don't you stick him in a prayer
and count to ten before my wife gets you.

That boy is a puddle in Beirut the paper says
    scraped up for singing in church
    too bad   too bad is a terrible tune
    It's no song at all how come you sing it?

I gave away that kidlike he was an old button
    Here old button get offa me
    I don't need you anymore
    go on get out of here
    get into the army
    sew yourself onto the colonel's shirt

    or the captain's fly   jackass
    don't you have any sense
    don't you read the papers
    why are you leaving now?

GRACE PALEY (B. 1922)

MICHAEL LONGLEY POET

19 January 1992

I hope the enclosed will be of some use to you.

Best wishes

Michael Longley

A favourite poem is not necessarily the best poem by a poet whom one admires more than all – or even most – other poets. For me it is a piece which took me completely by surprise once, and continues to do so without my ever being able to comprehend its 'meaning' or follow its processes. A spell has been cast. 'Fern Hill' by Dylan Thomas; Yeats's 'Byzantium'; 'Tall Nettles' by Edward Thomas; 'Innocence' by Patrick Kavanagh; 'Mayfly' by Louis MacNeice; D H Lawrence's 'Bavarian Gentians' are all candidates for the dubious privilege of being My Favourite Poem. (And I have confined myself to this century.)

I choose 'Voyages II' by the American poet Hart Crane. It is the high-point of a sequence of lyrics, each one a great psalm to the sea. Sensuous yet spiritual, unabashed in its erotic embrace, unembarrassed by its own over-reaching rhetoric, Crane's incantation risks failing ludicrously. Instead, here is a poem which has everything. After hundreds of readings it remains for me a revelation. When Hart Crane wrote at this altitude his genius became a small part of the universe, one of its wonders.

Voyages (II)

—And yet this great wink of eternity,
Of rimless floods, unfettered leewardings,
Samite sheeted and processioned where
Her undinal vast belly moonward bends,
Laughing the wrapt inflections of our love;

Take this Sea, whose diapason knells
On scrolls of silver snowy sentences,
The sceptred terror of whose sessions rends
As her demeanors motion well or ill
All but the pieties of lovers' hands.

And onward, as bells off San Salvador
Salute the crocus lustres of the stars,
In these poinsettia meadows of her tides,—
Adagios of islands, O my Prodigal,
Complete the dark confessions her veins spell.

Mark how her turning shoulders wind the hours,
And hasten while her penniless rich palms
Pass superscription of bent foam and wave,—
Hasten, while they are true,—sleep, death, desire,
Close round one instant in one floating flower.

Bind us in time, O Seasons clear, and awe.
O minstrel galleons of Carib fire,
Bequeath us to no earthly shore until
Is answered in the vortex of our grave
The seal's wide spindrift gaze toward paradise.

HART CRANE (1899–1932)

P.S. My favourite line of poetry is the last line of 'Voyages III': *'Permit me voyage, love, into your hands . . .'*

EILÍS NÍ DHUIBHNE

WRITER

25 January 1994

Dear Ewan, Áine and Christopher,

Thank you very much for your letter, asking me to send you the name of my favourite poem for Lifelines. *Of course I am very happy to do this, and appreciate very much being asked.*

Like most people, probably, I have a number of favourite poems, including poems that I loved when I first read them and which made an impact on me at the time, and poems, sometimes the same, that go through my head very often. If I were picking one from the first group, it would be 'When you are old and grey and full of sleep', *the poem by Yeats based on a sonnet by Ronsard, which my husband quoted to me when he proposed. It is the ideal poem for this situation. Who could resist* 'But I have loved the pilgrim soul in you . . .'? *In fact, I think love poems are the most primary and natural kinds of poem. Those and nature poems. The one I will finally select as my favourite is one in which love and nature are combined:* 'Leaba Shíoda', *by Nuala Ní Dhomhnaill. I like that because it is an honest, unabashedly romantic and passionate poem of a woman's love for a man, the kind of poem you sometimes get as a traditional song but seldom as a literary poem by an Irishwoman. The bit I like best is the* 'skin – like milk being poured from jugs at dinnertime'. *I think that, and many of the other images, are lovely.*

Good luck with the project.

Eilís Ní Dhuibhne

When You are Old

When you are old and grey and full of sleep,
And nodding by the fire, take down this book,
And slowly read, and dream of the soft look
Your eyes had once, and of their shadows deep;

How many loved your moments of glad grace,
And loved your beauty with love false or true,
But one man loved the pilgrim soul in you,
And loved the sorrows of your changing face;

And bending down beside the glowing bars,
Murmur, a little sadly, how Love fled
And paced upon the mountains overhead
And hid his face amid a crowd of stars.

W B YEATS (1865–1939)

['*When You Are Old*' was also chosen by Anthony Clare (*Lifelines*), Mary Finan (*Lifelines 3*) and Anthony Roche *(Lifelines 3)*.

Anthony Clare wrote:
I choose it because it never fails to move me when I read it, because it evokes the sweet, aching agony of nostalgia and ageing, and the elusive, endlessly sought human love that every one of us seeks and because when I recite it myself I immediately feel my kinship, however slight, with the greatest poet in the English language in this century.

Mary Finan wrote:
'*When You Are Old' by W B Yeats is a translation of Ronsard's poem 'Quand Tu Sera Vieille.' I have always felt that it was one of the most beautiful love poems ever written. Everyone wants to be loved for the kind of person they are, rather than who they are or how they look.*

I find I get fonder of this poem as the decades pass by. Rather like Agatha Christie who, when asked what it was like being married to an archaeologist, replied 'Wonderful, darling, the older I get the more interesting he finds me!'

Anthony Roche wrote:
My favourite poet is W B Yeats. Yeats is not a directly confessional poet. The circumstances of his life which may have given rise to the poem are transformed by the act of imagination; there is always, as he says, a phantasmagoria. But Yeats carries the original emotion with him and embodies it in the poem in ways that others can share. There are many of his poems that have meant a great deal to me at various times in my life. I have chosen 'When You Are Old' for two related reasons: it was read by Anna Hayes on the occasion of my marriage to her daughter, Katy, and the seventh line speaks to what I love about my wife.]

Leaba Shíoda

Do chóireoinn leaba duit
i Leaba Shíoda
sa bhféar ard
faoi iomrascáil na gcrann
is bheadh do chraiceann ann
mar shíoda ar shíoda
sa doircheacht
am lonnaithe na leamhan.

Craiceann a shníonn
go gléineach thar do ghéaga
mar bhainne á dháil as crúiscíní
am lóin
is tréad gabhar ag gabháil thar chnocáin
do chuid gruaige
cnocáin ar a bhfuil faillte arda
is dhá ghleann atá domhain.

Is bheadh do bheola taise
ar mhilseacht shiúcra
tráthnóna is sinn ag spaisteoireacht
cois abhann
is na gaotha meala
ag séideadh thar an Sionna
is na fiúisí ag beannú duit
ceann ar cheann.

Na fiúisí ag ísliú
a gceann maorga
ag umhlú síos don áilleacht
os a gcomhair
is do phriocfainn péire acu
mar shiogairlíní
is do mhaiseoinn do chluasa
mar bhrídeog.

Ó, chóireoinn leaba duit
i Leaba Shíoda
le hamhascarnach an lae
i ndeireadh thall
is ba mhór an pléisiúr dúinn
bheith géaga ar ghéaga
ag iomrascáil
am lonnaithe na leamhan.

Labasheedy (The Silken Bed)

I'd make a bed for you
in Labasheedy
in the tall grass
under the wrestling trees
where your skin
would be silk upon silk
in the darkness
when the moths are coming down.

Skin which glistens
shining over your limbs
like milk being poured
from jugs at dinnertime;
your hair is a herd of goats
moving over rolling hills,
hills that have high cliffs
and two ravines.

And your damp lips
would be as sweet as sugar
at evening and we walking
by the riverside
with honeyed breezes
blowing over the Shannon
and the fuchsias bowing down to you
one by one.

The fuchsias bending low
their solemn heads
in obeisance to the beauty
in front of them
I would pick a pair of flowers
as pendant earrings
to adorn you
like a bride in shining clothes.

O I'd make a bed for you
in Labasheedy,
in the twilight hour
with evening falling slow
and what a pleasure it would be
to have our limbs entwine
wrestling
while the moths are coming down.

NUALA NÍ DHOMHNAILL (B.1952)　　　TRANSLATED BY THE AUTHOR

Dear Caroline,

I enclose a small poem for Lifelines 3. *I only got your letter today. I hope I'm not too late!*
All the best,

Michael Hartnett

'How goes the night, boy?...'

The night before Patricia's funeral in 1951,
I stayed up late talking to my father.

How goes the night, boy?
    The moon is down:
    dark is the town
    in this nightfall.
How goes the night, boy?
    Soon is her funeral,
    her small white burial.
She was my three-years child,
her honey hair, her eyes
small ovals of thrush-eggs.
How goes the night, boy?
    It is late: lace
    at the window
    blows back in the wind.
How goes the night, boy?
    Oh, my poor white fawn!
How goes the night, boy?
    It is dawn.

MICHAEL HARTNETT (1941–1999)

JOHN KELLY BROADCASTER

Dear Ralph, Caroline and Gareth,

Thank you very much for the invitation to contribute to Lifelines. *I have long admired the project. My favourite poem at time of writing is 'Star' by Paddy Kavanagh.*

Kavanagh, the great Ulster poet, has always been a favourite – for his affection, his crankiness, his genuine mysticism, his vulnerability and his wisdom. This short poem is simple, obviously beautiful and yet quite extraordinary – it gets me in the heart, the head, the gut – and somewhere else that only the likes of Kavanagh has any proper sense of. It seems to connect with some other part of me that is often no more than a woolly and potential thing. Kavanagh almost always (for me anyway) puts some shape on things and helps me to know what I don't quite know and this, I feel, is the true poetic achievement. I'm also a sucker for pure melancholic beauty – read it and weep.

Good luck with the project.

Regards,

John Kelly

A Star

Beauty was that
Far vanished flame,
Call it a star
Wanting better name.

And gaze and gaze
Vaguely until
Nothing is left
Save a grey ghost-hill.

Here wait I
On the world's rim
Stretching out hands
To Seraphim.

PATRICK KAVANAGH (1904–1967)

PHILIPPA SUTHERLAND ARTIST

Dear Dónal, Caroline and Stephanie,

Thank you so much for your letter about Lifelines.

I wouldn't say that I have a 'favourite' poem. When I received your letter last week I was about to leave for work in Galway and to stay on the north coast of County Clare for a couple of days, so my choice was very much influenced by this particular set of circumstances.

To begin with I think the apparent subject matter of 'Some More Trees' – weather, sky and trees – resonated with my surroundings, but I think its appeal to me lay more in its use of language and its tone. The vocabulary is quite everyday but the careful placing of every word, of their repeated and contrasting sounds and structures, creates a fluctuating energy and a sense of the extraordinary. The tone produced is somehow ambiguous, suggesting not only a physical environment, but also a complex and uncertain state of mind and the poem moves seamlessly between these exterior and interior worlds. I liked the poet's referencing of another poet's words. ['Some More Trees' uses the end words of John Ashberry's 'Some Trees'] It reminds me of the practice in music of sampling or of the way my own ideas and work feels structured as much by all the books I've read or images I've seen as by my own lived experiences.

    With best wishes for the success of your project and thanks for considering me as a possible contributor.

Philippa Sutherland

Some More Trees

For John Ashbery

A fine mist coats each
leaf. Wind moves like speech
through laden boughs, a performance
which, given the chance,

will astonish the morning.
Clouds meanwhile, are agreeing
with me that I
should make an effort, at least try

to say exactly what they are.
They hang there.
I stare at them, hoping soon
to be able to explain

how they were invented.
The trees are surrounded
By charged air, bird noises,
Waves of light. Something emerges

from the centre of the morning.
I watch it moving
Nervously, with reticence,
caught-up in its own defence.

C J ALLEN

22 January 1992

Dear Nicola, Paula, Alice,

Thank you for your letter and my apologies for the delay in replying. I don't know that I have a favourite poem; but certainly among my favourites I would include Derek Mahon's 'A Disused Shed in Co. Wexford'.

The reasons? It is a poem that heartbreakingly dwells on and gives voice to all those peoples and civilisations that have been lost and/or destroyed. Since it is set in Ireland, with all the characteristic features of an Irish 'Big House' ruin, it speaks with a special sharpness to the present moment and the fear, rampant in Northern Ireland, of communities that fear they too might perish and be lost, with none to speak for them.

Yours sincerely,

Seamus Deane

A Disused Shed in Co. Wexford

Let them not forget us, the weak souls among the asphodels.
— Seferis, *Mythistorema*

For J G Farrell

Even now there are places where a thought might grow—
Peruvian mines, worked out and abandoned
To a slow clock of condensation,
An echo trapped for ever, and a flutter
Of wild-flowers in the lift-shaft,
Indian compounds where the wind dances
And a door bangs with diminished confidence,
Lime crevices behind rippling rain-barrels,
Dog corners for bone burials;
And in a disused shed in Co. Wexford,

Deep in the grounds of a burnt-out hotel,
Among the bathtubs and the washbasins
A thousand mushrooms crowd to a keyhole.
This is the one star in their firmament
Or frames a star within a star.
What should they do there but desire?
So many days beyond the rhododendrons
With the world waltzing in its bowl of cloud,
They have learnt patience and silence
Listening to the rooks querulous in the high wood.

They have been waiting for us in a foetor
Of vegetable sweat since civil war days,
Since the gravel-crunching, interminable departure
Of the expropriated mycologist.
He never came back, and light since then
Is a keyhole rusting gently after rain.
Spiders have spun, flies dusted to mildew
And once a day, perhaps, they have heard something—
A trickle of masonry, a shout from the blue
Or a lorry changing gear at the end of the lane.

There have been deaths, the pale flesh flaking
Into the earth that nourished it;
And nightmares, born of these and the grim
Dominion of stale air and rank moisture.
Those nearest the door grow strong—
'Elbow room! Elbow room!'
The rest, dim in a twilight of crumbling
Utensils and broken pitchers, groaning
For their deliverance, have been so long
Expectant that there is left only the posture.

A half century, without visitors, in the dark—
Poor preparation for the cracking lock
And creak of hinges; magi, moonmen,
Powdery prisoners of the old regime,
Web-throated, stalked life triffids, racked by drought
And insomnia, only the ghost of a scream
At the flash-bulb firing-squad we wake them with
Shows there is life yet in their feverish forms.
Grown beyond nature now, soft food for worms,
They lift frail heads in gravity and good faith.

They are begging us, you see, in their wordless way,
To do something, to speak on their behalf
Or at least not to close the door again.
Lost people of Treblinka and Pompeii!
'Save us, save us,' they seem to say,
'Let the god not abandon us
Who have come so far in darkness and in pain.
We too had our lives to live.
You with your light meter and relaxed itinerary,
Let not our naive labours have been in vain!'

DEREK MAHON (B. 1941)

['*A Disused Shed in Co. Wexford*' was also chosen by Kevin Barry in *Lifelines 2*. Kevin Barry wrote:

The poem I have selected is 'A Disused Shed in Co. Wexford' *by Derek Mahon. Born in Belfast in 1941, Mahon has become one of Ireland's most respected poets of the twentieth century. I choose* 'A Disused Shed in Co. Wexford' *because of its objective beauty. The poem has extraordinary scope. Its title remembers a shed which had first been imagined in J G Farrell's comic colonial novel,* Troubles. *Its rhythms remember W H Auden's* 'In Memory of Sigmund Freud'. *Its narrative remembers the innumerable and, therefore, the unnameable dead. The poem is about being almost forgotten. The resources of hope are asserted in its first lines with scepticism. Its last lines do not let us, its anonymous readers, off the hook.*]

GWEN O'DOWD ARTIST

30 March 1994

Dear Ewan, Áine and Christopher,

I am sending this poem 'Chicory, Chicory Dock', *written by my father, for inclusion in* Lifelines. *One of many he wrote during his lifetime for the various literary competitions he entered in the* Irish Times, Dublin Opinion *and many other publications over the years. I certainly think it's a very entertaining piece and sound advice for any perplexed gardeners. The best of luck with your project, I hope you get a very healthy response.*

Best wishes,

Gwen O'Dowd

Chicory Chicory Dock

I am an expert on all kinds of weeds
From common types to more exotic breeds,
Because my garden's full of every sort
From nettles to plantain and swallow-wort.
A creeping thing called bindweed chokes my plants
And even fruit trees if it gets the chance—
Its proper name's *convolvulus arvensis*
And it's a thing would drive you from your senses.
I dig and pull and spray and hoe
But still the damn things thrive and grow.

On television I see lawns being laid
And manicured to each obedient blade
With never once a single weed in sight
And so I'm left with thinking I'm not right.
My lawn is hardly what you'd call first-class—
It's mostly weeds with an odd patch of grass.
Although I conscientiously comply
With what the seedsman's packets specify,
And listen to the best of counsel,
I end up with a load of groundsel.

Goutweed, goosegrass, dock and thistles spread
Where I should have fine fruit and flowers instead
And where asparagus and peas I nourish,
It's only dandelions and spurge that flourish.
I once tried sowing seeds the wrong way up,
And got a crop of creeping buttercup.
My wife came out and looked at this and said
'That comes from standing Nature on its head.'
She said she'd like some cherry trees,
But then she's very hard to please.

Take berries (rasp or straw or even goose)—
I plant them and protect them from abuse,
But creepy greeny things with long tap roots
Come up in Spring and smother all the shoots.
And every year I fight an endless battle
With charlock, melilot and yellow rattle.
But now I've got a plot, that is to say,
A plan that came to me the other day.
This brilliant thought to me occurred,
Though you may think it quite absurd.

It seemed to me, or so at least I reasoned,
That nobody could keep a garden decent
By sowing, hoeing, spraying every Spring,
When there before my eyes, the very thing
Was at my feet and underneath my nose:
The thing, no matter what, that always grows.
Weeds never wither, wilt nor even wane
Though bruised and battered time and time again.
And so my weeds I'll cultivate
And grow to love the things I hate.

I'll root out all the dahlias and clematis
And give the lowly weed a higher status.
Out go potatoes, cabbages and peas
And in come dock and others as I please.
With vigour I'll uproot herbaceous borders
And fill the space with twitch till further orders.
I'll cut down apple trees without remorse,
And maybe plant a bush or two of gorse.
And very happy we will be,
My wife, my weedery and me.

'Come see my garden, Maud,' I'll proudly say,
(Maud's not her name but that is by the way.)
'Here's shepherd's purse and coltsfoot and some twitch
And buttonweed transplanted from a ditch.
And see the moss—it's full of scores and scores
Of very busy hard to get at spores,
And over here we've chickweed and fat hen,
(I think we'll call this part the Poultry Pen.)
And here's a thing I grew from seed,
It is a very weedy weed.'

So never more I'll need to hoe and mow,
But merely stand and watch my garden grow,
With just the odd dig at my scutch and such,
But I won't have to labour over much.
And people from all parts will come to see
What can be done with weedy husbandry.
But if I find that too much cultivation
Breeds in my weeds ideas above their station
And leaves them free to grow or not,
I'll concrete in the whole damn lot.

FRANK O'DOWD (1921–1991)

HUGH BRADY   ACADEMIC

UCD, Office of the President
5 May 2006

Dear Dónal, Caroline & Stephanie,

Thank you for inviting me to choose a favourite poem for Wesley College's Lifelines Project. I wish you every success in your work for Concern.

   My selection is 'To the Memory of Some I Knew Who are Dead and Who Loved Ireland', *written by George William Erskine Russell (Æ) in December 1917.*

   I chose this poem in the first instance because of its reference to two of UCD's most distinguished historic figures, Tom Kettle and Thomas MacDonagh. Both MacDonagh and Kettle, as the poem's title suggests, gave their lives for Ireland in different ways which have been the subject of much debate and discussion since.

   Tom Kettle, who was killed on 9 September 1916 during the attack on Ginchy in France in the First World War, had been appointed Professor of National Economics at UCD in 1910. Thomas MacDonagh was appointed Lecturer in English in UCD in 1911 and was executed for his part in the 1916 Rising on 3 May 1916.

   In this year of anniversary celebrations, it is instructive to note how, as early as Christmas 1917, Æ had managed to detect a common strand of values – patriotic values at that – in the various figures of Pearse, Connolly, the great figures of the co-operative movement Alan Anderson and Will Redmond, as well as MacDonagh and Kettle. As President of a university, I spend a good deal of my time trying to bring together a great diversity of highly talented people and their ideas to advance what is UCD's stated – and unashamedly patriotic, in the best sense – objective of serving Ireland in the wider world.

The last quatrain of this poem, with its image of unity, 'one river', coming together from many and often conflicting sources, 'dreams/ that clashed together in our night', continues to inspire in this effort.

With renewed wishes for the success of the Lifelines project,

Sincerely yours,

Hugh R Brady

To the Memory of Some I Knew Who are Dead and Who Loved Ireland

Their dream had left me numb and cold,
    But yet my spirit rose in pride,
Refashioning in burnished gold
    The images of those who died,
Or were shut in the penal cell.
    Here's to you, Pearse, your dream not mine,
But yet the thought, for this you fell,
    Has turned life's water into wine.

You who have died on Eastern hills
    Or fields of France as undismayed,
Who lit with interlinked wills
    The long heroic barricade,
You, too, in all the dreams you had,
    Thought of some thing for Ireland done.
Was it not so, Oh, shining lad,
    What lured you, Alan Anderson?

I listened to high talk from you,
    Thomas MacDonagh, and it seemed
The words were idle, but they grew
    To nobleness by death redeemed.
Life cannot utter words more great
    Than life may meet by sacrifice,
High words were equalled by high fate,
    You paid the price. You paid the price.

You who fought on fields afar,
    That other Ireland did you wrong
Who said you shadowed Ireland's star,
    Nor gave you laurel wreath nor song.
You proved by death as true as they,
    In mightier conflicts played your part,
Equal your sacrifice may weigh,
    Dear Kettle, of the generous heart.

The hope lives on age after age,
    Earth with its beauty might be won
For labour as a heritage,
    For this has Ireland lost a son.
This hope unto a flame to fan
    Men have put life by with a smile,
Here's to you Connolly, my man,
    Who cast the last torch on the pile.

You too, had Ireland in your care,
    Who watched o'er pits of blood and mire,
From iron roots leap up in air
    Wild forests, magical, of fire;
Yet while the Nuts of Death were shed
    Your memory would ever stray
To your own isle. Oh, gallant dead—
    This wreath, Will Redmond on your clay.

Here's to you, men I never met,
    Yet hope to meet behind the veil,
Thronged on some starry parapet,
    That looks down upon Innisfail,
And sees the confluence of dreams
    That clashed together in our night,
One river, born from many streams,
    Roll in one blaze of blinding light.

December, 1917

GEORGE RUSSELL (Æ) (1867–1935)

To my mind a poem should be like a piece of music – different pieces mean different things to us at various times of our lives. At the same time a truly fine poem is constantly changing, and no matter how many times we read it, something new will reach out. The poem I have chosen is one such. It's a poem written for my daughter, by Michael Hartnett in 1987, and is the last poem in his collection Poems to Younger Women *(1988) published by Gallery Press. I try to read it at least once a year, to see how it changes and grows as my daughter does. It reminds me of a happy time when we lived in Chapelizod and Michael was a part of our lives.*

It's a poem about the beginning of life and the end of life. About an ancient Ireland and one yet to come. It's about destruction and danger. It is also about love and hope. It's a gift from a lovely friend. As long as this poem exists, I will have my daughter, Bonnie.

Christine Dwyer Hickey

For my God-daughter, B.A.H.

Fish in the river where you live
turn their poisoned silver to the sky
and chemical air from woodlice-like machines
assault the lichens and they die.
This is our city, my lovely girl —
I must warn you from the very start.
This place, this land has an ugliness
that could warp the most devoted heart.
Still, I send my wish to you,
to Chapelizod by the river bend
(lovers set sail from here before
—or were lovers at their journey's end —
and came to grief on the Cornish shore):
may you have the blessed eyes
to see those people in whom joy survives
and leaves like dragons' footprints
embossed on gravel drives
and magenta seep through the Phoenix trees
from extraordinary skies.
For the heart can stay unwarped
in these most inhuman days
and one cobweb threading rain
can civilise a race —
for there is an Ireland, where
trees suddenly fly away
and leave their pigeons, baffled,
standing in the air.

MICHAEL HARTNETT (1941–1999)

Dear Ewan Gibson,

Thank you for your letter. I'm sending comments on Langston Hughes's 'A Dream Deferred' for the next collection. I wish you much success with this collection as well.

Sincerely,

Gloria Naylor

Harlem

What happens to a dream deferred?

Does it dry up
like a raisin in the sun?
Or fester like a sore—
And then run?
Does it stink like rotten meat?
Or crust and sugar over—
like a syrupy sweet?

Maybe it just sags
like a heavy load.

Or does it explode?

LANGSTON HUGHES (1902–1967)

This is one of my favorite poems and I liked it so much that I used it as an epigraph for my first novel, The Women of Brewster Place. *Part of the 'humanness' of being human is our ability to dream. There may be greater dreams for some, humbler dreams for others but, regardless of the degradation in any given circumstance, hope is innate within the human heart. So our ability to dream cannot be destroyed, even if it is reduced to only planning for the next meal – or a desire to be left totally alone. But here Langston Hughes talks about the dangers to the human spirit when dreams are thwarted. The language appears simple at first, but carefully examining each of the repercussions for a deferred dream, we can chart the behavior for individuals, societies, or entire nations that have despaired and given up.*

Gloria Naylor

Vassar

3 February 1994

Dear Ewan, Áine and Chris,

This astounding sonnet is high on the list of my favorite poems because of the way it manages to treat its subject – the death of one of Hopkins's parishioners – in a manner both tender and rugged. I also love it because of the vivid, economic, and apt portrait it gives of the blacksmith himself, 'Big-boned and hardy-handsome,' and because of the dexterity and speed with which it moves from objective description to direct, intimate address – from 'Sickness broke him,' to 'Child, Felix, poor Felix Randal.' There's such great swift sureness of speech in it, too, which you can hear in the athletic balance it can hold between formal restraints and emotional outburst. What also leaves me mesmerised with admiration is the way Hopkins manages to mix – in an utterly unsentimental way – religious consolation and real human pain: they can temper but never, for him, cancel one another. And that great last line strikes home with the effect of a series of sharp, decisive, final hammer-blows – violent and musical – leaving us with that 'bright and battering sandal' which could be forged for Pegasus himself. The fact of so many things (emotional, spiritual, intellectual, technical) all working so well together, in a poem that is itself partly a celebration of work, never ceases to be a wonder and a satisfaction to me.

Many thanks for asking me to participate in this good work of yours. Blessings on it.

Eamon Grennan

Felix Randal

Felix Randal the farrier, O he is dead then? my duty all ended,
Who have watched his mould of man, big-boned and hardy–handsome
Pining, pining, till time when reason rambled in it and some
Fatal four disorders, fleshed there, all contended?

Sickness broke him. Impatient he cursed at first, but mended
Being anointed and all; though a heavenlier heart began some
Months earlier, since I had our sweet reprieve and ransom
Tendered to him. Ah well, God rest him all road ever he offended!

This seeing the sick endears them to us, us too it endears.
My tongue had taught thee comfort, touch had quenched thy tears,
Thy tears that touched my heart, child, Felix, poor Felix Randal;

How far from then forethought of, all thy more boisterous years,
When thou at the random grim forge, powerful amidst peers,
Didst fettle for the great grey drayhorse his bright and battering sandal!

GERARD MANLEY HOPKINS (1844–1889)

['*Felix Randal*', '*A Christmas Childhood*'by Patrick Kavanagh, and his own poem, '*Confiteor*' were Cyril Cusack's choices in *Lifelines*. Cyril Cusack wrote:

Let me congratulate you on this very original and laudable effort of yours to succour the poor people of the Third World. The effort deserves every support.

Now, another thing, it is not clear to me whether you wish to have a poem selected from my own two slender volumes of published poetry or rather a poem I favour from the work of major poets. I think probably the latter, but to choose my 'favourite poem' of the many that appeal to me obviously presents a difficulty.

However, I think my only plan is to suggest two poems which for me have a special appeal, one by Hopkins, the other by Kavanagh; and one from myself.

My reasons for these preferences are almost impossible to articulate because they are scarcely rational, rather are they intuitive. I respond to them emotionally, perhaps because I am an actor.

However, I may say that I relate to 'A Christmas Childhood' because — vide the title — it is a pure evocation of the poet's childhood, of a child's intake of beauty in so many forms and images, and through the experiences and details of his country life and home in its beginnings, a perfect recall of true innocence, spirtually significant and sustaining into age. And, of course, it is tenderly, exquisitely rendered in the verse.

This poem I have spoken for audience on occasions, once in the National Concert Hall and again on Irish television, and on each occasion I found myself or, rather should I say, lost myself in identification with the poet as a child.

With this, as with 'Felix Randal', let it be said that identification with the poet is the most desirable condition for the rendering of true poetry, allowing no intrusion of 'theatricality' or pretence, or even a priority of technical excellence. And what endears me to this particular poem of Hopkins is the passionate, near Christlike, compassion for 'child Felix, poor Felix Randal', the farrier. And, however difficult, I would say, as in my experience, that the emotion will carry the speaker, identifying with the poet, even through the delicate intricacies of the verse. 'Felix Randal' some years ago I was privileged to commit to record and I treasure the compliment I had from a fellow Jesuit of the poet-priest: that in hearing the record it was as though for him, in some mysterious way, he were listening to Gerald Manley Hopkins himself.

For my own poem let it suffice that, as an actor, my preference for this over other poems I have written rests in the title.]

3 January 1997

Dear Ralph, Caroline and Gareth,

Thank you for your invitation to choose a poem for Lifelines 3. *I am extremely flattered to have been asked to be part of this excellent project.*

I have a problem with the word 'favourite', however. I am always astonished that people can have a favourite colour, for example. How can anyone prefer red to blue or green to yellow (or vice versa or vice versa)? Yellow is my favourite colour for walls and for jerseys for people with copper-coloured hair and especially for egg yolks, but I can't think of a colour I would like less for a pair of shoes or a sandwich.

It's the same with poems. I love poems that are funny and make me smile. And I love poems that are sad and make me cry. I love poems that are clear and translucent and sing to me off the page. And I love poems that are dense and thick and have to be mined for meaning. It's not that there aren't poems I prefer. Of course there are. But I don't have a single favourite poem; I have lots of favourites.

Which is all very fine, but where does it leave me with the task in hand? Precisely nowhere. So then I tried to think less about the idea of favourites and a bit more about the function of Lifelines – *the poetic function, that is, rather than the fund-raising one – and it struck me that one of the great things about this project is the way it brings readers and poems together, sometimes in unexpected ways. So in the end I decided to choose a new poem – this one's new to me at any rate and, since it's from a recent collection, it may be new to other people too – and one that people would be sure to be touched by, whoever they are and whatever their preoccupations; and so I chose this lovely springtime poem by Kerry Hardie.*

May
for Marian

The blessèd stretch and ease of it —
heart's ease. The hills blue. All the flowering weeds
bursting open. Balm in the air. The birdsong
bouncing back out of the sky. The cattle
lain down in the meadow, forgetting to feed.
The horses swishing their tails.
The yellow flare of furze on the near hill.
And the first cream splatters of blossom
high on the thorns where the day rests longest.

All hardship, hunger, treachery of winter forgotten.
This unfounded conviction: forgiveness, hope.

KERRY HARDIE (B. 1951)

Isn't that just . . . well, isn't it just! What more can I say?

Beir beannacht,

Siobhán Parkinson

Dear Dónal, Caroline and Stephanie,

I'm delighted that Lifelines *is to appear again. I remember the previous volumes with affection and admiration. Congratulations on its rejuvenation, and on your commitment to the developing world.*

After much cur agus cúiteamh, *I have decided to plump for 'What Were They Like?' by the American poet Denise Levertov, a poem published in book form in 1967. I remember reading it first when teaching in New South Wales in 1972, and being mesmerised by its beauty and anger, which are formalised in quiet, heartbreaking rhythms.*

I think the poem's power, which transcends its immediate context – the Vietnam war – comes from its evocation of a harmonious, traditional society in lines that recall the delicate, ceremonious conventions of oriental poetry. The images linger in the mind. They veer perhaps towards cliché, but the poem is, after all, an outsider's probing of what she imagines are the effects of war on an unfamiliar, exotic society.

The poem's unusual form – six questions followed by six answers – allows for shifts in tone. The questions do not mention war. They are almost anthropological, with an emphasis on the exotic. This allows the imagined respondent, who is familiar with the effects of the war, to use a tone of quiet rebuke: 'Sir, laughter is bitter to the burnt mouth.' At a time when terms such napalm and Agent Orange were entering our vocabulary, this was a line of extraordinary power. I believe the poem retains this power, and that the horror of war, and the poet's anger at what she sees as a war without any justification, are intensified into memorableness by her evocation of an idyllic, harmonious world being destroyed by a war which she refers to just a few times in telling detail.

A sad and bitter poem, but its concentration on the value and beauty of what war destroys, places a vision of hope in opposition to a vision of destruction.

Beir beannacht,

Paddy Bushe

What Were They Like?

1) Did the people of Viet Nam
    use lanterns of stone?
2) Did they hold ceremonies
    to reverence the opening of buds?
3) Were they inclined to quiet laughter?
4) Did they use bone and ivory,
    jade and silver, for ornament?
5) Had they an epic poem?
6) Did they distinguish between speech and singing?

1) Sir, their light hearts turned to stone.
    It is not remembered whether in gardens
    stone lanterns illumined pleasant ways.
2) Perhaps they gathered once to delight in blossom,
    but after their children were killed
    there were no more buds.
3) Sir, laughter is bitter to the burned mouth.
4) A dream ago, perhaps. Ornament is for joy.
    All the bones were charred.
5) It is not remembered. Remember,
    most were peasants; their life
    was in rice and bamboo.
    When peaceful clouds were reflected in the paddies
    and the water buffalo stepped surely along terraces,
    maybe fathers told their sons old tales.
    When bombs smashed those mirrors
    there was time only to scream.
6) There is an echo yet
    of their speech which was like a song.
    It was reported their singing resembled
    the flight of moths in moonlight.
    Who can say? It is silent now.

DENISE LEVERTOV (1923–1997)

Princeton
30 January 1997

Dear Ralph Croly,

Thanks for your recent letter. My favorite poem is Robert Frost's 'After Apple-Picking'. It's beautifully nuanced, haunting, and profound in its suggestion of a life so passionately lived, or a career so energetically mined, that it has utterly satiated its original appetite. But what mystery in Frost's rhythms and words! It's just a perfect poem.

Joyce Carol Oates

After Apple-Picking

My long two-pointed ladder's sticking through a tree
Toward heaven still,
And there's a barrel that I didn't fill
Beside it, and there may be two or three
Apples I didn't pick upon some bough.
But I am done with apple-picking now.
Essence of winter sleep is on the night,
The scent of apples: I am drowsing off.
I cannot rub the strangeness from my sight
I got from looking through a pane of glass
I skimmed this morning from the drinking trough
And held against the world of hoary grass.
It melted, and I let it fall and break.
But I was well
Upon my way to sleep before it fell,
And I could tell
What form my dreaming was about to take.
Magnified apples appear and disappear,
Stem end and blossom end,
And every fleck of russet showing clear.
My instep arch not only keeps the ache,
It keeps the pressure of a ladder-round.
I feel the ladder sway as the boughs bend.
And I keep hearing from the cellar bin
The rumbling sound
Of load on load of apples coming in.
For I have had too much
Of apple-picking: I am overtired
Of the great harvest I myself desired.
There were ten thousand thousand fruit to touch,
Cherish in hand, lift down, and not let fall.

For all
That struck the earth,
No matter if not bruised or spiked with stubble,
Went surely to the cider-apple heap
As of no worth.
One can see what will trouble
This sleep of mine, whatever sleep it is.
Were he not gone,
The woodchuck could say whether it's like his
Long sleep, as I describe its coming on,
Or just some human sleep.

ROBERT FROST (1874–1963)

[Ciaran Carson also chose 'After Apple-Picking' in Lifelines 2. Ciaran Carson wrote:
My favourite poem is 'After Apple-Picking' *by Robert Frost, which I have loved ever since I came across it in a school anthology. It's a beautifully subtle piece of work, in which the craft is almost invisible. As my old English teacher, Brother Hickey, told us at the time, 'Every line in the poem rhymes with another one, though you'd hardly know it when you read it out.'*

After some thirty years of reading it off and on, I am not entirey clear what it's all about, though the ordinary speech rhythms lull you into thinking that you know. The last lines are especially mysterious. Memory, anticipation, art, time . . . the big themes are all in there: emotion recollected in tranquillity. I've just read it again, and it gets better every time.]

PAULINE McLYNN ACTOR

1997

Dear All,

Enclosed is a poem for inclusion in Lifelines 3, *and a little piece as to why. If it has been done before (it hasn't, has it?), please let me know and I'll find another.*

Good luck with the venture,

Pauline McLynn

A lot of my favourite poems have already been covered in the previous two volumes in this series. But here's one from Michael Gorman that I love. Like me, he was born in Sligo and has lived in Galway (I grew up there). And I had the pleasure of hearing him read this aloud in 1984 at the launch of his book, Waiting for the Sky to Fall. *To me it describes an Ireland that we're leaving behind as we approach the twenty-first century, and that we are leaving it is no harm, I think. And it reminds me in a bitter-sweet way of my child-hood and especially summers spent in Sligo.*

The People I Grew Up With Were Afraid

The people I grew up with were afraid.
They were alone too long in waiting-rooms,
in dispensaries and in offices whose functions
they did not understand.

To buck themselves up, they thought
of lost causes, of 'Nature-boy'
O'Dea who tried to fly
from his bedroom window;
of the hunch-backed, little typist
who went roller-skating at Strandhill.
Or, they re-lived the last afternoon
of Benny Kirwin, pale, bald,
Protestant shop-assistant in Lydons' drapery.
One Wednesday, the town's half-day,
he hanged himself from a tree
on the shore at Lough Gill.

And what were they afraid of? Rent
collectors, rate collectors, insurance men.
Things to do with money. But,
especially of their vengeful God.
On her death-bed, Ena Phelan prayed
that her son would cut his hair.

Sometimes, they return to me,
Summer lunchtimes, colcannon
for the boys, back-doors
of all the houses open, the
news blaring on the radios.
Our mother's factory pay-packet
is sitting in the kitchen press
and our father, without
humour or relief, is
waiting for the sky to fall.

MICHAEL GORMAN (B. 1952)

A 'favourite poem' is an elusive idea – one likes different poems for different reasons at different times in different moods. But I'll nominate Larkin's 'Whitsun Weddings', which would be remarkable as descriptive prose if it were in prose, and is miraculous in its organisation as poetry; and mainly for the last two lines, most of all for the final three words which always give me a kick, after hundreds of readings (and which Kingsley Amis somewhere says are meaningless).

Tom Stoppard

The Whitsun Weddings

That Whitsun, I was late getting away:
    Not till about
One-twenty on the sunlit Saturday
Did my three-quarters-empty train pull out,
All windows down, all cushions hot, all sense
Of being in a hurry gone. We ran
Behind the backs of houses, crossed a street
Of blinding windscreens, smelt the fish-dock; thence
The river's level drifting breadth began,
Where sky and Lincolnshire and water meet.

All afternoon, through the tall heat that slept
    For miles inland,
A slow and stopping curve southwards we kept.
Wide farms went by, short-shadowed cattle, and
Canals with floatings of industrial froth;
A hothouse flashed uniquely: hedges dipped
And rose: and now and then a smell of grass
Displaced the reek of buttoned carriage-cloth
Until the next town, new and nondescript,
Approached with acres of dismantled cars.

At first, I didn't notice what a noise
    The weddings made
Each station that we stopped at: sun destroys
The interest of what's happening in the shade,
And down the long cool platforms whoops and skirls
I took for porters larking with the mails,
And went on reading. Once we started, though,
We passed them, grinning and pomaded, girls
In parodies of fashion, heels and veils,
All posed irresolutely, watching us go,

As if out on the end of an event
    Waving goodbye
To something that survived it. Struck, I leant
More promptly out next time, more curiously,
And saw it all again in different terms:
The fathers with broad belts under their suits
And seamy foreheads; mothers loud and fat;
An uncle shouting smut; and then the perms,
The nylon gloves and jewellery-substitutes,
The lemons, mauves, and olive-ochres that

Marked off the girls unreally from the rest.
    Yes, from cafés
And banquet-halls up yards, and bunting-dressed
Coach-party annexes, the wedding-days
Were coming to an end. All down the line
Fresh couples climbed aboard: the rest stood round;
The last confetti and advice were thrown,
And, as we moved, each face seemed to define
Just what it saw departing: children frowned
At something dull; fathers had never known

Success so huge and wholly farcical;
    The women shared
The secret like a happy funeral;
While girls, gripping their handbags tighter, stared
At a religious wounding. Free at last,
And loaded with the sum of all they saw,
We hurried towards London, shuffling gouts of steam.
Now fields were building-plots, and poplars cast
Long shadows over major roads, and for
Some fifty minutes, that in time would seem

Just long enough to settle hats and say
    I nearly died,
A dozen marriages got under way.
They watched the landscape, sitting side by side
— An Odeon went past, a cooling tower,
And someone running up to bowl — and none
Thought of the others they would never meet
Or how their lives would all contain this hour.
I thought of London spread out in the sun,
Its postal districts packed like squares of wheat:

There we were aimed. And as we raced across
    Bright knots of rail
Past standing Pullmans, walls of blackened moss
Came close, and it was nearly done, this frail
Travelling coincidence; and what it held
Stood ready to be loosed with all the power
That being changed can give. We slowed again,
And as the tightened brakes took hold, there swelled
A sense of falling, like an arrow-shower
Sent out of sight, somewhere becoming rain.

PHILIP LARKIN (1922–1985)

CATHERINE BYRNE   ACTOR

20 January 1997

Dear Ralph, Caroline and Gareth,

I just loved Lifelines *and* Lifelines 2 *and feel honoured to be asked to contribute to*
Lifelines 3. *I have chosen Seamus Heaney's* 'At the Wellhead' *as it recalls an especially
happy theatrical memory for me. In 1995 during rehearsals for Brian Friel's* Molly
Sweeney, *many discussions took place concerning the portrayal of the Blind Woman, who
is the play's namesake, and the part I was attempting to play.*

   *At the end of a long day, Brian showed me this wonderful poem, and I was profoundly
moved by it. 'What a marvellous description of her eyes,' I said. 'Could we have that
tomorrow at 10 a.m.?' smoothly requested the playwright.*

   I could but try.

Best wishes and much love,

Catherine Byrne

At the Wellhead

Your songs, when you sing them with your two eyes closed
As you always do, are like a local road
We've known every turn of in the past —
That midge-veiled, high-hedged side-road where you stood
Looking and listening until a car
Would come and go and leave you lonelier
Than you had been to begin with. So, sing on,
Dear shut-eyed one, dear far-voiced veteran,

Sing yourself to where the singing comes from,
Ardent and cut off like our blind neighbour
Who played the piano all day in her bedroom.
Her notes came out to us like hoisted water
Ravelling off a bucket at the wellhead
Where next thing we'd be listening, hushed and awkward.

That blind-from-birth, sweet-voiced, withdrawn musician
Was like a silver vein in heavy clay.
Night water glittering in the light of day.
But also just our neighbour, Rosie Keenan.
She touched our cheeks. She let us touch her braille
In books like books wallpaper patterns came in.
Her hands were active and her eyes were full
Of open darkness and a watery shine.

She knew us by our voices. She'd say she 'saw'
Whoever or whatever. Being with her
Was intimate and helpful, like a cure
You didn't notice happening. When I read
A poem with Keenan's well in it, she said,
'I can see the sky at the bottom of it now.'

SEAMUS HEANEY (B. 1939)

MICHEÁL Ó MUIRCHEARTAIGH   BROADCASTER

2006

The poem 'To a Skylark' has been a favourite of mine since it first came to my notice while at school. It hit a chord principally because it described with a most magical and musical anthology of words a sound I was very familiar with almost from birth.

It was the one that greeted me as I roamed through the fields in my early childhood and it seemed then every bit as fascinating as the lyrics in that superb opening verse of Shelley's depiction of the charms of a skylark's performance.

Thanks be to God the lark population is as large as ever and I look forward to my frequent trips into the open countryside simply to hear one of the wonders of the aural world. One does not have to travel far beyond the bounds of any town or city to hear larks in full flow and they seem at their heavenly best when soaring and singing simultaneously above the many golf courses of Ireland.

It is obvious from the poem that Shelley was both impressed and inspired by nature's free show running daily from dawn to early afternoon – 'like an unbodied joy whose race is just begun'.

Micheál Ó Muircheartaigh

from *To A Skylark*

Hail to thee, blithe Spirit!
   Bird thou never wert,
That from Heaven or near it,
   Pourest thy full heart
In profuse strains of unpremeditated art.

Higher still and higher
    From the earth thou springest
Like a cloud of fire;
    The blue deep thou wingest,
And singing still dost soar, and soaring ever singest.

In the golden light'ning
    Of the sunken Sun,
O'er which clouds are bright'ning,
    Thou dost float and run,
Like an unbodied joy whose race is just begun.

*

What thou art we know not;
    What is most like thee?
Frrom rainbow clouds there flow not
    Drops so bright to see
As from thy presence showers a rain of melody.

We look before and after,
    And pine for what is not:
Our sincerest laughter
    With some pain is fraught;
Our sweetest songs are those that tell of saddest thought.

Yet, if we could scorn
    Hate, and pride, and fear;
If we were things born
    Not to shed a tear,
I know not how thy joy we ever should come near.

Better than all measures
    Of delightful sound,
Better than all treasures
    That in books are found,
Thy skill to poet were, thou scorner of the ground!

Teach me half the gladness
    That thy brain must know;
Such harmonious madness
    From my lips would flow,
The world should listen then, as I am listening now.

PERCY BYSSHE SHELLEY (1792–1822)

HAROLD PINTER

10 March 1997

Dear Ralph Croly, Caroline Dowling and Gareth McCluskey,

This is certainly my favourite love poem. It is the most tender of poems and its voice is like no other.

Yours sincerely,

Harold Pinter

I Leave This at Your Ear
for Nessie Dunsmuir

I leave this at your ear for when you wake,
A creature in its abstract cage asleep.
Your dreams blindfold you by the light they make.

The owl called from the naked-woman tree
As I came down by the Kyle farm to hear
Your house silent by the speaking sea.

I have come late but I have come before
Later with slaked steps from stone to stone
To hope to find you listening for the door.

I stand in the ticking room. My dear, I take
A moth kiss from your breath. The shore gulls cry.
I leave this at your ear for when you wake.

W S GRAHAM (1918–1986)

MARIAN KEYES NOVELIST

12 January 1997

Dear Ralph, Caroline and Gareth,

Thank you very much for your letter asking me to contribute to Lifelines 3. *I'm honoured to be asked and delighted to be part of such a worthy project. My favourite poem – and has been for as long as I can remember – is 'The Wayfarer', the very last poem that Pádraig Pearse wrote, shortly before he was executed.*

It conveys with exquisite poignancy how laughably short our little lives are. And I also find it fascinating to be given a glimpse into his head at such a unique, terrible time – it's almost like having a type of bizarre live video link-up with the past.

I'm deeply moved by the courage shown in the poem, by Pearse's unflinching acceptance of his fate, as he already mourns his own passing.

I wish you great success with the venture and thanks again for asking me to contribute.

Yours sincerely,

Marian Keyes

The Wayfarer

The beauty of the world hath made me sad,
This beauty that will pass;
Sometimes my heart hath shaken with great joy
To see a leaping squirrel in a tree,
Or a red lady-bird upon a stalk,
Or little rabbits in a field at evening,
Lit by a slanting sun,
Or some green hill where shadows drifted by
Some quiet hill where mountainy man hath sown
And soon would reap; near to the gate of Heaven;
Or children with bare feet upon the sands
Of some ebbed sea, or playing on the streets
Of little towns in Connacht,
Things young and happy.
And then my heart hath told me:
These will pass,
Will pass and change, will die and be no more,
Things bright and green, things young and happy;
And I have gone upon my way
Sorrowful.

PÁDRAIG PEARSE (1879–1916)

JAMES HANLEY   ARTIST

1 February 1994

Dear Ewan, Áine and Christopher,

Many thanks for your kind invitation to nominate my favourite poem for your forthcoming publication. I am delighted to accept your offer, and I congratulate your efforts for such an interesting project and towards such a worthwhile end.

I have many favourite poems and it was difficult to select one that would be of real interest to a reader of the collection. Many of the poems I considered would be too well known, or at least the poets involved would be too well known.

I decided therefore to select a poem by Oliver Dunne, a young poet and friend of mine. We went to university together and since then Oliver has pursued post-graduate work, written reviews and published his own poetry. His unique style and quirky black humour appeals to me, and is not unlike a thread of humour that runs through my own work.

I wish you all the best of luck with Lifelines *and hope that it will be a success.*

Yours sincerely,

James Hanley

Uh-Oh

(The last words spoken by the captain of the spaceship Challenger*)*

uh-oh
he said

they were
at
the pinnacle
of human
achievement

they wore
white space-suits

he had talked
to
the president
on the
telephone
the day before

little boys
played with
models
of their
spaceship

they were headed
straight up

he had kissed
his girl-friend
the night before

tired his mind
on other things

she touched
his tense muscles

'it's just a job
to those guys'

his mother couldn't
think of what
to give him

settled on
home-made jam
for his wife

it was a life
he hadn't
really chosen

he had just
over-achieved

what had the
president
said?

his wife asked

oh, i don't know

it wasn't like
they were going
to the moon

that had been
done
already

good luck, i suppose

good luck
yes
that was probably it

that was probably
what the president
had said

words to that effect

and now the little
meter
had gone red
all of a sudden
and there was
nothing he could do

no split-second
decision

taken out
of his hands

just a little
surprised

that the routine
should be
interrupted
like that

OLIVER DUNNE (B.1961)

I like this poem because, knowing Oliver, I can relate to his quirky vision of life. It is not dissimilar to a thread of black humour that is in my own painting. The simplicity of the language and its easy flow mocks the grandeur of the event without offending the victims. The arrogance so often close to achievement is exposed as pure folly. The flight had become routine. All that sophistication could not compensate for human error. The banality of the President's words, for me, sums up the feeling that tragedy is soon forgotten. Myths collapse. It's yesterday's news. Life goes on.

James Hanley

ROBERT PINSKY POET

10 March 1993

Dear Ewan Gibson, Áine Jackson and Christopher Pillow:

Thanks for your letter about your planned anthology. Good luck to you in this excellent project.

Difficult though it is for me to choose one poem as a favourite, my choice seems clear: 'Sailing to Byzantium' by William Butler Yeats.

It is a great poem, but many of my reasons for choosing it are personal, even coincidental. It happens to be the first poem of its caliber that I recognized with an inner conviction, and the first that I got by heart. Also, when I ask myself about the poem's central place for me, it seems obvious that I must have been attracted by the way it implies a definition of my vocation, the study and pursuit of poetry. The poem associates the art of poetry not only with music, the art I strove to master before I made a lifework of poetry, but also with certain arts of the hand: mosaic-making and a kind of jeweler's tinkering, efforts to make something beautiful by hammering and assembling many different pieces, a kind of undertaking that I think has had some kind of special appeal for me. I think that the poem's idea of poetry as musical, historical, and involving a kind of improvisatory skill – the inventive fitting together of disparate pieces to create something that has pattern or animation – appeals to me quite apart from any glorification of poetry.

But I do have to admit that the glorification has appealed to me, too: the heroic and possibly extravagant terms in which Yeats beseeches the help of his singing masters – 'Consume my heart away; sick with desire/And fastened to a dying animal/It knows not what it is' – continue to move me, continue to express a tremendous reality. These lines present the glory of struggle, however: of effort rooted in desperate yearning. The poem's title denotes a process.

It occurs to me that a still more personal reason for my particular attachment to this poem, out of so many that I revere, may be that unlike other profound works by, for instance, George Herbert, John Donne or Gerard Manley Hopkins, 'Sailing to Byzantium' stands somewhat apart from or beyond Christianity: reading it, I need not feel any sharpening of my sense that the poems I love best, and the language to which I devote my life, are somehow divided from me, or less mine to love, simply because they are Christian, while I – a pagan humanist raised as an Orthodox Jew – am not Christian. Perhaps Yeats's 'holy city', being at least half pagan, has represented for me a kind of holiness to

---

which I have felt intuitively welcome. Byzantium represents a spiritual force not as secular as that in great poems by Keats or Stevens. In Yeats's words and images I sensed at once, before I learned anything about his ideas – some of them perhaps foolish in themselves – the vision of a spiritual reality that includes historical religion, but reaches beyond it. That inclusion, and that reaching, continue to have a powerful significance for me.

When I was seventeen I typed out the words of 'Sailing to Byzantium' and stuck the page on my kitchen wall, above the toaster. Now many years later my thoughts about poetry still return often to such phrases as 'the artifice of eternity', or 'Whatever is begotten, born, and dies' or that other triad, 'Of what is past, or passing, or to come'. And in such thoughts, or on a more mundane level whenever I think about my profession of teaching writing and literature, I come inevitably to the words 'Nor is there singing school but studying/Monuments of its own magnificence.' The principle in these lines – that one learns by paying close attention to the most magnificent, enduring models to be found – is endlessly humbling and inspiring.

Robert Pinsky

[John Montague also chose 'Sailing to Byzantium' in *Lifelines*. John Montague wrote:
It is hard for me to choose one poem, but If I had to it would probably be 'Sailing to Byzantium'. I love its defiance, its clangour, and while I have no desire to be a golden bird, I recognise and enjoy the final flourish, oratorical though it be!]

Sailing to Byzantium

I

That is no country for old men. The young
In one another's arms, birds in the trees,
—Those dying generations—at their song,
The salmon-falls, the mackerel-crowded seas,
Fish, flesh, or fowl, commend all summer long
Whatever is begotten, born, and dies.
Caught in that sensual music all neglect
Monuments of unageing intellect.

II

An aged man is but a paltry thing,
A tattered coat upon a stick, unless
Soul clap its hands and sing, and louder sing
For every tatter in its mortal dress,
Nor is there singing school but studying
Monuments of its own magnificence;
And therefore I have sailed the seas and come
To the holy city of Byzantium.

III

O sages standing in God's holy fire
As in the gold mosaic of a wall,
Come from the holy fire, perne in a gyre,
And be the singing-masters of my soul.
Consume my heart away; sick with desire
And fastened to a dying animal
It knows not what it is; and gather me
Into the artifice of eternity.

IV

Once out of nature I shall never take
My bodily form from any natural thing,
But such a form as Grecian goldsmiths make
Of hammered gold and gold enamelling
To keep a drowsy Emperor awake;
Or set upon a golden bough to sing
To lords and ladies of Byzantium
Of what is past, or passing, or to come.

W B Yeats (1865–1939)

4 January 1997

Dear Ralph, Caroline and Gareth,

Thank you for inviting me to contribute to the next volume of Lifelines.

It is an honour to do so. I have greatly admired the diverse literary richness of the earlier volumes and the manner in which the proceeds have helped to alleviate suffering in the Third World.

Hilaire Belloc, like his friend and contemporary G K Chesterton, is no longer a fashionable figure, but the energy of 'The Winged Horse', the sheer exuberance and joy of its many rhythms, has made it very special to me since I first came across it many years ago. It is not a great poem but it has those difficult-to-define qualities that make it unforgettable.

Yours sincerely,

Kevin Casey

The Winged Horse

It's ten years ago today you turned me out o' doors
To cut my feet on flinty lands and stumble down the shores
And I thought about the all-in-all, oh more than I can tell!
But I caught a horse to ride upon and I rode him very well,
He had flames behind the eyes of him and wings upon his side
And I ride, and I ride!

I rode him out of Wantage and I rode him up the hill,
And there I saw the Beacon in the morning standing still,
Inkpen and Hackpen and southward and away
High through the middle airs in the strengthening of the day,
And there I saw the channel-glint and England in her pride
And I ride, and I ride!

And once a-top of Lambourne down towards the hill of Clere
I saw the Host of Heaven in rank and Michael with his spear,
And Turpin out of Gascony and Charlemagne the Lord
And Roland of the marshes with his hand upon his sword
For the time he should have need of it, and forty more beside
And I ride, and I ride!

For you that took the all-in-all, the things you left were three.
A loud voice for singing and keen eyes to see
And a spouting well of joy within that never yet was dried!
And I ride.

HILAIRE BELLOC (1870–1953)

Dear Lifeliners,

My chosen poem is the lyrics of the song 'Like a Rolling Stone' *by Bob Dylan.*

  The first time poetry came alive for me was hearing Bob Dylan sing it, shortly after I left school. In the classroom, poetry had been something to analyse and struggle through, and here was a man who delivered his lines incantationally, to music. It was a strong, vivid sensation which pulled you deeper in. The style of the language in 'Like a Rolling Stone' *is still what I look for in poetry. I'm not into poems as intellectual crossword puzzles, castrated things leached of guts and blood. The language in* 'Like A Rolling Stone' *is not vague and precious. The images are concrete and visual, conjuring pictures and stories, and so rich that I can listen to them. Here I am, twenty years later, still amused. 'At Napoleon in rags. And the language that he used . . .'*

Best wishes,

Philip

Like a Rolling Stone

> Once upon a time you dressed so fine
> You threw the bums a dime in your prime, didn't you?
> People'd call, say, 'beware doll, you're bound to fall'
> You thought they were all kiddin' you
> You used to laugh about
> Everybody that was hangin' out
> Now you don't talk so loud
> Now you don't seem so proud
> About having to be scrounging for your next meal.
>
> How does it feel
> How does it feel
> To be without a home
> Like a complete unknown
> Like a rolling stone?
>
> You've gone to the finest school all right, miss lonely
> But you know you only used to get juiced in it
> And nobody has ever taught you how to live on the street
> And now you find out you're gonna have to get used to it
> You said you'd never compromise
> With the mystery tramp, but now you realize
> He's not selling any alibis
> As you stare into the vacuum of his eyes
> And ask him do you want to make a deal?

How does it feel
How does it feel
To be on your own
With no direction home
Like a complete unknown
Like a rolling stone?

You never turned around to see the frowns on the jugglers and the clowns
When they all come down and did tricks for you
You never understood that it ain't no good
You shouldn't let other people get your kicks for you
You used to ride on the chrome horse with your diplomat
Who carried on his shoulder a Siamese cat
Ain't it hard when you discover that
He really wasn't where its at
After he took from you everything he could steal.

How does it feel
How does it feel
To be on your own
With no direction home
Like a complete unknown
Like a rolling stone?

Princess on the steeple and all the pretty people
They're drinkin', thinkin' that they got it made
Exchanging all kinds of precious gifts and things
But you'd better lift your diamond ring, you'd better pawn it babe
You used to be so amused
At Napoleon in rags and the language that he used
Go to him now, he calls you, you can't refuse
When you got nothing, you got nothing to lose
You're invisible now, you got no secrets to conceal.

How does it feel
How does it feel
To be on your own
With no direction home
Like a complete unknown
Like a rolling stone?

BOB DYLAN (B. 1941)

SELIMA HILL

18 February 1997

Dear Ralph, Caroline and Gareth,

Thank you for your letter about Lifelines.
My favourite poem is this anonymous, title-less poem:

> Westron wynde when wyll thow blow
> the smalle rayne downe can rayne —
> Cryst if my love wer in my armys
> and I yn my bed agayne!

ANONYMOUS

I love all its reckless 'w's and 'y's; I love the way it seems to fly somewhere beyond spelling, punctuation, grammar, even meteorology; the way it reminds us how beautiful and sad things are. Poets today don't seem to let themselves write like this, and poetry is so good at it. In fact, that's what it's for. I wish I wrote more lyrically myself and I don't know why I don't. It may be old-fashioned, but I like poetry not only to play but to yearn.

Any one of the magical poems in Michael Longley's Gorse Fires (1991) or The Ghost Orchid (1995) would be my contemporary choice.

Thank you again for inviting me to contribute; I am delighted to be involved and wish the anthology every possible success.

Selima Hill

15 January 1997

Dear Ralph, Caroline and Gareth,

Thank you for your letter. I am honoured that you should want me to choose a poem for the new Lifelines *anthology. I think it is a wonderful idea and greatly to your credit that you are working so hard to make it happen. Here is the poem I have chosen, followed by a few lines on my choice.*

September Evening
Deer at Big Basin

When they talk about angels in books
I think what they mean is this sudden
arrival: this gift of an alien country
we guessed all along,

and how these deer are moving in the dark,
bound to the silence, finding our scent in their way
and making us strange, making us all that we are
in the fall of the light,

as if we had entered the myth
of one who is risen, and one who is left behind
in the gap that remains,

a story that gives us the questions we wanted to ask,
and our sense of our presence as creatures,
about to be touched.

JOHN BURNSIDE (B.1955)

I have many favourite poems – it isn't easy to select one – but this is a favourite poem from a Scots poet whose work I love because of his sense of the visionary in the ordinary, and because of the intent quietness of his voice.

Good luck in your enterprise,

Kerry Hardie

Dear Dónal, Caroline, and Stephanie,

Thank you for inviting me to contribute to Lifelines, *and sorry about my late reply.*

   Although I have no favourite poem, there are some poems I return to repeatedly. Really special and rare poems appear fresh and new with each reading. One of these is George Herbert's 'Love (III)'. This has always seemed to me as near perfection as poetry gets. In one way it is very simple (I won't use the word 'deceptively'), it describes the gradual seduction of the soul by divine love. But it entwines images of divine and profane love in a sophisticated and playful way: 'Who made the eyes but I?', for example, puns on the idea of amorously 'making eyes', and God as the creator of those eyes. If John Donne's metaphysical poetry is all sound and fury and exhortation: 'Batter my heart, three person'd God', Herbert's is always mild and serene and gleaming. This poem has the supernatural beauty of a prayer. The French religious philosopher Simone Weil loved it and had her first mystical experience while reciting it to herself like a mantra. But even if you are not religious, 'Love (III)' is a demonstration of the perfection of which language is capable, and it is deeply moving whether you regard it as a perfect prayer, or a perfect poem, or both at the same time.

   All the very best with the Lifelines *project.*

Yours,

Caitríona O'Reilly

Love (III)

Love bade me welcome: yet my soul drew back,
      Guiltie of dust and sinne.
But quick-ey'd Love, observing me grow slack
      From my first entrance in,
Drew nearer to me, sweetly questioning,
      If I lack'd any thing.

A guest, I answer'd, worthy to be here:
      Love said, You shall be he.
I the unkinde, ungratefull? Ah my deare,
      I cannot look on thee.
Love took my hand, and smiling did reply,
      Who made the eyes but I?

Truth Lord, but I have marr'd them: let my shame
      Go where it doth deserve.
And know you not, sayes Love, who bore the blame?
      My deare, then I will serve.
You must sit down, sayes Love, and taste my meat:
      So I did sit and eat.

GEORGE HERBERT (1593–1633)

1997

Dear Ralph, Caroline and Gareth,

Thank you for asking me to select a poem. I do so with pleasure. This is called 'Málaga' and it is by Pearse Hutchinson. I wish you and your venture every success.

Yours with all best wishes,

Colm Tóibín

I love how sensuous this poem is, how steeped it is in the pleasure of sights and smells. I love how the complex diction plays against the ballad rhythms and the simple rhyme scheme. It seems to me to be a quintessential Irish poem because I can hear in its rhythms the sound of a Gaelic poem, and I can feel the sense of wonder and joy and release of someone being in the south of Europe who is used to the north. It is a poem that never fails to make me feel happy and glad to be alive.

Málaga
(for Sammy Sheridan)

The scent of unseen jasmine on the warm night beach.

The tram along the sea-road all the way from town
through its wide open sides drank unseen jasmine down.
Living was nothing all those nights but that strong flower,
whose hidden voice on darkness grew to such mad power
I could have sworn for once I travelled through full peace
and even love at last had perfect calm release
only by breathing in the unseen jasmine scent,
that ruled us and the summer every hour we went.

The tranquil unrushed wine drunk on the daytime beach.
Or from an open room all that our sight could reach
was heat, sea, light, unending images of peace;
and then at last the night brought jasmine's great release —
not images but calm uncovetous content,
the wide-eyed heart alert at rest in June's own scent.

In daytime's humdrum town from small child after child
we bought cluster on cluster of the star flower's wild
white widowed heads, re-wired on strong weed stalks they'd trimmed
to long green elegance; but still the whole month brimmed
at night along the beach with a strong voice like peace;
and each morning the mind stayed crisp in such release.

Some hint of certainty, still worth longing I could teach,
lies lost in a strength of jasmine down a summer beach.

PEARSE HUTCHINSON (B. 1927)

April 1994

Dear Ewan, Áine and Christopher,

I was really delighted to receive your letter requesting me to contribute to your new edition of Lifelines. *To be honest, I am not a great reader of poetry books. However, I was given two copies of* Lifelines *last year; one by Wesley College when I had the great pleasure of presenting prizes at Prize Day. These two copies are placed strategically around the house and I have now discovered the joy of reading poems at odd quiet moments of the day, whilst also enjoying the comments accompanying them.*

Poetry has always been significant to me in the context of its setting to music. Of all the many songs I am familiar with, either from performing them myself or listening to others performing them, one particular song and poem continues to haunt me. W B Yeats's 'He Wishes for the Cloths of Heaven' is set to music by the English composer Thomas Frederick Dunhill. In this simple and evocative setting the composer, I feel, has enhanced Yeats's poem, so that the poignancy of the words linger on in the memory.

Wishing you continued success with this wonderful project.

Yours sincerely,

Judith Woodworth

He Wishes for the Cloths of Heaven

Had I the heavens' embroidered cloths,
Enwrought with golden and silver light,
The blue and the dim and the dark cloths
Of night and light and the half-light,
I would spread the cloths under your feet:
But I, being poor, have only my dreams;
I have spread my dreams under your feet;
Tread softly because you tread on my dreams.

W B YEATS (1865–1939)

['*He Wishes for the Cloths of Heaven*' has been chosen also by Brian Boydell, Brian Leyden and Michael Mortell in *Lifelines 2* and by Paul Carson in *Lifelines 3*.]

Brian Boydell wrote:

When asked to name my favourite poem, musical composition or composer, I find it impossible to give a simple reply. My taste changes with the passing of time, and with changes of mood. I cannot therefore name 'my favourite poem'. The answer might well be different tomorrow, or next year, or from what I might have named a decade ago.

The poetry of W B Yeats has, however, remained very special for me for as long as sixty years. It evokes the timeless magic of the Irish landscape which has inspired so much of my music.

The three early poems of Yeats which have constantly held a special place in my mind have all been firmly implanted through musical settings: the first I have set myself, the other two are included in Peter Warlock's wonderfully moving song-cycle entitled 'The Curlew'.

Brian Leyden wrote:

What to choose? There is Patrick Kavanagh's master-work, 'The Great Hunger'. A poem I love, though big and awkward like the man himself. And I treat it as a poem to read, not recite. No. It will have to be W B Yeats. the young and the living poets object. But if I give in to those clamouring voices, this letter will never be written. 'He Wishes for the Cloths of Heaven' is easily remembered, heartfelt and utterly Romantic. Not exactly a party piece, but I have found it useful when concerned by in-laws and relations who tell me being a writer is fine, but would I not like a proper job?

Michael Mortell wrote:

'He wishes for the Cloths of Heaven' by W B Yeats has been a poem close to my heart since I first read it about fifteen years ago. In this short poem, Yeats captures for me the two great abiding elements of love – its magic and its frailty.

Paul Carson wrote:

There is one poem I recall vividly and which I enjoyed. It is by William Butler Yeats, 'He Wishes for the Cloths of Heaven'. It is particularly apt in medicine because so many of our patients are so unwell they have nothing left but their dreams.]

ARTHUR MILLER PLAYWRIGHT

10 February 1997

How about 'The Diviner' by Heaney?

>Cut from the green hedge a forked hazel stick . . .

The poem evokes the magic of the creative person, the one who knows without knowing, who is in touch with hidden, ultimate things. And in so few words!

Arthur Miller

The Diviner

Cut from the green hedge a forked hazel stick
That he held tight by the arms of the V:
Circling the terrain, hunting the pluck
Of water, nervous, but professionally

Unfussed. The pluck came sharp as a sting.
The rod jerked with precise convulsions,
Spring water suddenly broadcasting
Through a green hazel its secret stations.

The bystanders would ask to have a try.
He handed them the rod without a word.
It lay dead in their grasp till, nonchalantly,
He gripped expectant wrists. The hazel stirred.

SEAMUS HEANEY (B. 1939)

Stand Magazine
5 February 1997

Dear Ralph, Caroline and Gareth,

You have asked me for a few lines for Lifelines; *here they are:*

> Earth! have they gone into you?
> Somewhere they must have gone,
>
> And flung on your hard back
> Is their souls' sack,
> Emptied of God-ancestralled essences.

This comes from 'Dead Man's Dump' by Isaac Rosenberg, a poet killed in the First World War who, even more than the Christian Wilfred Owen, attempted to consider the spiritual problems of what killing each other entails. These lines engage with this, I believe.

Yours,

Jon Silkin

Dead Man's Dump

> The plunging limbers over the shattered track
> Racketed with their rusty freight,
> Stuck out like many crowns of thorns,
> And the rusty stakes like sceptres old
> To stay the flood of brutish men
> Upon our brothers dear.
>
> The wheels lurched over sprawled dead
> But pained them not, though their bones crunched,
> Their shut mouths made no moan,
> They lie there huddled, friend and foeman,
> Man born of man, and born of woman,
> And shells go crying over them
> From night till night and now.
>
> Earth has waited for them
> All the time of their growth
> Fretting for their decay:
> Now she has them at last!
> In the strength of their strength
> Suspended — stopped and held.

What fierce imaginings their dark souls lit
Earth! have they gone into you?
Somewhere they must have gone,
And flung on your hard back
Is their souls' sack,
Emptied of God-ancestralled essences.
Who hurled them out? Who hurled?

None saw their spirits' shadow shake the grass,
Or stood aside for the half-used life to pass
Out of those doomed nostrils and the doomed mouth,
When the swift iron burning bee
Drained the wild honey of their youth.

What of us, who flung on the shrieking pyre,
Walk, our usual thoughts untouched,
Our lucky limbs as on ichor fed,
Immortal seeming ever?
Perhaps when the flames beat loud on us,
A fear may choke in our veins
And the startled blood may stop.

The air is loud with death,
The dark air spurts with fire
The explosions ceaseless are.
Timelessly now, some minutes past,
These dead strode time with vigorous life,
Till the shrapnel called 'an end!'
But not to all. In bleeding pangs
Some borne on stretchers dreamed of home,
Dear things, war-blotted from their hearts.

A man's brains splattered on
A stretcher-bearer's face;
His shook shoulders slipped their load,
But when they bent to look again
The drowning soul was sunk too deep
For human tenderness.

They left this dead with the older dead,
Stretched at the cross roads.
Burnt black by strange decay,
Their sinister faces lie
The lid over each eye,
The grass and coloured clay
More motion have than they,
Joined to the great sunk silences.

Here is one not long dead;
His dark hearing caught our far wheels,
And the choked soul stretched weak hands
To reach the living world the far wheels said,
The blood-dazed intelligence beating for light,
Crying through the suspense of the far torturing wheels
Swift for the end to break,
Or the wheels to break,
Cried as the tide of the world broke over his sight.

Will they come? Will they ever come?
Even as the mixed hoofs of the mules,
The quivering-bellied mules,
And the rushing wheels all mixed
With his tortured upturned sight,
So we crashed round the bend,
We heard his weak scream,
We heard his very last sound,
And our wheels grazed his dead face.

ISAAC ROSENBERG (1890–1918)

FIACH MACCONGHAIL   THEATRE DIRECTOR

2006

Dear Dónal, Caroline and Stephanie

Many apologies for not replying to you any sooner. Thank you for inviting me to participate in this great project, indeed I have the previous publications stacked conveniently on my bookshelf.

I would like to pick a poem by Michael Hartnett. I have never met him and I discovered his immense poetry only four years ago. In my opinion his poetry gives such a devastating, honest account of life and humanity in Ireland and I do think that he has not gained the wide recognition he deserved. It was he who said that 'the act of poetry is a rebel act' and his powerful poems help me engage with where I live and how I should make sense of family, friends and language.

I would like to include 'Poem for Lara, 10' in your collection as it is a simple love poem to his own daughter and the wonderful 'grace' or blessing he wishes to bestow on her with the last two lines. My second daughter Luisne is 10 this year and there is no other way that I can tell her how much I love her, than through this poem.

Go fada buan do shaothar.

Hope this is OK.

Best and good luck.

Fiach Mac Conghail
Amharclann na Mainistreach/The Abbey Theatre

Poem for Lara, 10

An ashtree on fire
the hair of your head
coaxing larks
with your sweet voice
in the green grass,
a crowd of daisies
playing with you,
a crowd of rabbits
dancing with you,
the blackbird
with its gold bill
is a jewel for you,
the goldfinch
with its sweetness
is your music.
You are perfume,
you are honey,
a wild strawberry:
even the bees think you
a flower in the field.
Little queen of the land of books,
may you always be thus,
may you ever be free
        from sorrow-chains.

Here's my blessing for you, girl,
and it is no petty grace —
may you have the beauty of your mother's soul
        and the beauty of her face.

MICHAEL HARTNETT (1941–1999)

17 January 1988

Dear Julie, Jonathan and Duncan,

Thank you for asking me to contribute to your book in aid of the Third World. Naturally I'm happy to do so, but I find it an extra-ordinarily difficult task. Because I'm involved with poetry all the time I have hundreds of favourite poems, and I'm constantly adding new ones or changing my mind about old ones. I couldn't possibly settle for one. (Also some of them are far too long for your purpose.)

So what I'm sending you is a poem which has been one of my favourites for a long time: John Donne's sonnet 'Death be not proud' (not a very original choice, I'm afraid). Like many people's favourites, it's one that I've known by heart since I was at school: this means that I don't need to look it up when I want to be reminded of it; it's a permanent fixture in my mind. It's the kind of poem that would be comforting in circumstances of desperation or extremity, such as in prison or during a war – or so I imagine. It was included in the second book of poetry I ever bought (at 16; the first was by T S Eliot). I'm enclosing a copy of the text in the original spelling.

And good luck with the project!

Yours sincerely,

Fleur Adcock

Death Be Not Proud

Death be not proud, though some have called thee
Mighty and dreadfull, for, thou art not soe,
For, those, whom thou think'st, thou dost overthrow,
Die not, poore death, nor yet canst thou kill mee.
From rest and sleepe, which but thy pictures bee,
Much pleasure, then from thee, much more must flow,
And soonest our best men with thee doe goe,
Rest of their bones, and soules deliverie.
Thou are slave to Fate, Chance, kings, and desperate men,
And dost with poyson, warre, and sicknesse dwell,
And poppie, or charmes can make us sleepe as well,
And better then thy stroake; why swell'st thou then?
One short sleepe past, wee wake eternally,
And death shall be no more; death, thou shalt die.

JOHN DONNE (1572–1631)

March 1993

Dear People,

Your anthology seems a wonderful one; I am honored to be invited to contribute. Impossible, though, to name a favorite poem. Instead, I'll name the first poems I loved (which still move me). I learned to read, was taught to read, very early, and found my way into various anthologies; I loved best Shakespeare's songs (was most haunted by 'O Mistress Mine') and Blake's Songs of Innocence (most, 'The Little Black Boy'). I understood, probably, very little of them, in terms of sense. I couldn't have been more than five or six years old. But the tone spoke; I heard the sorrow in Shakespeare's music, the grave heartbreaking simplicity of Blake, and in both an (apparently) artless directness, which came to seem to me the ideal of art.

These reasons are simple-minded; the poems, of course, are amazements.

Sincerely,

Louise Glück

from *Twelfth Night II (iii)*

O mistress mine, where are you roaming?
O stay and hear, your true love's coming,
    That can sing both high and low.
Trip no further, pretty sweeting;
Journeys end in lovers' meeting,
    Every wise man's son doth know.

What is love? 'Tis not hereafter;
Present mirth hath present laughter;
    What's to come is still unsure.
In delay there lies no plenty,
Then come kiss me, sweet and twenty;
    Youth's a stuff will not endure.

WILLIAM SHAKESPEARE (1564–1616)

The Little Black Boy

from *Songs of Innocence*

My mother bore me in the southern wild,
And I am black, but O! my soul is white;
White as an angel is the English child:
But I am black as if bereav'd of light.

My mother taught me underneath a tree,
And sitting down before the heat of day,
She took me on her lap and kisséd me,
And pointing to the east, began to say:

'Look on the rising sun: there God does live,
And gives his light, and gives his heat away;
And flowers and trees and beasts and men receive
Comfort in morning, joy in the noon day.

'And we are put on earth a little space,
That we may learn to bear the beams of love,
And these black bodies and this sun-burnt face
Is but a cloud, and like a shady grove.

'For when our souls have learn'd the heat to bear,
The cloud will vanish; we shall hear his voice,
Saying: "Come out from the grove, my love & care,
And round my golden tent like lambs rejoice." '

Thus did my mother say, and kisséd me;
And thus I say to little English boy.
When I from black and he from white cloud free,
And round the tent of God like lambs we joy,

I'll shade him from the heat till he can bear
To lean in joy upon our father's knee;
And then I'll stand and stroke his silver hair,
And be like him, and he will then love me.

WILLIAM BLAKE (1757–1827)

CLAIRE KILROY NOVELIST

2006

Hello all,

Please find attached a few words on Kavanagh's 'Advent'. If it's too long, let me know and I'll shorten it, or indeed, if you're just looking for a one-sentence answer, take the last sentence.

Thanks again for asking me to contribute, it was really nice to go back and think about a well-loved poem.

Claire

The arresting narrative drama of 'Advent's' opening declaration grasps the imagination immediately. Kavanagh draws on the intimacy and urgency of the direct address, and spears it with that abrupt hyphen: 'We have tested and tasted too much, lover –' The reader is spellbound, almost fearful: What have the lovers done, to bring them to this impasse? What is this dangerous stolen entity they now wish to return to Doom?

There are four presences in this most spiritual of love poems: the speaker, his lover, Doom, and wonder. Wonder is evoked as a shy and elusive creature, almost a wild animal. It can be enticed in through a chink, but only if it is a narrow chink; it can be 'charmed' into a room if that room is bare and 'Advent-darkened'; it can be perceived from a distance in 'a black slanting Ulster hill'. In the presence of wonder, the world is transformed. It becomes fascinating once more, as fascinating and as astounding as it was to the eyes of a child.

However, the poet's childlike enchantment is now combined with an adult sensibility, and is therefore touched by sadness – the dreeping hedges are 'heart-breaking' in their strangeness. Kavanagh is all too aware of the precariousness of the lovers' situation. 'Please God,' he implores, 'we shall not ask for reason's payment.' But it is the human condition to 'search', to 'ask', and to 'analyse'. The state of wonder cannot be sustained. Advent, after all, lasts for just four Sundays. This poignant fragility is fully realised in the delicate closing image of the January flower. I am moved, each time I read this poem, by Kavanagh's tremendous desire to protect and nurture innocence, by the great tenderness he pours upon the unassuming.

COLIN MARTIN ARTIST

3 May 2006

Dear Dónal, Caroline and Stephanie

Many thanks for your invitation to contribute to Lifelines. *I have chosen 'Advent' by Patrick Kavanagh.*

Kavanagh's poetry creates an awareness and a deeper consciousness of the redemption and mystery that is to be found in the familiar if we choose to look closer.

I wish you all every success with New and Collected Lifelines.

Yours sincerely,

Colin Martin

214 LIFELINES NEW AND COLLECTED

Advent

We have tested and tasted too much, lover –
Through a chink too wide there comes in no wonder.
But here in this Advent-darkened room
Where the dry black bread and the sugarless tea
Of penance will charm back the luxury
Of a child's soul, we'll return to Doom
The knowledge we stole but could not use.

And the newness that was in every stale thing
When we looked at it as children: the spirit-shocking
Wonder in a black slanting Ulster hill,
Or the prophetic astonishment in the tedious talking
Of an old fool, will awake for us and bring
You and me to the yard gate to watch the whins
And the bog-holes, cart-tracks, old stables where Time begins.

O after Christmas we'll have no need to go searching
For the difference that sets an old phrase burning –
We'll hear it in the whispered argument of a churning
Or in the streets where the village boys are lurching.
And we'll hear it among simple, decent men, too,
Who barrow dung in gardens under trees,
Wherever life pours ordinary plenty.
Won't we be rich, my love and I, and please
God we shall not ask for reason's payment,
The why of heart-breaking strangeness in dreeping hedges,
Nor analyse God's breath in common statement.
We have thrown into the dust-bin the clay-minted wages
Of pleasure, knowledge and the conscious hour –
And Christ comes with a January flower.

PATRICK KAVANAGH (1904–1967)

['*Advent*' was also chosen by Eithne Carr in *Lifelines 2*. Eithne Carr wrote:
My choice of poem for you is Patrick Kavanagh's 'Advent'. Last Christmas, copies of this were given out at Barna Church in Galway, and since then I have had my copy pinned up over my kitchen table. Each time I read it, and I often do, some different image stands out for me. The poem renews my hope and belief in the beauty of the everyday.]

University College Dublin
17 March 1994

Dear Ewan, Áine and Christopher,

When I studied English Literature as an undergraduate I never read even one line of American poetry or prose, much to my shame and regret. Years later a friend in Dublin introduced me to the writings of Jack Kerouac, Allen Ginsberg, Emily Dickinson, William Carlos Williams and, of course, Walt Whitman, among many others. I was thrilled with discovery after discovery. I even went to the City Lights Bookshop while on business in San Francisco and sat and read Ginsberg's Howl *in the midst of the browsers.*

More than any other poet, Walt Whitman's strength, honesty, compelling rhythm, disciplined pace, and perfect choice of words lead me to select a piece of his 'Song of Myself' *as my choice for inclusion in your anthology. These lines tell me so much about the energy, loneliness, self-reliance, and austerity of the sophisticated American mind.*

Very best wishes,

Terry Dolan

from *Song of Myself*

1
I celebrate myself, and sing myself,
And what I assume you shall assume,
For every atom belonging to me as good belongs to you.

I loafe and invite my soul,
I lean and loafe at my ease observing a spear of summer grass.
My tongue, every atom of my blood, form'd from this soil, this air,
Born here of parents born here from parents the same, and their parents the same,
I, now thirty-seven years old in perfect health begin,
Hoping to cease not till death.

Creeds and schools in abeyance,
Retiring back a while sufficed at what they are, but never forgotten,
I harbor for good or bad, I permit to speak at every hazard,
Nature without check with original energy.

. . . .

6

A child said *What is the grass?* fetching it to me with full hands,
How could I answer the child? I do not know what it is any more than he.

I guess it must be the flag of my disposition, out of hopeful green stuff woven.

Or I guess it is the handkerchief of the Lord,
A scented gift and remembrancer designedly dropt,
Bearing the owner's name someway in the corners, that we may see and remark, and
    say *Whose?*

Or I guess the grass is itself a child, the produced babe of the vegetation.

Or I guess it is a uniform hieroglyphic,
And it means, Sprouting alike in broad zones and narrow zones,
Growing among black folks as among white,
Kanuck, Tuckahoe, Congressman, Cuff, I give them the same, I receive them the same.

And now it seems to me the beautiful uncut hair of graves.

Tenderly will I use you curling grass,
It may be you transpire from the breasts of young men,
It may be if I had known them I would have loved them,
It may be you are from old people, or from offspring taken soon out of their mothers' laps,
And here you are the mothers' laps.

This grass is very dark to be from the white heads of old mothers,
Darker than the colorless beards of old men,
Dark to come from under the faint red roofs of mouths.

O I perceive after all so many uttering tongues,
And I perceive they do not come from the roofs of mouths for nothing.

I wish I could translate the hints about the dead young men and women,
And the hints about old men and mothers, and the offspring taken soon out of their laps.

What do you think has become of the young and old men?
And what do you think has become of the women and children?

They are alive and well somewhere,
The smallest sprout shows there is really no death,
And if ever there was it led forward life, and does not wait at the end to arrest it,
And ceas'd the moment life appear'd.

All goes onward and outward, nothing collapses,
And to die is different from what any one supposed, and luckier.

WALT WHITMAN (1819–1892)

Dear Dónal, Caroline, Stephanie

Sorry for leaving it so late, but here goes:

Being from south Monaghan, I know I should pick something by Kavanagh. And I love a poem called 'Home Is So Sad' by Philip Larkin, because it's heartbreaking.

But by complete contrast, the last book of poetry I read was The Best of Ogden Nash, *and I'm still laughing at it.*

So I'll nominate this one instead. It's called 'Very Like a Whale'.

Yours apologetically,

Frank McNally

Very Like a Whale

One thing that literature would be greatly the better for
Would be a more restricted employment by authors of simile and
      metaphor.
Authors of all races, be they Greeks, Romans, Teutons or Celts,
Can't seem just to say that anything is the thing it is but have
      to go out of their way to say that it is like something else.
What does it mean when we are told
That the Assyrian came down like a wolf on the fold?
In the first place, George Gordon Byron had had enough experience
To know that it probably wasn't just one Assyrian, it was a lot
      of Assyrians.
However, as too many arguments are apt to induce apoplexy and thus
      hinder longevity,
We'll let it pass as one Assyrian for the sake of brevity.
Now then, this particular Assyrian, the one whose cohorts were gleaming
      in purple and gold,
Just what does the poet mean when he says he came down like a wolf
      on the fold?
In heaven and earth more than is dreamed of in our philosophy there
      are a great many things,
But I don't imagine that among them there is a wolf with purple
      and gold cohorts or purple and gold anythings.
No, no, Lord Byron, before I'll believe that this Assyrian was actually
      like a wolf I must have some kind of proof;
Did he run on all fours and did he have a hairy tail and a big red
      mouth and big white teeth and did he say Woof woof?
Frankly I think it very unlikely, and all you were entitled to say,
      at the very most,

Was that the Assyrian cohorts came down like a lot of Assyrian cohorts
        about to destroy the Hebrew host.
But that wasn't fancy enough for Lord Byron, oh dear me no, he had
        to invent a lot of figures of speech and then interpolate them,
With the result that whenever you mention Old Testament soldiers
        to people they say Oh yes, they're the ones that a lot of wolves
        dressed up in gold and purple ate them.
That's the kind of thing that's being done all the time by poets,
        from Homer to Tennyson;
They're always comparing ladies to lilies and veal to venison,
And they always say things like that the snow is a white blanket
        after a winter storm.
Oh it is, is it, all right then, you sleep under a six-inch blanket
        of snow and I'll sleep under a half-inch blanket of unpoetical
        blanket material and we'll see which one keeps warm,
And after that maybe you'll begin to comprehend dimly,
What I mean by too much metaphor and simile.

OGDEN NASH (1902–1971)

GABRIEL FITZMAURICE   POET

24 January 1994

Dear Ewan, Áine and Christopher,

Many thanks for your invitation to submit a favourite poem for your consideration. I am honoured.

I have so very many favourite poems, and a number of favourite poets, that to choose one above another is a bit like choosing between my children! So, apart from saying that almost everything by Emily Dickinson, and a lot of Seán Ó Ríordáin immediately spring to mind, I'll go for something else.

I believe in poetry, in its power to influence and enlighten people, in its power to make us examine our lives. One such piece has always moved me. It's from Chapter 6 of Saint Matthew's Gospel, from The Sermon on the Mount. *(In fact, Brenda and I chose it as the Gospel reading for our wedding.) It is a hymn to living in the present. It is a calling to the good: if we are right with ourselves, we will be right with the world. There's a good God in Whose love we live. I've puzzled and pondered over this text for years trying to square it with the troubles of this world, and can only conclude that, ultimately, they are of our own making. If we are our brothers' keepers, we should look after each other. Anyway, here is the text. It's from the King James Version of 1611.*

I wish you all the best with the new Lifelines. *You are doing the world of good – not only for the Developing World, but also for the developing world of poetry! God bless the work!*

Gabriel Fitzmaurice

from *The Gospel according to St Matthew*

Translated out of the original tongues and with the former translations diligently compared and revised. By His Majesty's Special command. Authorised King James Version.

Therefore I say unto you, Take no thought for your life, what ye shall eat, or what ye shall drink; nor yet for your body, what ye shall put on. Is not the life more than meat, and the body than raiment?

Behold the fowls of the air: for they sow not, neither do they reap, nor gather into barns; yet your heavenly Father feedeth them. Are ye not much better than they?

Which of you by taking thought can add one cubit unto his stature?

And why take ye thought for raiment? Consider the lilies of the field, how they grow; they toil not, neither do they spin.

And yet I say unto you, That even Solomon in all his glory was not arrayed like one of these.

Wherefore, if God so clothe the grass of the field, which today is, and tomorrow is cast into the oven, *shall He* not much more *clothe* you, O ye of little faith?

Therefore take no thought, saying, What shall we eat? or, What shall we drink? or, Wherewithal shall we be clothed?

(For after all these things do the Gentiles seek:) for your heavenly Father knoweth that ye have need of all these things.

But seek ye first the kingdom of God, and his righteousness; and all these things shall be added unto you.

Take therefore no thought for the morrow: for the morrow shall take thought for the things of itself. Sufficient unto the day *is* the evil thereof.

MATTHEW 6: 25-34

Dear Dónal, Caroline and Stephanie,

It's an honour to be asked. I've enjoyed the previous Lifelines *and all for a good cause, charity and indeed poetry. May you have lots of luck and success with the project.*

My favourite poem – to pick a particular from thousands – is always shifting, it depends on the mood or the day; the day job naturally involves reading a lot of poetry. I've recently been re-reading the poems of Samuel Beckett, with the year that's in it. I read him first in my late teens or early twenties and his short poems really appealed to me, in the way that short poems always appeal to younger readers wanting to write; they make it look feasible.

Someone once said that all writers start out as poets, and Beckett, better known as a playwright and novelist, had an odd fidelity to writing and translating poetry all his life. His career begins with a poem, 'Whorescope', one of the few I don't care for, and closes with a poem, 'Comment dire' or 'What is the word', written in hospital the year before he died, and this is my favourite or chosen poem.

The poem first appeared as a last work alongside Beckett's obituaries; at the time I'd been keeping any newspaper cuttings that related to him for some years. I still have the scrapbooks and files of cuttings; it's probably fair to say I was a bit of a Beckett anorak back then!

The poem is very much a missive from the seventh age. The poet is trying to remember the word and, of course, 'the word' has all sorts of biblical connotations. In a lifetime where words were everything; he is now reduced to grappling for them. The poet is acutely conscious of the unravelling of what's been learnt and the folly in even trying to record or set the process down. Repetitions in the poem create a mournful music and while the word remains elusive, Beckett has succeeded in creating music.

Joe Woods

What is the Word

folly —
folly for to —
for to —
what is the word —
folly from this —
all this —
folly from all this —
given —
folly given all this —
seeing —
folly seeing all this —
this —
what is the word —
this this —
this this here —

all this this here —
folly given all this —
seeing —
folly seeing all this this here —
for to —
what is the word —
see —
glimpse —
seem to glimpse —
need to seem to glimpse —
folly for to need to seem to glimpse —
what —
what is the word —
and where —
folly for to need to seem to glimpse what where —
where —
what is the word —
there —
over there —
away over there —
afar —
afar away over there —
afaint —
afaint afar away over there what —
what —
what is the word —
seeing all this —
all this this —
all this this here —
folly for to see what —
glimpse —
seem to glimpse —
need to seem to glimpse —
afaint afar away over there what —
folly for to need to seem to glimpse afaint afar
                                        away over there what —
what —
what is the word —

what is the word

SAMUEL BECKETT (1906–1989)

Dear Ewan, Áine and Christopher,

Thank you for inviting me to participate in Lifelines.

I have chosen as my favourite poem, 'The River-Merchant's Wife: A Letter', written by the Chinese poet Li Po c. 750. This vivid poem about a young wife's longing for her absent husband has been translated many times into many languages, but this 'free' version by Ezra Pound is justly famous. It is a brilliant evocation of youthful longing. It was not until you asked me to choose a favourite poem, that I realised what an influence this one has been on my own writing.

The use of detail – the bamboo stilts, blue plums, the river of swirling eddies, the monkeys, moss, paired butterflies and narrows make this poem as alive in the twentieth century as it was in the eighth.

The use of place names appeals to me, but most of all I love the poignant understatement of the teenage wife's longing for her absent husband.

The very best of luck with your project.

Warm wishes,

Anne Kennedy

The River-Merchant's Wife: A Letter

While my hair was still cut straight across my forehead
I played about the front gate, pulling flowers.
You came by on bamboo stilts, playing horse,
You walked about my seat, playing with blue plums.
And we went on living in the village of Chokan:
Two small people, without dislike or suspicion.

At fourteen I married My Lord you.
I never laughed, being bashful.
Lowering my head, I looked at the wall.
Called to, a thousand times, I never looked back.

At fifteen I stopped scowling,
I desired my dust to be mingled with yours
Forever and forever and forever.
Why should I climb the lookout?

At sixteen you departed.
You went into far Ku-to-yen by the river of swirling eddies,
And you have been gone five months.
The monkeys make sorrowful noise overhead.

You dragged your feet when you went out.
By the gate now, the moss is grown, the different mosses,
Too deep to clear them away!
The leaves fall early this autumn, in wind.
The paired butterflies are already yellow with August
Over the grass in the West garden;
They hurt me. I grow older.
If you are coming down through the narrows of the river Kiang,
Please let me know beforehand,
And I will come out to meet you
        As far as Cho-fu-Sa.

Li Po (701–762)
Translated from the Chinese by Ezra Pound (1885–1972)

DEREK MAHON POET

19 January 1988

Dear Miss Grantham and friends,

I don't know if it's necessarily my favourite poem, but it's one I like very much: 'The Moose' by Elizabeth Bishop. The title is a pun on 'The Muse', and the poem describes a bus journey at night from Nova Scotia to Boston during which a moose appears on the road, to everyone's delighted astonishment. It's a poem about the magical in the ordinary, a poem about poetry itself in a sense: one of the great underrated poems of the century. I recommend it to all those who want to know what poetry means, and wish you well in your efforts on behalf of the Third World.

Sincerely,

Derek Mahon

The Moose

For Grace Bulmer Bowers

From narrow provinces
of fish and bread and tea,
home of the long tides
where the bay leaves the sea
twice a day and takes
the herrings long rides,

where if the river
enters or retreats
in a wall of brown foam
depends on if it meets
the bay coming in,
the bay not at home;

where, silted red,
sometimes the sun sets
facing a red sea,
and others, veins the flats'
lavender, rich mud
in burning rivulets;

on red, gravelly roads,
down rows of sugar maples,
past clapboard farmhouses
and neat, clapboard churches,
bleached, ridged as clamshells,
past twin silver birches,

through late afternoon
a bus journeys west,
the windshield flashing pink,
pink glancing off of metal,
brushing the dented flank
of blue, beat-up enamel;

down hollows, up rises,
and waits, patient, while
a lone traveller gives
kisses and embraces
to seven relatives
and a collie supervises.

Goodbye to the elms,
to the farm, to the dog.
The bus starts. The light
grows richer; the fog,
shifting, salty, thin,
comes closing in.

Its cold, round crystals
form and slide and settle
in the white hens' feathers,
in gray glazed cabbages,
on the cabbage roses
and lupins like apostles;

the sweet peas cling
to their wet white string
on the whitewashed fences;
bumblebees creep
inside the foxgloves,
and evening commences.

One stop at Bass River.
Then the Economies —
Lower, Middle, Upper;
Five Islands, Five Houses,
where a woman shakes a tablecloth
out after supper.

A pale flickering, Gone.
The Tantramar marshes
and the smell of salt hay.
An iron bridge trembles
and a loose plank rattles
but doesn't give way.

On the left, a red light
swims through the dark:
a ship's port lantern.
Two rubber boots show,
illuminated, solemn.
A dog gives one bark.

A woman climbs in
with two market bags,
brisk, freckled, elderly.
'A grand night. Yes, sir,
all the way to Boston.'
She regards us amicably.

Moonlight as we enter
the New Brunswick woods,
hairy, scratchy, splintery;
moonlight and mist
caught in them like lamb's wool
on bushes in a pasture.

The passengers lie back.
Snores. Some long sighs.
A dreamy divagation
begins in the night,
a gentle, auditory,
slow hallucination . . . .

In the creakings and noises,
an old conversation
—not concerning us,
but recognizable, somewhere,
back in the bus:
Grandparents' voices

uninterruptedly
talking, in Eternity:
names being mentioned,
things cleared up finally;
what he said, what she said,
who got pensioned;

deaths, deaths and sicknesses;
the year he remarried;
the year (something) happened.
She died in childbirth.
That was the son lost
when the schooner foundered.

He took to drink. Yes.
She went to the bad.
When Amos began to pray
even in the store and
finally the family had
to put him away.

'Yes . . .' that peculiar
affirmative. 'Yes . . .'
A sharp, indrawn breath,
half groan, half acceptance,
that means 'Life's like that.
We know *it* (also death).'

Talking the way they talked
in the old featherbed,
peacefully, on and on,
dim lamplight in the hall,
down in the kitchen, the dog
tucked in her shawl.

Now, it's all right now
even to fall asleep
just as on all those nights.
— Suddenly the bus driver
stops with a jolt,
turns off his lights.

A moose has come out of
the impenetrable wood
and stands there, looms, rather,
in the middle of the road.
It approaches; it sniffs at
the bus's hot hood.

Towering, antlerless,
high as a church,
homely as a house
(or, safe as houses).
A man's voice assures us
'Perfectly harmless. . . .'

Some of the passengers
exclaim in whispers,
childishly, softly,
'Sure are big creatures.'
'It's awful plain.'
'Look! It's a she!'

Taking her time,
she looks the bus over,
grand, otherworldly.
Why, why do we feel
(we all feel) this sweet
sensation of joy?

'Curious creatures,'
says our quiet driver,
rolling his r's.
'Look at that, would you.'
Then he shifts gears.
For a moment longer,

by craning backward,
the moose can be seen
on the moonlit macadam;
then there's a dim
smell of moose, an acrid
smell of gasoline.

ELIZABETH BISHOP (1911–1979)

['*The Moose*' was also chosen by David Leavitt in *Lifelines*. David Leavitt wrote:
*Thanks very much for your letter. The poem I've decided to send you is '*The Moose*' by Elizabeth
Bishop. It's rather a long poem as you can see.*
 *I think the reason I love this poem so much is because, magically, it articulates everything that
seems to me to be important about experiences – how the 'homely' can so easily glide into the
'otherwordly'; how a moose, caught in the twin beams of a Boston-bound bus, can transcend its
own earthliness to become something both more and less than human, generating a 'sweet sensation
of joy'. There is a calmness to the language of this poem, an ease and simplicity that belies the reality
of its making. (It took Bishop years to compose.) And it contains some of the most breathtaking
descriptions of nature that I've ever read. (In particular, I shall never forget 'the sweet peas cling to
their wet, white string'.)*]

When I was growing up, we were always taught that our physical and our spiritual yearnings were completely separate. And not just separate but irreconcilable. Our spiritual or religious impulses, we were informed again and again in different ways, were essentially good. They were to be nurtured, developed and expressed, at every opportunity. The biggest problem which we were likely to encounter in this great and worthy enterprise would in fact be presented by our physical, sensual desires. These were to be discouraged, repressed and ultimately routed. They were the enemy of spirituality. They were essentially bad.

In this dualistic view of the world, sex was the root possibly not of all but certainly of most evil. I could never accept this. Some resilient instinct burned strongly enough to reject the weight of the fearsome indoctrination we were subjected to. Desire, sensuality, sexual expression – these to me felt intrinsically like good things. Why should they be branded otherwise?

Confirmation of these feelings was hard to come by in art and literature. In a world of dogmatism and blunt commandments, we learned about the sins of the flesh and most of the poetry and novels we were fed reinforced the message. Ultimately this would be one of the great attractions for me of rock 'n' roll – a milieu where the concept of sin was turned inside out and the pleasures of the flesh were celebrated. But to those who were uncomfortable with the received dualism, to encounter a poet like John Donne was a startling, life-affirming revelation . . .

Here was a man who began writing in the sixteenth century who spoke in a wonderfully contemporary voice. It seemed to me, in my teens, as I began to grapple with aesthetic questions, that one of the great challenges facing artists in the 20th Century was to achieve the reconciliation of body and soul, of the sensual and the cerebral, the erotic and the spiritual – and yet when I read 'The Sunne Rising' *and* 'To His Mistris Going to Bed' *I realised that John Donne had achieved precisely this balance all of 400 years ago.*

'To His Mistris Going to Bed' *is cinematic in its power. It draws you in to a moment of shared intimacy without ever becoming cloying. The tone is humorous at times but never raffish. Desire is celebrated audaciously and yet with great dignity. And there is, finally, a mystical quality about the poem's evocation of the universe of pleasure which unfolds through the wonderful uninhibited meeting of man and woman as equals in the act of sexual passion and love.*

Dualism be damned! This is where it's at.

Niall Stokes

To His Mistris Going to Bed

Come, Madam, come, all rest my powers defy,
Until I labour, I in labour lie.
The foe oft-times having the foe in sight,
Is tired with standing though they never fight.
Off with that girdle, like heaven's zone glistering,

But a far fairer world encompassing.
Unpin that spangled breastplate which you wear,
That th' eyes of busy fools may be stopped there.
Unlace yourself, for that harmonious chime
Tells me from you, that now 'tis your bed time.
Off with that happy busk, which I envy,
That still can be, and still can stand so nigh.
Your gown going off, such beauteous state reveals,
As when from flowery meads th' hill's shadow steals.
Off with that wiry coronet and show
The hairy diadem which on you doth grow;
Now off with those shoes, and then safely tread
In this love's hallowed temple, this soft bed.
In such white robes heaven's angels used to be
Received by men; thou angel bring'st with thee
A heaven like Mahomet's paradise; and though
Ill spirits walk in white, we easily know
By this these angels from an evil sprite,
Those set our hairs, but these our flesh upright.
    Licence my roving hands, and let them go
Before, behind, between, above, below.
O my America! my new-found-land,
My kingdom, safeliest when with one man manned,
My mine of precious stones, my empery,
How blessed am I in this discovering thee!
To enter in these bonds, is to be free;
Then where my hand is set, my seal shall be.
    Full nakedness! All joys are due to thee.
As souls unbodied, bodies unclothed must be,
To taste whole joys. Gems which you women use
Are like Atlanta's balls, cast in men's views,
That when a fool's eye lighteth on a gem,
His earthly soul may covet theirs, not them.
Like pictures, or like books' gay coverings made
For laymen, are all women thus arrayed;
Themselves are mystic books, which only we
Whom their imputed grace will dignify
Must see revealed. Then, since that I may know,
As liberally, as to a midwife, show
Thyself: cast all, yea, this white linen hence,
There is no penance, much less innocence.
    To teach thee, I am naked first, why then
What needst thou have more covering than a man?

JOHN DONNE (1572–1631)

Dear Dónal, Caroline and Stephanie

Thank you for the invitation to name my favourite poem for the new edition of the Lifelines Project. I have a particular liking for some of Seamus Heaney's poems, especially those that link different times and places. There are two especially that appeal to me. First is 'Digging' which, although one of his very early poems, reminds us of the massive transformation that has occurred in Ireland over the last forty years, to the importance of the pen rather than the spade, the importance of our creative ideas rather than muscle. Second is his recent 'The Tollund Man in Springtime' which links across greater periods of time. It imagines how that human, sacrificed so long ago and preserved in the bog, would have viewed what has happened with our civilisation since. It is mysterious but wonderful. This would be my overall favourite.

    Wishing you every success with a very creative and worthy project.

Sincerly yours

John Hegarty

The Tollund Man in Springtime

Into your virtual city I'll have passed
Unregistered by scans, screens, hidden eyes,
Lapping time in myself, an absorbed face
Coming and going, neither god nor ghost,
Not at odds or at one, but simply lost
To you and yours, out under seeding grass
And trickles of kesh water, sphagnum moss,
Dead bracken on the spreadfield, red as rust.
I reawoke to revel in the spirit
They strengthened when they chose to put me down
For their own good. And to a sixth-sensed threat:
Panicked snipe offshooting into twilight,
Then going awry, larks quietened in the sun,
Clear alteration in the bog-pooled rain.

Scone of peat, composite bog-dough
They trampled like a muddy vintage, then
Slabbed and spread and turned to dry in the sun –
Though never kindling-dry the whole way through –
A dead-weight, slow-burn lukewarmth in the flue
Ashless, flameless, its very smoke a sullen
Waft of swamp-breath . . . And me, so long unrisen,
I knew that same dead weight in joint and sinew
Until a spade-plate slid and soughed and plied
At my buried ear, and the levered sod
Got lifted up; then once I felt the air
I was like turned turf in the breath of God,
Bog-bodied on the sixth day, brown and bare,
And on the last, all told, unatrophied.

*

My heavy head. Bronze-buffed. Ear to the ground.
My eye at turf level. Its snailskin lid.
My cushioned cheek and brow. My phantom hand
And arm and leg and shoulder that felt pillowed
As fleshily as when the bog pith weighed
To mould me to itself and it to me
Between when I was buried and unburied.
Between what happened and was meant to be.
On show for years, while all that lay in wait
Still waited. Disembodied. Far renowned.
Faith placed in me, me faithless as a stone
The harrow turned up when the crop was sown.
Out in the Danish night I'd hear soft wind
And remember moony water in a rut.

*

'The soul exceeds its circumstances.' Yes.
History not to be granted the last word
Or the first claim . . . In the end I gathered
From the display-case peat my staying powers,
Told my webbed wrists to be like silver birches,
My old uncallused hands to be young sward,
The spade-cut skin to heal, and got restored
By telling myself this. Late as it was,
The early bird still sang, the meadow hay
Still buttercupped and daisied, sky was new.
I smelled the air, exhaust fumes, silage reek,
Heard from my heather bed the thickened traffic
Swarm at a roundabout five fields away
And transatlantic flights stacked in the blue.

Cattle out in rain, their knowledgeable
Solid standing and readiness to wait,
These I learned from. My study was the wet,
My head as washy as a head of kale,
Shedding water like the flanks and tail
Of every dumb beast sunk above the cloot
In trampled gaps, bringing their heavyweight
Silence to bear on nosed-at sludge and puddle.
Of another world, unlearnable, and so
To be lived by, whatever it was I knew
Came back to me. Newfound contrariness.
In check-out lines, at cash-points, in those queues
Of wired, far-faced smilers, I stood off,
Bulrush, head in air, far from its lough.

*

Through every check and scan I carried with me
A bunch of Tollund rushes – roots and all –
Bagged in their own bog-damp. In an old stairwell
Broom cupboard where I had hoped they'd stay
Damp until transplanted, they went musty.
Every green-skinned stalk turned friable,
The drowned-mouse fibres withered and the whole
Limp, soggy cluster lost its frank bouquet
Of weed leaf and turf mould. Dust in my palm
And in my nostrils dust, should I shake it off
Or mix it in with spit in pollen's name
And my own? As a man would, cutting turf,
I straightened, spat on my hands, felt benefit
And spirited myself into the street.

SEAMUS HEANEY (B. 1939)

20 January 1988

Dear Julie, Jonathan and Duncan,

Although I read poetry as often as I'm allowed, and though I keep an emergency supply in my head, I still have no difficulty in choosing one poem from among the many that I admire. It is the elegy which Chidiock Tichborne wrote for himself as he awaited execution in the Tower of London in 1586. He was twenty-eight years of age and had been condemned to death for his part in a plot on the Queen. His response to his plight is a dignified one – he neither screams nor shouts; but the cry he emits is a piercing and moving one, nonetheless. In trying to puzzle out the riddle of his own early death, Tichborne speaks for all those who have been condemned to premature death, including those who starve as a result of injustice, indifference or greed.

Thank you for allowing me to be associated with your laudable project.

Best wishes,

Dennis O'Driscoll

Tichborne's Elegy

written with his own hand in the Tower before his execution.

My prime of youth is but a frost of cares,
My feast of joy is but a dish of pain,
My crop of corn is but a field of tares,
And all my good is but vain hope of gain;
The day is past, and yet I saw no sun,
And now I live, and now my life is done.

My tale was heard and yet it was not told,
My fruit is fall'n and yet my leaves are green,
My youth is spent and yet I am not old,
I saw the world and yet I was not seen;
My thread is cut and yet it is not spun,
And now I live, and now my life is done.

I sought my death and found it in my womb,
I looked for life and saw it was a shade,
I trod the earth and knew it was my tomb,
And now I die, and now I was but made;
My glass is full, and now my glass is run,
And now I live, and now my life is done.

CHIDIOCK TICHBORNE (1558–1586)

ALISON DYE NOVELIST

18 April 1994

Dear Ewan, Áine and Chris,

Thank you very much for your letter asking for a favourite poem.

I was surprised to discover that my first reaction to your request was to travel in my mind not to poetry I read in the present day, but to a poem I first knew and loved almost thirty years ago in college, a poem that took hold of me and apparently never let go, called up now by your letter.

The poem is 'Kubla Khan' *by Samuel Taylor Coleridge (1772–1843). Its first lines, indelibly imprinted on my unconscious, are:*

> In Xanadu did Kubla Khan
> A stately pleasure dome decree:
> Where Alph, the sacred river, ran
> Through caverns measureless to man
>   Down to a sunless sea.

I am not a poet, and certainly not a critic of poetry, so my reasons for responding so deeply to 'Kubla Khan' *are not in any way academic. I remain enthralled with its stunning, shining, dream-like images of peace and light – but also gripped by its ominous, foreboding sense of dread which makes one worry indeed for the beauty and romance ('And All should cry, Beware! Beware! . . . And close your eyes with holy dread'). The 'miracle of rare device/A sunny pleasure-dome with caves of ice' also contains the foreshadowing, to my eyes and ears, of much darker prospects: the ocean into which the sacred river runs is 'lifeless' and 'sunless', and as it reaches this sea from the caverns measureless to man, 'Kubla heard from far/Ancestral voices prophesying war!'*

I find the language of the poem absolutely riveting. One is caught off balance by the subtle, seductive way in which it brings alive, and together, the opposing forces of death and life, peace and war, light and dark. One cannot be complacent in the stately pleasure dome, although the poem tempts one to float along: darkness is nibbling at the pleasing surface. Things are not as they seem.

For me, the juxtaposition of the two possibilities creates a complex, provocative, and irreconcilable tension—perhaps this is why I have never forgotten the poem.

I am also struck as I write this that 'Kubla Khan' *may be quite appropriate to the interest of* Lifelines: *our relative plenty is in stark contrast to the suffering your anthology seeks to help relieve. Both exist, and one is very difficult indeed to reconcile with the other. Again, a relatively rosy state of being is at odds with realities elsewhere that cannot be denied.*

I am afraid I have written far more than the few lines you asked for. My apologies.

I am also enclosing a copy of my first novel, which I would like to donate to the school, in the hopes of encouraging new young writers.

Best wishes with your project, and I am certainly grateful that you thought to include me.

Yours sincerely,

Alison Dye

Kubla Khan

In Xanadu did Kubla Khan
A stately pleasure-dome decree:
Where Alph, the sacred river, ran
Through caverns measureless to man
    Down to a sunless sea.
So twice five miles of fertile ground
With walls and towers were girdled round:
And there were gardens bright with sinuous rills,
Where blossomed many an incense-bearing tree;
And here were forests ancient as the hills,
Enfolding sunny spots of greenery.

But oh! that deep romantic chasm which slanted
Down the green hill athwart a cedarn cover!
A savage place! as holy and enchanted
As e'er beneath a waning moon was haunted
By woman wailing for her demon-lover!
And from this chasm, with ceaseless turmoil seething,
As if this earth in fast thick pants were breathing,
A mighty fountain momently was forced:
Amid whose swift half-intermitted burst
Huge fragments vaulted like rebounding hail,
Or chaffy grain beneath the thresher's flail:
And 'mid these dancing rocks at once and ever
It flung up momently the sacred river.
Five miles meandering with a mazy motion
Through wood and dale the sacred river ran,
Then reached the caverns measureless to man,
And sank in tumult to a lifeless ocean:
And 'mid this tumult Kubla heard from far
Ancestral voices prophesying war!
    The shadow of the dome of pleasure
    Floated midway on the waves;
    Where was heard the mingled measure
    From the fountain and the caves.
It was a miracle of rare device,
A sunny pleasure-dome with caves of ice!
    A damsel with a dulcimer
    In a vision once I saw:
    It was an Abyssinian maid,
    And on her dulcimer she played,

Singing of Mount Abora.
Could I revive within me
Her symphony and song,
To such a deep delight 'twould win me,
That with music loud and long,
I would build that dome in air,
That sunny dome! those caves of ice!
And all who heard should see them there,
And all should cry, Beware! Beware!
His flashing eyes, his floating hair!
Weave a circle round him thrice,
And close your eyes with holy dread,
For he on honey-dew hath fed,
And drunk the milk of Paradise.

SAMUEL TAYLOR COLERIDGE (1772–1843)

OLIVE BRAIDEN   CHAIR, ARTS COUNCIL

2006

The Dead

The dead are always looking down on us, they say,
while we are putting on our shoes or making a sandwich,
they are looking down through the glass-bottom boats of heaven,
as they row themselves slowly through eternity.

They watch the tops of our heads moving below on earth,
and when we lie down in a field or on a couch,
drugged perhaps by the hum of a warm afternoon,
they think we are looking back at them,

which makes them lift their oars and fall silent
and wait, like parents, for us to close our eyes.

BILLY COLLINS (B. 1941)

*This is one of my favourite poems. It appeals to me because it is a different and amusing
stance rather than the very sad and hopeless feeling we get when we think of our friends
and family who have died. I think it would be particularly helpful for children to read
after the initial grieving period, when someone special dies. I don't find it at all morbid.*
   Wishing you good luck with your very interesting venture

Regards,

Olive

RTÉ
23 January 1994

Dear Ewan, Áine and Christopher,

Enclosed please find my choice of poetry – 'The Windhover' by Gerard Manley Hopkins.
    I always come back to 'The Windhover' mainly because it was the first poem to cast a sheltering shadow over my life. Up to encountering Hopkins's masterpiece for my Leaving Certificate in 1976, I don't think I understood the power, grace, release and deep kaleidoscope that is good poetry.
    Every word seems carefully hewn from wood, stonily chiselled from granite, and unleashed from the farrier's grasp to soar, inspire and thrill.
    The imaginative power of language alliterating its way through the onomatopoeia of carefully chosen words and phrases is but a gateway to the wide world – a world I can thankfully say I recently returned to, asking myself all the while where I'd been all those years. It is also a reminder that good poetry contains deep understandings that maybe are not of this world.
Yours sincerely,
Joe Duffy

The Windhover

To Christ our Lord

I caught this morning morning's minion, kingdom of daylight's
    dauphin, dapple-dawn-drawn Falcon, in his riding
    Of the rolling level underneath him steady air, and striding
High there, how he rung upon the rein of a wimpling wing
In his ecstasy! then off, off forth on swing,
    As a skate's heel sweeps smooth on a bow-bend: the hurl and gliding
    Rebuffed the big wind. My heart in hiding
Stirred for a bird,—the achieve of, the mastery of the thing!

Brute beauty and valour and act, oh, air, pride, plume, here
    Buckle! AND the fire that breaks from thee then, a billion
Times told lovelier, more dangerous, O my chevalier!

    No wonder of it: shéer plód makes plough down sillion
Shine, and blue-bleak embers, ah my dear,
    Fall, gall themselves, and gash gold-vermilion.

GERARD MANLEY HOPKINS (1844–1889)

['*The Windhover*' was also chosen by Desmond O'Grady in *Lifelines 3*. Desmond O'Grady wrote:

A thirty-three year old – the age of Christ on the cross – converted Catholic, Hopkins was ordained a priest the year he wrote this 'Italian' sonnet, in 1877. When I first read the poem, in an Irish Cistercian boarding school, I was sixteen and had never heard of Hopkins. His startling language baffled me. What it all meant eluded me. Was this 'modern' poetry? Hearing the poem read by my teacher Mr Cole I was captivated, pleasured by its musically swingy, jumpy rhythms and accents – conducted with Tom Cole's palms, elbows, head, shoulders, legs and feet – by its alliteration, assonance, dissonance, its eccentric juxtaposition of simple and strange words. It was like reading aloud the numbers in mathematical formulae that spell the meaning of the equation, which I was then beginning to see as a kind of poetry, painting, silent music. The sounds, rhythms and emphases of Hopkins's poem harmonised with old Gaelic poems I knew by heart, without understanding them fully either, for the same reasons. But, moved by them, their meaning didn't matter. Their music stirred my soul. This was dramatic lyric, the highest form of poetry, of art, of human expression.

With study, Hopkins's challenging craft clarified. This gave me the added enjoyment of his word jamming and line enjambment. It evoked Anglo-Saxon and Gaelic poetry and the English of Dylan Thomas's poems. What Hopkins called 'inscape', Dedalus–Joyce called the whatness or thingness of things. Like him, Hopkins's method was implosive, to effect an explosive revelation or meaning. This connected for me with Joyce's concept and method of verbal epiphany and situation epiphany, the whatness of words and state of things. Also, Hopkins's, still jumpy to me, 'sprung-rhythm' and pauses or stops evoked associations with classical music, bell ringing, jazz, while his 'inscape' connected with the Cubism of Picasso – all of which I was discovering, adolescently becoming aware of joyfully together with my secret, spiritual selfness. In class Mr Thomas Cole asked: 'Which is more important in a poem: what the poet says or how he says it?' What was said often sounded mundane or incomprehensible to me. How it was said often expanded my awareness of things and situations. How Hopkins had made 'The Windhover' hit me between the eyes as new, daring, modern, exciting. Yet its basic form was the sonnet, its techniques classical. For me 'The Windhover' was Hopkins's epiphany of himself as person, priest, poet momentarily aware of God's divine nature, of his own human nature, of his spiritual, aesthetic and creative self who, like the hawk momentarily hovering before he whistles down the wind, may pounce on his prey of chosen words that will give expression to that self-awareness in a poem which is his prayer for strength to 'rebuff the big wind' of life's gusts of doubt and despair. This 'happening', 'inscape', 'epiphany' reveals God to Hopkins in all creation, from the poised, wingspread kestrel, symbol of the God of peace, to Hopkins himself as priest wingspread between hope and despair, by way of God-Man-Lord Christ between life and death, vocation and revelation, on the cross and back to the mundane reality of the hawk that is the inscape of the priest and poet's epiphany. The poem is Hopkins's exalting prayer to his lord-God in celebration of life and the joyous living of it. Similar experiences had come to my adolescent self on long cross-country walks and religious retreats at boarding school.

As a teenager, this was my start at enjoying poetry. It refocused the world around me forever. It stimulated my own first verses. Today, Hopkins was sixteen years dead at my age now and I haven't grown wings strong enough for flight yet, never mind windhovering.

One of my own favourite poems is 'Professor Kelleher and the Charles River'. *It was written during the winter of 1963–64 while I was studying Celtic and Irish literature at Harvard University. It is a simple poem at first reading. On the naturalistic level a professor and a student are walking and talking on the banks of the Charles River in Cambridge, New England. It is springtime's beginning. The professor talks of the past. The student listens and is reminded of childhood walks on the Shannon River in Ireland with an uncle who told him stories of the past. This touches the poet in the student who subconsciously becomes aware of the, like the river, flowing past of time, of the seasons changing, now out of winter into spring. This is all written in six six-line stanzas with a flexible five beat rhythm and a fixed rhyme scheme – except in the last stanza where one rhyme is broken.*

On the social level we have an Irish-American professor of Harvard and an Irish-European student of his who is also a poet. In age they span two generations of Irish in America from the labouring Irish emigrants that produced the professor to the new Irish academic emigrants that the student–poet represents and both at the most prestigious university in America. With names like Kelleher and O'Grady, they are Irish Catholic. They pass the graveyard of Protestant New Englanders. The poet is reminded of his father rowing on the Shannon river and he thinks of the ploughman brother across the Atlantic common to both poet and professor.

On the historic level both professor and student–poet embody the history of Irish Catholic emigration and the history of Irish culture in Europe and America.

On the symbolic level the two rivers generally and the Charles in particular evoke the passing of time and life; the spring brings new life and flow; the Atlantic receives both rivers and continues to erode the coasts of both continents. At this point we reach the mythic level, where the young poet–student, with this poem forming in his mind, and the ageing professor with the past in his, begin their ageless struggle of dying and bearing. Here too the struggle between the Classic and the Romantic, the Apollonian and Dionysian begins like some ancient dance. Out of this emerges the deliberate echo of Yeats's lines as he must, with the professor, give ground to the new academic and poetic generation being born this spring in this poem. Mythically, behind all this emerges the foundation of the poem which is the underlying theme of the Oresteia of Greek myth and Aeschylus's tragic trilogy. The poet–student acknowledges the past and Yeats but is looking up-river to the birth of a new life and order in the future generations who will be the lights of a new awareness and order. This is the pyramidal base of the poem in Western cultural history from where the reader looks up through the peak of the pyramid which is the epiphanic moment of a teacher and student walking and talking.

Writing this poem helped me to manage more matter than I had in previous poems. Without this step I would never have begun The Dying Gaul *that autumn in Rome.*]

Professor Kelleher and the Charles River

The Charles river reaps here like a sickle. April
Light sweeps flat as ice on the inner curve
Of the living water. Overhead, far from the wave, a dove
White gull heads inland. The spring air, still
Lean from winter, thaws. Walking, John
Kelleher and I talk on the civic lawn.

West, to our left, past some trees, over the ivy walls,
The clock towers, pinnacles, the pillared university yard,
The Protestant past of Cambridge New England selfconsciously dead
In the thawing clay of the Old Burying Ground. Miles
East, over the godless Atlantic, our common brother,
Ploughing his myth-muddy fields, embodies our order.

But here, while the students row by eights and fours on the river —
As my father used to row on the Shannon when, still a child,
I'd cross Thomond Bridge every Sunday, my back to the walled
And turreted castle, listening to that uncle Mykie deliver
His version of history — I listen now to John Kelleher
Unravel the past a short generation later.

Down at the green bank's nerve ends, its roots half in the river,
A leafing tree gathers refuse. The secret force
Of the water worries away the live earth's under-surface.
But his words, for the moment, hold back time's being's destroyer
While the falling wave on both thighs of the ocean
Erodes the coast, at its dying conceptual motion.

Two men, one young, one old, stand stopped acrobats in the blue
Day, their bitch river to heel. Beyond,
Some scraper, tower or ancestral house's gable end.
Then, helplessly, as in some ancient dance, the two
Begin their ageless struggle, while the tree's shadow
With all its arms, crawls on the offal-strewn meadow.

Locked in their mute struggle there by the blood-loosed tide
The two abjure all innocence, tear down past order —
The one calm, dispassionate, clearsighted, the other
Wild with ecstasy, intoxicated, world mad.
Surely some new order is at hand;
Some new form emerging where they stand.

Dusk. The great dim tide of shadows from the past
Gathers for the end — the living and the dead.
All force is fruitful. All opposing powers combine.
Aristocratic privilege, divine sanction, anarchy at last
Yield the new order. The saffron sun sets.
All shadows procession in an acropolis of lights.

DESMOND O'GRADY (B.1935)

3 February 1994

Dear Wesley College Students,

Yes, I do know about Lifelines. *Indeed I even bought copies for my friends. As probably one of Ranelagh's Greatest Egoists, I was, I confess, a touch bothered that your former Fifth Years hadn't deigned to ask me for my Personal Poetry Choice before now. However, with the help of my local Parish Priest (presently chaplain to the Chippendales) I got over it and am duly humbled and grateful to finally be included.*

I'd love to choose Roger McGough, particularly 'Discretion is the Better Part of Valerie' because Roger was one of the first men I ever fell in love with. We held hands in Edinburgh for a whole week.

Not only is McGough an excellent poet but he also understands how poetry should be taught, besides which he's the only poet I've ever heard performing his own work properly. However, as I'm sure lots of your respondees will be choosing him, I'm prepared to offer an alternative.

Here are some short poems from one of the best anthologies I've ever come across. These are delicious translations by Graeme Wilson from the 7th, 8th and 9th century Japanese, which show how little in terms of human emotion ever seems to change. Something which delights and puzzles me at the same time.

With best regards to you all,

Jeananne Crowley

Discretion

Discretion is the better part of Valerie
(though all of her is nice)
lips as warm as strawberries
eyes as cold as ice
the very best of everything
only will suffice
not for her potatoes
and puddings made of rice

Not for her potatoes
and puddings made of rice
she takes carbohydrates
like God takes advice
a surfeit of ambition
is her particular vice
Valerie fondles lovers
like a mousetrap fondles mice

And though in the morning
she may whisper: 'it was nice'
you can tell by her demeanour
that she keeps her love on ice
but you've lost your hardearned heart
now you'll have to pay the price
for she'll kiss you on the memory
and vanish in a trice

Valerie is corruptible
but known to be discreet
Valerie rides a silver cloud
where once she walked the street.

ROGER MCGOUGH (B.1937)

A Grain of Sand

No. I shall not die for love.
I lack the discipline
To face the waves and drown in them.
My nature is to spin
Around and around like a grain of sand
Whenever a tide flows in.

ANONYMOUS (LATE SEVENTH CENTURY)

Plum Trees

Those plum-slips that we planted
My darling wife and I.
Stand now in the garden
As thick around and high
As full-grown trees.

I stare at them.

How high their branches float
Upon these tears which blind me
As grief thickens in my throat

OTOMO NO TIBITO (665–731)

Pearl Diver

No one dives to the ocean-bottom
Just like that:
One does not learn the skills involved
At the drop of a hat
It's those skills slow-learnt in the depths of love
That I'm working at.

LADY NAKATOMI (EARLY EIGHTH CENTURY)

The poem I select is No. 29 from John Berryman's 77 Dream Songs. *Begins: 'There sat down once... etc.'*

John Berryman's 77 Dream Songs *is the book of poetry I return to most. This particular poem for a wickedly merciful laugh on the nights when there is nothing to hang on to but the sweaty bars of the dock, when the evidence is stacking up against you and the jury gasps and covers its mouth during the reconstruction of your every precious hour back to the very start. The poem is a desperate bruised mouthful of hope. Hang on, it says, these hands may be trembling but they are innocent. These eyes have never scowled at beauty. Everybody is present yet and uncorrected. Nobody's missing is there?*

Hope that's OK.

Sean

from *The Dream Songs*

29
There sat down, once, a thing on Henry's heart
só heavy, if he had a hundred years
& more, & weeping, sleepless, in all them time
Henry could not make good.
Starts again always in Henry's ears
the little cough somewhere, an odour, a chime.

And there is another thing he has in mind
like a grave Sienese face a thousand years
would fail to blur the still profiled reproach of. Ghastly,
with open eyes, he attends, blind.
All the bells say: too late. This is not for tears;
thinking.

But never did Henry, as he thought he did,
end anyone and hacks her body up
and hide the pieces, where they may be found.
He knows: he went over everyone, & nobody's missing.
Often he reckons, in the dawn, them up.
Nobody is ever missing.

JOHN BERRYMAN (1914–1972)

26 January 1988

Dear Julie, Jonathan and Duncan,

Thanks very much for your letter and for the invitation to contribute to the book. My sincere congratulations on your initiative and dedication in producing a book – I have some idea of the amount of perseverance and sheer hard labour involved. It is terrible that such efforts should have any place in a supposedly civilised world, that other people's lives should depend on them. But so long as they do we are all prisoners of conscience.

I hope you like the poem I've chosen. It's by the Chilean Nobel Prize winner Pablo Neruda, who died of a heart-attack during the savage coup in his country in 1973. I've chosen it both because I think it's a wonderful poem and because I think it's appropriate to the inspiration of your book: our responsibility not to ignore the suffering of our fellow human beings. This is what I'd like to say about it:

Pablo Neruda's poem is both a work of great formal beauty and a statement of the insufficiency of beauty in an ugly world. Neruda, a poet of the magical and the mysterious, was Chile's consul in Madrid at the time of the Spanish Civil War. There, through the friendship of fellow-poets like Federico Garcia Lorca (the 'Federico' of the poem), murdered by the Fascists, he discovered his responsibility to his fellow man in the face of barbarity and atrocity. What is wonderful about the poem, however, is that the devastation of death is set against the vigour, colour and flow of life. The poem is tragic but also an affirmation of the joy of living. Against the accusation that he no longer writes 'pure poetry', Neruda puts forward both a vision of the richness of humanity and an invocation of the terror of its destruction by the Fascist bombing of Madrid. I can never read it without a mixture of horror, anger and hope.

Good luck with the entire project,

All the best,

Fintan O'Toole

I'm Explaining a Few Things

You are going to ask: and where are the lilacs?
and the poppy-petalled metaphysics?
and the rain repeatedly spattering
its words and drilling them full
of apertures and birds?

I'll tell you all the news.

I lived in a suburb,
a suburb of Madrid, with bells,
and clocks, and trees.

From there you could look out
over Castille's dry face:
a leather ocean.

    My house was called
the house of flowers, because in every cranny
geraniums burst: it was
a good-looking house
with its dogs and children.

    Remember, Raul?
Eh, Rafael?
    Federico, do you remember
From under the ground
my balconies on which
the light of June drowned flowers in your mouth?
                Brother, my brother!

Everything
loud with big voices, the salt of merchandises,
pile-ups of palpitating bread,
the stalls of my suburb of Arguelles with its statue
like a drained inkwell in a swirl of hake:
oil flowed into spoons,
a deep baying
of feet and hands swelled in the streets,
metres, litres, the sharp
measure of life,
    stacked-up fish,
the texture of roofs with a cold sun in which
the weather vane falters,
the fine, frenzied ivory of potatoes,
wave on wave of tomatoes rolling down to the sea.

And one morning all that was burning,
one morning the bonfires
leapt out of the earth
devouring human beings —
and from then on fire,
gunpowder from then on,
and from then on blood.
Bandits with planes and moors
bandits with finger-rings and duchesses,
bandits with black friars spattering blessings
came through the sky to kill children
and the blood of children ran through the streets
without fuss, like children's blood.

Jackals that the jackals would despise,
stones that the dry thistle would bite on and spit out,
vipers that the vipers would abominate!

Face to face with you I have seen the blood
of Spain tower like a tide
to drown you in one wave
of pride and knives!

Treacherous
generals:
see my dead house,
look at broken Spain:
from every house burning metal flows
instead of flowers,
from every socket of Spain
Spain emerges
and from every dead child a rifle with eyes,
and from every crime bullets are born
which one day will find
the bull's eye of your hearts.

And you will ask: why doesn't his poetry
speak of dreams and leaves
and the great volcanoes of his native land?

Come and see the blood in the streets.
Come and see
the blood in the streets.
Come and see the blood
in the streets!

PABLO NERUDA (1904–1973)
(Translated by Nathaniel Tar)

4 January 1990

Dear Joann, Jacki and Carolyn,

Many thanks for inviting me to participate in this worthy venture.

A favourite poem of mine is 'Coal for Mike' by Brecht. As I understand it, the poem is about unconditional love, which is rare enough.

Also the vivid imagery in the poem allows one to play back the story of the poem again and again, whether standing in a queue waiting for stamps, or going home on the bus.

Success to you.

Slán go fóill,

Rita Ann Higgins

Coal for Mike

I have heard that in Ohio
At the beginning of this century
A woman lived in Bidwell
Mary McCoy, widow of a railroad man
Mike McCoy by name, in poverty.

But every night from the thundering trains of the Wheeling Railroad
The brakemen threw a lump of coal
Over the picket fence into the potato patch
Shouting hoarsely in their haste:
For Mike!

And every night when the lump of coal for Mike
Hit the back wall of the shanty
The old woman got up, crept
Drunk with sleep into her dress and hid away the lump of coal
The brakemen's present to Mike, who was dead but
Not forgotten.

The reason why she got up so long before daybreak and hid
Their gifts from the sight of the world was so that
The brakemen should not get into trouble
With the Wheeling Railroad.

This poem is dedicated to the comrades
Of the brakeman Mike McCoy
(Whose lungs were too weak to stand
The coal trains of Ohio)
For comradeship.

BERTOLT BRECHT (1898–1956)
(Translated by Edith Anderson)

JENNIFER JOHNSTON

NOVELIST

20 January 1988

Dear Three,

Thank you for your letter.

I can't possibly let you have the text of my favourite poem, as I have quite a few . . . and anyway I expect that lots of people will send you the same poems over and over again. Here, however is a short poem that I like very much and it seems to have relevance to what you are trying to do.

It is called 'Fairy Tale'. It is written by a Czech poet called Miroslav Holub. I don't know how you pronounce that, but that doesn't matter. It is simple, truthful and sad and filled with beautiful imagination.

It has for me the innocence and simplicity of a child's painting, bright, honest, unselfconscious, and the sad wisdom of the adult; all wrapped up into such a few lines.

I hope you like it also.

Good luck with the project and have a happy 1988.

Yours in friendship,

Jennifer Johnston

Fairy Tale

He built himself a house,
    his foundations,
    his stones,
    his walls,
    his roof overhead,
    his chimney and smoke,
    his view from the window.

He made himself a garden,
    his fence,
    his thyme,
    his earthworm,
    his evening dew.

He cut out his bit of sky above.

And he wrapped the garden in the sky
and the house in the garden
and packed the lot in a handkerchief
and went off
lone as an arctic fox
through the cold
unending
rain
into the world.

MIROSLAV HOLUB (1923–1998)
(From the Czech, translated by George Theiner)

1 February 1988

Dear Julie, Jonathan, Duncan,

I know Adrian Mitchell and have heard him reading his poetry from time to time, but even though he has written poems which may have stronger messages, poetry against war of all kinds, nothing ever struck me as being so immediate and something that everyone could understand as this. We have all been in a playground of some sort or other, there has always been violence and hurt and cruelty. I saw this as a child and as a teacher. People pick on others often without any idea of the damage and the hurt they have caused.

But the end of the poem is very true and very full of hope. When you are older and more or less grown up it becomes easier to take charge of your own life and not to feel a victim of the bullies and those who wound you with words or with war in the Killing Ground.

All the best,

Maeve Binchy

Back in the Playground Blues

I dreamed I was back in the playground, I was
    about four feet high
Yes dreamed I was back in the playground,
    standing about four feet high
Well the playground was three miles long and
    the playground was five miles wide.

It was broken black tarmac with a high wire
    fence all around
Broken black dusty tarmac with a high fence
    running all around
And it had a special name to it, they called
    it The Killing Ground.

Got a mother and a father, they're one
    thousand years away
The rulers of The Killing Ground are coming
    out to play
Everybody thinking: 'Who they going to play
    with today?'

    Well you get it for being Jewish
    And you get it for being black
    Get it for being chicken
    And you get it for fighting back
    You get it for being big and fat
    Get it for being small
    Oh those who get it get it and get it
    For any damn thing at all

Sometimes they take a beetle, tear off its
    six legs one by one
Beetle on its black back, rocking in the
    lunchtime sun
But a beetle can't beg for mercy, a beetle's
    not half the fun.

I heard a deep voice talking, it had that
    iceberg sound,
'It prepares them for Life' – but I have
    never found
Any place in my life worse than The Killing Ground.

ADRIAN MITCHELL (B. 1932)

KATIE DONOVAN WRITER

1994

'Gan do Chuid Éadaigh'/'Nude' *by Nuala Ní Dhomhnaill is one of my favourite poems. I like the poet's subversion of the perspective of the traditional love poem, wherein a male poet gives an admiring description of his beloved's physical charms. Instead we have a female poet casting a loving and appreciative eye on her man's nakedness. She takes on the authoritative role of observer, which is so often presumed to be a male preserve. I like her frank expression of fierce and exultant possessiveness towards her lover's body. Her tongue-in-cheek tone takes pleasure in flouting the convention that only men should admit to these feelings.*

I enjoy the fact that her male translator, Paul Muldoon, enters the fun-loving spirit of the poem (I am assuming that the 'la-di-da' is his inspired addition). No doubt reassuring for many men, this poem shows that so-called caveman appeal can't hold a candle to silky snow-white skin with its own distinctive scent.

Ní Dhomhnaill writes openly about the body in a way that Irish women poets have not done before, perhaps because, like Virginia Woolf, they encountered a block in their imaginations when it came to writing about a subject which was considered taboo: unclean, improper. Mary O'Malley, Mary O'Donnell and Maighread Medbh are other Irish poets who are following in her footsteps.

Our cultural heritage includes legendary women of earth goddess proportions such as the lusty warrior, Queen Medbh, and Cuchulainn's wife, 'great-bladdered Emer'. These women were not shy about the physical side of their lives. Perhaps the wheel is turning full circle, and we are shrugging off a relatively recent, imported strain of prudery. The great number of Irish women poets writing today, and the wide scope of their subject matter, augurs well for the future.

Katie Donovan

Gan do Chuid Éadaigh

Is fearr liom tú
gan do chuid éadaigh ort,
do léine shíoda
is do charabhat,
do scáth fearthainne faoi t'ascaill
is do chulaith
trí phíosa faiseanta
le barr feabhais táilliúrachta,

do bhróga ar a mbíonn
i gcónaí snas,
do lamhainní craiceann eilite
ar do bhois,
do hata *crombie*
feircthe ar fhaobhar na cluaise—
ní chuireann siad aon ruainne
le do thuairisc,

mar thíos fúthu
i ngan fhios don slua
tá corp gan mhaisle, mháchail
nó míbhua
lúfaireacht ainmhí allta,
cat mór a bhíonn amuigh
san oíche
is a fhágann sceimhle ina mharbhshruth.

Do ghuailne leathan fairsing
is do thaobh
chomh slím le sneachta séidte
ar an sliabh;
do dhrom, do bhásta singil
is i do ghabhal
an rúta
go bhfuil barr pléisiúrtha ann.

Do chraiceann atá chomh dorcha
is slím
le síoda go mbeadh tiús veilbhite
ina shníomh
is é ar chumhracht airgid luachra
nó meadhg na habhann
go ndeirtear faoi
go bhfuil suathadh fear is ban ann.

Mar sin is dá bhrí sin
is tú ag rince liom anocht
cé go mb'fhearr liom tú
gan do chuid éadaigh ort,
b'fhéidir nárbh aon díobháil duit
gléasadh anois ar an dtoirt
in ionad leath ban Éireann
a mhilleadh is a lot.

Nuala Ní Dhomhnaill (b.1952)

Nude

The long and short
of it is I'd far rather see you nude—
your silk shirt
and natty

tie, the brolly under your oxter
in case of a rainy day,
the three-piece seersucker
suit that's so incredibly trendy,

your snazzy loafers
and, la-di-da,
a pair of gloves
made from the skin of a doe,

then, to top it all, a crombie hat
set at a rak-
ish angle—none of these add
up to more than the icing on the cake.

For, unbeknownst to the rest
of the world, behind the outward
show lies a body unsurpassed
for beauty, without so much as a wart

or blemish, but the brill-
iant slink of a wild animal, a dream-
cat, say, on the prowl,
leaving murder and mayhem

in its wake. Your broad, sinewy
shoulders and your flank
smooth as the snow
on a snow-bank.

Your back, your slender waist,
and, of course,
the root that is the very seat
of pleasure, the pleasure-source.

Your skin so dark, my beloved,
and soft
as silk with a hint of velvet
in its weft,

smelling as it does of meadowsweet
or 'watermead'
that has the power, or so it's said,
to drive men and women mad.

For that reason alone, if for no other,
when you come with me to the dance tonight
(though, as you know, I'd much prefer
to see you nude)

it would probably be best
for you to pull on your pants and vest
rather than send
half the women of Ireland totally round the bend.

Translated by Paul Muldoon

['*Gan do Chuid Éadaigh*' was also chosen by Katy Hayes in *Lifelines 3*, with a translation by the author. Katy Hayes wrote:
Thank you for your invitation. The poem I have chosen, enclosed here in Irish and with an English translation, is 'Gan do Chuid Éadaigh' by Nuala Ní Dhomhnaill. Poems about male beauty are so rare that, when one comes across such a delightful one as this, it has the same arresting power as beauty itself.]

EILEEN DUNNE   NEWSCASTER

15 April 1985

Please find enclosed two pieces – at least one of which I hope you'll find suitable.

'Desiderata' isn't really a poem – I know, but it's a piece that means a lot to me. Like most teenagers in the Seventies, I had a poster of it on my wall, and then of course there was the record – a firm favourite. I went to Manor House school in Raheny, and when I was leaving in 1975 we had a graduation Mass. 'Desiderata' was on the back page of the missalettes we got that day, and I have always thought that it was excellent advice for the nuns to send us out into the world with.

As for Prévert – well this little poem epitomises for me the power and simplicity of the French language, especially when it comes to romance and the like.

So I hope this is all of some use to you. Good luck with your project and do send me a copy of the book when it comes out (I'll pay for it of course!).

Yours sincerely,

Eileen Dunne

Paris at Night

Trois allumettes une à une allumées dans la nuit
La première pour voir ton visage tout entier
La seconde pour voir tes yeux
La dernière pour voir ta bouche
Et l'obscurité tout entière pour me rappeler tout cela
En te serrant dans mes bras.

JACQUES PRÉVERT (1900–1977)

Desiderata

Go placidly amid the noise and haste and remember what peace there may be in silence. As far as possible without surrender be on good terms with all persons. Speak your truth quietly and clearly; and listen to others, even the dull and ignorant – they too have their story. Avoid loud and aggressive persons; they are vexations to the spirit. If you compare yourself with others, you may become vain and bitter; for always there will be greater and lesser persons than yourself. Enjoy your achievements as well as your plans. Keep interested in your own career, however humble – it is a real possession in the changing fortune of time. Exercise caution in your business affairs, for the world is full of trickery. But let this not blind you to what virtue there is; many persons strive for high ideals, and everywhere life is full of heroism. Be yourself, especially do not feign affection. Neither be cynical about love; for in the face of all aridity and disenchantment it is as perennial as the grass. Take kindly the counsel of the years, gracefully surrendering the things of youth. Nurture strength of spirit to shield you in sudden misfortune. But do not distress yourself with imaginings. Many fears are born of fatigue and loneliness. Beyond a wholesome discipline, be gentle with yourself.

You are a child of the universe, no less than the trees and the stars; you have a right to be here. And whether or not it is clear to you, no doubt the universe is unfolding as it should. Therefore be at peace with God, whatever you conceive Him to be. And whatever your labours and aspirations in the noisy confusion of life, keep at peace with your soul. With all its sham, drudgery and broken dreams, it is still a beautiful world. Be careful. Strive to be happy.

BEN ELTON COMEDIAN

Dear Nicola, Paula and Alice,

To tell you the truth I have read very little poetry since leaving school. It is an omission I regret but one cannot do everything. I find it difficult enough keeping up with the prose I wish to read. Therefore I'm afraid I do not have a favourite poem. I know this is not a very helpful reply, but there you go. Were you to ask me to name my favourite poet I would answer Shakespeare, but to choose one piece from his endlessly inspiring work would be impossible.

Favourites aside, you might be surprised to hear that the single piece of verse that has most moved me is a quote from the lyric of Cliff Richard's old hit 'The Young Ones'. It was in 1984 when The Young Ones *TV show which I had co-written was a big hit. Rik Mayall and I were on tour together. After the show we always signed autographs for those that wanted them. One night a mother came back with her son, he was about eleven and was, she explained, a colossal* Young Ones *fan, adding that he did not have long to live. The boy was embarrassed and tongue-tied, and of course nobody really knew what to say, so his mother asked Rik to write something for the boy on a tour poster. I did not envy Rik at that moment; what can you write, off the cuff, to a dying boy who adores you? In what I feel was a moment of inspiration, Rik wrote a quote from Cliff's old song which Rik had sung over the titles of the series. He wrote 'Young Ones shouldn't be afraid'. The boy and his mother seemed much moved by this thought, as indeed was I.*

Not great poetry I'll admit, but good writing can sometimes be as much about context as content and I shall always remember that line. As Noël Coward (whose lyrics I also adore) once said, 'strange how potent cheap music can be.'

Huge best wishes for the book,

Yours sincerely,

Ben Elton

CATHERINE PHIL MACCARTHY POET

Dear Ewan, Áine and Chris,

Thanks for inviting me to participate in your wonderful project for hunger relief. I am full of admiration for Lifelines *and hope you make a fortune with your next book.*

My favourite poem is 'The Pomegranate' by Eavan Boland. I love it for the beauty and intimacy of the private world it reveals – the sleeping child, her can of Coke, the uncut fruit, her mother's resolve to say nothing. It makes instant and magical changes always from legend to life, in a voice that is never less than exhilarating for its urgency and ability to surprise. At the heart of the poem is love and loss, at once ritualized and totally formless.

Good luck with your work.

Yours sincerely,

Catherine Phil MacCarthy

The Pomegranate

The only legend I have ever loved is
the story of a daughter lost in hell.
And found and rescued there.
Love and blackmail are the gist of it.
Ceres and Persephone the names.
And the best thing about the legend is
I can enter it anywhere. And have.
As a child in exile in
a city of fogs and strange consonants,
I read it first and at first I was
an exiled child in the crackling dusk of
the underworld, the stars blighted. Later
I walked out in a summer twilight
searching for my daughter at bed-time.
When she came running I was ready
to make any bargain to keep her.
I carried her back past whitebeams
and wasps and honey-scented buddleias.
But I was Ceres then and I knew
winter was in store for every leaf
on every tree on that road.
Was inescapable for each one we passed.
And for me.

        It is winter
and the stars are hidden.
I climb the stairs and stand where I can see
my child asleep beside her teen magazines,
her can of Coke, her plate of uncut fruit.
The pomegranate! How did I forget it?
She could have come home and been safe
and ended the story and all
our heart-broken searching but she reached
out a hand and plucked a pomegranate.
She put out her hand and pulled down
the French sound for apple and
the noise of stone and the proof
that even in the place of death,
at the heart of legend, in the midst
of rocks full of unshed tears
ready to be diamonds by the time
the story was told, a child can be
hungry. I could warn her. There is still a chance.
The rain is cold. The road is flint-coloured.

The suburb has cars and cable television.
The veiled stars are above ground.
It is another world. But what else
can a mother give her daughter but such
beautiful rifts in time?
If I defer the grief I will diminish the gift.
The legend will be hers as well as mine.
She will enter it. As I have.
She will wake up. She will hold
the papery flushed skin in her hand.
And to her lips. I will say nothing.

EAVAN BOLAND (B.1944)

['*The Pomegranate*' was also chosen by Lia Mills in *Lifelines 3*. Lia Mills wrote:
Thank you for your letter asking me to nominate a poem for Lifelines 3. *You've given me days of anguish because I find it very difficult to choose one 'favourite'. There are many poems that I love and return to, at different times and for different reasons. However, I've finally settled on 'The Pomegranate', by Eavan Boland.*
   Good luck with compiling the anthology. It's a brilliant idea, and I'm very glad to be included in it.
   The legend of Demeter (Ceres) and Persephone has always been a favourite of mine, because it can see us through almost anything. The levels of meaning in the myth are both general and personal, and will probably never be exhausted. 'The Pomegranate' is a recognition of that, and is a reminder of the sustaining and imaginative power of literature, its continuing relevance. I love this poem because its language and imagery make it live and because, while it recognises loss, it also believes in renewal. It is a moving, powerful expression of creativity and of maternal love.]

PATRICIA McKENNA POLITICIAN

23 January 1997

Dear Ralph, Caroline and Gareth,

Thanks a million for your letter requesting details of my favourite poem: 'On Raglan Road' *by Patrick Kavanagh. I hope that you will bend the rules a tiny bit for me, as most people think of this work as a song, rather than a poem.*
   Best of luck with the new edition of Lifelines. *The previous editions were extremely impressive and I look forward to seeing the fruits of your work.*
   Le gach dea-ghuí,

Patricia McKenna

'On Raglan Road' *is one of the most beautiful things ever written. So many people's experiences of life and love are contained in the lines:*

> I saw the danger, yet I walked along the enchanted way,
> And I said, let grief be a fallen leaf at the dawning of the day.

I always thought that nobody could come even close to Luke Kelly's version of this song, but I was proven wrong when I heard Sinéad O'Connor's haunting rendition recently.
   Like myself, Kavanagh grew up in Monaghan and then moved to Dublin, where his finest poems were written. His poems, especially the ones he wrote on the banks of the

Grand Canal, show that you can find serenity and peace amid the hustle and bustle of Dublin life and highlight how everything must be done to preserve the capital's heritage.

On Raglan Road

On Raglan Road on an autumn day I met her first and knew
That her dark hair would weave a snare that I might one day rue;
I saw the danger, yet I walked along the enchanted way,
And I said, let grief be a fallen leaf at the dawning of the day.

On Grafton Street in November we tripped lightly along the ledge
Of the deep ravine where can be seen the worth of passion's pledge,
The Queen of Hearts still making tarts and I not making hay –
O I loved too much and by such, by such, is happiness thrown away.

I gave her gifts of the mind, I gave her the secret sign that's known
To the artists who have known the true gods of sound and stone
And word and tint. I did not stint for I gave her poems to say
With her own name there and her own dark hair like clouds over fields of May.

On a quiet street where old ghosts meet I see her walking now
Away from me so hurriedly my reason must allow
That I had wooed not as I should a creature made of clay –
When the angel woos the clay he'd lose his wings at the dawn of day.

PATRICK KAVANAGH (1904–1967)

['*On Raglan Road*' has been chosen five times – by Ken Bourke in *Lifelines*, by Jimmy Murphy in *Lifelines 2* and by Seamus Hosey, Tom Garvin and Patricia McKenna in *Lifelines 3*.]

Ken Bourke wrote:
My choice is 'On Raglan Road' by Patrick Kavanagh. I like this poem for its romance, its tragedy, and its evocation of Dublin. I am particularly fond of the sung version by Luke Kelly. I sing it myself, often on my own, but also in company, when I'm let.

Jimmy Murphy wrote:
I suppose if I was to have a favourite poem it would be a poem that would stir up in me a fond memory that was lost in whereever memories lose themselves. Yeats's 'He wishes for the cloths of heaven' is one and, if I was to choose a favourite, then Kavanagh's 'On Raglan Road' is it.
  I don't know what he intended, but it's a poem of unrequited love to me. And whether we're ready or not, one day we will all trip lightly along the ledge of our own 'quiet street . . .'.

Seamus Hosey wrote:
I am delighted to nominate 'On Raglan Road' by Patrick Kavanagh as a favourite poem of mine. Like so many of Kavanagh's poems it manages to combine simplicity with profundity. This, I think, is a great love poem and I can never read it without hearing the voice of Luke Kelly bringing it so dramatically to life to the air of 'The Dawning of the Day'. This poem by Patrick Kavanagh seems to me a perfect exposition of Joyce's line which says it all: 'We lived and loved and laughed and left.'

Tom Garvin wrote:

I would like to nominate 'On Raglan Road', by Patrick Kavanagh. It has many resonances for me, not least that of watching Luke Kelly sing it in Dublin thirty years ago. The poem evokes the city as it was in the 1950s in its use of familiar placenames. It is an urban ballad, and a love song. I like it also because of its descent from Irish tradition. My grandfather, John Daly of Clonakility, West Cork, born about 1870, sang its ancestor as his favourite song ('The Dawning of the Day'). He taught it to me as a child. As a boy in Ring College, County Waterford, I was taught the eighteenth-century Kerry version, 'Fáinne Geal an Lae'.

'On Raglan Road' symbolises a continuity of singing tradition over two centuries, from Irish to English and from rural to urban. All three versions are about a man's love for a woman.]

JOANNA TROLLOPE   NOVELIST

20 January 1997

Dear Ralph, Caroline and Gareth,

Here is my choice for the new Lifelines. *I think it's a wonderful idea and I hope it's a huge success.*

   With very best wishes,

Yours sincerely,

Joanna Trollope

Heaven-Haven
A nun takes the veil

I have desired to go
       Where springs not fail,
To fields where flies no sharp and sided hail
       And a few lilies blow.

And I have asked to be
       Where no storms come,
Where the green swell is in the havens dumb,
       And out of the swing of the sea.

GERARD MANLEY HOPKINS (1844–1889)

I think we all hope to get to some kind of heaven, somewhere, and this expression of it seems to me not only peaceful but also poignant, which makes it very human. I also like the pictures in it.

JAMIE MCKENDRICK POET

28 February 1994

Dear Ewan Gibson, Áine Jackson, Christopher Pillow,

Many thanks for your invitation to the new Lifelines *anthology. I feel very honoured, and I'm sorry for the delay in replying. I hope it isn't too late to send in – a small 'eternity' here too.*

  The poem I finally settled for is Emily Dickinson's 'Because I could not stop for Death'. *All best wishes for your anthology.*

Yours sincerely,

Jamie McKendrick

> Because I could not stop for Death—
> He kindly stopped for me—
> The Carriage held but just Ourselves—
> And Immortality.
>
> We slowly drove—He knew no haste
> And I had put away
> My labor and my leisure too,
> For His Civility—
>
> We passed the School, where Children strove
> At Recess—in the Ring—
> We passed the Fields of Gazing Grain—
> We passed the Setting Sun—
>
> Or rather—He passed Us—
> The Dews drew quivering and chill—
> For only Gossamer, my Gown—
> My Tippet—only Tulle—
>
> We paused before a House that seemed
> A Swelling of the Ground—
> The Roof was scarcely visible—
> The Cornice—in the Ground—
>
> Since then—'tis Centuries—and yet
> Feels shorter than the Day
> I first surmised the Horses' Heads
> Were toward Eternity—

EMILY DICKINSON (1830–1886)

What I most admire in this poem is its small compass and enormous span – a curve which links the everyday to forever. Dickinson is one of the few poets who can give an abstraction like 'Eternity' a distinct physical presence. Especially here, where the subject is time.

Rhythmically the poem slows down then breathlessly accelerates time, elongates and foreshortens it, until by the final '–' any conventional idea of duration is in shreds.

Jamie McKendrick

JOHN QUINN BROADCASTER

26 January 1994

Dear Ewan, Áine and Christopher,

Thank you for the honour of inviting me to contribute to Lifelines 2. *I enjoy leafing through the first* Lifelines *and commend your predecessors on their initiative. As to my own selection, I initially thought of choosing something by Kavanagh or Hopkins – but then I remembered the enclosed little poem which I like very much. Let me tell you why.*

Twenty years ago, as editor with an educational publishing company, I compiled a series of English anthologies for senior standards in primary schools. As well as including established poets I was anxious to give a platform to the writing of children of that day. Patricia Heeney was then aged twelve and a pupil of Duleek National School, Co. Meath. For me, her poem 'Things I Like' has simplicity, a directness and a freshness that time has not withered. There is the reassurance of the familiar, allied to a natural poetic rhythm. (Where are you now, Patricia? I hope you are still writing . . .)

I hope you and your readers will derive as much pleasure from this poem as I do. Good luck with Lifelines 2.

John Quinn

Things I Like

> Bark of our dog to welcome us home,
> Croak of a frog on the commons;
> Trot of a horse,
> Heather and gorse on Bellewstown hill;
> Bleat of a lamb,
> Gurgling and laughing of Curleys' baby
> In her pram.

PATRICIA HEENEY (BORN C.1962)

Dear Collette Lucy, Joy Marshall, Steven Given:

Thank you for your letter. I enclose the text of a poem which you might like to use in your anthology. Celan's poetry is very difficult to translate, so I hope you can carry the German as well as the English translation. Even though many readers will not know German, the look of the original is important.

I wish you the best of luck with your venture.

John Banville

Psalm

Niemand knetet uns weider aus Erde und Lehm,
niemand besprict unsern Staub.
Niemand.

Gelobt seist du, Niemand.
Dir zulieb wollen
wir blühn.
Dir
entgegen.

Ein Nichts
waren wir, sind wir, werden
wir bleiben, blühend:
die Nichts—, die
Niemandsrose.

Mit
dem Griffel seelenhell
dem Staubfaden himmelswüst,
der Krone rot
vom Purpurwort, das wir sangen
über, o über
dem Dorn.

PAUL CELAN (1920–1970)

There is no single poem which I would describe as my favourite. However, here is the text of a very beautiful poem, which I think would be particularly suitable for your anthology. It is by Paul Celan (1920–1970), a Jewish poet who wrote in German. As a child during World War II he was a prisoner in a Romanian Labour camp. His parents were killed by the Nazis. Out of these terrible experiences he created a heartbreaking poetry.

Psalm

No one moulds us again out of earth and clay,
no one conjures our dust.
No one.

Praised be your name, no one.
For your sake
we shall flower.
Towards
you.

A nothing
we were, are, shall
remain, flowering;
the nothing —, the
no one's rose.

With our pistil soul-bright
with our stamen heaven-ravaged
our corolla red
with the crimson word which we sang
over, o over
the thorn.

PAUL CELAN (1920–1970)
(Translated by Michael Hamburger)

[Richard Kearney also chose '*Psalm*' in *Lifelines*. Richard Kearney wrote:
*This poem by the modern German Jewish poet, Paul Celan, is, for me, a cry of hope from the
darkest abyss. It celebrates the defiant power of song even as one struggles through the darkest night
of the soul or the most despairing hour of history. The 'I Am' of the Bible is here invoked in the
contemporary idiom of the 'no one' – a power of love which can become present to us even in those
times it appears most absent.*]

TESS GALLAGHER   POET

1 May 1993

Dear Ewan Gibson, et al,

Thank you for your letter.
   Your project seems quite a good one and I will enclose a copy of the poem 'What the
Doctor Said' *by Raymond Carver, which is from his last book entitled* A New Path to
the Waterfall.
   *Now as to why this is a favorite poem of mine: Raymond Carver was able to write this
poem in the aftermath of having received the dire news that his lung cancer, which had
progressed to the brain, had then spread to the one remaining lung. What's amazing
to me is that horror, humor and mortality all coexist in this poem. The humanity of*

the speaker in the poem is what astounds me every time I re-read the poem. I feel the predicament of the doctor having to deliver such news and trying to clock himself in the facticity of counting the tumors. I feel the razor sharp irony of the speaker, how it coexists with his desperate need to cling to hope, and then the amazing way in which the speaker grasps the hands of the very one who has delivered the news of his death. It is as if he has seen the highest choice and, in a way, vanquished death by thanking the messenger who has by then begun to assume an almost ridiculous air. It is the speaker whose stature is enlarged, even if it is 'habit' which delivers him from that impossible, yet unavoidable news. Ray wrote the poem and then fulfilled its news with his death barely two months later, on 2 August 1988. Except for the Buddhist monks who used to write a brief haiku, then put down their pens and die, I don't know any contemporary example of a writer giving us such a poem under the pressure of his own imminent death. I love its spiritual dimension which is delivered so offhandedly that it takes hold of us the way sunlight takes hold of roses and weeds alike.

I hope this is sufficient to explain my predilection for this poem by my late husband. Sincere best wishes,

Tess Gallagher

What the Doctor Said

He said it doesn't look good
he said it looks bad in fact real bad
he said I counted thirty-two of them on one lung before
I quit counting them
I said I'm glad I wouldn't want to know
about any more being there than that
he said are you a religious man do you kneel down
in forest groves and let yourself ask for help
when you come to a waterfall
mist blowing against your face and arms
do you stop and ask for understanding at those moments
I said not yet but I intend to start today
he said I'm real sorry he said
I wish I had some other kind of news to give you
I said Amen and he said something else
I didn't catch and not knowing what else to do
and not wanting him to have to repeat it
and me to have to fully digest it
I just looked at him
for a minute and he looked back it was then
I jumped up and shook hands with this man who'd just given me
something no one else on earth had ever given me
I may even have thanked him habit being so strong

RAYMOND CARVER (1939–1988)

JEREMY IRONS ACTOR

Dear Joann, Jacki and Carolyn,

Thank you for your letter regarding Lifelines. *Herewith my poem, the author is unknown to me. It is my favourite poem since it deals with risk and trust and the magic that occurs sometimes when you do either.*

Come to the Edge

Come to the edge.
We might fall.
Come to the edge.
It's too high!
COME TO THE EDGE!
And they came,
and he pushed,
and they flew

CHRISTOPHER LOGUE (B. 1926)

I hope this will suffice and I wish you good luck in your efforts.

Yours sincerely,

Jeremy Irons

NOEL MONAGHAN POET

20 April 2006

Delighted to hear from you re my choice of favourite poem for inclusion in Lifelines.

My favourite poem is The Great Hunger *by Patrick Kavanagh. I have chosen this poem above the thousands of poems I have read over the years because it relates most to me. Coming as I do from Granard, County Longford, one might expect I would be tempted by 'The Deserted Village' by Goldsmith, a much-loved pastoral poem of the midlands ... But No. I love* The Great Hunger, *an anti-pastoral poem with a passion.*

Patrick Maguire, the protagonist in the poem, hardly ever achieves a rudimentary consciousness. The poem attempts to answer the great questions ... What is life? What is man? ... The poem's stark realism is haunting. Kavanagh is not viewing the Irish peasantry from the safety of Thoor Ballylee. Kavanagh, the poet, has first-hand experience and is out there in the fields with Maguire picking the potatoes.

Because the poem is 759 lines long, it would be foolish to think you could publish it in its entirety, so I've chosen the following lines.

Let me wish you continued success with your great adventure.

Le Gach Dea Ghuí,

Noel Monaghan

from *The Great Hunger*
from XIII

The peasant is the unspoiled child of Prophecy,
The peasant is all virtues – let us salute him without irony –
The peasant ploughman who is half a vegetable,
Who can react to sun and rain and sometimes even
Regret that the Maker of Light had not touched him more intensely,
Brought him up from the sub-soil to an existence
Of conscious joy. He was not born blind.
He is not always blind: sometimes the cataract yields
To sudden stone-falling or the desire to breed.

The girls pass along the roads
And he can remember what man is,
But there is nothing he can do.
Is there nothing he can do?
Is there no escape?
No escape, no escape.

The cows and horses breed,
And the potato-seed
Gives a bud and a root and rots
In the good mother's way with her sons;
The fledged bird is thrown
From the nest – on its own.
But the peasant in his little acres is tied
To a mother's womb by the wind-toughened navel-cord
Like a goat tethered to a stump of a tree –
He circles around and around wondering why it should be.
No crash,
No drama.
That was how his life happened.
No mad hooves galloping in the sky,
But the weak, washy way of true tragedy –
A sick horse nosing around the meadow for a clean place to die.

PATRICK KAVANAGH (1904–1967)

The Ark, A Cultural Centre for Children,
Temple Bar
28 January 1997

Dear Ralph, Caroline and Gareth,

Thank you for your letter inviting me to contribute to Lifelines 3. *I am delighted to be asked as I have enjoyed the previous books immensely and consider it a wonderful project.*

The problem now of course is that the previous books contain many dozens of 'my favourite poems'. However, that fact liberates me to propose a poem I like a great deal: 'Though There Are Torturers' by Michael Coady.

This is one of those poems that has lodged for years in the recesses of my mind, surfacing occasionally and with such a quiet insistence that I have realised it matters to me. Apart from its craft, I choose it for its values: I think that the dark side of humanity is so evident in contemporary life that we need to remember that our nature is also distinguished by capacities and dispositions which are joyful and graceful.

With renewed thanks and best wishes for another successful Lifelines,

Yours sincerely,

Martin Drury

Though There Are Torturers

Though there are torturers in the world
There are also musicians.

Though, at this moment, men
Are screaming in prisons
There are jazzmen raising storms
Of sensuous celebration
And orchestras releasing
Glories of the spirit.

Though the image of God
Is everywhere defiled
A man in West Clare
Is playing the concertina,
The Sistine Choir is levitating
Under the dome of St Peter's
And a drunk man on the road
Is singing for no reason.

MICHAEL COADY (B.1939)

23 April 2006

Dear Friends,

While it is not possible to select a favourite poem, I can name one of my favourites by one of my favourite poets: 'A Feaver' by John Donne.

Why? Perhaps because it was one of my earliest encounters with great poetry, as a teenager. The combination of a romantic conceit with the sophistry of the words and thoughts, the absolute convergence of subject matter and literary form, have continued to impress me and influence my own approach to the problems of art.

With all good wishes for the success of your project,

Stephen McKenna

A Feaver

Oh do not die, for I shall hate
    All women so, when thou art gone,
That thee I shall not celebrate,
    When I remember, thou wast one.

But yet thou canst not die, I know,
    To leave this world behind, is death,
But when thou from this world wilt go,
    The whole world vapours with thy breath.

Or if, when thou, the world's soul, go'st,
    It stay, 'tis but thy carcase then,
The fairest woman, but thy ghost,
    But corrupt worms, the worthiest men.

O wrangling schools, that search what fire
    Shall burn this world, had none the wit
Unto this knowledge to aspire,
    That this her feaver might be it?

And yet she cannot waste by this,
    Nor long bear this torturing wrong,
For more corruption needful is
    To fuel such a fever long.

These burning fits but meteors be,
    Whose matter in thee is soon spent.
Thy beauty, and all parts, which are thee,
    Are unchangeable firmament.

Yet 'twas of my mind, seizing thee,
    Though it in thee cannot perséver.
For I had rather owner be
    Of thee one hour, than all else ever.

John Donne (1572–1631)

In my view, 'The Ballad of Reading Gaol' is Oscar Wilde's finest poetic piece. It captures perfectly the intense sadness of man facing certain death, the loneliness of a condemned prisoner, and the pitiful self-interest of fellow inmates – yet their profound heartfelt sympathy for him.

It is a sad and deeply moving poem which I always enjoy returning to. It helps put a perspective on those things in life which we feel are so important but are not really so.

Michael W J Smurfit

from *The Ballad of Reading Gaol*

IV
There is no chapel on the day
    On which they hang a man:
The Chaplain's heart is far too sick,
    Or his face is far too wan,
Or there is that written in his eyes
    Which none should look upon.

So they kept us close till nigh on noon,
    And then they rang the bell,
And the warders with their jingling keys
    Opened each listening cell,
And down the iron stair we tramped,
    Each from his separate Hell.

Out into God's sweet air we went,
    But not in wonted way,
For this man's face was white with fear,
    And this man's face was grey,
And I never saw sad men who looked
    So wistfully at the day.

I never saw sad men who looked
    With such a wistful eye
Upon the little tent of blue
    We prisoners called the sky,
And at every happy cloud that passed
    In such strange freedom by.

But there were those amongst us all
     Who walked with downcast head,
And knew that, had each got his due,
     They should have died instead:
He had but killed a thing that lived,
     Whilst they had killed the dead.

For he who sins a second time
     Wakes a dead soul to pain,
And draws it from its spotted shroud,
     And makes it bleed again,
And makes it bleed great gouts of blood,
     And makes it bleed in vain!

* * * *

They hanged him as a beast is hanged:
     They did not even toll
A requiem that might have brought
     Rest to his startled soul,
But hurriedly they took him out,
     And hid him in a hole.

They warders stripped him of his clothes,
     And gave him to the flies:
They mocked the swollen purple throat,
     And the stark and staring eyes:
And with laughter loud they heaped the shroud
     In which the convict lies.

The Chaplain would not kneel to pray
     By his dishonoured grave:
Nor mark it with that blessed Cross
     That Christ for sinners gave,
Because the man was one of those
     Whom Christ came down to save.

Yet all is well; he has but passed
     To Life's appointed bourne:
And alien tears will fill for him
     Pity's long-broken urn,
For his mourners will be outcast men,
     And outcasts always mourn.

OSCAR WILDE (1854–1900)

['*The Ballad of Reading Gaol*' was also chosen by Michele Souter in *Lifelines*.
Michele Souter wrote:
Thank you for writing to me. I have enjoyed reading the past editions of Lifelines *and my choice for your next edition is Oscar Wilde's poem, 'The Ballad of Reading Gaol'. I find it so moving and evocative of the circumstances in which he found himself. I only hope it isn't too long for inclusion in your book.*]

I was honoured to be asked to submit my favourite poem for inclusion in Lifelines. *Thank you so much . Picking a favourite has been very hard. There are so many I really like for all sorts of different reasons. 'The Village Blacksmith' made me fancy men with strong and sinewy arms, and 'To Bring the Dead To Life' still chills me. But the one I kept coming back to was 'Cargoes', by John Masefield.*

I learnt it by heart in primary school and loved it from the beginning. It made me curious. I wanted to know what a 'Quinquireme' was, and where was 'Ophir'? What was an 'isthmus' and a 'gold moidore'?

This was the poem that made me want to be a writer. It taught me a lot about writing. How the way you use words can create images in your mind. It taught me about language and pace and rhythm. In the first two verses you feel as if you are there, rowing home to haven, or passing those palm-green shores. You're in another beautiful, colourful ancient world. Then it's back to reality in the last verse, the pace quickens and you're butting through the Channel on the hard-working little British coaster. And I suppose, it takes me right back to my childhood too.

Catherine MacPhail

Cargoes

Quinquireme of Nineveh from distant Ophir,
Rowing home to haven in sunny Palestine,
With a cargo of ivory,
And apes and peacocks,
Sandalwood, cedarwood, and sweet white wine.

Stately Spanish galleon coming from the Isthmus,
Dipping through the Tropics by the palm-green shores,
With a cargo of diamonds,
Emeralds, amethysts,
Topazes, and cinnamon, and gold moidores.

Dirty British coaster with a salt-caked smoke-stack,
Butting through the Channel in the mad March days,
With a cargo of Tyne coal,
Road-rails, pig-lead,
Firewood, iron-ware, and cheap tin trays.

JOHN MASEFIELD (1878–1967)

19 January 1988

Dear Compilers, all,

Glad to be included in your anthology. Hope you like my choice. I cannot say it's my favourite poem of all time, but I found my wife Kathleen reading it recently and it tickled my heart, for three reasons:

(1) I've been insulted, abused and kicked by TV viewers and radio listeners so often through the years, that I'm sadistically delighted when I see someone else getting a lash – even if they're dead.

(2) I'm a firm believer in the maxim that if you're going to do someone down, you should do a thorough job; and I think you'll agree that Amanda Ros does a thorough job on her hated lawyer. No pussyfooting or skirting the issue here – she lets her readers know precisely her opinion of the offending corpse.

(3) Anyone who has had a run-in with the legal profession in this country will relish the poem.

Gay Byrne

Amanda Ros was born in County Down. Lived 1860–1939. She had a major grudge against people in the legal profession, for whatever reason I do not know.

Jamie Jarr

Here lies a blooming rascal
Once known as Jamie Jarr;
A lawyer of the lowest type,
Who loved your name to char.
Of clownish ways and manners,
He aped at speaking fine,
Which proved as awkward to him
As a drawing-room to swine.

I stood while the ground was hollowed
To admit this pile of stink;
They placed the coffin upside down
(The men upon the brink).
How the stony mould did thunder
Upon the coffin's rump,
The fainter grew the rattle
The deeper Jamie sunk.

His mouth now shut for ever,
His lying tongue now stark —
His 'paws' lie still, and never more
Can stab you in the dark.
Earth is by far the richer,
Hell—one boarder more—
Heaven rejoices to be free
From such a legal 'bore'.

AMANDA ROS (1860–1939)

FAY WELDON NOVELIST

Dear Ewan Gibson,

How about Kipling's 'If'? An old-fashioned poem, suggesting out-of-date self-control, and very stiff-upper-lipped, but nevertheless it had a profound influence.

With best wishes,

Fay Weldon

If—

If you can keep your head when all about you
    Are losing theirs and blaming it on you,
If you can trust yourself when all men doubt you,
    But make allowance for their doubting too;
If you can wait and not be tired by waiting,
    Or being lied about, don't deal in lies,
Or being hated, don't give way to hating,
    And yet don't look too good, nor talk too wise:

If you can dream—and not make dreams your master;
    If you can think—and not make thoughts your aim;
If you can meet with Triumph and Disaster
    And treat those two impostors just the same;
If you can bear to hear the truth you've spoken
    Twisted by knaves to make a trap for fools,
Or watch the things you gave your life to, broken,
    And stoop and build 'em up with worn-out tools:

If you can make one heap of all your winnings
    And risk it on one turn of pitch-and-toss,
And lose, and start again at your beginnings
    And never breathe a word about your loss;
If you can force your heart and nerve and sinew
    To serve your turn long after they are gone,
And so hold on when there is nothing in you
    Except the Will which says to them: 'Hold on!'

If you can talk with crowds and keep your virtue,
    Or walk with Kings—nor lose the common touch,
If neither foes nor loving friends can hurt you,
    If all men count with you, but none too much;
If you can fill the unforgiving minute
    With sixty seconds' worth of distance run,
Yours is the Earth and everything that's in it,
    And—which is more—you'll be a Man, my son!

RUDYARD KIPLING (1865–1936)

26th April 1985

Thank you for your letter. One of my favourite poems is Seamus Heaney's 'Bogland' — from
Door into the Dark. *This is not simply because he dedicated the poem to me, which
naturally pleased me very much, but because he and I had been together at the poem's
beginnings. Seamus and I and our families had spent Hallowe'en together in McFadden's
Hotel at Gortahork in County Donegal. And he came with me when I went out sketching in
the car. It was a dry luminous Autumn, and after the hot summer of that year the bogland
was burnt the colour of marmalade. We all stood on the beach watching marvellous sunsets,
and, in the twilight let off fireworks from the sand dunes to please our children. The poem is
a celebration for me of a very happy and creative time in both our lives.*

Good luck with your project,

T P Flanagan

Bogland
for T P Flanagan

We have no prairies
To slice a big sun at evening —
Everywhere the eye concedes to
Encroaching horizon,

Is wooed into the cyclops' eye
Of a tarn. Our unfenced country
Is bog that keeps crusting
Between the sights of the sun.

They've taken the skeleton
Of the Great Irish Elk
Out of the peat, set it up,
An astounding crate full of air.

Butter sunk under
More than a hundred years
Was recovered salty and white.
The ground itself is kind, black butter

Melting and opening underfoot,
Missing its last definition
By millions of years.
They'll never dig coal here,

Only the waterlogged trunks
Of great firs, soft as pulp.
Our pioneers kept striking
Inwards and downwards,

Every layer they strip
Seems camped on before.
The boglands might be Atlantic seepage.
The wet centre is bottomless.

SEAMUS HEANEY (B. 1939)

HUGHIE O'DONOGHUE ARTIST

2006

Dear All,

I discovered poetry quite late – not really understanding what it was as a youngster. This was probably as a result of the fact that the timetable at the school I attended did not allow me to study both Art and English Literature.

The poem I have chosen is from the first book of poetry that I ever bought. It is short and simple but it connected with me in a very powerful way. It was published in 1971, the year that I met my wife Clare and a year when I spent a lot of time travelling on trains through the industrial towns of northern England. When I read the poem it takes me directly back to that time.

Hughie O'Donoghue

I Caught a Train That Passed the Town Where you Lived

I caught a train that passed the town where you lived.

On the journey I thought of you.
One evening when the park was soaking
You hid beneath trees, and all round you dimmed itself
as if the earth were lit by gaslight.
We had faith that love would last forever.

I caught a train that passed the town where you lived.

BRIAN PATTEN (B. 1946)

28 January 1994

Dear Ewan, Áine and Christopher,

Thank you for inviting me to contribute a favourite poem to the next Lifelines. *I would be delighted, both because the money you raise goes to help others and because the previous* Lifelines *were such fascinating anthologies, full of old favourites and, for me anyway, exciting new discoveries.*

Choosing one poem is almost impossible. But this one by the Czech writer Miroslav Holub seems very suitable for the times we live in.

Good luck,

Margrit Cruickshank

The Door

Go and open the door.
    Maybe outside there's
    a tree, or a wood,
    a garden,
    or a magic city.

Go and open the door.
    Maybe a dog's rummaging.
    Maybe you'll see a face,
or an eye,
or the picture
            of a picture.

Go and open the door.
    If there's a fog
    it will clear.

Go and open the door.
    Even if there's only
    the darkness ticking,
    even if there's only
    the hollow wind,
    even if
            nothing
                is there,
go and open the door.

At least
there'll be
a draught.

MIROSLAV HOLUB (B.1923)
Translated by Ian Milner

February 1994

Robin Flower was an Englishman with a deep love of Ireland and its Gaelic tradition. He was a distinguished scholar and worked for some years compiling The Catalogue of Irish Manuscripts *in the British Museum.*

But Robin Flower's interest in Gaelic Ireland was not confined to the dusty volumes in the Museum; for him the living speech of the Gaelic world was equally important. In this he found an oral literature which he saw as a rich part of an old European civilisation.

From 1910 onwards for about 20 years he spent long holidays in the Great Blasket, a Gaelic speaking island off the Kerry coast, three miles out on the Atlantic, 'the ultimate shore of the old world', as he described it himself.

The people of the Great Blasket made Flower one of themselves and from them he wrote down their folktales and folksongs and translated into English one of the great classic books on life on the Blaskets, written in Irish by his friend Tomás O'Crohan (An tOileánach, The Islandman), who lived there all his life.

But Robin Flower was a writer and a poet in his own right and his book The Western Island *or* The Great Blasket *is a delightful account in prose of his own experiences there and also includes some of his original poems.*

'Solitude' is one of these poems and evokes the loneliness and strange unearthly experience he felt on the Great Blasket when 'a mist came from the sea and took the world away.' But all is well as the sun breaks through and the mountain peaks of Slemish and Brandon appear again in their high glory and seem to be physical symbols of a timeless, mystical world.

Ciarán Mac Mathúna

Solitude

They could not stack the turf in that wet spring,
And the cold nights were icy in our bones,
And so we burned furze and the rusted bracken.
I climbed the hill alone
And by the old fort gathered in the sun
Red fern and crackling furze;
And, as I worked, a mist came from the sea
And took the world away,
And left me islanded in that high air,
Where the trenched doon broods silent on the hill.
I do not know what shapes were in the mist,
But solitude was made more solitary
By some re-risen memory of the earth
That gathered round my loneliness,
And threatened with the dead my living breath.
I could have cried aloud for my sharp fear,
But the mist thinned and withered, and the sun
At one swift stride came through.
They passed those shadowy threats,
And the great company of Ireland's hills,
Brandon and Slemish and the lesser brethren,
Stood up in the bright air,
And on the other side the sea,
The illimitable Atlantic, rolled and shone.

ROBIN FLOWER (1881–1946)

Tao and Unfitness at Inistiogue on the River Nore

Noon

The black flies kept nagging in the heat.
Swarms of them, at every step, snarled
off pats of cow dung spattered in the grass.

Move, if you move, like water.

The punts were knocking by the boathouse, at full tide.
Volumes of water turned the river curve
hushed under an insect haze.

                                      Slips of white,
trout bellies, flicked in the corner of the eye
and dropped back onto the deep mirror.

Respond. Do not interfere. Echo.

Thick green woods along the opposite bank
climbed up from a root-dark recess
eaved with mud-whitened leaves.

                   *

In a matter of hours all that water is gone,
except for a channel near the far side.
Muck and shingle and pools where the children
wade, stabbing flatfish.

Afternoon

Inistiogue itself is perfectly lovely,
like a typical English village, but a bit sullen.
Our voices echoed in sunny corners
among the old houses; we admired
the stonework and gateways, the interplay
of roofs and angled streets.

The square, with its 'village green', lay empty.
The little shops had hardly anything.
The Protestant church was guarded by a woman
of about forty, a retainer, spastic
and indistinct, who drove us out.

An obelisk to the Brownsfoords and a Victorian
Celto-Gothic drinking fountain, erected
by a Tighe widow for the villagers,
'erected' in the centre. An astronomical-looking
sundial stood sentry on a platform
on the corner where High Street went up out of the square.

We drove up, past a long-handled water pump
placed at the turn, with an eye to the effect,
then out of town for a quarter of a mile
above the valley, and came to the dead gate
of Woodstock, once home of the Tighes.

*

The great ruin presented its flat front
at us, sunstruck. The children disappeared.
Eleanor picked her way around a big fallen branch
and away along the face toward the outbuildings.
I took the grassy front steps and was gathered up
in a brick-red stillness. A rook clattered out of the dining room.

A sapling, hooked thirty feet up
in a cracked corner, held out a ghost-green
cirrus of leaves. Cavities
of collapsed fireplaces connected silently
about the walls. Deserted spaces, complicated
by door-openings everywhere.

There was a path up among the bushes and nettles
over the beaten debris, then a drop, where bricks
and plaster and rafters had fallen into the kitchens.
A line of small choked arches . . . The pantries, possibly.

Be still, as though pure.

A brick, and its dust, fell.

Nightfall

The trees we drove under in the dusk
as we threaded back along the river through the woods
were no mere dark growth, but a flitting-place
for ragged feeling, old angers and rumours.

Black and Tan ghosts up there, at home
on the Woodstock heights: an iron mouth
scanning the Kilkenny road: the house
gutted by the townspeople and burned to ruins.

The little Ford we met, and inched past, full of men
we had noticed along the river bank during the week,
disappeared behind us into a fifty-year-old night.
Even their caps and raincoats . . .

Sons, or grandsons. Poachers.
                                        Mud-tasted salmon
slithering in a plastic bag around the boot,
bloodied muscles, disputed since King John.

The ghosts of daughters of the family
waited in the uncut grass as we drove
down to our mock-Austrian lodge and stopped.
                            *
We untied the punt in the half-light, and pushed out
to take a last hour on the river, until night.
We drifted, but stayed almost still.
The current underneath us
and the tide coming back to the full
cancelled in a gleaming calm, punctuated
by the plop of fish.

Down on the water . . . at eye level . . . in the little light
remaining overhead . . . the mayfly passed in a loose drift,
thick and frail, a hatch slow with sex,
separate morsels trailing their slack filaments,
olive, pale evening dun, imagoes, unseen eggs
dropping from the air, subimagoes, the river filled
with their nymphs ascending and excited trout.

Be subtle, as though not there.

We were near the island—no more than a dark mass
on a sheet of silver—when a man appeared in mid-river
quickly and with scarcely a sound, his paddle touching
left and right of the prow, with a sack behind him.
The flat cot's long body slid past effortless
as a fish, sinewing from side to side,
as he passed us and vanished.

THOMAS KINSELLA (B. 1928)

*Thomas Kinsella's poems look informal at first, but they quickly reveal intricate structures.
He aptly describes how he writes and 'tests' the success of his own poetry in a poem called*
'Worker in Mirror at his Bench':

He bends closer, testing the work.
The bright assembly begins to turn in silence.
The answering brain glitters — one system
answering another.

What I love about his poem 'Tao and Unfitness' is this sense of a poem as a 'bright assembly' and of poem-reading as a kind of telepathic lightning or 'glitter'. 'Tao and Unfitness' assembles dozens of overlapping connections even as it moves rapidly between different kinds of observation, the travel-guide description of Inistiogue's square and then the diary-like lines on the poet's wife and children wandering into different parts of the old Tighe mansion, the historical context of the back-road poachers and then the nature notes on mayflies over the river, brilliantly described images appearing and disappearing and interspersed with surprising Tao injunctions. I feel like a whole world has been made newly visible as the poem ends and the 'flat cot' or boat vanishes downriver.

John McAuliffe

PÁDRAIG J DALY POET

24 January 1994

Dear Ewan, Áine and Christopher,

I am very sorry for not getting back to you sooner. There seemed to be so much stuff to get through in the after-Christmas period. Good luck for your venture.

  It is an honour and a pleasure to be associated with it.

Sincerely,

Pádraig J Daly

When trying to choose a favourite poem, I found myself swamped by the possibilities. I thought of the bleak, 'H'M' by R S Thomas; of John F Deane's heartbreaking 'On a Dark Night'; and of Pearse Hutchinson's superbly sensuous 'Málaga'.
Finally, however, I settled on 'Swineherd', a poem by Eileán Ní Chuilleanáin. It is a poem that creates its own world. It offers us an intact and complete imaginative experience. It leads us into the mysterious, perhaps fairytale, time and place of swineherds and Portuguese lay-sisters.

  I love the poem above all for its breathtaking evocation of quiet and silence:

I want to lie awake at night
Listening to cream crawling to the top of the jug
And the water lying soft in the cistern.

They are lines to kill for. Writing about them now reminds me of how I first came across Eileán Ní Chuilleanáin's poems in newspapers and magazines; and of how imaginatively liberating they were for me then; and they still are.

Swineherd

'When all this is over', said the swineherd,
'I mean to retire, where
Nobody will have heard about my special skills
And conversation is mainly about the weather.

I intend to learn how to make coffee, at least as well
As the Portuguese lay-sister in the kitchen
And polish the brass fenders every day.
I want to lie awake at night
Listening to cream crawling to the top of the jug
And the water lying soft in the cistern.

I want to see an orchard where the trees grow in straight lines
And the yellow fox finds shelter between the navy-blue trunks,
Where it gets dark early in summer
And the apple-blossom is allowed to wither on the bough.'

EILEÁN NÍ CHUILLEANÁIN (B.1942)

DERMOT SEYMOUR   ARTIST

2006

Recovery

*When I sit down on Henry St,/faint and funny I/think of what has become me . . ./
Aftershock they call it./Four days after the event!/The event happened whilst I crossed the
shortcut from lunch./I misjudged the duck, hit the crossbar of a fence/thump, pain, stars./
Back at work, I felt a trickle. Then a flood of wet./Soaked in blood I was!/ I returned to
the fence/and upon four rusty nails hung a sliver of scalp./To the Doctor with haste./Get
ye straight to A&E./With a split head, thoughts of lockjaw, tetanus jab, I think of Dermot
Healey's 'Recovery'.*

All the Best,
Dermot Seymour

Recovery

in memory of Charlie McGovern

1

The first thing I hear is women's voices,
the next a priest withdrawing from me.
A friend leaves by the bedside
Berryman's *Seven Addresses to the Lord*
which I must have asked for

and then you
climb in the window

(funny to fall asleep at last
in the ladies' ward and outside
the drunken gardener falling
asleep under
the purple plum).

2

Night nurses water the flowers;
St Joseph guards my window
a giant shadow thrown across the room at night in prayer.
And after being moved from the women's ward
they find room for me in the men's.
Charlie, after a lifetime of coughing,
lies across from me.

You can make any tree weep, he explains,
if you train it. A man in the corridor drops dead
after weighing himself on the scales.
Did the second hand register his soul leaving,
flying off? And a woman is saying:
It will be easy to satisfy me now,
I wouldn't dream of spending
half the night up now,
Oh God, no.

3

When your head begins to swing to the right
we'll correct the tendency,
when your head begins to swing to the left
just shout for me, the doctor said,

and then the veins begin to gather
like gnarled roots
at the back of my head.

4

You're one of the lucky ones, says the doctor,
Usually they die.
The one sure thing is
it can never happen to you again.
That's something, I suppose,
I say.

5

In a local news item in the *Anglo-Celt*
a man is described who died
after receiving a prick
from a rose in his garden,
the following week
his brother was shot by gangsters
in New York.

So what do you make of news like that?
I feel like Virginia Woolf
when she stood under the vast dome of the British Museum

and felt as if she were a single thought
in that huge broad forehead.

6

How many thoughts can you cram into a day?
How many of us are in this world
rising up and doing a little,
going some of the way,
being there at the time,
in the early morning meeting them
down the side streets,
the sound of shoes, steps being washed down,
coal dropped into a hole in the street?

An example of sublime skepticism
is the man who discovered purgatory.

Charlie McGovern,
after a lifetime in the air force
where he saw coffins come back from Vietnam
filled with dope,
left his apartment in the States,
just turned the key in the lock,
and came home to die in Ireland.

And then today
Charlie McGovern
saw an X-ray of his lung
which he prayed was not his,
one big white mushroom

rising over Glengevlin.

7
Poor Charlie,
highest nut in the wood,
man of the limestone-white neck,
now you are heartbroken and fallen on hard times,

a herb of grace is needed for your wound
or young women who in the heat-haze of noon
might pluck for you *moonógs*
from down at the black rocks;

not for show you constantly shrug your shoulders
and stay awake most of the night,
your last horse stands in the gorse haggard
looking at the same spot for days,

your dogs have strayed from you
to the Maguires and the O'Rourkes
and sometimes you stop at the gate
watching for them, whistling,

and Pilib, when winter freshened his wound,
departed beyond the wounded Boyne,
he sends neither message nor friends to bring good news
but the heart has only what it is accustomed to,

so you follow with affection tales of his,
news of great victories,
thousands of foreigners dead,
while in your innermost heart

you found the shaft
enter his heart,
and his memory in your mind
will long be a reproach to you —

Pilib breathless in death
propped up in his coffin
like in the prow of a currach.
Afterwards you cross through Dowra

like a man astray in the head
and try luring birds from the cliffs
that you might have some sign of the future,
acknowledgement from the blackfaced queen

that she might send you easy peace terms.
But the news is not good.
The last time I saw you you were trying to sit up in the Home.
They were shooting the hereafter into your veins.

8
In the miraculous country of silk
where the horse runs with one foot
poised on the wings of a swallow

and the natives refrain from saying
the names of women who are called by the names of flowers
or the names of men who are called by the names of birds

lest they awake a sleeping ancestor,
so, Charlie, I say your name low.
As I recovered you were dying,

the priest suddenly came out from behind the screen,
and across sand and muffled stones
the undercurrent bore your soul away.

9
In Killygowen
all rested and well
I feel another
heart beating by my side,
joy all round.

The first day I go to town,
an off-duty soldier speaking of grief
congratulated me
with a flick of his fingers,
'I saw you at the funeral,'

he says.
I look at him a long time
trying to gauge who has died.
'It was good of you,' he says, 'to come.'
'It was nothing,' I replied.

DERMOT HEALY (B. 1947)

SHARON OLDS POET

New York
1992

Dear Paula Griffin, Nicola Hughes and Alice McEleney,

Thank you kindly for your letter. I am honored to be asked and happy to comply. What a fine project!

Here are two favorites of mine – 'Oatmeal' by Galway Kinnell, so homey and beautiful, earthy and sublime and funny, singing in that great unique Kinnell line of food for the body and the spirit (and honoring poetry parents); and, if I might have two, Toi Derricotte's 'Before Making Love' (from Captivity), which has for me a Keatsian quality and a political/intimate ferocity and beauty I much admire.

My respects and gratitude,

Sharon Olds

Oatmeal

I eat oatmeal for breakfast.
I make it on the hot plate and put skimmed milk on it.
I eat alone.
I am aware it is not good to eat oatmeal alone.
Its consistency is such that it is better for your mental health if
    somebody eats it with you.
That is why I often think up an imaginary companion to have breakfast with.
Possibly it is even worse to eat oatmeal with an imaginary companion.
Nevertheless, yesterday morning, I ate my oatmeal—porridge, as he called it—
    with John Keats.
Keats said I was absolutely right to invite him: due to its glutinous texture, gluey
    lumpishness, hint of slime, and unusual willingness to disintegrate, oatmeal
    should not be eaten alone.
He said that in his opinion, however, it is perfectly OK to eat it with an imaginary
    companion,
and that he himself had enjoyed memorable porridges with Edmund Spenser and
    John Milton.
Even if eating oatmeal with an imaginary companion is not as wholesome as Keats
    claims, still, you can learn something from it.
Yesterday morning, for instance, Keats told me about writing the 'Ode to a
    Nightingale.'
He had a heck of a time finishing it—those were his words— 'Oi 'ad a 'eck of a
    toime,' he said, more or less, speaking through his porridge.
He wrote it quickly, on scraps of paper, which he then stuck in his pocket,
but when he got home he couldn't figure out the order of the stanzas, and he and a
    friend spread the papers on a table, and they made some sense of them, but he
    isn't sure to this day if they got it right.

An entire stanza may have slipped into the lining of his jacket through a hole in
the pocket.

He still wonders about the occasional sense of drift between stanzas,

and the way here and there a line will go into the configuration of a Moslem at
prayer, then raise itself up and peer about, and then lay itself down slightly off
the mark, causing the poem to move forward with a reckless, shining wobble.

He said someone told him that later in life Wordsworth heard about the scraps of
paper on the table, and tried shuffling some stanzas of his own, but only made
matters worse.

I would not have known about any of this but for my reluctance to eat oatmeal
alone.

When breakfast was over, John recited 'To Autumn.'

He recited it slowly, with much feeling, and he articulated the words lovingly, and
his odd accent sounded sweet.

He didn't offer the story of writing 'To Autumn,' I doubt if there is much of one.

But he did say the sight of a just-harvested oat field got him started on it,

and two of the lines, 'For Summer has o'er-brimmed their clammy cells' and 'Thou
watchest the last oozing hours by hours,' came to him while eating oatmeal
alone.

I can see him—drawing a spoon through the stuff, gazing into the glimmering
furrows, muttering.

Maybe there is no sublime; only the shining of the amnion's tatters.

For supper tonight I am going to have a baked potato left over from lunch.

I am aware that a leftover baked potato is damp, slippery, and simultaneously
gummy and crumbly,

and therefore I'm going to invite Patrick Kavanagh to join me.

GALWAY KINNELL (B. 1927)

Before Making Love

I move my hands over your face,
closing my eyes, as if blind;
the cheek bones, broadly spaced,
the wide thick nostrils of the African,
the forehead whose bones push
at both sides as if the horns
of fallen angels lie just under,
the chin that juts forward with pride.
I think of the delicate skull of the Taung child—
earliest of human beings
emerged from darkness—whose geometry
brings word of a small town of dignity
that all the bloody kingdoms rest on.

TOI DERRICOTTE (B. 1941)

MICHAEL COLGAN THEATRE DIRECTOR

Gate Theatre
1994

Dear Ewan, Áine and Christopher,

Thank you for yours. Apologies for the delay. The poem is from a series of short poems entitled Light Music *by Derek Mahon and is entitled 'Absence'. These six lines are so simple and so heart rending that you know that Mahon is a poet of extraordinary ability. It is short but very powerful and very moving.*

Will this do?

Michael Colgan

> *Absence*
> *from Light Music*
>
> I wake at night
> in a house white
> with moonlight.
>
> Somewhere my son,
> his vigour, his laughter;
> somewhere my daughter.

DEREK MAHON (B.1941)

JOHN CONNOLLY NOVELIST

2006

My introduction to this poem ['somewhere i have never travelled'], *and to E E Cummings, came through Woody Allen. Not personally, I hasten to add. Woody didn't call one evening to urge, in angst-ridden Brooklynese, that I should read* 'somewhere I have never travelled', *although that would make for a far better story and enable me to drop references to Woody Allen into my everyday conversation. ('As Woody Allen said to me . . .', for example, or 'How Woody Allen and I laughed!')*

No, the rather more mundane truth is that I went to see Woody Allen's film Hannah And Her Sisters *at the Screen Cinema in Dublin shortly after it came out. I was a big Woody Allen fan. I once took a girl to see a double bill of* Annie Hall *and* Manhattan *on our first date together. I was 16 and she was 15. It was also our last date together, probably because I took her to see a double bill of* Annie Hall *and* Manhattan. *She wanted to see* Terms of Endearment *but I suspected that* Terms of Endearment *was not for me and, since I was paying, a double bill at the Cameo next door was cheaper. Still, even I had to admit that, halfway through* Manhattan, *I was starting to sag a little. But that was what people did on proper dates, right? They went to see black and white movies at arthouse cinemas and talked about them in coffee shops afterwards. At least, that was what people did in Woody Allen movies, which may be where I went wrong.*

Anyway, Hannah And Her Sisters *uses intertitles to break up the action, so at one point the screen goes* black *and the last line of Cummings's poem appears on the screen. It reads:*

nobody,not even the rain,has such small hands

I thought that I had never read such a startling line of poetry. The film was released in 1986, so I was probably 18 when I saw it and perhaps more susceptible to grand romantic gestures than I am now. In the film, Elliot (played by Michael Caine) sends the poem to his sister-in-law Lee (Barbara Hershey), with whom he is infatuated. The poem moves her to tears. I had never seen anyone moved to tears by a poem before, not in a film and certainly not in real life, although I was pretty certain that it probably happened. It just didn't happen to anyone I knew.

But I loved that line of poetry, even with its peculiar punctuation. (There should be a single space after the first comma, and another single space after the last comma, but that's Cummings for you.) It was, I think, the first line of verse that ever resonated with me in quite that way. I decided that I had to hunt down the poem. It took me a while, and I ended up ordering quite a few volumes of Cummings's poetry from Fred Hanna's bookshop before I found it. This was no bad thing, although I admit it was a little frustrating at the time. Forced to work through the books of poetry in an effort to find the poem I was seeking, I ended up reading more of Cummings's work than I might otherwise have done if the search had proved easier and had ended more quickly. They were the first books of poetry that I had ever bought for myself, and they were certainly among the first poems I had read out of choice rather than because they formed part of the school syllabus.

Cummings became 'my' poet. I read each of the books as they arrived from America, often both baffled and delighted by the games Cummings played with punctuation and lettering. Admittedly, some of the poems were more straightforward than others, and I struggled a bit with more than a couple. There was poem 57 *in the* Xaipe *collection, for example, the first two lines of which read:*

(im) c-a-t (mo)
b,i;l:e

What does that mean? 'I am a mobile cat', perhaps? It was like no poetry that I had ever read before. Even though I didn't understand it, I liked it because it was different and because I had discovered it for myself.

Eventually I received a copy of ViVa, *a collection dating from 1931. 'somewhere I have never travelled' was poem number LVII. All of that searching was worth the effort. Even if the rest of Cummings's work had been terrible, which it was not, poem number LVII would still have been worth the effort. I love the subtle eroticism of 'you open always petal by petal myself as Spring opens/(touching skilfully ,mysteriously)her first rose', and the image of that same flower closing in the verse that follows. I love the simple profundity of the lover's acknowledgement that there are things about his beloved that he 'cannot touch because they are too near'. I love that image of the snow 'carefully everywhere descending'. And I love that final line, so simple yet so breathtakingly beautiful.*

In the winter of 1988, I fell in love for the first time. I copied out 'somewhere I have never travelled' and placed it in the Christmas card that I gave to the woman whom I loved. It was the only way I could tell her how I felt, because I was still young and I didn't have the words to explain it for myself, or I didn't trust myself enough to say them. She was older than I was and she cried when she read it, just like Barbara Hershey did in

Hannah And Her Sisters. *Over the course of our relationship, I gave her other poems by Cummings, but none ever had quite the impact of this one.*

In the end, things fell apart between us. I learned, as Richard Ford puts it in his novel The Sportswriter *(which I read, with uncanny timing, as we were breaking up), that it 'is possible to love someone, and no one else, and still not live with that one person or even see her'. But* 'somewhere I have never travelled' *remained my poem. I had discovered it, I had tracked it down, and the process of finding it awakened in me both a love for the poet and for the language of poetry. It is a little unfashionable now to express admiration for Cummings, but I don't care. I still think this is the most beautiful love poem I have ever read.*

John Connolly

> somewhere i have never travelled,gladly beyond
> any experience,your eyes have their silence:
> in your most frail gesture are things which enclose me,
> or which i cannot touch because they are too near
>
> your slightest look easily will unclose me
> though i have closed myself as fingers,
> you open always petal by petal myself as Spring opens
> (touching skilfully,mysteriously)her first rose
>
> or if your wish be to close me,i and
> my life will shut very beautifully,suddenly,
> as when the heart of this flower imagines
> the snow carefully everywhere descending;
>
> nothing which we are to perceive in this world equals
> the power of your intense fragility:whose texture
> compels me with the colour of its countries,
> rendering death and forever with each breathing
>
> (i do not know what it is about you that closes
> and opens;only something in me understands
> the voice of your eyes is deeper than all roses)
> nobody,not even the rain,has such small hands

E E Cummings (1894–1962)

['*somewhere i have never travelled,gladly beyond*' was also chosen by Philip Davison in *Lifelines 3*. On 6 February 1997, Philip Davison wrote:
My choice of poem is 'somewhere i have never travelled,gladly beyond', *by E E Cummings. It seems we never have doubts about what we are drawn to in others, but have only the vaguest notion of what others see in us. This poem does more than illuminate the power of attraction. Somehow, it suggests, though we may fail to seize the moment, there is still cause for celebration – and perhaps the moment has not yet passed.*]

GORDON SNELL WRITER

Dear Editors,

Thank you for asking me to submit a poem I like for Lifelines 3. *I have chosen W H Auden's poem 'Lullaby'.*

I first read this poem when I was around 17, and have liked it ever since. It is melodiously lyrical, while still having the quirky and startling array of words that's typical of Auden's style. It manages to be robust and optimistic in the midst of a melancholy view of the transient nature of life.

The best of success to your excellent project.

Sincerely,

Gordon Snell

Lullaby

Lay your sleeping head, my love,
Human on my faithless arm;
Time and fevers burn away
Individual beauty from
Thoughtful children, and the grave
Proves the child ephemeral:
But in my arms till break of day
Let the living creature lie,
Mortal, guilty, but to me
The entirely beautiful.

Soul and body have no bounds:
To lovers as they lie upon
Her tolerant enchanted slope
In their ordinary swoon,
Grave the vision Venus sends
Of supernatural sympathy,
Universal love and hope;
While an abstract insight wakes
Among the glaciers and the rocks
The hermit's carnal ecstasy.

Certainty, fidelity
On the stroke of midnight pass
Like vibrations of a bell
And fashionable madmen raise
Their pedantic boring cry:
Every farthing of the cost,
All the dreaded cards foretell,
Shall be paid, but from this night
Not a whisper, not a thought,
Not a kiss nor look be lost.

Beauty, midnight, vision dies:
Let the winds of dawn that blow
Softly round your dreaming head
Such a day of welcome show
Eye and knocking heart may bless,
Find our mortal world enough;
Noons of dryness find you fed
By the involuntary powers,
Nights of insult let you pass
Watched by every human love.

January 1937

W H AUDEN (1907–1973)

ENDA WYLEY   POET

2006

Dear Dónal, Caroline and Stephanie,

I became a mother for the first time eleven months ago and since then I have found myself being drawn to poems about parenthood.

One of my favourites is 'Walking Away' by Cecil Day Lewis. I find the feeling of the father 'letting go' of his young son so moving in this poem that I often find myself thinking about it. After all, the best poems are those that stay with you long after putting them down – the ones that you hear unexpectedly in your head when you are just doing ordinary things.

For me, 'Walking Away' by Cecil Day Lewis is such a poem.

Lots of luck with your book and thank you for including my choice.

Enda Wyley

Walking Away
For Sean

It is eighteen years ago, almost to the day—
A sunny day with the leaves just turning,
The touch-lines new-ruled — since I watched you play
Your first game of football, then, like a satellite
Wrenched from its orbit, go drifting away

Behind a scatter of boys. I can see
You walking away from me towards the school
With the pathos of a half-fledged thing set free
Into a wilderness, the gait of one
Who finds no path where the path should be.

That hesitant figure, eddying away
Like a winged seed loosened from its parent stem,
Has something I never quite grasp to convey
About nature's give-and-take — the small, the scorching
Ordeals which fire one's irresolute clay.

I had worse partings, but none that so
Gnaws at my mind still. Perhaps it is roughly
Saying what God alone could perfectly show—
How selfhood begins with a walking away,
And love is proved in the letting go.

CECIL DAY LEWIS (1904–1972)

JOSEPH BRODSKY POET

New York
11 April 1993

Dear Mr Gibson, Ms Jackson and Mr Pillow,

I would say that my favorite poem is 'Desert Places' by Robert Frost. As for the reasons for my choice, my feelings about this poem are not reducible to a few lines. The poem is a few lines itself: you're better off reading them than anything I would have to say about them.

Yours sincerely,

Joseph Brodsky

Desert Places

Snow falling and night falling fast, oh, fast
In a field I looked into going past,
And the ground almost covered smooth in snow,
But a few weeds and stubble showing last.

The woods around it have it—it is theirs.
All animals are smothered in their lairs.
I am too absent-spirited to count;
The loneliness includes me unawares.

And lonely as it is, that loneliness
Will be more lonely ere it will be less—
A blanker whiteness of benighted snow
With no expression, nothing to express.

They cannot scare me with their empty spaces
Between stars—on stars where no human race is.
I have it in me so much nearer home
To scare myself with my own desert places.

ROBERT FROST (1874-1963)

10 February 1997

Dear Ralph Croly, Caroline Dowling and Gareth McCluskey,

Thank you for your letter outlining the background to the Lifelines *anthology. I would have thought that at this stage it needs little introduction, being something of a national institution and a very worthy one at that. I'm honoured to be included among those asked to name their favourite poem. Making that choice was enjoyable but not at all easy. The short list included Ted Hughes's 'The Horses', Emily Dickinson's 'My Life it stood a Loaded Gun', the opening section of Eliot's 'East Coker', Eavan Boland's 'A Ballad of Home' and finally Wallace Stevens's 'Le Monocle de Mon Oncle'. I have selected Ted Hughes's 'The Horses' from his collection,* The Hawk in the Rain. *It was a poem I read so often in the Seventies that I came to know it off by heart. So I no longer actually read it but periodically stumble into it. I particularly enjoy the enormous leap it makes in the final stanza, boldly catapulting itself right out of the static domain of description. It is as if the whole process by which experience becomes memory is captured in that leap.*

Again thank you for the opportunity to contribute to Lifelines. *I wish you every success with the project.*

Sincerely,

James Ryan

The Horses

I climbed through woods in the hour-before-dawn dark.
Evil air, a frost-making stillness,

Not a leaf, not a bird, —
A world cast in frost. I came out above the wood

Where my breath left tortuous statues in the iron light.
But the valleys were draining the darkness

Till the moorline — blackening dregs of the brightening grey —
Halved the sky ahead. And I saw the horses:

Huge in the dense grey — ten together —
Megalith-still. They breathed, making no move,

With draped manes and tilted hind-hooves,
Making no sound.

I passed: not one snorted or jerked its head.
Grey silent fragments

Of a grey silent world.

I listened in emptiness on the moor-ridge.
The curlew's tear turned its edge on the silence.

Slowly detail leafed from the darkness. Then the sun
Orange, red, red erupted.

Silently, and splitting to its core tore and flung cloud,
Shook the gulf open, showed blue,

And the big planets hanging —.
I turned

Stumbling in the fever of a dream, down towards
The dark woods, from the kindling tops,

And came to the horses.
                              There, still they stood,
But now steaming and glistening under the flow of light,

Their draped stone manes, their tilted hind-hooves
Stirring under a thaw while all around them

The frost showed its fires. But still they made no sound.
Not one snorted or stamped,

Their hung heads patient as the horizons
High over valleys, in the red levelling rays —

In din of the crowded streets, going among the years, the faces,
May I still meet my memory in so lonely a place

Between the streams and the red clouds, hearing curlews,
Hearing the horizons endure.

TED HUGHES (1930–1998)

TED HUGHES   POET

1994

Dear Lifelines,

Since I let my mail grow in a corner, like a mutant mushroom that I daren't eat, often I don't see for a long time what comes when I'm away. Forgive me for this delay in answering your letter.

I expect I'm too late. Maybe not.

My favourite poem is 'Dónal Óg' in Lady Gregory's translation. Why is this my favourite? I think no short poem has ever hit me so hard, or stayed with me so closely.

There's my reason why.

All my best to you.

Ted Hughes

Dónal Óg

It is late last night the dog was speaking of you;
the snipe was speaking of you in her deep marsh.
It is you are the lonely bird through the woods;
and that you may be without a mate until you find me.

You promised me, and you said a lie to me,
that you would be before me where the sheep are flocked;
I gave a whistle and three hundred cries to you,
and I found nothing there but a bleating lamb.

You promised me a thing that was hard for you,
a ship of gold under a silver mast;
twelve towns with a market in all of them,
and a fine white court by the side of the sea.

You promised me a thing that is not possible,
that you would give me gloves of the skin of a fish;
that you would give me shoes of the skin of a bird;
and a suit of the dearest silk in Ireland.

When I go by myself to the Well of Loneliness,
I sit down and I go through my trouble;
when I see the world and do not see my boy,
he that has an amber shade in his hair.

It was on that Sunday I gave my love to you;
the Sunday that is last before Easter Sunday.
And myself on my knees reading the Passion;
and my two eyes giving love to you for ever.

My mother said to me not to be talking with you today,
or tomorrow, or on the Sunday;
it was a bad time she took for telling me that;
it was shutting the door after the house was robbed.

My heart is as black as the blackness of the sloe,
or as the black coal that is on the smith's forge;
or as the sole of a shoe left in white halls;
it was you put that darkness over my life.

You have taken the east from me; you have taken the west from me;
you have taken what is before me and what is behind me;
you have taken the moon, you have taken the sun from me;
and my fear is great that you have taken God from me!

Anonymous
From the Irish (translated by Lady Augusta Gregory)

Dear Ralph, Caroline and Gareth,

Please forgive my late reply. Enclosed is a copy of a poem I like: Milton's sonnet 'Methought I saw my late espousèd saint'.

Sonnet XXIII

Methought I saw my late espousèd saint
    Brought to me like Alcestis from the grave,
    Whom Jove's great son to her glad husband gave,
    Rescued from death by force, though pale and faint.
Mine, as whom washed from spot of child-bed taint
    Purification in the Old Law did save,
    And such as yet once more I trust to have
    Full sight of her in Heaven without restraint,
Came vested all in white, pure as her mind.
    Her face was veiled, yet to my fancied sight
    Love, sweetness, goodness, in her person shined
So clear as in no face with more delight.
    But O, as to embrace me she inclined,
    I waked, she fled, and day brought back my night.

JOHN MILTON (1608–1674)

I find this poem very moving. Milton wrote it about his second wife, Katherine Woodcock, whom he married in 1656. It is generally accepted that Milton was totally blind at this stage and so never actually saw what she looked like. They had a daughter together in 1657, but both mother and child died in 1658.

    What I find so touching about the poem is that even though Milton meets his dead wife in a dream, her face is covered with a veil, and so he still doesn't see how she looked. And to me that's a shocking and unsettling detail.

    Considering that Milton is famous for epic works about religion and politics, this is a rare and intriguing glimpse of his personal feelings. And it's interesting to note that he is thought to have begun work on his most well-known poem, Paradise Lost, *that same tragic year.*

    The best of luck with Lifelines 3.

Yours,

Conor McPherson

20 February 1992

Dear Paula,

I wish to acknowledge receipt of your letter received in early January which unfortunately got mislaid during renovations to my office.

You asked for my favourite poem and the reasons why and I hope I am not too late with my contribution for Lifelines IV. *My favourite poem is* 'Stony Grey Soil' *by Patrick Kavanagh and I first encountered this poem while studying English for my Leaving Cert at the Presentation Convent, Clondalkin.*

As an 18-year-old, I immediately identified with the theme of the love/hate relationship between the poet and his native Monaghan soil. The stony grey soil of the title reminds me of the terrain of East Galway where I was born and where I have spent many happy holidays. It is symbolic of the way of life associated with the land – harsh, mundane and full of strife. Yet this same land has also produced his poetic inspirations.

What I particularly like about the poem is the way in which Kavanagh manages to link up the sterility and frustration of farm life with the physical beauty and grace that only working so close to nature can produce.

The first five verses are very accusing in tone – he blames the stony grey soil of Monaghan for his lack of freedom and spontaneity as a child, yet in the final three verses he acknowledges, very calmly, the significance of his early environment as a major influence on his early development.

Hope the above is of benefit to you.

Sincerely,

Mary Harney
Minister for Environmental Protection

Stony Grey Soil

O stony grey soil of Monaghan
The laugh from my love you thieved;
You took the gay child of my passion
And gave me your clod-conceived.

You clogged the feet of my boyhood
And I believed that my stumble
Had the poise and stride of Apollo
And his voice my thick-tongued mumble.

You told me the plough was immortal!
O green-life-conquering plough!
Your mandril strained, your coulter blunted
In the smooth lea-field of my brow.

You sang on steaming dunghills
A song of cowards' brood,
You perfumed my clothes with weasel itch,
You fed me on swinish food.

You flung a ditch on my vision
Of beauty, love and truth.
O stony grey soil of Monaghan
You burgled by bank of youth!

Lost the long hours of pleasure
All the women that love young men.
O can I still stroke the monster's back
Or write with unpoisoned pen

His name in these lonely verses
Or mention the dark fields where
The first gay flight of my lyric
Got caught in a peasant's prayer.

Mullahinsha, Drummeril, Black Shanco –
Wherever I turn I see
In the stony grey soil of Monaghan
Dead loves that were born for me.

PATRICK KAVANAGH (1904–1967)

ALLEN GINSBERG   POET

New York
9 March 1993

Dear Wesley College Editors:

If a favorite poem by another is requested, put Shelley's 'Hymn to Intellectual Beauty'
among elder poets and/or Blake's 'Auguries of Innocence'.

Or Gregory Corso's 'The Whole Mess . . . Almost' *from his book* Herald of the
Autocthonic Spirit. *This represents the present century.*

*I thought about the sublime transcendental penetration of Shelley's yearning for
permanent beauty, while flying across America yesterday – and realized how much more
permanent his vision was than Matthew Arnold's passing disapproval of Shelley's all too
human and altogether appropriate Spiritual ambition.*

Blake's poem's full of practical and karmic wisdom.

*Corso's poem is a condensation of enormous suffering alchemized into pure wisdom
in the open space (Sunyata, or natural emptiness) of Human mind.*

Yours,

Allen Ginsberg

[due to space restrictions, one of Allen Ginsberg's choices is included in this edition]

The Whole Mess ... Almost

I ran up six flights of stairs
to my small furnished room
opened the window
and began throwing out
those things most important in life

First to go, Truth, squealing like a fink:
'Don't! I'll tell awful things about you!'
'Oh yeah? Well, I've nothing to hide ... OUT!'
Then went God, glowering & whimpering in amazement:
'It's not my fault! I'm not the cause of it all!' 'OUT!'
Then Love, cooing bribes: 'You'll never know impotency!
All the girls on *Vogue* covers, all yours!'
I pushed her fat ass out and screamed:
'You always end up a bummer!'
I picked up Faith Hope Charity
all three clinging together:
'Without us you'll surely die!'
'With you I'm going nuts! Goodbye!'

Then Beauty ... ah, Beauty—
As I led her to the window
I told her: 'You I loved best in life
... but you're a killer; Beauty kills!'
Not really meaning to drop her
I immediately ran downstairs
getting there just in time to catch her
'You saved me!' she cried
I put her down and told her: 'Move on.'

Went back up those six flights
went to the money
there was no money to throw out.
The only thing left in the room was Death
hiding beneath the kitchen sink:
'I'm not real!' It cried
'I'm just a rumor spread by life ...'
Laughing I threw it out, kitchen sink and all
and suddenly realized Humor
was all that was left—
All I could do with Humor was to say:
'Out the window with the window!'

GREGORY CORSO (1930–2001)

Hi Caroline,

Picking a favourite poem is a nightmare!! But one of my absolute favourites, competing with Yeats, Auden and Heaney, is 'Do not go gentle into that good night' by Dylan Thomas.

It's so emotive: Dylan Thomas just reaches inside you with his words and pulls at your soul, which is what poetry is about, for me. When my father died, I'd have loved to have read this poem at his funeral but didn't, as I wasn't up to reading anything at all. But this poem sums up life, death and pain so vividly: how precious life is, how we've got to battle to cling onto it and yet, how we'll all lose that battle one day.

Hope this is OK, Caroline, and what you had in mind.

Best,

Cathy

'Do not go gentle into that good night'

Do not go gentle into that good night,
Old age should burn and rave at close of day;
Rage, rage against the dying of the light.

Though wise men at their end know dark is right,
Because their words had forked no lightning they
Do not go gentle into that good night.

Good men, the last wave by, crying how bright
Their frail deeds might have danced in a green bay,
Rage, rage against the dying of the light.

Wild men who caught and sang the sun in flight,
And learn, too late, they grieved it on its way,
Do not go gentle into that good night.

Grave men, near death, who see with blinding sight
Blind eyes could blaze like meteors and be gay,
Rage, rage against the dying of the light.

And you, my father, there on the sad height,
Curse, bless, me now with your fierce tears, I pray.
Do not go gentle into that good night.
Rage, rage against the dying of the light.

DYLAN THOMAS (1914–1953)

14 January 1997

Dear Ralph Croly, Caroline Dowling and Gareth McCluskey,

I have today received your letter and I identify my choice for your Lifelines 3, *together with a few words of apologia, below.*

Yrs. &e.,

Peter Reading

No worst, there is none

No worst, there is none. Pitched past pitch of grief,
More pangs will, schooled at forepangs, wilder wring.
Comforter, where, where is your comforting?
Mary, mother of us, where is your relief?
My cries heave, herds-long; huddle in a main, a chief
Woe, wórld-sorrow; on an áge-old anvil wince and sing —
Then lull, then leave off. Fury had shrieked 'No ling–
ering! Let me be fell: force I must be brief'.

   O the mind, mind has mountains; cliffs of fall
Frightful, sheer, no-man-fathomed. Hold them cheap
May who ne'er hung there. Nor does long our small
Durance deal with that steep or deep. Here! creep,
Wretch, under a comfort serves in a whirlwind: all
Life death does end and each day dies with sleep.

GERARD MANLEY HOPKINS (1844–1889)

This 'sonnet of desolation' (like the one beginning 'I wake and feel the fell of dark, not day') plumbs the depths of despair and the agonising tension between faith and doubt. There is, however, an implicit stoical resilience in the elaborate and original construction of Hopkins's Petrarchan fourteen-liner, and a Beckett-like grimness in confronting life's onslaughts: 'No worst, there is none'; 'Here! creep,/Wretch, under a comfort serves in a whirlwind: all/Life death does end and each day dies with sleep.'

Dear Lifelines Team,

Thank you for inviting me to contribute to your new project.
I would like to present a poem by the English Poet Rodney Pybus, called 'Not Only Forms'.
I came across this some years ago in a book published in 1982 which I found in a second-hand bookshop. I responded to it immediately. It is a wonderfully resonant poem and echoes much of what I am trying to get at in my own work.

Donald Teskey

Not Only Forms

Not long since, we combed
the shoreline of this western foreland
among the jetsam of weather, tide
and all things that diminish
through the hourglass of air,

trying for purchase
on the sliding stones, these difficult
peninsular relics
rounded bones
and pounded forms
of the earth's violent slow decay –

a place where crows come in their black
twilight clusters
for raucous scouring
and picking over;

hammer in hand, mind pacing,
you fossicked for spoors
of what's locked, original,

oldest lithographs
of what brought us here
to the mad pebble-dashed hurtle
of this planet

Always the continuing
preamble of form:

the curt consonance
of stones, their milled gravel
under-foot, and the tide's drawn
vowel receding
over the bay's wide tongue,

those sombre mud-flats
that take the earth right out
to meet the sky:
a complex speech
you tried for size, attesting
to weighed syllables
and potential music.

One lumpen limestone block
the sea'd rolled smooth
you split with a blow,
surprised the quick faint scent
of ancient chemistry escaping,
and found each half sharing
the fossil's image,
bi-valve across the break –
delicate drypoint
of a radiating fan
in its storm of stone:
both image and narrative.

Presiding friend, hierophant
of authentic making,
you held to the joy
of insight striking, not
only the entrancing rigid forms;

later, you gave me half,
a gift to match across
the break. In return
I bring you this, less durable
but form of a kind, this still hardening speech.

Yes, a gift against the times.

RODNEY PYBUS (B. 1938)

29 January 1994

Dear Friends,

I hope I can squeeze a few lines out, giving reasons for the choice of one of my favourite poems, which is 'I Sing the Body Electric' by Walt Whitman.

One of the reasons I like the poem so much is that it completely encapsulates a man's passion for his fellow man or woman, and shows such an enthusiasm, such a basic, whole-hearted love for humanity that manifests itself in line after line of the most exquisite language. I never tire of reading this poem and it happily eschews the preciousness of poetry and gives poetry a powerful masculinity and passion and lack of self-consciousness that makes 'I Sing the Body Electric' one of my all-time favourites.

I hope this will do.

Yours sincerely,

Steven Berkoff

from *I Sing the Body Electric*

II
The love of the body of man or woman balks account, the body itself
    balks account,
That of the male is perfect, and that of the female is perfect.

The expression of the face balks account,
But the expression of a well-made man appears not only in his face,
It is in his limbs and joints also, it is curiously in the joints of his hips
    and wrists,
It is in his walk, the carriage of his neck, the flex of his waist and knees,
    dress does not hide him,

The strong sweet quality he has strikes through the cotton and broad-
    cloth,
To see him pass conveys as much as the best poem, perhaps more,
You linger to see his back, and the back of his neck and shoulder-side.

The sprawl and fullness of babes, the bosoms and heads of women, the
    folds of their dress, their style as we pass in the street, the contour of
    their shape downwards,
The swimmer naked in the swimming-bath, seen as he swims through
    the transparent green-shine, or lies with his face up and rolls silently
    to and fro in the heave of the water,
The bending forward and backward of rowers in row-boats, the
    horseman in his saddle,

Girls, mothers, house-keepers, in all their performances,
The group of laborers seated at noon-time with their open dinner
    kettles, and their wives waiting,
The female soothing a child, the farmer's daughter in the garden or cow-
    yard,
The young fellow hoeing corn, the sleigh-driver driving his six horses
    through the crowd,

The wrestle of wrestlers, two apprentice-boys, quite grown, lusty, good-
    natured, native-born, out on the vacant lot at sundown after work,
The coats and caps thrown down, the embrace of love and resistance,
The upper-hold and under-hold, the hair rumpled over and blinding the
    eyes;
The march of firemen in their own costumes, the play of masculine
    muscle through clean-setting trowsers and waist-straps,
The slow return from the fire, the pause when the bell strikes suddenly
    again, and the listening on the alert,
The natural, perfect, varied attitudes, the bent head, the curv'd neck and
    the counting;
Such-like I love—I loosen myself, pass freely, am at the mother's breast with
    the little child,
Swim with the swimmers, wrestle with wrestlers, march in line with the
    firemen, and pause, listen, count.

WALT WHITMAN (1819–1892)

MYLES DUNGAN

BROADCASTER

19 April 1985

Dear Collette, Joy and Steven,

Congratulations on having a very good idea. When the book comes out anthologists and writers of gimmick tomes the world over (given to compiling books such as Desert Island Menus/Laundry Lists/10 Best Films of the rich and famous) will grind their teeth and grunt 'why didn't I think of that?' I must get the wife to get me a new agent for Christmas.

*   In my youth poetry was something to be learned by heart first and appreciated afterwards. I liked most of it but then what you do at school tends to be like a poetic K-Tel compilation album (Now that's what I call Poetry – eighteenth-century). The trick was to be able to recite it at great speed last thing at night in the hope that you could steer your way slowly around the same course the following morning. Accordingly one of my favourite poems was one that went:*

*   'InxanadudidKublakhanastatelypleasuredomedecreewherealphthesacredriverran-throughcavernsmeasurelesstomandowntoasunlesssea – (pause for breath) – a poem which I have recently discovered was actually written by Frankie Goes to Hollywood and not Samuel Taylor Coleridge as my teacher would have me believe.*

Since those days of innocence my tastes have become more esoteric and frankly quite elitist. During what I would describe as My Middle Period I developed a taste for the obscure and extremely personal statements of E Jarvis Thribb (17) in Private Eye. *He belies his years (he has, in fact, been seventeen for about twenty years). The apparent simplicity of his verse is merely a ploy to deter those who do not have eyes to see. Clever and sensitive people like me have the ability to ignore the utter banality of the language, the artless blandness of the sentiments and the pedestrian metre and go straight to the gaps between the verses wherein lies the incandescence of the man. Thribb is to the gap on the printed page what Pinter is to the theatrical pause.*

Take for example his sad little elegy to the jazz pianist Eubie Blake who died at the age of a hundred.

So Farewell
Then Eubie
Blake.

Noted Jazz
Pianist and
Composer.
Aged 100

Eubie
A strange name.

Keith says
That possibly
your initials
Were U B

Hence the
Name.

I wonder

But aside from all that you want to know what my favourite poem is. For me the best poetry is brief and incisive. Good comedy should also be equally sharp. My problem is that I tend to like to see the two on some sort of combination. This doesn't mean that I loathe poets who are not a barrel of laughs. It just means that I am so crassly Philistinitic that I tend to agree with Pope that 'true wit is nature to advantage dressed/what oft was thought but ne'er so well expressed' – except that I mean wit in its more commonly accepted sense and I see it as being heightened by humour in poetic form. Rhyme helps a lot. One of the funniest things I've ever seen on stage in recent years was an adaptation by (the poet) Derek Mahon for 'Field Day' of a French farce which he re-titled High Times. *It was written in rhyme and this served to heighten the hilarity.*

Put it down to a black sense of humour which desires to see poetry perverted by humour for vaguely subversive purposes. Or just put it down to idiosyncrasy but the kind of thing I like best is done by Roger McGough. Here are two examples:

Sad Aunt Madge

As the cold winter evenings drew near
Aunt Madge used to put extra blankets
over the furniture, to keep it warm and cosy.
Mussolini was her lover, and life
was an outoffocus rosy tinted spectacle.

but neurological experts
with kind blueeyes
and gentle voices
small white hands
and large Rolls Royces
said that electric shock treatment
should do the trick
it did . . .

today after 15 years of therapeutic tears
and an awful lot of ratepayers' shillings
down the hospital meter
sad Aunt Madge
no longer tucks up the furniture
before kissing it goodnight
and admits
that her affair with Mussolini
clearly was not right
particularly in the light
of her recently announced engagement
to the late pope.

ROGER McGOUGH (B. 1937)

Motorway

The politicians
(who are buying huge cars with hobnailed wheels
    the size of merry-go-rounds)
    have a new plan.
    They are going to
    put cobbles
    in our eyesockets
    and pebbles
    in our navels
    and fill us up
    with asphalt
    and lay us
    side by side
so that we can take a more active part
    in the road
    to destruction.

ROGER McGOUGH (B. 1937)

I like Dylan Thomas as well. Honest I do!
Yours sincerely,
Myles Dungan

Dear Dónal, Caroline and Stephanie,

Samuel Johnson famously said of John Donne that images in his poems were 'yoked together by violence'. It's still a surprisingly common complaint: that Donne's love of complex metaphor obscures the emotional content of his poetry, that he's being clever for the sake of being clever. But the apparent distance between subject matter and style is exactly what I love about a poem like 'A Valediction: of the Book'. It's deliberately, audaciously and mischievously difficult: the poet's initial declaration to his lover that the letters she writes him are actually a form of literature, is then pursued, through a kind of intellectual labyrinth, to the point where the reader begins to lose the thread of the original comparison. It seems strained and implausible that love letters should be like theological tomes, legal textbooks or political tracts: what, if anything, does this tell us about love? That it is a form of knowledge, every bit as valuable as religion or science? Or that it is merely a rhetorical exercise, just as abstract and empty as the dry texts of lawyers and theologians? And what are we to make of the poet's final sly demand of his beloved: essentially, that she quit his sight, all the better to test their love?

'A Valediction: of the Book' is, in a way, the perfect demonstration of T S Eliot's comment: 'A thought to Donne was an experience; it modified his sensibility.' There is no distance between how Donne thinks and how he feels: his lovers and his books are part of the same poetic universe. But I'd go further than Eliot: Donne, I think, found thinking not just emotional but actually erotic. He thinks ideas are sexy and, as a corollary, that his lover is an intellectual. But that means that ideas can be just as absurd and illusory as human passion too: the urges of philosophers and ardent lovers are equally thrilling and equally suspect. None of which confusion stops him producing a poetry that is utterly ravishing in terms of its language. It may be a learned language (as in this poem, when he uses the terminology of alchemy or navigation) but it is also a charged, excited lexicon – 'subliming', 'eclipses', 'schismatic': these words are full of both physical and intellectual significance for Donne. Whenever I hear a critic disparage a writer for being 'too' intellectual or 'merely' emotional, I think of this poem, which plays elaborate games with the distinction between the two, and maybe suggests that there is no difference after all.

Brian Dillon

A Valediction: of the Book

I'll tell thee now (dear love) what thou shalt do
    To anger destiny, as she doth us;
    How I shall stay, though she eloign me thus,
And how posterity shall know it too;
        How thine may out-endure
        Sibyl's glory, and obscure
        Her who from Pindar could allure,
    And her, through whose help Lucan is not lame,
And her, whose book (they say) Homer did find, and name.

Study our manuscripts, those myriads
    Of letters, which have past 'twixt thee and me;
    Thence write our annals, and in them will be
To all whom love's subliming fire invades,
        Rule and example found;
        There the faith of any ground
        No schismatic will dare to wound,
    That sees, how Love this grace to us affords,
To make, to keep, to use, to be these his records.

This book, as long-lived as the elements,
    Or as the world's form, this all-gravèd tome
    In cypher writ, or new made idiom;
We for Love's clergy only are instruments;
        When this book is made thus,
        Should again the ravenous
        Vandals and Goths invade us,
    Learning were safe; in this our universe,
Schools might learn sciences, spheres music, angels verse.

Here Love's divines—since all divinity
    Is love or wonder—may find all they seek,
    Whether abstract spiritual love they like,
Their souls exhaled with what they do not see;
        Or, loth so to amuse
        Faith's infirmity, they choose
        Something which they may see and use;
    For, though mind be the heaven, where love doth sit,
Beauty a convenient type may be to figure it.

Here more than in their books may lawyers find,
    Both by what titles mistresses are ours,
    And how prerogative these states devours,
Transferr'd from Love himself, to womankind;
        Who, though from heart and eyes,
        They exact great subsidies,
        Forsake him who on them relies;
    And for the cause, honour, or conscience give;
Chimeras vain as they or their prerogative.

Here statesmen—or of them, they which can read—
    May of their occupation find the grounds;
    Love, and their art, alike it deadly wounds,
If to consider what 'tis, one proceed.
        In both they do excel
        Who the present govern well,
        Whose weakness none doth, or dares tell;
    In this thy book, such will there something see,
As in the Bible some can find out alchemy.

Thus vent thy thoughts; abroad I'll study thee,
    As he removes far off, that great heights takes;
    How great love is, presence best trial makes,
But absence tries how long this love will be;
        To take a latitude
        Sun, or stars, are fitliest view'd
        At their brightest, but to conclude
    Of longitudes, what other way have we,
But to mark when and where the dark eclipses be?

JOHN DONNE (1572–1631)

Dear Ewan Gibson, Áine Jackson and Christopher Pillow,

I have just got back from two months in America to find your letter and I am so sorry that, through nobody's fault, you have not had a reply about your excellent project.

I would feel honoured to be able to contribute to your Lifelines *if it helps in any way. I particularly support projects to maintain clean water supplies to people.*

What causes us to like certain poems is often as little to do with reasons and literary judgement as other matters of taste. My reaction to words, on the page as well as spoken, is a physiological one no less than that to pictures and music. I react to what I call grammar, the ways of words, as I do to combinations of shapes and colours and food. In this poem I find the progress of the separate sentences somehow pleasing to my inner ear, as if a step is made, tested, and then another very carefully added. The grammatical structure itself exemplifies this quiet watchful concentration on getting at the meaning, as when you are watching animals feeding at dusk you have to be still enough and concentrated, for them to feel you are part of the night.

More clearly, I like this poem because I love summer nights when it is balmy enough to leave doors and windows open all night and not know it, no separation between inner and outer; and because it reminds me of the extreme yet somehow peaceful excitement of feeling what one is thinking, one's bloodstream involved with the presence of the writer of the book one has taken to an upper window to catch the last of the light on such a summer night.

The House was Quiet and the World was Calm

The house was quiet and the world was calm.
The reader became the book; and summer night

Was like the conscious being of the book.
The house was quiet and the world was calm.

The words were spoken as if there was no book,
Except that the reader leaned above the page,

Wanted to lean, wanted much most to be
The scholar to whom his book is true, to whom

The summer night is like a perfection of thought.
The house was quiet because it had to be.

The quiet was part of the meaning, part of the mind:
The access of perfection to the page.

And the world was calm. The truth in a calm world,
In which there is no other meaning, itself

Is calm, itself is summer and night, itself
Is the reader leaning late and reading there.

WALLACE STEVENS (1879–1955)

To say what I like about Wordsworth's Prelude *would take as much space as one of the fourteen books of that great epic. It should be read through as a narrative, preferably in no shorter sections than a book at a time, at least the first couple of readings. The cumulative roll of Wordsworth's narrative line, his superb ear, his command of vocabulary of course give pleasure. I personally like* The Prelude *perhaps because it is a work I've read closely and often, at first in my teens; and I think my own thinking about human beings in society (i.e. my political development) developed through reading Wordsworth. I have picked out some lines from Book X but at least from the beginning of the book should be read to give the context. The lines exemplify Wordsworth's mastery at exact, moving psychological analysis and description of human thinking and feeling. I value Wordsworth for his honesty. With George Orwell, Samuel Johnson and Virginia Woolf, he is the most honest writer I know. In* The Prelude *he takes us through a political education. He sets down, not a particular dogma, but what it feels like to think and feel politically. Heart-rending sadness at the Revolution betrayed, at hope lost, the idealist disillusioned, the true patriot helpless – these are portrayed in these books of* The Prelude *as nowhere else I know in English literature except for George Orwell's* Homage to Catalonia *and the ending of William Morris's* A Dream of John Ball, *surely the saddest end to a book in English.*

from *The Prelude*
Book X. Residence in France [1850 version]

What, then, were my emotions, when in arms
Britain put forth her freeborn strength in league,
Oh, pity and shame! with those confederate Powers!
Not in my single self alone I found,
But in the minds of all ingenuous youth,
Change and subversion from that hour. No shock
Given to my moral nature had I known
Down to that very moment; neither lapse
Nor turn of sentiment that might be named
A revolution, save at this one time;
All else was progress on the self-same path
On which, with a diversity of pace,
I had been travelling: this a stride at once
Into another region. As a light
And pliant harebell, swinging in the breeze
On some grey rock—its birthplace—so had I
Wantoned, fast rooted on the ancient tower
Of my belovèd country, wishing not
A happier fortune than to wither there:
Now was I from that pleasant station torn
And tossed about in whirlwind. I rejoiced,
Yea, afterwards—truth most painful to record!—
Exulted, in the triumph of my soul,
When Englishmen by thousands were o'erthrown,
Left without glory on the field, or driven,
Brave hearts! to shameful flight. It was a grief,—
Grief call it not, 'twas anything but that,—
A conflict of sensations without name,
Of which *he* only, who may love the sight
Of a village steeple, as I do, can judge,
When, in the congregation bending all
To their great Father, prayers were offered up,
Or praises for our country's victories;
And, 'mid the simple worshippers, perchance
I only, like an uninvited guest
Whom no one owned, sate silent, shall I add,
Fed on the day of vengeance yet to come?

WILLIAM WORDSWORTH (1770–1850)

I'm sure the above is too long. I found it impossible to do 3 'sound bites' per great work. I thought that as it's students doing it they could learn something of the poems, not just my personal feelings.

Yours sincerely,

Jenny Joseph

28 April 1997

Dear Ralph, Caroline and Gareth,

I have always liked Robert Hayden's poem, 'Those Winter Sundays', very much. These days a lot of writing seems to be about selling everyone close to you down the river, so Robert Hayden's fidelity is striking and a bit humbling. Another great American poet, James Wright, said the strongest word in the poem for him was the last one, 'offices', from the French office, meaning a religious service after dark. Anyway, I know I took my own parents for granted, too. Maybe we all do a little.

Best wishes,

Michael Gorman

Those Winter Sundays

Sundays too my father got up early
and put his clothes on in the blueblack cold,
then with cracked hands that ached
from labor in the weekday weather made
banked fires blaze. No one ever thanked him.

I'd wake and hear the cold splintering, breaking.
When the rooms were warm, he'd call,
and slowly I would rise and dress,
fearing the chronic angers of that house,

Speaking indifferently to him,
who had driven out the cold
and polished my good shoes as well.
What did I know, what did I know
of love's austere and lonely offices?

ROBERT HAYDEN (1913–1980)

DAVID MARCUS EDITOR

Dear Áine, Ewan and Christopher,

(Although an ardent feminist, I still believe in putting ladies first!) – I am delighted to be associated with your noble venture and thank you for inviting me.

I enclose my choice, a poem by the American poet, E E Cummings. It has no title – Cummings never gave his poems titles – and it is absolutely vital that it be printed exactly as enclosed with the poet's typographical oddities.

Good luck to you all.

Yours,

David Marcus

> mr youse needn't be so spry
> concernin questions arty
>
> each has his tastes but as for i
> i likes a certain party
>
> gimme the he-man's solid bliss
> for youse ideas i'll match youse
>
> a pretty girl who naked is
> is worth a million statues

E E CUMMINGS (1894–1962)

The typographical experiments cultivated by the American poet, E E Cummings, served to alienate many readers and critics. The loss was, and still is, theirs. One of the most accomplished craftsmen of his age and a lyric poet who had few superiors, he was a master of every mode. The poem of his I have chosen would, in our silly politically correct times, probably be reviled as male sexist. Male? But naturally; that's what he was. Sexist? But that's to ignore his use of the sexual dichotomy to express his view that life was more important than art. Ms youse needn't be so spry.

15 February 1997

Dear Ralph, Caroline and Gareth,

Thanks very much for your January letter. I'm sorry to be late in answering it.

I would like to nominate the 51st psalm as my choice for your anthology, and I leave it to you to select whichever translation you prefer. Like many catholic Christians, I would have grown up with the revised Standard version (for devotional purposes) and with the King James psalter (for literary pleasure), and have gone on more recently to the English edition of the Jerusalem Bible and to the New English Bible, but I have no way of knowing which, if any, is the senior or the sounder likeness to the original work in the Writings. The most influential treatment of this particular psalm is possibly the Vulgate setting by Allegri which Mozart is supposed to have notated on his shirt-cuff during a service in the Sistine Chapel.

I love this poem for the same reasons everybody else does, and that in itself is one of the most refreshing things about biblical and liturgical texts. They allow you to skip the quest for the prestige of an original insight, which is the aim of so much educated reading. The 51st psalm embodies our strange and damaged lives in the heartbreaking loveliness of a language which draws radical theological values from humdrum human states. It cannot be read and overcome, it can only be re-read and undergone; and it therefore frees us from the tedium of having rapid and ready opinions about it such as we're supposed to have in the present age of soundbytes, stop-press amnesia and media blink-think. Instead, it accompanies us in silence through all our stars and disasters as long as we choose to live.

It can do that because its author is neither here nor there, all autograph and no biography. The life of his work continues without him in the work of our lives, and the reader benefits from this impersonality by achieving from time to time the grace of his own anonymity before it. For a moment, he or she is a self and not an ego. In addition, the hodge-podge production of any part of scripture – which is after all creativity by committee, translations from translations, English from Latin from Greek and Hebrew – reminds us that the relationship between a reader and a text is more higgledy-piggledy than any straightline enlightenment model of devour-and-digest, that great work can be done in solidarity and not in solitude, and that the intimacy of print calls into being a community of very different dead and dying readers across many cultures and centuries for whom the verses of the 51st psalm signify not just the familiarity of a mood or the foreignness of a mode, not just impressionism or expressivity, but something pure and imperfect, a presence past all our projections.

Best wishes,

Aidan Mathews

Psalm 51

To the chief Musician, A Psalm of David, when Nathan the prophet came unto him, after he had gone to Bath-sheba.

1 Have mercy upon me, O God, according to thy loving kindness: according unto the multitude of thy tender mercies blot out my transgressions.

2 Wash me thoroughly from mine iniquity, and cleanse me from my sin.

3 For I acknowledge my transgressions: and my sin *is* ever before me.

4 Against thee, thee only, have I sinned, and done this *evil* in thy sight: that thou mightest be justified when thou speakest, and be clear when thou judgest.

5 Behold, I was shapen in iniquity; and in sin did my mother conceive me.

6 Behold, thou desirest truth in the inward parts: and in the hidden part thou shalt make me to know wisdom.

7 Purge me with hyssop, and I shall be clean: wash me, and I shall be whiter than snow.

8 Make me to hear joy and gladness; *that* the bones *which* thou hast broken may rejoice.

9 Hide thy face from my sins, and blot out all mine iniquities.

10 Create in me a clean heart, O God; and renew a right spirit within me.

11 Cast me not away from thy presence; and take not thy holy spirit from me.

12 Restore unto me the joy of thy salvation; and uphold me *with thy* free spirit.

13 *Then* will I teach transgressors thy ways; and sinners shall be converted unto thee.

14 Deliver me from bloodguiltiness, O God, thou God of my salvation: *and* my tongue shall sing aloud of thy righteousness.

15 O Lord, open thou my lips; and my mouth shall shew forth thy praise.

16 For thou desirest not sacrifice; else would I give *it*: thou delightest not in burnt offering.

17 The sacrifices of God *are* a broken spirit: a broken and contrite heart, O God, thou wilt not despise.

18 Do good in thy good pleasure unto Zion: build thou the walls of Jerusalem.

19 Then shalt thou be pleased with the sacrifices of righteousness, with burnt offering and whole burnt offering: then shall they offer bullocks upon thine altar.

AUTHORISED KING JAMES VERSION

Dear Ralph Croly, Caroline Dowling and Gareth McCluskey,

Thank you for asking me to contribute – and please forgive me for having brooded so long over my answer.

My poem is 'The Trout', by John Montague. I heard John Montague read this in Cork nearly 30 years ago, and remember it as my first 'grown-up' experience of poetry. At school I had fallen under the sensual spell of Wordsworth and Yeats, as young people readily do.

This poem, and Montague's reading of it, taught me that words have an even stronger magic: the power to reach where neither sense nor mind alone will serve us, and tickle great truth.

Eamonn Lawlor

The Trout
for Barrie Cooke

Flat on the bank I parted
Rushes to ease my hands
In the water without a ripple
And tilt them slowly downstream
To where he lay, tendril-light,
In his fluid sensual dream.

Bodiless lord of creation,
I hung briefly above him
Savouring my own absence,
Senses expanding in the slow
Motion, the photographic calm
That grows before action.

As the curve of my hands
Swung under his body
He surged, with visible pleasure.
I was so preternaturally close
I could count every stipple
But still cast no shadow, until

The two palms crossed in a cage
Under the lightly pulsing gills.
Then (entering my own enlarged
Shape, which rode on the water)
I gripped. To this day I can
Taste his terror on my hands.

JOHN MONTAGUE (B. 1929)

EMMA DONOGHUE NOVELIST

1994

Dear Ewan, Áine, and Christopher,

I've heard of these excellent books before; best of luck with this year's. It's not often that poems get to fill hungry mouths.

  My favourite poem is one of Emily Dickinson's that begins 'Wild Nights—Wild Nights!''

  I've loved Dickinson's startling poems ever since my mother recited them to me when I was small. As a 14-year-old lesbian I happened to read somewhere that Emily Dickinson had been in love with her sister-in-law; this confirmed my hunch that writers didn't have to be 'normal', didn't have to obey any rules but their own hearts. 'Wild Nights' conjures up the mixture of danger and safety found in the best kind of love.

Good luck again, and thanks for asking me.

Emma Donoghue

Wild Nights—Wild Nights!
Were I with thee
Wild Nights should be
Our luxury!

Futile—the Winds—
To a Heart in port—
Done with the Compass—
Done with the Chart!

Rowing in Eden—
Ah, the Sea!
Might I but moor—Tonight—
In Thee!

EMILY DICKINSON (1830–1886)

BRENDAN KENNELLY

POET

18 April 1985

Collette, Joy, Steven,

Thank you for writing to me. I think my favourite poem in the English language is 'The Garden of Love' by William Blake. I like it because it is a celebration of freedom.

Yours sincerely,

Brendan Kennelly

The Garden of Love

I went to the Garden of Love,
And saw what I never had seen:
A Chapel was built in the midst,
Where I used to play on the green.

And the gates of this Chapel were shut
And Thou shalt not. writ over the door;
So I turn'd to the Garden of Love,
That so many sweet flowers bore,

And I saw it was filled with graves,
And tomb-stones where flowers should be:
And Priests in black gowns, were walking their rounds,
And binding with briars, my joys & desires.

WILLIAM BLAKE (1757–1827)

RICHARD MURPHY

POET

5 January 1992

Dear Nicola, Paula and Alice,

Thank you for your New Year's Day letter about your anthology. I hope it will be successful.

I enclose my contribution: a poem by Pasternak called 'Bread' in an English version by Michael Harari, followed by my comments.

With best wishes,

Richard Murphy

Bread

With half a century to pile,
　　Unwritten, your conclusions,
　　By now, if you're not a halfwit,
You should have lost a few illusions,

　　Grasped the pleasure of study,
The laws and secrets of success,
The curse of idleness, the heroism
　　Needed for happiness;

　　That the powerful kingdom of beasts,
The sleepy kingdom of vegetation
　　Await their heroes, giants,
Their altars and their revelation;

That first of all the revelations,
　　Father of living and dead,
Gift to the generations, growth
　　Of the centuries, is bread;

And a harvest field is not just wheat
　　But a page to understand,
　　Written about yourself
In your remote forefather's hand,

His very word, his own amazing
　　Initiative among the birth,
　　Sorrow and death that circle
　　Their set ways round the earth.

BORIS PASTERNAK (1890–1960)
(English version by Michael Harari)

*Boris Pasternak's poem 'Bread' in the English version by Michael Harari has been a
favourite poem of mine since a friend showed it to me about fifteen years ago. It was then
a purifying antidote to the toxic effects of creative writing at Iowa during the coldest
winter on record. It still seems to have a mysterious power to say everything under the sun
in a way that sounds new. I can't imagine what gets lost in this translation, apart from
rhyme, because the poetry comes through with visionary force.*

If that sounds grandiloquent, it's because I think Pasternak has taken a high risk in daring to make a conclusive comment on what life seems to him to be all about. Wisely he uses the admonishing tone of voice of an alter ego or a conscience or the muse. He addresses himself as 'you': and you as a reader feel yourself drawn inside his thought process, becoming transformed into a better person as you read.

The great metaphor of the harvest field, as 'a page to understand/written about yourself/ in your remote forefather's hand' is, at least, an original way of seeing the link between the discovery of agriculture and the invention of writing. The biblical word forefather may suggest God, but at earth level it projects our unknown primitive ancestors, perhaps in the valleys of the Jordan and the Euphrates, whose 'amazing initiative' began the process that has enabled us to probe beyond the farthest visible stars.

The word forefather, like mankind, may disturb readers affected by the feminist assault on sexist vocabulary. Since seed was cast in a fenced field, and bread baked, women have done much of the work, while men have been waging war. I don't think Pasternak, or his translator, intended the word forefather to exclude the idea of motherhood, but to be inclusive. If he'd used a neuter word, such as 'originator', humanity would have been drained out of his poem at its climax. Instead, without losing his foothold on the ground, he rises to a new affirmation of the mythical link between bread and the word, or logos. To express the search through the self and the cosmos for salvation, he uses a tone of voice unflawed by religiosity.

Before he works this beneficial magic, he rings bells as common as those that chime from village or city clock towers. If the clichés in the first two stanzas sound banal, their banality is soon transmuted into the poem's myth. And the bread is revealed as the truth. Pasternak had suffered through the famine caused by Stalin's policy of collectivisation, the terror under Stalin, and the horrors of war. He had earned the moral authority with which he speaks of 'the heroism needed for happiness'.

'Bread' was written in the mid-Fifties. Bearing this in mind while reading the final stanza, I recall the first sputnik moving across the sky before dawn over Dublin, where I watched it from the cattle-markets. Russia was then winning the space race by an 'amazing initiative', putting a dog into orbit. The unfortunate creature received a lethal injection when its job of contributing to a triumph of human technology was finished. In a sense that is literal and shocking, the dog on its doomed voyage underscores and confirms Pasternak's final metaphor of the 'birth, sorrow and death that circle their set ways round the earth'. The poem has become all the more relevant in the winter of 1991–1992, when a great number of desperate people in Russia and the Third World cannot obtain enough bread.

Richard Murphy

GLENDA JACKSON ACTOR

January 1992

Dear Nicola, Paula and Alice,

Thank you for your letter. I don't really have a favourite poem, but I would choose
'Not Waving, but Drowning' by Stevie Smith, because I share her feeling.
   Best wishes for your book and I hope it will raise a wonderful sum of money.

Yours sincerely,

Glenda Jackson

Not Waving But Drowning

Nobody heard him, the dead man,
But still he lay moaning:
I was much further out than you thought
And not waving but drowning.

Poor chap, he always loved larking
And now he's dead
It must have been too cold for him his heart gave way,
They said.

Oh, no no no, it was too cold always
(Still the dead one lay moaning)
I was much too far out all my life
And not waving but drowning.

STEVIE SMITH (1902–1971)

['*Not Waving But Drowning*' was also chosen by Sara Berkeley in *Lifelines* and Leland Bardwell in *Lifelines 2*.

Sara Berkeley wrote:
My favourite poem is Stevie Smith's 'Not Waving but Drowning'. It may seem like a morbid poem but I like it because it is so matter-of-fact and simple. I think of it often when I'm waving to people and hope they don't imagine I'm drowning, and sometimes I think of it when I'm drowning and wish someone would realise I wasn't waving.

Leland Bardwell wrote:
I have chosen this poem because, as in all Stevie Smith's work, there is the duality of absurdity and pain. These twelve lines, therefore, with their beautiful lyrical quality, epitomise the daftness and trip-wire existence of the poet.]

Hi there,

As requested, here is my selected poem for New and Collected Lifelines, *and the reason for my choice.*

    Thank you again for inviting me to contribute. I wish you all the very best with the project, and hope it proves to be as successful as previous editions!

With best wishes,

Matt Whyman

Poetry has always intimidated me. I can read a much-loved classic, and just fail to get it. Don't get me wrong. I love words, reading and writing. It's just something I have always considered to be for people with more intelligence than me. My only exception to this is the work of Charles Bukowski. Before I had read anything by him, I knew more about his life than I did about his prose or poetry. That he was a self-confessed slob, drifter and drinker somehow made me think his stuff must be more accessible, and I wasn't wrong.

    Bukowski's work is raw, bawdy, funny, joyful, skewed, startling, tragic and moving. That's some achievement here, using such a spare amount of words.

A Radio with Guts

it was on the 2nd floor on Coronado Street
I used to get drunk
and throw the radio through the window
while it was playing, and, of course,
it would break the glass in the window
and the radio would sit there on the roof
still playing
and I'd tell my woman,
'Ah, what a marvelous radio!'
the next morning I'd take the window
off the hinges
and carry it down the street
to the glass man
who would put in another pane.
I kept throwing that radio through the window
each time I got drunk
and it would sit there on the roof
still playing—
a magic radio
a radio with guts,
and each morning I'd take the window
back to the glass man.

I don't remember how it ended exactly
though I do remember
we finally moved out.
there was a woman downstairs who worked in
the garden in her bathing suit,
she really dug with that trowel
and she put her behind up in the air
and I used to sit in the window
and watch the sun shine all over that thing
while the music played.

CHARLES BUKOWSKI (1920–1994)

FIONA SHAW   ACTOR

10 January 1990

Dear Joann, Jacki and Carolyn,

Thank you so very much for inviting me to be part of your anthology. I am truly honoured, particularly as I think your predecessors asked me and due to my infinite moves my reply was never sent.

Anyway good luck with this and I do hope it's another sell-out.

You have asked a difficult question. 'Favourite' is always hard for a fanatic, so I have approached this by trying to narrow down the possibilities to a favourite poet.

I have decided that it is Yeats and I am full of trepidation that too many of your poems will be Yeats choices. Mine is either: 'The Song of Wandering Aengus' and I really don't know why. I don't intellectually understand the poem but I think it's great because the moment you start reading it you are transported to another place, the inside of someone else's vision, and you travel swiftly through landscape and time even to the end of life with the yearning speaker and then you wake up at the end of the poem having had the beatific rest of unravelling sleep.

If too many chose that poem I would like to offer the alternative of 'The Second Coming'. I love this poem because it frightens me!

Best wishes,

Yours, with gratitude,

Fiona Shaw

The Song of Wandering Aengus

I went out to the hazel wood,
Because a fire was in my head,
And cut and peeled a hazel wand,
And hooked a berry to a thread;
And when white moths were on the wing,
And moth-like stars were flickering out,
I dropped the berry in a stream
And caught a little silver trout.

When I had laid it on the floor
I went to blow the fire aflame,
But something rustled on the floor,
And some one called me by my name:
It had become a glimmering girl
With apple blossom in her hair
Who called me by my name and ran
And faded through the brightening air.

Though I am old with wandering
Through hollow lands and hilly lands,
I will find out where she has gone,
And kiss her lips and take her hands;
And walk among long dappled grass,
And pluck till time and times are done
The silver apples of the moon,
The golden apples of the sun.

W B YEATS (1865–1939)

The Second Coming

Turning and turning in the widening gyre
The falcon cannot hear the falconer;
Things fall apart; the centre cannot hold;
Mere anarchy is loosed upon the world,
The blood-dimmed tide is loosed, and everywhere
The ceremony of innocence is drowned;
The best lack all conviction, while the worst
Are full of passionate intensity.

Surely some revelation is at hand;
Surely the Second Coming is at hand.
The Second Coming! Hardly are those words out
When a vast image out of *Spiritus Mundi*
Troubles my sight: somewhere in sands of the desert
A shape with lion body and the head of a man,
A gaze blank and pitiless as the sun,
Is moving its slow thighs, while all about it
Reel shadows of the indignant desert birds.
The darkness drops again; but now I know
That twenty centuries of stony sleep
Were vexed to nightmare by a rocking cradle,
And what rough beast, its hour come round at last,
Slouches towards Bethlehem to be born?

W B YEATS (1865–1939)

['*The Song of Wandering Aengus*' was also chosen by Charles Haughey and Seamus Brennan in *Lifelines*, and by Carol Ann Duffy in *Lifelines 2*; '*The Second Coming*' was chosen by Louis Le Brocquy in *Lifelines*.

Charles Haughey wrote:
The language and imagery are exquisite. It is full of romance, mystery and magic.

Seamus Brennan wrote:
I have been thinking since I received your letter about my favourite poem. Different verses have come to mind, but I have opted for the one which first struck me – 'The Song of Wandering Aengus' by W B Yeats.

My reasons for nominating this poem are more difficult to articulate. I am putting to paper some random thoughts which come to mind:

The words have stayed in my mind over so many years; they must have impacted to a greater degree than I previously realised.

The opening lines bring to my mind an image of a person confused, but from that opening Yeats weaves a most serene, peaceful and tranquil picture with absolute simplicity, in a manner only a master poet can do.

Carol Ann Duffy wrote:
'*The Song of Wandering Aengus*' *by W B Yeats is my favourite poem. I first read it when I was 15 or so and I still, thankfully, find it as beautiful now as I did then. It was almost instantly memorable and the last two lines on that first reading were like a small punch in the stomach. I've recently taken great pleasure from a recording of the poem, with music, by Christy Moore.*

Louis Le Brocquy wrote:
The poem which means most to me, after all, is Yeats's 'The Second Coming'. What are my reasons? Yeats himself replies with his own question in 'Steam and Sun at Glendalough':

What motion of the sun or stream
Or eyelid shot the gleam
That pierced my body through?]

Wesley College
1992

Dear Julie, Jonathan and Duncan,

Thank you for inviting me to submit a favourite poem in the latest edition of Lifelines.

I choose 'Schoolmaster' because of the way I remember my days in the old St Patrick's Cathedral Grammar School (a new school is to be opened by the Taoiseach next month) and the variety of the teaching styles of Miss Dunbar and the schoolmasters there. All of them had at least one great gift in common – the ability to inspire. Albert Schweitzer has written 'I do not believe that we can put into anyone ideas which are not in him anyway. As a rule there are in everyone some good ideas, like tinder. But much of this tinder catches fire only when it meets some flame or spark from outside; that is, from some other person.'

With every good wish,

Yours sincerely,

Kenneth Blackmore

Schoolmaster

Oh yes, yes, I remember him well,
though I do not know if I would recognise him now:
nobody grows any younger, or better,
and boys grow into much the sort of men one would suppose
though sometimes the moustaches bewilder
and one finds it hard to reconcile one's memory of a small
none-too-clean urchin lying his way unsuccessfully out of his homework
with a fierce and many-medalled sergeant-major with three children
or a divorced chartered accountant;
and it is hard to realise
that some little tousled rebellious youth whose only claim
to fame among his contemporaries was his undisputed right
to the championship of the spitting contest
is now perhaps one's own bank manager.
Oh yes, I remember him well, the boy you are searching for:
he looked like most boys, no better, brighter, or more respectful;
he cribbed, mitched, spilt ink, rattled his desk and
garbled his lessons with the worst of them;
he could smudge, hedge, smirk, wriggle, wince,
whimper, blarney, badger, blush, deceive, be
devious, stammer, improvise, assume
offended dignity or righteous indignation as though to the manner born;
sullenly and reluctantly he drilled, for some small
crime, under Sergeant Bird, so wittily nicknamed

Oiseau, on Wednesday half-holidays,
appeared regularly in detention classes,
hid in the cloakroom during algebra,
was, when a newcomer, thrown, into the bushes of the
Lower Playground by the bigger boys;
and threw newcomers into the bushes of the Lower
Playground when *he* was a bigger boy;
he scuffled at prayers,
he interpolated, smugly, the time-honoured wrong
irreverent words into the morning hymns,
he helped to damage the headmaster's rhubarb,
was thirty third in trigonometry,
and, as might be expected, edited the School Magazine.

DYLAN THOMAS (1914–1953)

JOHN HARRIS   EDUCATOR

Wesley College
28 May 1997

Dear Ralph, Caroline and Gareth,

I appreciate very much your kind invitation to contribute to Lifelines 3. *I find it very difficult to choose a favourite poem, as my feelings about particular poems or styles of poetry can vary according to my mood at the time. However, I have decided to choose 'Concert-Interpretation' by Siegfried Sassoon on this occasion.*

The poem appeals to me because it captures so accurately how difficult it can be for any new creative form to gain acceptance initially – as clearly was the case with the initial exposure to the works of Stravinsky, the subject of the poem. The second reason it appeals to me so much is because of the way in which the poet makes this an orchestral work in words. To listen to it read aloud evokes so strikingly the sound of Stravinsky's music.

I congratulate you most warmly for your initiative in compiling Lifelines 3 *and for your support for such a worthy cause.*

Yours sincerely,

John W Harris

Concert-Interpretation
(Le Sacré du Printemps)

The audience pricks an intellectual Ear . . .
Stravinsky . . . *Quite the Concert of the Year!*

Forgetting now that none-so-distant date
When they (or folk facsimilar in state
Of mind) first heard with hisses — hoots — guffaws —
This abstract Symphony (they booed because
Stravinsky jumped their Wagner palisade
With modes that seemed cacophonous and queer),
Forgetting now the hullabaloo they made,
The Audience pricks an intellectual ear.

Bassoons begin . . . Sonority envelops
Our auditory innocence; and brings
To Me, I must admit, some drift of things
Omnific, seminal, and adolescent.
Polyphony through dissonance develops
A serpent-conscious Eden, crude but pleasant;
While vibro-atmospheric copulations
With mezzo-forte mysteries of noise
Prelude Stravinsky's statement of the joys
That unify the monkeydom of nations.

This matter is most indelicate indeed!
Yet one perceives no symptom of stampede.
The Stalls remain unruffled: craniums gleam:
Swept by a storm of pizzicato chords,
Elaborate ladies re-assure their lords
With lifting brows that signify 'Supreme!'
While orchestrated gallantry of goats
Impugns the astigmatic programme-notes.

In the Grand Circle one observes no sign
Of riot: peace prevails along the line.
And in the Gallery, cargoed to capacity,
No tremor bodes eruptions and alarms.
They are listening to this not-quite-new audacity
As though it were by someone dead, — like Brahms.

But savagery pervades Me; I am frantic
With corybantic rupturing of laws.
Come, dance, and seize this clamorous chance to function
Creatively, — abandoning compunction
In anti-social rhapsodic applause!
Lynch the conductor! Jugulate the drums!
Butcher the brass! Ensanguinate the strings!
Throttle the flutes! . . . Stravinsky's April comes
With pitiless pomp and pain of sacred springs . . .
Incendiarize the Hall with resinous fires
Of sacrificial fiddles scorched and snapping! . . .

Meanwhile the music blazes and expires;
And the delighted Audience is clapping.

Siegfried Sassoon (1886–1967)

CHRISTOPHER WOODS EDUCATOR

8 April 2006

Dear Dónal, Caroline and Stephanie,

Thank you very much for your kind invitation to contribute a poem to the New and
Collected Lifelines. *There are so many wonderful poems to choose from, but poetry
becomes magical when it speaks to me at the moment, and draws an image that I feel
is just right, now. So rather than give you an old favourite I am sending you this poem
by Sharon Olds which I came upon only recently. What appeals to me is that instant
recognition of the picture it paints, the beauty in things so ordinary, the message that the
best in life is right in front of us.*

*   All the very best with your work and I look forward very much to reading the collection.*

Yours sincerely,

Christopher Woods

Looking at Them Asleep

When I come home late at night and go in to kiss the children,
I see my girl with her arm curled around her head,
her face deep in unconsciousness—so
deeply centered she is in her dark self,
her mouth slightly puffed like one sated but
slightly pouted like one who hasn't had enough,
her eyes so closed you would think they have rolled the
iris around to face the back of her head,
the eyeball marble-naked under that
thick satisfied desiring lid,
she lies on her back in abandon and sealed completion,
and the son in his room, oh the son he is sideways in his bed,
one knee up as if he is climbing
sharp stairs up into the night,
and under his thin quivering eyelids you
know that his eyes are wide open and
staring and glazed, the blue in them so
anxious and crystally in all this darkness, and his
mouth is open, he is breathing hard from the climb
and panting a bit, his brow is crumpled
and pale, his long fingers curved,
his hand open, and in the center of each hand
the dry dirty boyish palm
resting like a cookie. I look at him in his
quest, the thin muscles of his arms
passionate and tense, I look at her with her
face like the face of a snake who has swallowed a deer,
content, content—and I know if I wake her she'll
smile and turn her face toward me though
half asleep and open her eyes and I
know if I wake him he'll jerk and say Don't and sit
up and stare about him in blue
unrecognition, oh my Lord how I
know these two. When love comes to me and says
What do you know, I say This girl, this boy.

SHARON OLDS (B. 1942)

18 May 1985

Dear Collette Lucy,

One of my favourite poems is 'Cuchulain Comforted' *by W B Yeats. Written a few days before his death, it is a mysterious and difficult poem, but one which seems to fulfil Yeats's stated ambition 'to hold in a single thought reality and justice'. It presents a confrontation between heroism and cowardice, between violence and resignation, between life and death, and communicates a deep sense of peace and understanding.*

Sincerely,

Seamus Heaney

Cuchulain Comforted

A man that had six mortal wounds, a man
Violent and famous, strode among the dead;
Eyes stared out of the branches and were gone.

Then certain Shrouds that muttered head to head
Came and were gone. He leant upon a tree
As though to meditate on wounds and blood.

A Shroud that seemed to have authority
Among those bird-like things came, and let fall
A bundle of linen. Shrouds by two and three

Came creeping up because the man was still.
And thereupon the linen-carrier said:
'Your life can grow much sweeter if you will

'Obey our ancient rule and make a shroud;
Mainly because of what we only know
The rattle of those arms make us afraid.

'We thread the needles' eyes, and all we do
All must together do.' That done, the man
Took up the nearest and began to sew.

'Now we must sing and sing the best we can,
But first you must be told our character:
Convicted cowards all, by kindred slain

'Or driven from home and left to die in fear.'
They sang, but had nor human tunes nor words,
Though all was done in common as before;

They had changed their throats and had the throats of birds.

W B YEATS (1865–1939)

19 January 1988

Dear Julie, Jonathan and Duncan,

I love good anthologies and Lifelines I *was unquestionably one of the best anthologies put together anywhere in recent years. I am looking forward immensely, therefore to* Lifelines II.

I have hundreds of 'favourite poems'. Here are some titles as they come to mind: 'To my Wife' *by Knut Hamsun;* 'Innocent When You Dream' *by Tom Waits;* 'One Art' *by Elizabeth Bishop;* 'In St Etheldreda's' *by Sara Berkeley;* 'Almost Communication' *by Rita Ann Higgins;* 'The Dark Sobrietee' *by Macdara Woods;* 'White Shirts in Childhood' *by Dermot Bolger;* 'Summertime in England' *by Van Morrison;* 'To Margot Heineman' *by John Cornford;* 'The Fall of Rome' *by W H Auden;* 'The Pleasant Joys of Brotherhood' *by James Simmon;* 'Sunday Morning' *by Wallace Stevens;* 'The Keen Stars Were Twinkling' *by Percy Shelley;* 'In Parenthesis' *by David Jones;* 'Voracities and Verities Sometimes are Interacting' *by Marianne Moore;* 'Lisdoonvarna' *by Christy Moore;* 'The Bronze Horseman' *by Aleksandr Pushkin;* 'On Raglan Road' *by Patrick Kavanagh;* 'Four Quartets' *by T S Eliot;* 'Everness' *by Jorge Luis Borges;* 'One Too Many Mornings' *by Bob Dylan;* 'The Collar-Bone Of A Hare' *by W B Yeats;* 'The Silken Tent' *by Robert Frost;* 'Thirty Bob A Week' *by John Davidson;* 'Of the Great and Famous Ever-to-be-honoured Knight, Sir Francis Drake, and of My Little-Little Self' *by Robert Hayman;* 'Return Thoughts' *by Anthony Cronin;* '7 Middagh Street' *by Paul Muldoon;* 'Ireland 1944' *by Francis Stuart;* 'Born in the USA' *by Bruce Springsteen;* 'Lament for Ignacio Sanchez Mejias' *by Federico Garcia Lorca;* 'Midnight Trolleybus' *by Bulat Okudjhava;* 'Let's Be Sad' *by Irina Ratushinskaya;* 'He Among Them Nightly Moving' *by John Stephen Moriarty;* 'A Bat on the Road' *by Seamus Heaney;* 'Barbara' *by Jacques Prévert;* 'Antarctica' *by Derek Mahon;* 'Intoxication' *by Boris Pasternak;* 'Skrymtymnym' *by Andrei Voznesensky;* 'The Princess of Parallelograms' *by Medbh McGuckian;* 'In the Luxembourg Gardens' *by Tom McCarthy* . . .

But the poem I would like you to play for me today is 'Shut Up, I'm Going To Sing You a Love Song' *by Ellen Gilchrist, an American word-magician who is the author of at least two stunning books of stories,* Victory Over Japan *and* In The Land of Dreamy Dreams.

I hope you collect buckets of money for the people of Ethiopia.

Salut,

Paul Durcan

Shut Up, I'm Going to Sing You A Love Song
for F S K

I dream to save you
I must leap from an ocean pier
into water of uncertain depth
You flail below me in a business suit
Knowing I must jump I frown
Knowing we will drown together
Knowing the dark sea will bloom for a moment
with the red hibiscus I refuse to wear
over either ear

Sighing I dive my special Red Cross dive
straight into the sea
which is deeper than either of us dreamed
it would be
Sit still there is nothing to fear
Undo my dress I am here you are here

ELLEN GILCHRIST (B. 1935)

(from *The Land Surveyors's Daughter*, 1980)

EAVAN BOLAND   POET

1985

Upon Julia's Clothes

Whenas in silks my Julia goes,
Then, then, methinks, how sweetly flows
The liquefaction of her clothes.

Next, when I cast mine eyes, and see
That brave vibration, each way free,
O, how that glittering taketh me!

ROBERT HERRICK (1591–1674)

This is written by Robert Herrick who died fourteen years after the Restoration in 1660. He has come to be known as a Caroline poet but I think the title is misleading. He is a late, upbeat and maverick Elizabethan. This is certainly one of my favourite poems. For a piece supposedly written by a court poet it practises remarkable thrift. I like the miserly economy of language played off against the wonderful, prosperous image of the woman in silks.

Notes on the Contributors

Fleur Adcock (p. 211) Poet (*Selected Poems*; *The Incident Book*; *Time Zones*), translator, critic and anthologist. Awarded the Queen's Gold Medal for Poetry 2006.

Bertie Ahern TD (p. 3) Politician. Leader of Fianna Fáil. Taoiseach.

Darina Allen (p. 102) Chef and founder of the Ballymaloe Cookery School. Author of *The Ballymaloe Cookery Course*.

Myrtle Allen (p. 66) Cookery expert and author (*The Ballymaloe Cookbook*).

Jeffrey Archer (p. 97) Writer (*Kane and Abel*; *As the Crow Flies*).

Simon Armitage (p 11) Poet (*Zoom!*; *Kid*; *Cloudcuckooland*). Writer (*All Points North*) and novelist (*Little Green Man*).

Kate Atkinson (p. 89) Novelist (*Behind the Scenes at the Museum*; *Emotionally Weird*; *Case Histories*).

Beryl Bainbridge (p. 45) Novelist (*The Dressmaker*; *The Bottle Factory Outing*; *Injury Time*; *Every Man for Himself*).

John Banville (p. 263) Novelist (*Kepler*; *The Book of Evidence*; *Shroud*; *The Sea* – winner of the Booker Prize, 2006).

Lynn Barber (p. 84) Journalist and author of *Mostly Men*.

Leland Bardwell Poet (p. 329) (*Dostoevsky's Grave, New and Selected Poems*; *The White Beach, New and Selected Poems*; *The Noise of Masonry Settling*), novelist, short-story writer and playwright.

Kevin Barry (p. 172) Professor of English, NUI Galway, writer and critic.

Eileen Battersby (p. 132) *Irish Times* literary correspondent, broadcaster and critic.

Sara Berkeley (p. 329) Poet (*Penn*; *Strawberry Thief*), novelist and short-story writer.

Steven Berkoff (p. 309) Playwright, actor, director, writer.

Maeve Binchy (p. 250) Novelist (*Light a Penny Candle*; *Firefly Summer*; *The Copper Beech*; *Night of Rain and Stars*), playwright (*Deeply Regretted By*).

Charlie Bird (p. 79) Chief news correspondent, RTÉ.

Kenneth Blackmore (p. 334) Retired principal of Wesley College, Dublin.

Eavan Boland (p. 341) Poet (*Night Feed*; *Outside History*; *The Lost Land*; *New Collected Poems*), writer (*Object Lessons*) and critic.

Rosita Boland (p. 10) Staff journalist, *The Irish Times*, Poet (*Muscle Creek*; *Dissecting the Heart*), writer (*Sea-Legs – Hitch-hiking the Coast of Ireland*; *A Secret Map of Ireland*).

Dermot Bolger (p. 124) Novelist (*Nightshift*; *The Journey Home*; *Father's Music*; *The Valparaiso Voyage*; *The Family on Paradise Pier*), playwright (*Lament for Arthur Cleary*; *In High Germany*; *Consenting Adults*), poet (*Taking My Letters Back: New & Selected Poems*), journalist and editor.

Ken Bourke (p. 259) Playwright (*Wild Harvest*).

Brian Boydell (p. 205) Composer.

John Boyne (p. 49) Author (*The Boy In The Striped Pyjamas*; *The Thief of Time*; *The Congress of Rough Riders*; *Crippen*; *Next of Kin*).

Hugh Brady (p. 174) President of UCD, University College Dublin.

Melvyn Bragg (p. 130) Novelist (*The Hired Man*; *Kingdom Come*; *Josh Lawton*; *The Maid of Buttermere*; *Credo*), writer (*The Adventure of English: The Biography of a Language*; *Twelve Books That Changed the World*), broadcaster, controller of Arts at Granada, President of the National Campaign for the Arts.

Olive Braiden (p. 237) Chairperson of the Arts Council.

Niamh Bhreathnach (p. 57) Labour councillor for Dún Laoghaire/Rathdown.

Seamus Brennan TD (p. 333) Politician. Minister for Social & Family Affairs.

Joseph Brodsky (p. 297) Russian poet (*A Part of Speech*; *To Urania*), winner of the 1987 Nobel Prize for literature. Deceased.

Melvin Burgess (p. 9) Author and winner of the Carnegie Medal (*The Cry of the Wolf*; *Junk*; *Doing It*; *Bloodtide*; *Bloodsong*; *Sara's Face*).

Paddy Bushe (p. 182) Poet/File (*Poems with Amergin; Teanga; Digging Towards the Light; Hopkins on Skellig Island; In Ainneoin na gCloch; The Nitpicking of Cranes*).

Catherine Byrne (p. 189) Actor on stage (*Dancing at Lughnasa; Molly Sweeney; Give Me Your Answer Do!*) and television (*Upwardly Mobile*).

Gay Byrne (p. 273) Former broadcaster and presenter of the *Late Late Show* on RTÉ television. Author of *The Time of My Life*. Chairperson of Road Safety Authority.

Ollie Campbell (p. 131) former rugby player.

John Carey (p. 65) Professor Emeritus of English at Merton College, Oxford, broadcaster, writer (*The Intellectual and the Masses; What Good are the Arts?*).

Eithne Carr (p. 215) Artist.

Ciaran Carson (p. 185) Poet (*The Irish for No; First Language*) and writer (*The Star Factory; Fishing for Amber*).

Paul Carson (p. 206) Novelist (*Scalpel*) and writer.

Kevin Casey (p. 198) Novelist (*A Sense of Survival; Dreams of Revenge*) short-story writer and critic.

Jung Chang (p. 12) Chinese writer (*Wild Swans; Mao*).

Anthony Clare (p. 165) Psychiatrist, writer, broadcaster.

Amy Clampitt Poet (p. 36) (*The Kingfisher; What the Light was Like; Archaic Figure; A Silence Opens*). Deceased.

Michael Coady (p. 61) Poet (*Two for a Woman, Three for a Man; Oven Lane; All Souls; One Another*). Winner of the Patrick Kavanagh Award 1979 and the O'Shaughnessy Poetry Award 2004.

J M Coetzee (p. 88) Novelist (*Waiting for the Barbarians; The Life and Times of Michael K; Disgrace; Slow Man*), writer (*Stranger Shores: Essays 1986–1999*) Awarded the Nobel Prize for Literature 2003 and twice winner of the Booker Prize.

Paddy Cole (p. 102) Musician.

Michael Colgan (p. 291) Director of the Gate Theatre.

Billy Collins (p. 19) Poet (*Nine Horses; Sailing Alone Around the Room: New and Selected Poems; Picnic, Lightning; The Art of Drowning; Questions About Angels; The Apple that Astonished Paris; Video-Poems; Pokerface*).

Evelyn Conlon (p. 161) Novelist, short-story writer, broadcaster and critic.

Marita Conlon-McKenna (p. 118) Novelist for teenagers (*Under the Hawthorn; No Goodbye; The Blue Horse; Tree; Wildflower Girl*) and adults (*The Magdalen*).

John Connolly (p. 291) Novelist (*The White Road; Dark Hollow; Every Dead Thing; The Black Angel*).

Barrie Cooke (p. 74) Artist.

Jeananne Crowley (p.242) Actor.

Margrit Cruickshank (p. 277) Author for children and teenagers (the *S.K.U.N.K.* books, including *S.K.U.N.K. and the Freak Flood Fiasco; A Monster Called Charlie* and *Circling the Triangle*).

Bill Cullen (p. 6) Head of Renault Ireland. Writer (*It's a Long Way from Penny Apples; Golden Apples*).

Cyril Cusack (p. 180) Actor (deceased).

Ita Daly (p.16) Novelist (*Ellen; Unholy Ghosts*), short-story writer, critic and broadcaster.

Pádraig J Daly (p. 283) Poet (*Poems, New and Selected; Out of Silence*) and Augustinian priest.

Philip Davison (p. 293) Novelist (*The Book-Thief's Heartbeat; Twist and Shout; The Illustrator; The Crooked Man*) and playwright (*The Invisible Mending Company*).

Richard Dawkins (p. 25) Scientist and writer (*River Out of Eden*).

Seamus Deane (p. 170) Poet (*History Lessons*), novelist (*Reading in the Dark*), author (*A Short History of Irish Literature*).

Greg Delanty (p. 70) Poet (*Cast in the Fire; Southward; American Wake; The Hellbox; The Ship of Birth; Collected Poems 1986–2006*).

Matthew Dempsey (p. 65) Journalist and editor of the *Farmers' Journal*.

Judi Dench (p. 73) Actor. Acclaimed roles include Cleopatra in *Antony and Cleopatra* at the National Theatre, London, Mistress Quickly in the film *Henry V* and Queen Elizabeth in *Shakespeare in Love*, for which she won an Oscar.

Dermot Desmond (p. 59) Businessman.

Brian Dillon (p. 314) Writer (*In the Dark Room*) and critic.

Eilís Dillon (p. 151) Novelist (*Across the Bitter Sea*), children's writer. Deceased.

Terry Dolan (p. 216) Writer, editor, broadcaster. Professor of Old and Middle English, UCD.

Emma Donoghue (p. 325) Novelist (*Stir Fry; Slammerkin*), playwright (*I Know My Own Heart*), writer (*Passion Between Women*) and broadcaster.

Katie Donovan (p. 251) Author (*Irish Women Writers: Marginalised by Whom?*), poet (*Watermelon Man*), journalist, selector with Brendan Kennelly and A N Jeffares of *Ireland's Women, Writers Past and Present*.

Anne Doyle (p. 1) Newscaster on RTÉ radio and television.

Roddy Doyle (p. 102) Novelist (*The Commitments; The Snapper; The Van; Paddy Clarke Ha Ha Ha; The Woman Who Walked Into Doors*) and playwright (*Brownbread; War*); writer (*Rory and Ita*).

Margaret Drabble, CBE (p. 2) Novelist (*A Summer Bird-Cage; The Millstone; The Needle's Eye; The Radiant Way; The Seven Sisters; The Red Queen*), biographer (*Arnold Bennett; Angus Wilson*), lecturer, critic and editor of *The Oxford Companion to English Literature*.

Martin Drury (p. 268) Theatre director and former director of The Ark, a cultural centre for children.

Carol Ann Duffy Poet (p. 333) (*Standing Female Nude; Selling Manhattan; Feminine Gospels; Out of Fashion; Rapture*), and playwright.

Joe Duffy (p. 238) Broadcaster and journalist. Presenter of *Liveline* on RTÉ Radio 1.

Robert Dunbar (p. 50) Lecturer, editor, writer and critic. Commentator on children's literature.

Myles Dungan (p. 310) Broadcaster, journalist and author.

Helen Dunmore (p. 24) Poet (*The Apple Fall; The Sea Skater; The Raw Garden*), novelist (*Zennor in Darkness; Burning Bright*) and short-story writer.

Eileen Dunne (p. 254) Newscaster on RTÉ radio and television.

Paul Durcan (p. 340) Poet (*The Berlin Wall Café; Daddy Daddy; Crazy About Women; A Snail in My Prime; The Art of Life*) and holder of the Ireland Chair Professor of Poetry.

Christine Dwyer Hickey (p. 177) Novelist (*The Gambler; Tatty*).

Alison Dye (p. 235) Novelist (*The Sense of Things; Memories of Snow; An Awareness of March*).

Lauris Edmond (p. 153) New Zealand poet (*Summer Near the Arctic Circle; New and Selected Poems*) and autobiographer (*Hot October; Bonfires in the Rain; The Quick Life*). Deceased.

Ben Elton (p. 256) Comedian, playwright, novelist (*Stark; Gridlock*).

Tracey Emin (p. 122) Artist and writer (*Strangeland*).

Peter Fallon (p. 77) Poet (*The First Affair; Winter Work; News of the World: Selected and New Poems; The Georgics of Virgil*), editor and founder of The Gallery Press.

Bernard Farrell (p. 144) Playwright (*I Do Not Like Thee Dr Fell; Canaries; Kevin's Bed*).

Brian Farrell (p. 8) Journalist, broadcaster and writer (*Chairman or Chief*) and biographer of Seán Lemass.

Mary Finan (p. 165) Chairperson of the RTÉ Authority.

Garret FitzGerald (p. 32) Author (*Towards a New Ireland; All in a Life –Autobiography*), politician, lecturer and academic. Former Taoiseach and leader of Fine Gael.

Penelope Fitzgerald (p. 18) English novelist (*Offshore* – winner of the Booker prize 1979, *The Beginning of Spring; The Gate of Angels; The Blue Flower*). Deceased.

Gabriel Fitzmaurice (p. 219) Poet (*The Father's Part*), teacher, editor (*Irish Poetry Now*) and broadcaster.

Christopher Fitz-Simon (p. 28) Writer, playwright and biographer (*The Irish Theatre; The Arts in Ireland; The Boys: A Biography of Micheál MacLiammóir and Hilton Edwards*). Former artistic director of the Abbey Theatre.

T P Flanagan (p. 275) Artist.

Roy Foster (p. 56) Professor of Irish History at Oxford. Writer (*Charles Stewart Parnell: The Man and His Family; Lord Randolph Churchill: A Political Life; Modern Ireland 1600–1972*). Biographer of W B Yeats.

Mildred Fox (p. 72) Politician, Independent TD.

Maureen Gaffney (p. 126) Chairperson of the National Economic and Social Forum. Writer and broadcaster.

Tess Gallagher (p. 264) American poet (*Stepping Outside; Instructions to the Double; Willingly; Amplitude: New and Selected Poems*) and short-story writer (*The Lover of Horses*).

Tom Garvin (p. 260) Professor of Politics at UCD and writer.

John Gielgud (p. 152) Actor. Deceased.

Allen Ginsberg (p. 303) American poet (*Howl and Other Poems*; *Kaddish and Other Poems*; *TV Baby Poems*; *The Fall of America: Poems of These States*). Deceased.

Louise Glück (p. 212) American poet (*Firstborn*; *The House on Marshland*; *Descending Figure*; *The Wild Iris*). Winner of the Pulitzer Prize.

Michael Gorman (p. 320) Poet (*Postcards from Galway*; *Waiting for the Sky to Fall*; *Up She Flew*).

Eamon Grennan (p. 179) Poet (*Wildly for Days*; *What Light There Is*; *As If It Matters*; *The Quick of It*; *Selected and New Poems*).

Vona Groarke (p. 48) Poet (*Shale*; *Other People's Houses*; *Flight*; *Juniper Street*). Broadcaster.

Mark Haddon (p. 78) Novelist (*The Curious Incident of the Dog in the Night-time*) and author of fifteen books for children. Illustrator and screenwriter. Winner of two BAFTA Awards.

James Hanley (p. 193) Artist. Portrait painter. Secretary of the RHA.

Kerry Hardie (p. 202) Poet (*A Furious Place*; *The Sky Didn't Fall*), winner of the 1996 Friends Provident National Poetry Competition, winner [with Sinead Morrissey] of the Michael Hartnett Award 2005 and novelist (*Hannie Bennett's Winter Marriage*; *The Bird Woman*).

Mary Harney, TD (p. 302) Minister in Irish government, Tánaiste, Leader of the Progressive Democrats.

John Harris (p. 335) Retired principal of Wesley College, Dublin.

Michael Hartnett (p. 167) Poet (*Anatomy of a Cliché*; *The Hag of Beare*; *Gipsy Ballads*; *A Farewell to English*; *Cúlú Íde: The Retreat of Ita Cagney*; *Inchicore Haiku*; *Poems to Younger Women*; *The Killing of Dreams*). Deceased.

Charles Haughey (p. 333) Politician and former Leader of Fianna Fáil. Deceased.

Katy Hayes (p. 254) Short-story writer (*Forecourt*) and novelist (*Curtains*; *Gossip*).

Dermot Healy (p. 12) Novelist (*Banished Misfortune*; *Fighting with Shadows*; *A Goat's Song*), poet (*The Ballyconnell Colours*; *What the Hammer*; *The Reed Bed*) and memoir writer (*The Bend for Home*).

Marie Heaney (p. 81) Writer (*Over Nine Waves: A Book of Irish Legends*; *Names Upon the Harp*) anthologist (*Heart Mysteries*) broadcaster, editor (*Sources*; *Sunday Miscellany*) and critic.

Seamus Heaney (p. 339) Poet (*Death of a Naturalist*; *North*; *Seeing Things*; *Electric Light*; *District and Circle*), critic (*Preoccupations*; *The Government of the Tongue*; *The Redress of Poetry*; *Finders Keepers*) and winner of the Nobel Prize for Literature 1995.

John Hegarty (p. 231) Provost of Trinity College, Dublin.

Chaim Herzog (p. 101) former President of Israel. Deceased.

Rita Ann Higgins (p. 248) Poet (*Goddess on the Mervue Bus*; *Philomena's Revenge*; *Throw in the Vowels*).

Selima Hill (p. 201) Poet (*The Accumulation of Small Acts of Kindness*; *Saying Hello at the Station*; *My Darling Camel*; *Little Book of Meat*; *Violet*).

Alan Hollinghurst (p. 34) Journalist and novelist (*The Swimming Pool Library*; *The Line of Beauty*).

Michael Holroyd (p. 150) Writer and biographer (*Lytton Strachey*; *Augustus John, G B Shaw*).

Miroslav Holub (p. 138) Czechoslovakian poet (*Go and Open the Door*; *Totally Unsystematic Zoology*) and scientist (*The Dimension of the Present Moment*). Deceased.

George Hook (p. 113) Broadcaster with Newstalk 106, journalist, sports commentator and writer (*Time Added On*).

Seamus Hosey (p. 259) Broadcaster and producer with RTÉ.

Nick Hornby (p. 42) Arsenal football fan, writer (*Fever Pitch*), novelist (*A Long Way Down*) and critic.

Declan Hughes (p. 22) Playwright (*I Can't Get Started*; *Digging For Fire*; *Love and a Bottle*; *New Morning*; *Halloween Night*; *Philip Newman's Weekend*) and novelist (*The Wrong Kind of Blood*).

Ted Hughes (p. 299) Poet (*Poetry in the Making*; *The Hawk in the Rain*; *Lupercal, Crow*), essayist (*Winter Pollen*). Deceased.

Sean Hughes (p. 55) Comedian and novelist (*The Detainees*; *It's What He Would Have Wanted*).

Jonathan Hunter (p. 108) Artist.

Jeremy Irons (p. 266) Actor. (*Brideshead Revisited*; *The French Lieutenant's Woman, The Mission*) Won an Oscar for *The Reversal of Fortune*.

Glenda Jackson, MP (p. 329) Actor (*Stevie; A Touch of Class*) and Member of Parliament (Labour Party).

Jennifer Johnston (p. 249) Novelist (*How Many Miles to Babylon; The Invisible Worm; This Is Not A Novel*) and playwright.

Jenny Joseph (p. 317) Poet (*The Unlooked-for Season; The Thinking Heart; Beyond Descartes; Selected Poems*).

Mark Joyce (p. 85) Artist.

Fergal Keane (p. 141) Broadcaster with the BBC and writer (*Letter to Daniel; All of These People*).

Madeleine Keane (p. 160) Journalist and critic. Literary editor, *Sunday Independent*.

Richard Kearney (p. 264) Writer and philosopher.

Brian Keenan (p. 82) Writer (*An Evil Cradling; Between Extremes*), novelist (*Turlough*).

Cathy Kelly (p. 305) Novelist (*Woman to Woman; She's the One; Past Secrets*).

Eamon Kelly (p. 127) Storyteller, author (*In My Father's Time*) and actor (played S B O'Donnell in the first production of Brian Friel's *Philadelphia Here I Come!*, September 1964). Deceased.

John Kelly (p. 168) Broadcaster (Presenter of *The View* on RTÉ television; presented *The Eclectic Ballroom* and *The Mystery Train* on RTÉ Radio 1), novelist (*Grace Notes and Bad Thoughts*), poet and writer (*Cool About the Ankles*).

Anne Kennedy (p. 223) Poet (*Buck Mountain Poems; The Dog Kubla Dreams; No; My Life*), broadcaster and photographer. Deceased.

Sr Stanislaus Kennedy (p. 38) Social worker and director of Focus Ireland. Writer (*Now is the Time; Gardening the Soul; Seasons of the Day*).

Brendan Kennelly (p. 326) Poet (*Cromwell; The Book of Judas; Poetry My Arse*), anthologist and Professor Emeritus of English at Trinity College, Dublin.

Pat Kenny (p. 39) Broadcaster on RTÉ radio and television. Presenter of the *Late Late Show*.

Marian Keyes (p. 192) Novelist (*Watermelon; Lucy Sullivan Is Getting Married; Sushi for Beginners; The Other side of the Story; Anybody Out There?*) and writer (*Under the Duvet*).

Bernadette Kiely (p. 160) Artist.

Claire Kilroy (p. 214) Novelist (*All Summer; Tenderwire*). Awarded the Rooney Prize 2004.

Philip King (p. 143) Broadcaster, musician, film maker.

Nick Laird (p. 86) Poet (*To A Fault*) and Novelist (*Utterly Monkey*). Awarded the Rooney Prize 2005.

Eamonn Lawlor (p. 324) Journalist and broadcaster. Presenter on Lyric FM.

Louis le Brocquy (p. 333) Artist.

Anne Le Marquand Hartigan (p. 134) Poet (*Long Tongue; Return Single; Now is a Moveable Feast; Immortal Sins; Nourishment*), playwright (*Beds; La Corbière*), artist.

David Leavitt (p. 228) Novelist (*Equal Affections; The Lost Language of Cranes*) and short-story writer.

Hermione Lee (p. 117) Critic, broadcaster, lecturer in English at Oxford University. Author of books on Virginia Woolf, Elizabeth Bowen, Philip Roth, Willa Cather.

Laurie Lee (p. 88) Writer (*Cider with Rosie; As I Walked Out One Midsummer Morning*) and poet. Deceased.

Brian Lenihan (p. 117) Senior Fianna Fáil politician, served as Tánaiste from 1987–1990. Deceased.

Doris Lessing (p. 8) Novelist (*The Grass is Singing; Martha Quest; The Golden Notebook; The Good Terrorist; The Fifth Child*), short-story writer, poet, autobiographer (*Under My Skin; Walking in the Shade*).

Brian Leyden (p. 205) Writer (*Departures*) and broadcaster.

Rosaleen Linehan (p. 26) Actor.

David Lodge (p. 115) Novelist (*Nice Work; Paradise News; Author, Author*), critic (*The Novelist at the Crossroads*) Professor Emeritus of English and the University of Birmingham.

Mary Lohan (p. 62) Artist.

Michael Longley (p. 163) Poet (*Man Lying on a Wall; Gorse Fires; The Weather in Japan; Snow Water; Collected Poems*), writer (*Tuppenny Stung*) and editor.

Brian Lynch (p. 75) Poet (*New and Renewed: Poems 1967–2004*) novelist (*The Winner of Sorrow*), art critic and scriptwriter.

P J Lynch (p. 69) Illustrator of children's books (*The Snow Queen; The King of Ireland's Son; The Christmas Miracle of Jonathan Toomey*) and writer (*East o' the Sun and West o' the Moon*).

Seán Lysaght (p. 66) Poet (*Noah's Irish Ark; The Clare Island Survey; Scarecrow; Erris*).

Ferdia MacAnna (p. 51) Broadcaster, writer (*Bald Head*), novelist (*The Last of the High Kings*).

John McAuliffe (p. 280) Poet (*A Better Life*). Winner of the RTÉ Poet of the Future Award 2000, the Séan Dunne National Poetry Award 2002. Director of the Poetry Now Festival.

Colum McCann (p. 33) Short-story writer (*Fishing the Sloe-Black River*) and novelist (*Songdogs; Underground Snow; Dancer*) and winner of the 1994 Rooney Prize.

Catherine Phil MacCarthy (p. 256) Poet (*This Hour of the Tide; The Blue Globe*) and novelist (*One Room an Everywhere*).

Molly McCloskey (p. 160) Novelist and short-story writer (*Solomon's Seal; The Beautiful Changes*).

Fiach MacConghail (p. 209) Director of The Abbey Theatre.

Frank McCourt (p. 54) Writer (*Angela's Ashes; Teacher Man*) and performer with his brother Malachy in a musical review about their Irish youth (*A Couple of Blaguards*).

Moy McCrory (p. 80) Short-story writer (*The Water's Edge; Bleeding Sinners*), novelist (*The Fading Shrine*).

Frank McDonald (p. 43) Environment correspondent of *The Irish Times*, author (*The Destruction of Dublin; Saving the City; Chaos at the Crossroads*) and co-author with Peigín Doyle (*Ireland's Earthen Homes*).

Mary McEvoy (p. 140) Actor.

Declan McGonagle (p. 89) Former Director of IMMA, Arts Administrator.

Medbh McGuckian (p. 27) Poet (*The Flower Master; Marconi's Cottage; The Book of the Angel; The Currach Requires No Harbours*).

John MacKenna (p. 157) Writer (*The Occasional Optimist; Castledermot and Kilkea; The Lost Village*), short-story writer (*The Fallen*) and novelist (*Clare*).

Jamie McKendrick (p. 261) Poet (*The Sirocco Room; The Kiosk on the Brink*).

Patricia McKenna (p. 258) Politician and MEP.

Stephen McKenna (p. 269) Artist.

Pauline McLynn (p. 185) Actor (roles include Mrs Doyle in *Father Ted*) and novelist (*Something for the Weekend; Better than a Rest; Right on Time*).

Liz McManus (p. 137) Politician and novelist (*Acts of Subversion*).

Frank McNally (p. 218) Staff Journalist with *The Irish Times*.

Conor McPherson (p. 301) Playwright (*The Good Thief; This Lime Tree Bower; St Nicholas; The Weir*) and screenwriter (*I Went Down*).

Ciarán Mac Mathúna (p. 278) Broadcaster. Presented *Mo Cheol Thú* on RTÉ Radio.

Catherine MacPhail (p. 272) Children's author (*Run, Zan, Run; Underworld; Missing; Roxy's Baby; Nemesis: Into the Shadows*).

Deirdre Madden (p. 92) Novelist (*Nothing is Black; One by One in the Darkness; Authenticity*).

Brenda Maddox (p. 129) Journalist, broadcaster and author (*Beyond Babel: New Directions in Communications; The Half-Parent: Living with Other People's Children; Married and Gay; Who's Afraid of Elizabeth Taylor; Nora: The Real Life of Molly Bloom*).

Alice Maher (p. 136) Artist.

Derek Mahon (p. 224) Poet (*The Hunt by Night; Antarctica; Harbour Lights; Collected Poems*), translator and anthologist.

David Marcus (p. 321) Former editor of 'New Irish Writing', *The Irish Press*. Editor of numerous anthologies, including *Modern Irish Love Stories and Alternative Love: Irish Lesbian and Gay Short Stories*). Novelist (*A Land Not Theirs; A Land in Flames*).

Colin Martin (p. 214) Artist.

Aidan Mathews (p. 322) Short-story writer (*Adventures in a Bathyscope; Lipstick on the Host*), playwright (*Exit/Entrance*), poet (*Windfalls; Minding Ruth*) and novelist (*Muesli at Midnight*).

Paula Meehan (p. 154) Poet (*Return and No Blame; The Man who was Marked by Winter; Dharmakaya*) and playwright.

Arthur Miller (p. 206) Playwright (*Death of a Salesman; The Crucible; A View from the Bridge; The American Clock*) and author (*Timebends*). Deceased.

Lia Mills (p 258) Novelist (*Another Alice; Nothing Simple*).

Noel Monaghan (p.266) Poet (*Snowfire; Curse of the Birds*).

John Montague (p. 196) Poet (*Forms of Exile; The Rough Field; The Great Cloak*) and writer (*Company*).

Derek Mooney (p. 19) Broadcaster on RTÉ radio and television.

Michael Mortell (p. 206) Fashion designer.

Andrew Motion (p. 6) Appointed Poet Laureate 1999 (*The Pleasure Steamers; Love in a Life; Salt Water; Selected Poems; Public Property*), novelist (*Pale Companions*), critic, editor and biographer (*Keats; Philip Larkin: A Writer's Life*).

Paul Muldoon (p. 47) Poet (*New Weather; Mules; Why Brownlee Left; Meeting the British; Madoc: A Mystery; The Annals of Chile; Horse Latitudes*) and editor (*The Faber Book of Contemporary Irish Poetry*).

Iris Murdoch (p. 29) Novelist (*The Sea, The Sea; The Black Prince; The Book and the Brotherhood*), playwright (*The Servants and the Snow*) and philosopher (*The Sovereignty of Good; Metaphysics as a Guide to Morals*). Deceased.

Jimmy Murphy (p. 259) Playwright (*Brothers of the Brush*).

Mike Murphy (p. 100) Retired RTÉ broadcaster and author (*Mike and Me*).

Richard Murphy (p. 326) Poet (*High Island; The Price of Stone; Collected Poems*).

Gloria Naylor (p. 178) African-American novelist (*The Women of Brewster Place; Linden Hills; Mama Day; Bailey's Café*).

John Neill (p. 51) Archbishop of Dublin and Bishop of Glendalough, Primate of Ireland and Metropolitan.

Nuala Ní Dhomhnaill (p. 103) Poet (*An Dealg Droighin; Selected Poems/Rogha Dánta*).

Éilís Ní Dhuibhne (p. 164) Short-story writer (*Blood and Water; Eating Women is not Recommended*) and novelist (*The Bray House; The Dancers Dancing*).

Christopher Nolan (p. 112) Poet (*Dam Bursts of Dreams*) and novelist (*Under the Eye of the Clock*).

Graham Norton (p. 1) Broadcaster, comedian (played Father Noel Furlong in *Father Ted*) and writer (*So Me*). Winner of numerous BAFTA Awards.

Julie O'Callaghan (p. 142) Poet (*Edible Anecdotes; What's What; No Can Do; The Book of Whispers*).

Philip Ó Ceallaigh (p. 199) Short-story writer (*Notes from a Turkish Whorehouse*). Awarded the Rooney Prize 2006.

Eóin O'Connor (p. 106) Artist.

Joseph O'Connor (p. 121) Novelist (*Cowboys and Indians; Star of the Sea*), playwright and short-story writer (*True Believers*).

John O'Donnell (p. 94) Poet (*Some Other Country; Icarus Sees His Father Fly*) and barrister.

Mary O'Donnell (p. 46) Poet (*Reading the Sunflowers in September; Spiderwoman's Third Avenue Rhapsody*) short-story writer and novelist.

Bernard O'Donoghue (p. 140) Poet (*Poaching Rights; The Absent Signifier; The Weakness; Gunpowder*) and writer on medieval English.

Hughie O'Donoghue (p. 276) Artist.

Gwen O'Dowd (p.172) Artist.

Dennis O'Driscoll (p. 234) Poet (*Kist; Hidden Extras; New and Selected Poems*) critic (*Troubled Thoughts, Majestic Dreams*) and editor (*The Bloodaxe Book of Poetry Quotations*).

Nuala O'Faolain (p. 89) Writer (*Are You Somebody?; Almost There; Chicago May*) journalist and novelist (*My Dream of You*).

Tomás Ó Fiaich (p. 80) Cardinal Bishop of Armagh and church leader. Deceased.

Desmond O'Grady (p. 239) Poet (*Chords and Orchestrations; Reilly; The Dark Edge of Europe; Off Licence; The Dying Gaul; Sing Me Creation*).

Andy O'Mahony (p. 67) Broadcaster with RTÉ and presenter of *Off the Shelf* and *Dialogue*.

Micheál Ó Muircheartaigh (p. 190) Sports Commentator and writer (*From Dún Síon to Croke Park*).

Caitríona O'Reilly (p. 203) Poet (*The Nowhere Birds; The Sea Cabinet*). Awarded the Rooney Prize 2002.

Emily O'Reilly (p. 54) Journalist, broadcaster and writer (*Candidate; Masterminds of the Right*) and Ombudsman.

Sean O'Reilly (p. 244) Short-story writer (*Curfew*), novelist (*Love and Sleep; The Swing of Things; Watermark*).

Cathal Ó Searcaigh (p. 52) Playwright and poet (*Súile Shuibhne; Ag Tnúth Leis an tSolas*).

Fintan O'Toole (p. 245) *Irish Times* Journalist, critic, broadcaster and author (*No More Heroes: A Radical Guide to Shakespeare; A Mass for Jesse James*).

Joyce Carol Oates (p. 184) American novelist (*Them; With Shuddering Fall; Marya: A Life*), short-story writer, poet and critic.

Sharon Olds (p. 289) American poet (*The Gold Cell; The Father; Blood, Tin, Straw; The Unswept Room*) and teacher of poetry workshops at New York University, Columbia University and Goldwater Hospital on Roosevelt Island in New York.

Don Paterson (p. 122) Poet (*Nil, Nil; God's Gift to Women*).

Jill Paton Walsh (p. 57) Novelist (*Lapsing; A School for Lovers; Knowledge of Angels*) and children's writer.

Glenn Patterson (p. 66) Novelist (*Burning Your Own; Fat Lad*).

Siobhán Parkinson (p. 181) Children's writer (*All Shining in the Spring; Amelia; No Peace for Amelia; Sisters – No Way!; Off We Go – The Country Adventure; Off We Go – The Dublin Adventure*) and editor (*Home: An Anthology of Modern Irish Writing*).

Robert Pinsky (p. 195) American poet (*Sadness and Happiness; An Exploration of America; History of My Heart*) and critic (*The Situation of Poetry*).

Harold Pinter (p. 192) Playwright (*The Birthday Party; The Caretaker; Ashes to Ashes; One for the Road; Mountain Language*). Awarded the Nobel Prize for Literature 2005.

James Plunkett (p. 58) Novelist (*Strumpet City; Farewell Companions*) and short-story writer (*The Trusting and the Maimed*).

Terry Prone (p. 82) Short-story writer (*Blood Brothers, Soul Sisters),* novelist (*Racing the Moon*), journalist, broadcaster, media consultant and managing director of Carr Communications).

Ann Quinn (p. 23) Artist.

Feargal Quinn (p. 120) Managing director of Superquinn.

John Quinn (p. 262) Novelist for teenagers (*The Summer of Lily and Esme*), broadcaster and producer with RTÉ.

Pat Rabbitte (p. 17) Politician. Leader of the Labour Party.

Peter Reading (p. 306) Poet (*For the Municipality's Elderly; Stet; Shitheads: New Poems; Collected Poems I and II*).

Anthony Roche (p. 165) Lecturer, broadcaster, critic and writer.

Neil Rudenstine (p. 64) Scholar, academic and President Emeritus of Harvard University, Cambridge, Massachusetts.

James Ryan (p. 298) Novelist (*Home from England; Dismantling Mr Doyle; Seeds of Doubt*).

Patricia Scanlan (p. 98) Novelist (*Finishing Touches; Divided Loyalties*).

Anna Scher (p. 112) Actor, author, director of the Anna Scher Theatre and co-author of *100+ Ideas for Drama.*

Michael Schmidt (p. 147) Poet (*Bedlam and the Oak Wood; The Love of Strangers; New and Selected Poems*), writer (*The Lives of the Poets*) and founder of Carcanet Press, Manchester, and Poetry Nation.

Michael Scott (p. 84) Children's writer (*Windlord; The Quest of the Sons of Tuireann*).

Dermot Seymour (p. 284) Artist.

Fiona Shaw (p. 331) Actor. Stage roles include Katharine in *The Taming of the Shrew* and the title role in *Hedda Gabler*. Film work includes *My Left Foot* and the Harry Potter films.

Carol Shields (p. 60) American-born Canadian novelist (*The Box Garden; Small Ceremonies; Mary Swann; Happenstance; The Republic of Love; The Stone Diaries; Unless*).

Jon Silkin (p. 207) Poet (*The Reordering of Stones; Nature with Man*).

Francesca Simon (p. 15) Author of the *Horrid Henry* books for children.

Jo Slade (p. 160) Poet (*In Fields I Hear Them Sing*), artist.

Michael Smurfit (p. 270) Businessman.

Gordon Snell (p. 294) Children's writer (*Cruncher Sparrow, High Flyer; The Mystery of Monk Island; The Tex and Sheelagh Omnibus*) and critic.

Michelle Souter (p. 271) Artist.

Tom Stoppard (p. 187) Playwright (*Rosencrantz and Guildenstern Are Dead; The Real Inspector Hound; The Dog it Was that Died; Indian Ink*).

Niall Stokes (p. 229) Editor of *Hot Press*.

Philippa Sutherland (p. 168) Artist.

Eamonn Sweeney (p. 98) Novelist (*Waiting for the Healer; The Photograph*), critic, journalist and broadcaster.

Mark Swords (p. 123) Artist.

Mother Teresa (p. 114) Missionary nun dedicated to serving the poor, the sick and the lonely. Founder of the Missionaries of Charity in Calcutta. Deceased.

Donald Teskey (p. 307) Artist.

Kate Thompson (p. 106) Novelist (*Switchers; The New Policeman; The Fourth Horseman*) Winner of the Guardian Prize, the Whitbread Prize, Four times winner of the Bisto Award.

Colm Tóibín (p. 204) Novelist (*The South; The Heather Blazing; The Story of the Night; The Master*) and writer (*Walking Along the Border; Homage to Barcelona*). Winner of the Impac Prize 2006.

Maura Treacy (p. 133) Novelist (*Scenes from a Country Wedding*) and short-story writer.

Joanna Trollope (p. 260) Novelist (*The Rector's Wife; The Choir; A Village Affair; A Passionate Man; The Men and the Girls; Second Honeymoon*), writer (*Britannia's Daughters*) and author of historical romantic period sagas using the pseudonym Caroline Harvey.

Lynne Truss (p. 4) Novelist and writer (*Eats, Shoots and Leaves; Talk to the Hand*).

Charles Tyrrell (p. 67) Artist.

Helen Vendler (p. 109) Scholar, critic, writer (*Part of Nature, Part of Us*). Editor of *The Harvard Book of Contemporary American Poetry*.

William Wall (p. 6) Poet (*Mathematics*) and novelist (*Alice Falling; Minding Children; The Map of Tenderness; This is the Country*).

Caroline Walsh (p. 146) Literary editor of *The Irish Times*, author (*The Homes of Irish Writers*) and editor (*Modern Irish Stories from the Irish Times; Virgins and Hyacinths; Arrows in Flight*).

Kathleen Watkins (p. 55) Broadcaster.

Fay Weldon (p. 274) Novelist (*Praxis; Affliction*).

Katharine Whitehorn (p. 149) Journalist with the *Observer*.

Matt Whyman (p. 330) Novelist and writer (*Boy Kills Man; Superhuman; XY; The Wild*).

Christopher Woods (p. 337) Principal of Wesley College, Dublin.

Denyse Woods [aka Denyse Devlin] (p. 40) Novelist (*Overnight to Innsbruch; The Catalpa Tree; Like Nowhere Else*).

Joseph Woods (p. 221) Poet (*Sailing to Hokkaido; Bearings*) and director of Poetry Ireland.

Macdara Woods (p. 16) Poet (*Stopping the Lights in Ranelagh; The Hanged Man was not Surrendering*).

Judith Woodworth (p. 205) Director of The National Concert Hall.

Enda Wyley (p. 295) Poet (*Eating Baby Jesus; Socrates in the Garden; Poems for Breakfast*).

Index of Poets and their Works

CONTRIBUTORS TO *Lifelines*

Fleur Adcock, Darina Allen, Sir Kingsley Amis (deceased), Martin Amis, Lord Jeffrey Archer, Simon Armitage, Margaret Atwood, Robert Ballagh, Mary Banotti, MEP, John Banville, Lynn Barber, Julian Barnes, Gerald Barry, Sebastian Barry, John Bayley, Mary Beckett, Emmet Bergin, Sara Berkeley, Pauline Bewick, Maeve Binchy, Kenneth Blackmore, Michael Blumenthal, Eavan Boland, Ken Bourke, Clare Boylan (deceased), Alicia Boyle (deceased), Kenneth Branagh, Richard Branson, Séamus Brennan, TD, Noel Browne (deceased), Helen Lucy Burke, Barbara Bush, A S Byatt, CBE, Gay Byrne, Ollie Campbell, Noelle Campbell-Sharp, Bunny Carr, Amy Clampitt (deceased), Anthony Clare, Adam Clayton, Don Cockburn, Shane Connaughton, Jilly Cooper, Elizabeth Cope, Wendy Cope, Anthony Cronin, William Crozier, Dorothy Cross, Cyril Cusack (deceased), Niamh Cusack, Cardinal Cahal Daly, Ita Daly, Derek Davis, Treasa Davison, Seamus Deane, Greg Delanty, Dame Judi Dench, Thomas Docherty, Patricia Donlon, Theo Dorgan, Anne Doyle, Maria Doyle, Margaret Drabble, CBE, Alan Dukes, TD, Myles Dungan, Eileen Dunne, Paul Durcan, Archbishop Robin Eames, Lauris Edmond, Felim Egan, Ben Elton, Peter Fallon, Brian Farrell, Desmond Fennell, Anne Fine, Mr Justice Thomas A Finlay, Garret FitzGerald, Mary FitzGerald, Theodora FitzGibbon (deceased), T P Flanagan, Bob Gallico, Sir John Gielgud (deceased), Ellen Gilchrist, Larry Gogan, Patrick Graham, Victor Griffin, Hugo Hamilton, Eithne Hand, Mary Harney, TD, Charles Haughey (deceased), Isabel Healy, Seamus Heaney, Margaret Heckler, Chaim Herzog (deceased), Tom Hickey, Rita Ann Higgins, Desmond Hogan, Alan Hollinghurst, Michael Holroyd, Miroslav Holub (deceased), Patricia Hurl, Jeremy Irons, Glenda Jackson, MP, Jennifer Johnston, Rónán Johnston, John Kavanagh, John B Keane (deceased), Richard Kearney, Sr Stanislaus Kennedy, Brendan Kennelly, Pat Kenny, Declan Kiberd, Benedict Kiely, Galway Kinnell, Thomas Kinsella, Mick Lally, Barry Lang, Mary Lavin (deceased), Sue Lawley, David Leavitt, Louis Le Brocquy, Laurie Lee (deceased), Mary Leland, Brian Lenihan, TD (deceased), Hugh Leonard, Doris Lessing, Rosaleen Linehan, David Lodge, Michael Longley, Seán Lucy (deceased), Joe Lynch, Ferdia MacAnna, Joan McBreen, Nell McCafferty, Mr Justice Niall McCarthy (deceased), Thomas McCarthy, Tom McCaughren, Margaret MacCurtain (Sr Benvenuta), Mary McEvoy, Michael McGlynn, Medbh McGuckian, Frank McGuinness, Sir Ian McKellen, Bernard MacLaverty, Bryan MacMahon (deceased), Sean McMahon, Flo McSweeney, Jimmy Magee, Alice Maher, Derek Mahon, Thelma Mansfield, Augustine Martin (deceased), Maxi, Paula Meehan, Maire Mhac an tSaoi, Sue Miller, John Montague, Mary Mooney, Brian Moore (deceased), Christy Moore, Andrew Motion, Dame Iris Murdoch (deceased), Mike Murphy, Richard Murphy, Tom Murphy, Kevin Myers, Doireann Ní Bhriain, Eilean Ní Chuilleanáin, Nuala Ní Dhomhnaill, David Norris, Conor Cruise O'Brien, Julie O'Callaghan, Eilís O'Connell, Joseph O'Connor, Ulick O'Connor, Mary O'Donnell, Dennis O'Driscoll, Cardinal Tomás Ó Fiaich (deceased), Emer O'Kelly, Sharon Olds, Michael O'Loughlin, Andy O'Mahony, Tony O'Malley (deceased), Liam Ó Murchú, Joseph O'Neill, Hilary Orpen, Micheal O'Siadhail, Fintan O'Toole, Lord David Owen, Geraldine Plunkett, James Plunkett (deceased), Maureen Potter (deceased), Kathy Prendergast, Sir V S Pritchett (deceased), Deirdre Purcell, Marian Richardson, Christopher Ricks, Vivienne Roche, Neil Rudenstine, Patricia Scanlan, Anna Scher, Fiona Shaw, Antony Sher, James Simmons (deceased), Archbishop George Otto Simms (deceased), Maria Simonds-Gooding, Ailbhe Smyth, Camille Souter, Michele Souter, Alan Stanford, Amelia Stein, Francis Stuart (deceased), Alice Taylor, Mother Teresa (deceased), Sue Townsend, William Trevor, Gerrit van Gelderen (deceased), Helen Vendler, Michael Viney, Martin Waddell, Kathleen Watkins, Padraic White, Macdara Woods.

CONTRIBUTORS TO *Lifelines 2*

Bertie Ahern, TD, Paul Andrews, SJ, John Arden, Neil Astley, Vincent Banville, Leland Bardwell, Ben Barnes, Kevin Barry, Bibi Baskin, John Behan, Ciaran Benson, Steven Berkoff, Agnes Bernelle, Wendell Berry, Harold Bloom, Seoirse Bodley, Veronica Bolay, Brian Bourke, Brian Boydell, Charles Brady (deceased), Conor Brady, Cecily Brennan, Rory Brennan, Joseph Brodsky (deceased), Denis Brown, Terence Brown, John Bruton TD, Julie Burchill, Donald Caird, Ciana Campbell, Moya Cannon, John Carey, Eithne Carr, Ciaran Carson, Charles Causley, Jung Chang, Siobhán Cleary, Michael Coady, Paddy Cole, Michael Colgan, Evelyn Conlon, Marita Conlon-McKenna, Róisín Conroy, Barrie Cooke, Emma Cooke, Art Cosgrove, Ingrid Craigie, John Creedon, Jeananne Crowley, Margrit Cruikshank, Pádraig J Daly, Brian D'Arcy, Michael Davitt, Gerald Dawe, Éamon de Buitléar, Eilís Dillon (deceased), Brian Dobson, Terry Dolan, Emma Donoghue, Katie Donovan, Mary Dorcey, Avril Doyle, Rose Doyle, Carol Ann Duffy, Joe Duffy, Anne Dunlop, Helen Dunmore, Sean Dunne (deceased), Alison Dye, Desmond Egan, Conor Fallon, Bernard Farrell, Eithne Fitzgerald, Gabriel Fitzmaurice, Christopher Fitz-Simon, Roy Foster, Maureen Gaffney, Tess Gallagher, Trevor Geoghegan, Máire Geoghegan-Quinn, Allen Ginsberg (deceased), Louise Glück, Richard Gorman, Tim Goulding, Bernadette Greevy, Eamon Grennan, Vona Groarke, Donald Hall, Daniel Halpern, James Hanley, Nigel Hawthorne (deceased), Michael D Higgins, Kathryn Holmquist, Nick Hornby, Kevin Hough, Sean Hughes, Ted Hughes (deceased), Gemma Hussey, Garry Hynes, Neil Jordan, Jenny Joseph, Mark Joyce, Madeleine Keane, Brian Keenan, Eamon Kelly (deceased), Maeve Kelly, Jim Kemmy (deceased), Anne Kennedy, Brian P Kennedy, Mary Kennedy, Jean Kennedy Smith, Philip King, Penelope Leach, Hermione Lee, Anne Le Marquand Hartigan, Brian Leyden, Edna Longley, Seán Lysaght, Sam McAughtry, Eugene McCabe, Patrick McCabe, Catherine Phil MacCarthy, Moy McCrory, Steve MacDonogh, Eleanor McEvoy, Barry McGovern, Jamie McKendrick, John MacKenna, Liz McManus, Ciarán Mac Mathúna, Deirdre Madden, Anne Madden Le Brocquy, David Malouf, David Marcus, Jim Mays, Leonard Michaels, Áine Miller, Mary Morrissey, Michael Mortell, Paul Muldoon, Jimmy Murphy, Gloria Naylor, Eilís Ní Dhuibhne, Christopher Nolan, Sharon O'Brien, Conor O'Callaghan, Gwen O'Dowd, Proinnsías Ó Duinn, Macdara Ó Fátharta, Colm O'Gaora, Fionn O'Leary, Olivia O'Leary, Jane O'Malley, Mary O'Malley, Brendan O'Reilly (deceased), Emily O'Reilly, Cathal Ó Searcaigh, Micheál Ó Súilleabháin, Seán Ó Tuama, Jay Parini, Don Paterson, Tom Paulin, Tim Pigott-Smith, Robert Pinsky, Annie Proulx, John Quinn, Richard W Riley, Lillian Roberts Finlay , Michèle Roberts, Adi Roche, Gabriel Rosenstock, Carol Rumens, James Scanlon, Vikram Seth, John Shinnors, Jo Slade, Art Spiegelman, Dick Spring, Niall Stokes, Eithne Strong, Imogen Stuart, Matthew Sweeney, R S Thomas (deceased), Carl Tighe, Maura Treacy, Charles Tyrrell, Jean Valentine, Edward Walsh, Dolores Walshe, John Waters, Fay Weldon, Hugo Williams, Judith Woodworth, Charles Wright, Nancy Wynne-Jones.

Contributors to *Lifelines 3*

Myrtle Allen, Brian Ashton, Michael Aspel, Kate Atkinson, R J Ayling, Ivy Bannister, Beryl Bainbridge, Eileen Battersby, Gerard Beirne, Niamh Bhreathnach, Mary Rose Binchy, Tony Blair, John Boland, Dermot Bolger, Betty Boothroyd, Angela Bourke, Paul Brady, Melvyn Bragg, Stephen Brennan, John Burnside, Catherine Byrne, Hayden Carruth, Paul Carson, Kevin Casey, Philip Casey, Barry Castle, Philip Castle, Patrick Chapman, Jeremy Clarkson, Harry Clifton, Dame Catherine Cookson (deceased), Ronnie Corbett, Andrea Corr, Tom Courtenay, Roz Cowman, Elaine Crowley, Michael Curtin, Philip Davison, Richard Dawkins, John F Deane, Eamon Delaney, Matthew Dempsey, Louis de Paor, Roddy Doyle, Martin Drury, Robert Dunbar, Terry Eagleton, Brian Fallon, Sebastian Faulks, Alex Ferguson CBE, Mary Finan, Fr Aengus Finucane, Penelope Fitzgerald (deceased), Marie Foley, Aisling Foster, Mildred Fox, Tom Garvin, Mary Gordon, Michael Gorman, Lady Valerie Goulding (deceased), Anita Groener, Andrew Hamilton, Charles Handy, Kerry Hardie, Dr John W Harris, Rolf Harris, Josephine Hart, Lara Harte, Michael Hartnett (deceased), Anne Haverty, Katy Hayes, Dermot Healy, Marie Heaney, Oscar Hijuelos, Selima Hill, Tobias Hill, Seamus Hosey, Brendan Howlin, Declan Hughes, John Hughes, Kathleen Jamie, Elizabeth Jolley, Lesley Joseph, Fergal Keane, Tony Keily, John Kelly, Frank Kermode, Marian Keyes, Tony Kushner, Soinbhe Lally, Eugene Lambert, Eamonn Lawlor, Jessie Lendennie, Denise Levertov (deceased), Gary Lineker, Antonia Logue, P J Lynch, Colum McCann, Molly McCloskey, Mike McCormack, Frank McCourt, Martin McDonagh, Frank McDonald, Michael McDowell, Declan McGonagle, Iggy McGovern, Tom MacIntyre, Patricia McKenna, Susan McKenna-Lawlor, Pauline McLynn, Conor McPherson, Austin McQuinn, Brenda Maddox, John Major, Aidan Mathews, Orla Melling, Arthur Miller (deceased), Lia Mills, Michael Mortell, Michael Mullen, Bríd Óg Ní Bhuachalla, Fionnuala Ní Chiosáin, Áine Ní Ghlinn, Betty Ann Norton, Joyce Carol Oates, Miriam O'Callaghan, Brendan O'Carroll, Bernard O'Donoghue, Desmond O'Grady, Nora Owen, Michael Parkinson, Siobhán Parkinson, Glenn Patterson, Stephen Pearce, Harold Pinter, Andy Pollak, Terry Prone, Ita Quilligan, Eimear Quinn, Feargal Quinn, Justin Quinn, Pauline Quirke, Jane Ray, Peter Reading, Jonathan Rhys Meyers, Rodney Rice, Anne Robinson, Tim Robinson, Anthony Roche, Frank Ronan, James Ryan, Mary Ryan, Trevor Sargent, Michael Schmidt, Michael Scott, Sir Harry Secombe (deceased), Will Self, Carol Shields, Jon Silkin (deceased), Peter Sirr, Dave Smith (pseudonym of David Jeddie), Michael Smurfit, Gordon Snell, Pauline Stainer, Sir Tom Stoppard, Eamonn Sweeney, Marilyn Taylor, Melanie Rae Thon, Colm Tóibín, Barbara Trapido, Joanna Trollope, William Wall, Jill Paton Walsh, Robert Welch, David Wheatley, Katharine Whitehorn, David Whyte, Susan Wicks, A N Wilson, Richard Wilson, Barbara Windsor.

ACKNOWLEDGEMENTS

For permission to reprint copyright material, the compilers, editor and publishers are grateful to the following:

Carcanet Press Ltd for 'Night Feed', 'The Journey' 'The Lost Land' and 'The Pomegranate' by Eavan Boland; The Random House House Group Ltd for 'September Evening' by John Burnside from *The Myth of the Twin*. 'Gravy', 'Happiness', 'Hummingbird', 'Late Fragment', 'Lemonade' and 'What the Doctor Said' from *All of Us* by Raymond Carver, published by Harvill. Reprinted by permission of The Random House Group Ltd; Harcourt Brace & Co for 'Ithaca' by C P Cavafy; Prof Michael Hamburger for 'Psalm' by Paul Celan (trans. Michael Hamburger); 'Vaucluse' by Harry Clifton by kind permission of The Gallery Press, Loughcrew, Oldcastle, County Meath, Ireland; 'Though There Are Torturers' by kind permission of Michael Coady and The Gallery Press, Loughcrew, Oldcastle, County Meath, Ireland from *Two for a Woman Three for a Man* (1980); 'Voyages II', from *Complete Poems of Hart Crane* by Hart Crane, ed. Marc Simon. © 1933, 1958, 1966 by Liveright Publishing Corporation. © 1986 by Marc Simon. Used by permission of Liveright Publishing Corporation; 'somewhere I have never travelled,gladly beyond', 'mr youse needn't be so spry' and 'Buffalo Bill's' are reprinted from *Collected Poems* 1904–1962, by E E Cummings, ed. George J Firmage, by permission of W W Norton & Company © 1991 by the Trustees for the E E Cummings Trust and George James Firmage; 'Before Making Love' from *Captivity*, by Toi Derricotte, © 1989 by Toi Derricotte. Reprinted by permission of the University of Pittsburgh Press; 'Prayer' is taken from *Mean Time* by Carol Ann Duffy, published by Anvil Press Poetry in 1993; Oliver Dunne for 'Uh-Oh' by Oliver Dunne; Paul Durcan for 'The Mantelpiece, after Vuillard' by Paul Durcan; 'After Apple-Picking', 'Desert Places' and 'Stopping by Woods on a Snowy Evening' from *The Poetry of Robert Frost* ed. Edward Connery Lathem, published by Jonathan Cape. Reprinted by permission of the Random House Group Ltd; Michael Gorman for 'The People I Grew Up With Were Afraid' by Michael Gorman; Margaret Snow for 'I Leave This at Your Ear' and 'The Alligator Girls' by W S Graham; 'May' from *A Furious Place* (1996) and The 'Terrain of Suffering: Frida Kahlo in Ireland' by Kerry Hardie by kind permission of Kerry Hardie and The Gallery Press, Loughcrew, Oldcastle, County Meath, Ireland; Tony Harrison for 'Long Distance II' by Tony Harrison. 'How goes the night, boy?...' from *Collected Poems* (1999) 'Poem for Lara, 10' from *Selected Poems* (1994) and 'For my God-daughter, B.A.H.' by Michael Hartnett by kind permission of the Estate of Michael Hartnett and The Gallery Press, Loughcrew, Oldcastle, County Meath, Ireland; 'Recovery' by Dermot Healy by kind permission of Dermot Healy and The Gallery Press, Loughcrew, Oldcastle, County Meath, Ireland; 'Masterpiece', 'Fairy Tale' and 'The Door' from *Poems Before and After* by Miroslav Holub, published by Bloodaxe Books (1991, 2006). Reproduced by permission of Bloodaxe Books; The Society of Authors for 'XXXII' from *A Shropshire Lad* by A E Housman; David Higham Associates for 'Harlem' from *Collected Poems of Langston Hughes* by Langston Hughes published by Alfred A Knopf Inc; 'Málaga' by Pearse Hutchinson by kind permission of The Gallery Press, Loughcrew, Oldcastle, County Meath, Ireland; 'Advent', 'Canal Bank Walk', 'Epic', 'In Memory of My Mother', On Raglan Road' 'Stony Grey Soil' and an excerpt from 'The Great Hunger' by Patrick Kavanagh are reprinted from *Collected Poems*, ed. Antoinette Quinn (Allen Lane, 2004) and 'The Star' and 'Street Corner